**Deborah Tannen** is Professor of Linguistics at Georgetown University in Washington DC. Born in Brooklyn, New York, she received her Ph.D in linguistics from the University of California, Berkeley and has been awarded fellowships and grants from many organisations including The Rockefeller Foundation, The National Endowment for the Humanities, and the National Science Foundation. With sixteen books and over seventy articles to her credit, she has been invited to lecture all over the world. Her internationally-renowned book, *You Just Don't Understand: Women and Men in Conversation* (Virago 1991), has been a phenomenal bestseller in the UK, the USA, Canada, Australia, Germany, Holland, Brazil and Hong Kong. Virago also publish *That's Not What I Meant!: How Conversational Style Makes or Breaks Relationships* (1992) and *Talking from 9 to 5: Women and Men in the Workplace: Language, Sex and Power* (1995). Her play, *An Act of Devotion*, is included in *Best Short Plays 1993–94*. She and her husband live outside Washington DC.

## ALSO BY DEBORAH TANNEN

That's Not What I Meant!:
How Conversational Style Makes or Breaks Relationships

You Just Don't Understand:
Women and Men in Conversation

Talking from 9 to 5:
Women and Men in the Workplace: Language, Sex, and Power

Scholarly Books:

Gender and Discourse
Talking Voices: Repetition, Dialogue and Imagery in Conversational
Discourse
Conversational Style: Analyzing Talk Among Friends
Lilika Nakos

Edited Books:

Framing in Discourse
Gender and Conversational Interaction
Linguistics in Context: Connecting Observation and Understanding
Languages and Linguistics: The Interdependence of Theory, Data and
Application
Perspectives on Silence
Coherence in Spoken and Written Discourse
Spoken and Written Language: Exploring Orality and Literacy
Analyzing Discourse: Text and Talk

# THE
# ARGUMENT
# CULTURE

---

Changing The Way We Argue And Debate

---

DEBORAH TANNEN

With British examples and additions by
Michael Leapman

*A Virago Book*

Published by Virago Press 1999
First published by Virago Press 1998

First published in the United States by Random House, Inc., New York

Copyright © Deborah Tannen 1998

All acknowledgments of permissions to reprint material are on
pages 334–336 which constitute
an extension of the copyright page

The moral right of the author has been asserted

A CIP catalogue record for this book is available from
the British Library

ISBN 1 86049 543 5

Typeset by Palimpsest Book Production Limited,
Polmont, Stirlingshire
Printed and bound in Great Britain by
Clays Ltd, St Ives plc

Virago
A Division of
Little, Brown and Company (UK)
Brettenham House
Lancaster Place
London WC2E 7EN

To
Miriam Tannen
and
Naomi Tannen

my sisters in every sense of the word

# Contents

# ACKNOWLEDGMENTS

I first talked about this book's central theme to a general audience at Renaissance Weekend in Hilton Head, North Carolina, December 1993. Given ten minutes to speak on 'Something that's been bugging me lately,' I had no idea how my thoughts on this topic would be received. The enthusiastic response encouraged me to undertake the research that led to this book, applying my concern with what I had been calling 'the culture of critique' in academia to society at large. And so, at the start, I want to thank Phil and Linda Lader for including me in this unique gathering, and all the generous Renaissance participants who let me know that my remarks struck a chord.

Bolstered by their responses, I submitted an essay on this subject as an op-ed piece to *The New York Times*. I would like to thank *The New York Times* editors who published that first foray as 'The Triumph of the Yell' in January 1994.

Over the next several years, as I developed the ideas and pursued the research that led to this book, my thinking was immeasurably enriched by presenting my work at academic conferences and by teaching seminars on the topic at Georgetown University. Colleagues who heard my talks and students in my classes offered invaluable insights, helped identify relevant research, and fueled my interest with their own. I would like to thank my seminar students in particular, as their engagement with the course material was an essential part of my research: Heidi Beall, Jeff Deby, Hiroko Furo, Debra Graham, Sage Graham, Atsuko Honda, Jessica Mackenzie, Keller Magenau, Nancy Marwin, Lee Ann McNerney, Ralitsa Mileva, Sigrid Norris, Kanako Ohara, Winnie Wing Fung Or, Eden Springer, Camelia Suleiman, Katharine Thomas Trites, Yuko Takakusaki, Mei-hui Tsai, Virginia Yelei Wake, Keli Yerian. Keller Magenau played a special role as research assistant for the section on law; it was she who unearthed and mined many of the sources I cite in that chapter. My thinking on sports was shaped fundamentally by Jeff Deby, who also led me to the literature cited in that section. Keli Yerian helped with research in the anthropological arena of how conflict is managed in other cultures.

My assistant Eve Burnett ably helped locate materials early on; her successor, David Robinson, was a dedicated and talented assistant as the fan was proverbially hit in the final stages of tracking down and checking sources and references. For making these assistants available to me, and for the multifaceted support I have received not only in recent years but for nearly two decades, I continue to be grateful to Georgetown University. I especially want to thank President Leo O'Donovan, Dean Richard Schwartz, and former dean James E. Alatis. I would also like to thank my fellow faculty in the linguistics department.

Generous friends and colleagues read and commented on an entire lengthy early draft of this book. For their gifts of time and wisdom I will always be grateful to A. L. Becker, Amitai Etzioni, Harriet Grant, Karl Goldstein, Susan Philips, and David Wise. I am equally grateful to those who read parts of the manuscript in draft, immeasurably improving the result: Sally Arteseros, Tom Brazaitis, Adrienne Davis, David Luban, Michael Macovski, Judy Mann, Marjorie Margolies-Mezvinsky, Carrie Menkel-Meadow, Patricia O'Brien, Bekah Perks, David Robinson, Richard Starnes, Naomi Tannen, and Joan Williams.

Many people who provided examples are named in the book; I am grateful to them, and to others who provided examples but are not there named, as well as to those who offered other types of insight or assistance: Thomas C. Albro II, Terri Allen, Susan Baer, Cheryl Chase, Carrie Crockett, Tom Dyja, Paul Ekman, Fred Erickson, Ralph Fasold, Richard Giannone, Karl Goldstein, Jerry Groopman, Rom Harré, Warren Hern, Caleen Sinette Jennings, Carl Jennings, Christina Kakava, Shari Kendall, David Larson, Lewis Libby, Mary Maggini, Joshua Marx, Nancy Marx, Barbara McGrael, Sarah Diane McShea, Yoshiko Nakano, Susie Napper, Joseph P. Newhouse, Renee O'Brien, Patricia O'Connor, Peter Patrick, June Phillips, Livia Polanyi, Dorothy Ross, Karin Ryding, Ron Scollon, Suzanne Wong Scollon, Miriam Tannen, Merrilyn Astin Tarlton, Lenore Weitzman, Etsuko Yamada, Haru Yamada.

My editor, Deb Futter, has been a joy, a precious source of guidance and encouragement; her infectious enthusiasm for the book has been a gift. My agent, Suzanne Gluck, has been vigilant and devoted throughout this project as she has been ever since she suggested to me that I write *You Just Don't Understand*.

I would also like to thank my editor at Virago, Lennie Goodings, who has likewise been a wise and stalwart partner since Virago published *You Just Don't Understand* in the UK. The British edition of *The Argument Culture* includes British examples added to the chapters on politics and the press. These examples, and the commentary accompanying them (which I naturally reviewed, tweaked, and slightly altered), were provided by Michael Leapman. I am grateful to him for his contributions. A complete list of the pages on which his additions appear is provided on page 322.

I thank, finally, my friends and colleagues for their patience and understanding when I withdrew from the normal interactions and responsibilities of life to immerse myself in writing this book. They all helped enormously, in their own ways. And once again I thank my family, without whom I cannot imagine doing anything, or wanting to: my parents, Dorothy and Eli Tannen, there from the start and never wavering; my sisters Miriam and Naomi, to whom this book is dedicated (as was the first book I ever wrote more than two decades ago); my in-laws, Addie and Al Macovski and Nancy Marx; and my husband, Michael Macovski – partner in life, partner in love, intellectual and spiritual friend.

# PREFACE TO THE
# BRITISH EDITION

In January 1998, while the American edition of this book was still in production, I found myself having dinner in Hong Kong, hearing from expatriate Americans that a new scandal had broken back home in Washington: the president was accused of having had inappropriate relations with a White House intern. The next day I read lengthy accounts of the scandal in international newspapers – and was awed by the parallels to forces I had described in this book, which at the time was written but not yet in print. The scandal, and all the developments leading up to it, seemed to have leapt off the pages of *The Argument Culture*.

The way the institutions of the press, politics, and the law had intertwined to create this scandal and divert Americans from the real problems facing our nation and the world constitute an emblematic example of what I am calling 'the argument culture.' Even the trivializing name by which it was identified, 'zippergate,' illustrates a point I make in the book: that appending the suffix '—gate' to one after another scandal serves both to exaggerate the significance of

any and all misdeeds and to minimize, retrospectively, the significance of those complex and egregious violations of constitutional
law subsumed under the name 'Watergate.'

Watergate came to light because a security guard discovered
a criminal break-in by chance. The Lewinsky scandal – like all
the mini-scandals that preceded it – came to light because of a
giant industry bent on creating scandals. Watergate snuck up on
reporters. Today reporters pounce on any hint of scandal.

Journalists, however, do not create scandals alone. The vicious
attacking of opponents by politicians has a long history, but it used
to be confined to election campaigns. Now it is a round-the-clock
business, fuelled by well-funded organizations that uncover or
invent damaging information to feed the media.

Then there's the law. By a process known as 'discovery,' lawyers
are allowed to question potential witnesses before a case goes to trial.
But the procedure is now used to harass and intimidate opponents.
Thus attorneys for Paula Jones used their client's sexual-harassment
suit as a pretext to hunt down rumors about the president's private
life and to grill unwilling witnesses with humiliating questions. Men
were questioned about their conversations; women were questioned
about their sex lives. Here, too, the media played a crucial role, as
the supposedly secret depositions were routinely leaked to the press,
who wasted no time in making them public.

Where did Jones' lawyers get the names of the women they
subpoenaed? In some cases from the media: it was *Newsweek*, for
example, that named Kathleen Willey. And how did Paula Jones
find – or get found by – the right-wing supporters who funded her
belated lawsuit? An *American Spectator* article full of rumors about
Bill Clinton's tenure as governor of Arkansas used her name. The
author of this article, David Brock, has since declared his remorse
and admitted in an open letter to the president that he was motivated
by a desire to damage him: 'I wasn't hot for this story in the interest
of good government or serious journalism. I wanted to pop you
right between the eyes.' In the spirit of the argument culture, his
original article was accepted as an easily understandable effort, but
his subsequent apology was greeted by derision and suspicion.

The harm done by dirt uncovered in the guise of 'discovery' takes
on a life of its own, regardless of its relevance to the case that
provided the license to dig it up. Judge Susan Webber Wright

ruled that the allegations regarding White House intern Monica Lewinsky were irrelevant to Jones' case. Eventually she threw out the case altogether, as lacking in substance. But independent counsel Kenneth Starr had the bit in his teeth and was not about to let it drop.

Ah, the independent counsel, the roiling center of this storm. The first special prosecutor was appointed in 1972 to investigate the Watergate coverup. This unusual step was necessary because members of the Justice Department, including the attorney general himself, were involved in the events to be investigated – events that permeated the conduct of government. But the independent counsel institution had gone out of control in sorcerer's apprentice fashion. Starr had moved far afield from Whitewater (the Arkansas land deal he was appointed to investigate), and most Americans believe his four-year investigation became a partisan attempt to destroy Bill Clinton. (When the independent counsel law came before Congress for renewal in 1999, Starr himself testified that it should be allowed to lapse.)

Why was an independent counsel appointed to investigate events that occurred long before the president took office? Because of the media drumbeat of stories fed by an operation headed by a former official of the 1988 and 1992 Republican presidential campaigns.

So goes the back-and-forth among politics, law, and the press, as all three institutions have become obsessed with stirring up no-holds-barred battles. Yet, thanks to the habit of viewing everything as a shootout between two characters in a Western film, the press reported developments in terms of victories and defeats for Clinton and Starr, or a 'showdown' between them, rather than exploring the long-term effects on the nation of such orchestrated and prolonged attacks on those who hold public office.

The world watched with incredulity as the House of Representatives impeached the president, and the Senate tried him, even as a majority of Americans continued to express their convictions that the president's private life should not be the basis for such drastic action, as well as their outrage at what they saw as the hypocrisy of Republican lawmakers, some of whose own private misdeeds were exposed in the process. Many citizens' responses were reminiscent of the Vietnam era: I heard callers to talk shows say that the spectacle of the impeachment made them feel like leaving the country; other callers identifying themselves as Republicans said they would never again vote for their own party. In the end, by a vote that split almost uniformly along party lines, the president remained in office, but many people shuddered at how close the vote was – and at the diversion of attention – the president's, the press and their own – from important national and international affairs.

As the scandal unfolded, journalists and pundits predicted that each new revelation would at last turn a majority of citizens against their president, yet each time their predictions proved false. The president's job approval ratings just kept going up. The most popular explanation for this phenomenon was that Americans selfishly cared only about their own material well-being, and were lulled into complacency by a strong economy. But this interpretation is belied by the facts. Complacency would be reflected by the president's approval ratings staying the same. That they kept going up evinced, I believe, the public's revulsion against the argument culture – a revulsion expressed as well in a ferocious backlash against both Starr and the press.

The concept underlying the argument culture is the notion of ritualized opposition, in contrast to the literal opposition of genuine disagreement. It is the Western tendency to view everything through the template of a battle metaphor, and to glorify conflict and aggression, in contrast to the Eastern emphasis on harmony as a way to defuse inevitable conflict. This concept has wide application as a means to understand our ways of communicating, in public and private. But illustrative examples must come from society at large. For this British edition, the chapters on the press and on politics include additional examples taken from the British context, which were provided, along with commentary, by journalist and writer Michael Leapman. The other chapters are unchanged from the original edition. Taken together, the chapters dramatize why we must stop and think about what the argument culture is, how it affects us, and what we can do to change the way we carry on our public conversations and arguments.

# 1

## FIGHTING FOR OUR LIVES

This is not another book about civility. 'Civility' suggests a superficial, pinky-in-the-air veneer of politeness spread thin over human relations like a layer of marmalade over toast. This book is about something deeper – our tendency to engage in ritualized, knee-jerk opposition, to turn everything into a metaphorical battle. It is about a pervasive warlike atmosphere that makes us approach public dialogue, and just about anything we need to accomplish, as if it were a fight. It is a tendency in Western culture in general, and in Britain and the United States in particular, that has a long history and a deep, thick, and far-ranging root system. It has served us well in many ways but in recent years has become so exaggerated that it is getting in the way of solving our problems. Our spirits are corroded by living in an atmosphere of unrelenting contention – an argument culture.

The argument culture urges us to approach the world – and the people in it – in an adversarial frame of mind. It rests on the assumption that opposition is the best way to get anything done: The best way to discuss an idea is to set up a debate; the best way to cover news is to find spokespeople who express the most extreme, polarized views and present them as 'both sides'; the best way to settle disputes is litigation that pits one party against the other; the best way to begin an essay is to attack someone; and the best way to show you're really thinking is to criticize.

Our public interactions have become more and more like having an argument with a spouse. Conflict can't be avoided in our public lives any more than we can avoid conflict with people we love. One of the great strengths of our society is that we can express these conflicts openly. But just as spouses have to learn ways of settling their differences without inflicting real damage on each other, so we, as a society, have to find constructive ways of resolving disputes and differences. Public discourse requires *making* an argument for a point of view, not *having* an argument – as in having a fight.

The war on drugs, the war on cancer, the battle of the sexes, politicians' turf battles – in the argument culture, war metaphors pervade our talk and shape our thinking. Nearly everything is framed as a battle or game in which winning or losing is the main concern. These all have their uses and their place, but they are not the only way – and often not the best way – to understand and approach our world. Conflict and opposition are as necessary as cooperation and agreement, but the scale is off balance, with conflict and opposition overweighted. In this book, I show how deeply entrenched the argument culture is, the forms it takes, and how it affects us every day – sometimes in useful ways, but often creating more problems than it solves, causing rather than avoiding damage. As a sociolinguist, a social scientist, I am trained to observe and explain language and its role in human relations, and that is my biggest job here. But I will also point toward other ways for us to talk to each other and get things done in our public lives.

The message of this book is not, 'Let's stop arguing and be nice to each other.' Quite the contrary, the message is, 'Let's look more closely at the effects of *ritualized* opposition, so we can have the *real* arguments.' The opposite of the argument culture is not being 'nice' and avoiding conflict; it is finding constructive ways of arguing, debating, and confronting conflict.

## THE BATTLE OF THE SEXES

My interest in the topic of opposition in public discourse intensified in the years following the publication of *You Just Don't Understand*, my book about communication between women and men. In the first year I appeared on many television and radio shows and was interviewed for many print articles in newspapers and magazines. For the most part, that coverage was extremely fair, and I was – and remain – indebted to the many journalists who found my ideas interesting enough to make them known to viewers, listeners, and readers. But from time to time – more often than I expected – I encountered producers who insisted on setting up a television show as a fight (either between the host and me or between another guest and me) and print journalists who made multiple phone calls to my colleagues, trying to find someone who would criticize my work. This got me thinking about what kind of information comes across on shows and in articles that take this approach, compared to those that approach topics in other ways.

At the same time, my experience of the academic world that had long been my intellectual home began to change. For the most part, other scholars, like most journalists, were welcoming and respectful in their responses to my work, even if they disagreed on specific points or had alternative views to suggest. But about a year after *You Just Don't Understand* became a best-seller – the wheels of academia grind more slowly than those of the popular press – I began reading attacks on my work that completely misrepresented it. I had been in academia for over fifteen years by then, and had valued my interaction with other researchers as one of the greatest rewards of academic life. Why, I wondered, would someone represent me as having said things I had never said or as having failed to say things I had said?

The answer crystallized when I put the question to a writer who I felt had misrepresented my work: 'Why do you need to make others wrong for you to be right?' Her response: 'It's an argument!' Aha, I thought, that explains it. When you're having an argument with someone, your goal is not to listen and understand. Instead, you use every tactic you can think of – including distorting what your opponent just said – in order to win the argument.

Not only the level of attention *You Just Don't Understand* received but, even more, the subject of women and men, triggered the tendency to polarize. This tendency to stage a fight on television or in print was posited on the conviction that opposition leads to truth. Sometimes it does. But the trouble is, sometimes it doesn't. I was asked at the start of more than one talk show or print interview, 'What is the most controversial thing about your book?' Opposition does not lead to truth when the most controversial thing is not the most important.

The conviction that opposition leads to truth can tempt not only members of the press but just about anyone seeking to attract an audience to frame discussions as a fight between irreconcilable opposites. Even the Smithsonian Institution, to celebrate its 150th anniversary, sponsored a series of talks billed as debates. They invited me to take part in one titled 'The Battle of the Sexes.' The organizer preempted my objection: 'I know you won't be happy with this title, but we want to get people interested.' This is one of many assumptions I question in this book: Is it necessary to frame an interchange as a battle to get people interested? And even if doing so succeeds in capturing attention, does it risk dampening interest in the long run, as audiences weary of the din and begin to hunger for more substance?

## THOUGHT-PROVOKING
## OR JUST PROVOCATIVE?

In the spring of 1995, Horizons Theatre in Arlington, Virginia, produced two one-act plays I had written about family relationships. The director, wanting to contribute to the reconciliation between Blacks and Jews, mounted my plays in repertory with two one-act plays by an African-American playwright, Caleen Sinnette Jennings. We had both written plays about three sisters that explored the ethnic identities of our families (Jewish for me, African-American for her) and the relationship between those identities and the American context in which we grew up. To stir interest in the plays and to explore the parallels between her work and mine, the theater planned a public dialogue between Jennings and me, to be held before the plays opened.

As production got under way, I attended the audition of actors for my plays. After the auditions ended, just before everyone headed home, the theater's public relations volunteer distributed copies of the flyer announcing the public dialogue that she had readied for distribution. I was horrified. The flyer announced that Caleen and I would discuss 'how past traumas create understanding and conflict between Blacks and Jews today.' The flyer was trying to grab by the throat the issue that we wished to address indirectly. Yes, we were concerned with conflicts between Blacks and Jews, but neither of us is an authority on that conflict, and we had no intention of expounding on it. We hoped to do our part to ameliorate the conflict by focusing on commonalities. Our plays had many resonances between them. We wanted to talk about our work and let the resonances speak for themselves.

Fortunately, we were able to stop the flyers before they were distributed and devise new ones that promised something we could deliver: 'a discussion of heritage, identity, and complex family relationships in African-American and Jewish-American culture as represented in their plays.' Jennings noticed that the original flyer said the evening would be 'provocative' and changed it to 'thought-provoking.' What a world of difference is implied in that small change: how much better to make people think, rather than simply to 'provoke' them – as often as not, to anger.

It is easy to understand why conflict is so often highlighted: Writers of headlines or promotional copy want to catch attention and attract an audience. They are usually under time pressure, which lures them to established, conventionalized ways of expressing ideas in the absence of leisure to think up entirely new ones. The promise of controversy seems an easy and natural way to rouse interest. But serious consequences are often unintended: Stirring up animosities to get a rise out of people, though easy and 'provocative,' can open old wounds or create new ones that are hard to heal. This is one of many dangers inherent in the argument culture.

---

## FOR THE SAKE OF ARGUMENT

In the argument culture, criticism, attack, or opposition are the predominant if not the only ways of responding to people or ideas.

I use the phrase 'culture of critique' to capture this aspect. 'Critique' in this sense is not a general term for analysis or interpretation but rather a synonym for criticism.

It is the *automatic* nature of this response that I am calling attention to – and calling into question. Sometimes passionate opposition, strong verbal attack, are appropriate and called for. No one knows this better than those who have lived under repressive regimes that forbid public opposition. The Yugoslavian-born poet Charles Simic is one. 'There are moments in life,' he writes, 'when true invective is called for, when it becomes an absolute necessity, out of a deep sense of justice, to denounce, mock, vituperate, lash out, in the strongest possible language.' I applaud and endorse this view. There are times when it is necessary and right to fight – to defend your country or yourself, to argue for right against wrong or against offensive or dangerous ideas or actions.

What I question is the ubiquity, the knee-jerk nature, of approaching almost any issue, problem, or public person in an adversarial way. One of the dangers of the habitual use of adversarial rhetoric is a kind of verbal inflation – a rhetorical boy who cried wolf: The legitimate, necessary denunciation is muted, even lost, in the general cacophony of oppositional shouting. What I question is using opposition to accomplish *every* goal, even those that do not require fighting but might also (or better) be accomplished by other means, such as exploring, expanding, discussing, investigating, and the exchanging of ideas suggested by the word 'dialogue.' I am questioning the assumption that *everything* is a matter of polarized opposites, the proverbial 'two sides to every question' that we think embodies open-mindedness and expansive thinking.

In a word, the type of opposition I am questioning is what I call 'agonism.' I use this term, which derives from the Greek word for 'contest,' *agonia*, to mean an automatic warlike stance – not the literal opposition of fighting against an attacker or the unavoidable opposition that arises organically in response to conflicting ideas or actions. An agonistic response, to me, is a kind of programmed contentiousness – a prepatterned, unthinking use of fighting to accomplish goals that do not necessarily require it.

## HOW USEFUL ARE FIGHTS?

Noticing that public discourse so often takes the form of heated arguments – of having a fight – made me ask how useful it is in our personal lives to settle differences by arguing. Given what I know about having arguments in private life, I had to conclude that it is, in many cases, not very useful.

In close relationships it is possible to find ways of arguing that result in better understanding and solving problems. But with most arguments, little is resolved, worked out, or achieved when two people get angrier and less rational by the minute. When you're having an argument with someone, you're usually not trying to understand what the other person is saying, or what in their experience leads them to say it. Instead, you're readying your response: listening for weaknesses in logic to leap on, points you can distort to make the other person look bad and yourself look good. Sometimes you know, on some back burner of your mind, that you're doing this – that there's a kernel of truth in what your adversary is saying and a bit of unfair twisting in what you're saying. Sometimes you do this because you're angry, but sometimes it's just the temptation to take aim at a point made along the way because it's an easy target.

Here's an example of how this happened in an argument between a couple who had been married for over fifty years. The husband wanted to join an HMO by signing over their Medicare benefits to save money. The wife objected because it would mean she could no longer see the doctor she knew and trusted. In arguing her point of view, she said, 'I like Dr B. He knows me, he's interested in me. He calls me by my first name.' The husband parried the last point: 'I don't like that. He's much younger than we are. He shouldn't be calling us by first name.' But the form of address Dr B. uses was irrelevant. The wife was trying to communicate that she felt comfortable with the doctor she knew, that she had a relationship with him. His calling her by first name was just one of a list of details she was marshaling to explain her comfort with him. Picking on this one detail did not change her view – and did not address her concern. It was just a way to win the argument.

We are all guilty, at times, of seizing on irrelevant details, distorting someone else's position the better to oppose it, when we're arguing with those we're closest to. But we are rarely dependent on these fights as sources of information. The same tactics are common when public discourse is carried out on the model of personal fights. And the results are dangerous when listeners are looking to these interchanges to get needed information or practical results.

Fights have winners and losers. If you're fighting to win, the temptation is great to deny facts that support your opponent's views and to filter what you know, saying only what supports your side. In the extreme form, it encourages people to misrepresent or even to lie. We accept this risk because we believe we can tell when someone is lying. The problem is, we can't.

Paul Ekman, a psychologist at the University of California, San Francisco, studies lying. He set up experiments in which individuals were videotaped talking about their emotions, actions, or beliefs – some truthfully, some not. He has shown these videotapes to thousands of people, asking them to identify the liars and also to say how sure they were about their judgments. His findings are chilling: Most people performed not much better than chance, and those who did the worst had just as much confidence in their judgments as the few who were really able to detect lies. Intrigued by the implications of this research in various walks of life, Dr Ekman repeated this experiment with groups of people whose jobs require them to sniff out lies: judges, lawyers, police, psychotherapists, and employees of the CIA, FBI, and ATF (Bureau of Alcohol, Tobacco, and Firearms). They were no better at detecting who was telling the truth than the rest of us. The only group that did significantly better were members of the U.S. Secret Service. This finding gives some comfort when it comes to the Secret Service but not much when it comes to every other facet of public life.

## TWO SIDES TO EVERY QUESTION

Our determination to pursue truth by setting up a fight between two sides leads us to believe that every issue has two sides – no more, no less: If both sides are given a forum to confront each other, all the relevant information will emerge, and the best case will be made for each side. But opposition does not lead to truth when an issue is not composed of two opposing sides but is a crystal of many sides. Often the truth is in the complex middle, not the oversimplified extremes.

We love using the word 'debate' as a way of representing issues: the abortion debate, the health care debate, the affirmative action debate – even 'the great backpacking vs. car camping debate.' The ubiquity of this word in itself shows our tendency to conceptualize issues in a way that predisposes public discussion to be polarized, framed as two opposing sides that give each other no ground. There are many problems with this approach. If you begin with the assumption that there *must* be an 'other side,' you may end up scouring the margins of science or the fringes of lunacy to find it. As a result, proven facts, such as what we know about how the earth and its inhabitants evolved, are set on a par with claims that are known to have no basis in fact, such as creationism.

The conviction that there are two sides to every story can prompt writers or producers to dig up an 'other side,' so kooks who state outright falsehoods are given a platform in public discourse. This accounts, in part, for the bizarre phenomenon of Holocaust denial. Deniers, as Emory University professor Deborah Lipstadt shows, have been successful in gaining television airtime and campus newspaper coverage by masquerading as 'the other side' in a 'debate.'

Appearance in print or on television has a way of lending legitimacy, so baseless claims take on a mantle of possibility. Lipstadt shows how Holocaust deniers dispute established facts of history, and then reasonable spokespersons use their having been disputed as a basis for questioning known facts. The actor Robert Mitchum, for example, interviewed in *Esquire*, expressed doubt about the Holocaust. When the interviewer asked about the slaughter of six million Jews, Mitchum replied, 'I don't know. People dispute that.' Continual reference to 'the other side' results in a pervasive conviction that everything has another side – with the result that people begin to doubt the existence of any facts at all.

## THE EXPENSE OF TIME AND SPIRIT

Lipstadt's book meticulously exposes the methods used by deniers to falsify the overwhelming historic evidence that the Holocaust occurred. That a scholar had to invest years of her professional life writing a book unraveling efforts to deny something that was about as well known and well documented as any historical fact has ever been – while those who personally experienced and witnessed it are still alive – is testament to another way that the argument culture limits our knowledge rather than expanding it. Talent and effort are wasted refuting outlandish claims that should never have been given a platform in the first place. Talent and effort are also wasted when individuals who have been unfairly attacked must spend years of their creative lives defending themselves rather than advancing their work. The entire society loses their creative efforts. This is what happened with scientist Robert Gallo.

Dr Gallo is the American virologist who codiscovered the AIDS virus. He is also the one who developed the technique for studying T-cells, which made that discovery possible. And Gallo's work was seminal in developing the test to detect the AIDS virus in blood, the first and for a long time the only means known of stemming the tide of death from AIDS. But in 1989, Gallo became the object of a four-year investigation into allegations that he had stolen the AIDS virus from Luc Montagnier of the Pasteur Institute in Paris, who had independently identified the AIDS virus. Simultaneous investigations by the National Institutes of Health, the office of Michigan Congressman John Dingell, and the National Academy of Sciences barreled ahead long after Gallo and Montagnier settled the dispute to their mutual satisfaction. In 1993 the investigations concluded that Gallo had done nothing wrong. Nothing. But this exoneration cannot be considered a happy ending. Never mind the personal suffering of Gallo, who was reviled when he should have been heralded as a hero. Never mind that, in his words, 'These were the most painful years and horrible years of my life.' The dreadful, unconscionable result of the fruitless investigations is that Gallo had to spend four years fighting the accusations instead of fighting AIDS.

The investigations, according to journalist Nicholas Wade, were sparked by an article about Gallo written in the currently popular spirit of demonography: not to praise the person it features but to bury him – to show his weaknesses, his villainous side. The implication that Gallo had stolen the AIDS virus was created to fill a requirement of the discourse: In demonography, writers must find negative sides of their subjects to display for readers who enjoy seeing heroes transformed into villains. The suspicion led to investigations, and the investigations became a juggernaut that acquired a life of its own, fed by the enthusiasm for attack on public figures that is the culture of critique.

## METAPHORS: WE ARE WHAT WE SPEAK

Perhaps one reason suspicions of Robert Gallo were so zealously investigated is that the scenario of an ambitious scientist ready to do anything to defeat a rival appeals to our sense of story; it is the kind of narrative we are ready to believe. Culture, in a sense, is an environment of narratives that we hear repeatedly until they seem to make self-evident sense in explaining human behavior. Thinking of human interactions as battles is a metaphorical frame through which we learn to regard the world and the people in it.

All language uses metaphors to express ideas; some metaphoric words and expressions are novel, made up for the occasion, but more are calcified in the language. They are simply the way we think it is natural to express ideas. We don't think of them as metaphors. Someone who says, 'Be careful: You aren't a cat; you don't have nine lives,' is explicitly comparing you to a cat, because the cat is named in words. But what if someone says, 'Don't pussyfoot around; get to the point'? There is no explicit comparison to a cat, but the comparison is there nonetheless, implied in the word 'pussyfoot.' This expression probably developed as a reference to the movements of a cat cautiously circling a suspicious object. I doubt that individuals using the word 'pussyfoot' think consciously of cats. More often than not, we use expressions without thinking about their metaphoric implications. But that doesn't mean those implications are not influencing us.

At a meeting, a general discussion became so animated that a participant who wanted to comment prefaced his remark by saying, 'I'd like to leap into the fray.' Another participant called out, 'Or share your thoughts.' Everyone laughed. By suggesting a different phrasing, she called attention to what would probably have otherwise gone unnoticed: 'Leap into the fray' characterized the lively discussion as a metaphorical battle.

Americans talk about almost everything as if it were a war. A book about the history of linguistics is called *The Linguistics Wars*. A magazine article about claims that science is not completely objective is titled 'The Science Wars.' One about breast cancer detection is 'The Mammogram War'; about competition among caterers, 'Party Wars' – and on and on in a potentially endless list. Politics, of course, is a prime candidate. One of innumerable possible examples, the headline of a story reporting that the Democratic National Convention nominated Bill Clinton to run for a second term declares, 'DEMOCRATS SEND CLINTON INTO BATTLE FOR A 2D TERM.' But medicine is as frequent a candidate, as we talk about battling and conquering disease.

Headlines are intentionally devised to attract attention, but we all use military or attack imagery in everyday expressions without thinking about it: 'Take a shot at it,' 'I don't want to be shot down,' 'He went off half cocked,' 'That's half the battle.' Why does it matter that our public discourse is filled with military metaphors? Aren't they just words? Why not talk about something that matters – like actions?

Because words matter. When we think we are using language, language is using us. As linguist Dwight Bolinger put it (employing a military metaphor), language is like a loaded gun: It can be fired intentionally, but it can wound or kill just as surely when fired accidentally. The terms in which we talk about something shape the way we think about it – and even what we see.

The power of words to shape perception has been proven by researchers in controlled experiments. Psychologists Elizabeth Loftus and John Palmer, for example, found that the terms in which people are asked to recall something affect what they recall. The researchers showed subjects a film of two cars colliding, then asked how fast the cars were going; one week later, they asked whether there had been any broken glass. Some subjects were asked, 'About how fast were the cars going when they bumped into each other?' Others were asked, 'About how fast were the cars going when they smashed into each other?' Those who read the question with the verb 'smashed' estimated that the cars were going faster. They were also more likely to 'remember' having seen broken glass. (There wasn't any.)

This is how language works. It invisibly molds our way of thinking about people, actions, and the world around us. Military metaphors train us to think about – and see – everything in terms of fighting, conflict, and war. This perspective then limits our imaginations when we consider what we can do about situations we would like to understand or change.

Even in science, common metaphors that are taken for granted influence how researchers think about natural phenomena. Evelyn Fox Keller describes a case in which acceptance of a metaphor led scientists to see something that was not there. A mathematical biologist, Keller outlines the fascinating behavior of cellular slime mold. This unique mold can take two completely different forms: It can exist as single-cell organisms, or the separate cells can come together to form multicellular aggregates. The puzzle facing scientists was: What triggers aggregation? In other words, what makes the single cells join together? Scientists focused their investigations by asking what entity issued the order to start aggregating. They first called this bosslike entity a 'founder cell,' and later a 'pacemaker cell,' even though no one had seen any evidence for the existence of such a cell. Proceeding nonetheless from the assumption that such a cell must exist, they ignored evidence to the contrary: For example, when the center of the aggregate is removed, other centers form.

Scientists studying slime mold did not examine the interrelationship between the cells and their environment, nor the interrelationship between the functional systems within each cell, because they were busy looking for the pacemaker cell, which, as eventually became evident, did not exist. Instead, under conditions of nutritional deprivation, each individual cell begins to feel the urge to merge with others to form the conglomerate. It is a reaction of the cells to their environment, not to the orders of a boss. Keller recounts this tale to illustrate her insight that we tend to view nature through our understanding of human relations as hierarchical. In her words, 'We risk imposing on nature the very stories we like to hear.' In other words, the conceptual metaphor of hierarchical governance made scientists 'see' something – a pacemaker cell – that wasn't there.

Among the stories many Americans most like to hear are war stories. According to historian Michael Sherry, the American war movie developed during World War II and has been with us ever since. He shows that movies not explicitly about war were also war movies at heart, such as westerns with their good guy-bad guy battles settled with guns. *High Noon*, for example, which became a model for later westerns, was an allegory of the Second World War: The happy ending hinges on the pacifist taking up arms. We can also see this story line in contemporary adventure films: Think of *Star Wars*, with its stirring finale in which Han Solo, having professed no interest in or taste for battle, returns at the last moment to destroy the enemy and save the day. And precisely the same theme is found in a contemporary low-budget independent film, *Sling Blade*, in which a peace-loving retarded man becomes a hero at the end by murdering the man who has been tormenting the family he has come to love.

---

## PUT UP YOUR DUKES

---

If war provides the metaphors through which we view the world and each other, we come to view others – and ourselves – as warriors in battle. Almost any human encounter can be framed as a fight between two opponents. Looking at it this way brings particular aspects of the event into focus and obscures others.

Framing interactions as fights affects not only the participants but also the viewers. At a performance, the audience, as well as the performers, can be transformed. This effect was noted by a reviewer in *The New York Times*, commenting on a musical event:

> **Showdown at Lincoln Center.** Jazz's ideological war of the last several years led to a pitched battle in August between John Lincoln Collier, the writer, and Wynton Marsalis, the trumpeter, in a debate at Lincoln Center. Mr Marsalis demolished Mr Collier, point after point after point, but what made the debate unpleasant was the crowd's blood lust; humiliation, not elucidation, was the desired end.

Military imagery pervades this account: the difference of opinions between Collier and Marsalis was an 'ideological war,' and the 'debate' was a 'pitched battle' in which Marsalis 'demolished' Collier (not his arguments, but him). What the commentator regrets, however, is that the audience got swept up in the mood instigated by the way the debate was carried out: 'the crowd's blood lust' for Collier's defeat.

This is one of the most dangerous aspects of regarding intellectual interchange as a fight. It contributes to an atmosphere of animosity that spreads like a fever. In a society that includes people who express their anger by shooting, the result of demonizing those with whom we disagree can be truly tragic.

But do audiences necessarily harbor within themselves a 'blood lust,' or is it stirred in them by the performances they are offered? Another arts event was set up as a debate between a playwright and a theater director. In this case, the metaphor through which the debate was viewed was not war but boxing – a sport that is in itself, like a debate, a metaphorical battle that pitches one side against the other in an all-out effort to win. A headline describing the event set the frame: 'AND IN THIS CORNER . . .,' followed by the subhead 'A Black Playwright and White Critic Duke It Out.' The story then reports:

> the face-off between August Wilson, the most successful black playwright in the American theater, and Robert Brustein, longtime drama critic for The New Republic and artistic director of the American Repertory Theatre in Cambridge, Mass. These two heavyweights had been battling in print since last June . . .
>
> Entering from opposite sides of the stage, the two men shook hands and came out fighting – or at least sparring.

Wilson, the article explains, had given a speech in which he opposed Black performers taking 'white' roles in color-blind casting; Brustein had written a column disagreeing; and both followed up with further responses to each other.

According to the article, 'The drama of the Wilson-Brustein confrontation lies in their mutual intransigence.' No one would question that audiences crave drama. But is intransigence the most appealing source of drama? I happened to hear this debate broadcast on the radio. The line that triggered the loudest cheers from the audience was the final question put to the two men by the moderator, Anna Deavere Smith: 'What did you each learn from the other in this debate?' The loud applause was evidence that the audience did not crave intransigence. They wanted to see another kind of drama: the drama of change – change that comes from genuinely listening to someone with a different point of view, not the transitory drama of two intransigent positions in stalemate.

To encourage the staging of more dramas of change and fewer of intransigence, we need new metaphors to supplement and complement the pervasive war and boxing match metaphors through which we take it for granted issues and events are best talked about and viewed.

## MUD SPLATTERS

Our fondness for the fight scenario leads us to frame many complex human interactions as a battle between two sides. This then shapes the way we understand what happened and how we regard the participants. One unfortunate result is that fights make a mess in which everyone is muddied. The person attacked is often deemed just as guilty as the attacker.

The injustice of this is clear if you think back to childhood. Many of us still harbor anger as we recall a time (or many times) a sibling or playmate started a fight – but both of us got blamed. Actions occur in a stream, each a response to what came before. Where you punctuate them can change their meaning just as you can change the meaning of a sentence by punctuating it in one place or another.

Like a parent despairing of trying to sort out which child started a fight, people often respond to those involved in a public dispute as if both were equally guilty. When champion figure skater Nancy Kerrigan was struck on the knee shortly before the 1994 Olympics in Norway and the then-husband of another champion skater, Tonya Harding, implicated his wife in planning the attack, the event was characterized as a fight between two skaters that obscured their differing roles. As both skaters headed for the Olympic competition, their potential meeting was described as a 'long-anticipated figure-skating shootout.' Two years later, the event was referred to not as 'the attack on Nancy Kerrigan' but as 'the rivalry surrounding Tonya Harding and Nancy Kerrigan.'

By a similar process, the Senate Judiciary Committee hearings to consider the nomination of Clarence Thomas for Supreme Court justice at which Anita Hill was called to testify are regularly referred to as the 'Hill-Thomas hearings,' obscuring the very different roles played by Hill and Thomas. Although testimony by Anita Hill was the occasion for reopening the hearings, they were still the Clarence Thomas confirmation hearings: Their purpose was to evaluate Thomas's candidacy. Framing these hearings as a two-sides dispute between Hill and Thomas allowed the senators to focus their investigation on cross-examining Hill rather than seeking other sorts of evidence, for example by consulting experts on sexual harassment to ascertain whether Hill's account seemed plausible.

## SLASH-AND-BURN THINKING

Approaching situations like warriors in battle leads to the assumption that intellectual inquiry, too, is a game of attack, counterattack, and self-defense. In this spirit, critical thinking is synonymous with criticizing. In many classrooms, students are encouraged to read someone's life work, then rip it to shreds. Though criticism is one form of critical thinking – and an essential one – so are integrating ideas from disparate fields and examining the context out of which ideas grew. Opposition does not lead to the whole truth when we ask only 'What's wrong with this?' and never 'What can we use from this in building a new theory, a new understanding?'

There are many ways that unrelenting criticism is destructive in itself. In innumerable small dramas mirroring what happened to Robert Gallo (but on a much more modest scale), our most creative thinkers can waste time and effort responding to critics motivated less by a genuine concern about weaknesses in their work than by a desire to find something to attack. All of society loses when creative people are discouraged from their pursuits by unfair criticism. (This is particularly likely to happen since, as Kay Redfield Jamison shows in her book *Touched with Fire*, many of those who are unusually creative are also unusually sensitive; their sensitivity often drives their creativity.)

If the criticism is unwarranted, many will say, you are free to argue against it, to defend yourself. But there are problems with this, too. Not only does self-defense take time and draw off energy that would better be spent on new creative work, but any move to defend yourself makes you appear, well, defensive. For example, when an author wrote a letter to the editor protesting a review he considered unfair, the reviewer (who is typically given the last word) turned the very fact that the author defended himself into a weapon with which to attack again. The reviewer's response began, 'I haven't much time to waste on the kind of writer who squanders his talent drafting angry letters to reviewers.'

The argument culture limits the information we get rather than broadening it in another way. When a certain kind of interaction is the norm, those who feel comfortable with that type of interaction are drawn to participate, and those who do not feel comfortable with it recoil and go elsewhere. If public discourse included a broad range of types, we would be making room for individuals with different temperaments to take part and contribute their perspectives and insights. But when debate, opposition, and fights overwhelmingly predominate, those who enjoy verbal sparring are likely to take part – by calling in to talk shows, writing letters to the editor or articles, becoming journalists – and those who cannot comfortably take part in oppositional discourse, or do not wish to, are likely to opt out.

This winnowing process is easy to see in apprenticeship programs such as acting school, law school, and graduate school. A woman who was identified in her university drama program as showing exceptional promise was encouraged to go to New York to study acting. Full of enthusiasm, she was accepted by a famous acting school where the teaching method entailed the teacher screaming at students, goading and insulting them as a way to bring out the best in them. This worked well with many of the students but not with her. Rather than rising to the occasion when attacked, she cringed, becoming less able to draw on her talent, not more. After a year, she dropped out. It could be that she simply didn't have what it took – but this will never be known, because the adversarial style of teaching did not allow her to show what talent she had.

## POLARIZING COMPLEXITY:
## NATURE OR NURTURE?

Few issues come with two neat, and neatly opposed, sides. Again, I have seen this in the domain of gender. One common polarization is an opposition between two sources of differences between women and men: 'culture,' or 'nurture,' on one hand and 'biology,' or 'nature,' on the other.

Shortly after the publication of *You Just Don't Understand*, I was asked by a journalist what question I most often encountered about women's and men's conversational styles. I told her, 'Whether the differences I describe are biological or cultural.' The journalist laughed. Puzzled, I asked why this made her laugh. She explained that she had always been so certain that any significant differences are cultural rather than biological in origin that the question struck her as absurd. So I should not have been surprised when I read, in the article she wrote, that the two questions I am most frequently asked are 'Why do women nag?' and 'Why won't men ask for directions?' Her ideological certainty that the question I am most frequently asked was absurd led her to ignore my answer and get a fact wrong in her report of my experience.

Some people are convinced that any significant differences between men and women are entirely or overwhelmingly due to cultural influences – the way we treat girls and boys, and men's dominance of women in society. Others are convinced that any significant differences are entirely or overwhelmingly due to biology: the physical facts of female and male bodies, hormones, and reproductive functions. Many problems are caused by framing the question as a dichotomy: Are behaviors that pattern by sex biological or cultural? This polarization encourages those on one side to demonize those who take the other view, which leads in turn to misrepresenting the work of those who are assigned to the opposing camp. Finally, and most devastatingly, it prevents us from exploring the interaction of biological and cultural factors – factors that must, and can only, be understood together. By posing the question as either/or, we reinforce a false assumption that biological and cultural factors are separable and preclude the investigations that would help us understand their interrelationship. When a problem is posed in a way that polarizes, the solution is often obscured before the search is under way.

## WHO'S UP? WHO'S DOWN?

Related to polarization is another aspect of the argument culture:

our obsession with ratings and rankings. Magazines and Sunday papers offer the 10, 50, or 100 best of everything: restaurants, mutual funds, hospitals, even judges. Newsmagazines tell us Who's up, Who's down, as in *Newsweek*'s 'Conventional Wisdom Watch' and *Time*'s 'Winners and Losers.' Rankings and ratings pit restaurants, products, schools, and people against each other on a single scale, obscuring the myriad differences among them. Maybe a small Thai restaurant in one neighborhood can't really be compared to a pricey French one in another, any more than judges with a vast range of abilities and beliefs can be compared on a single scale. And timing can skew results: Ohio State University protested to *Time* magazine when its football team was ranked at the bottom of a scale because only 29 percent of the team graduated. The year before it would have ranked among the top six with 72 percent.

After a political debate, analysts comment not on what the candidates said but on the question 'Who won?' After the president delivers an important speech, such as the State of the Union Address, expert commentators are asked to give it a grade. Like ranking, grading establishes a competition. The biggest problem with asking what grade the president's speech deserves, or who won and who lost a campaign debate, is what is not asked and is therefore not answered: What was said, and what is the significance of this for the country?

---

## AN ETHIC OF AGGRESSION

---

In an argument culture aggressive tactics are valued for their own sake. For example, a woman called in to a talk show on which I was a guest to say, 'When I'm in a place where a man is smoking, and there's a no-smoking sign, instead of saying to him "You aren't allowed to smoke in here. Put that out," I say, "I'm awfully sorry, but I have asthma, so your smoking makes it hard for me to breathe. Would you mind terribly not smoking?" Whenever I say this, the man is extremely polite and solicitous, and he puts his cigarette out, and I say, "Oh, thank you, thank you!" as if he's done a wonderful thing for me. Why do I do that?'

I think this woman expected me to say that she needs assertiveness training to learn to confront smokers in a more aggressive manner.

Instead, I told her that there was nothing wrong with her style of getting the man to stop smoking. She gave him a face-saving way of doing what she asked, one that allowed him to feel chivalrous rather than chastised. This is kind to him, but it is also kind to herself, since it is more likely to lead to the result she desires. If she tried to alter his behavior by reminding him of the rules, he might well rebel: 'Who made you the enforcer? Mind your own business!' Indeed, who gives any of us the authority to set others straight when we think they're breaking rules?

Another caller disagreed with me, saying the first caller's style was 'self-abasing' and there was no reason for her to use it. But I persisted: There is nothing necessarily destructive about conventional self-effacement. Human relations depend on the agreement to use such verbal conventions. I believe the mistake this caller was making – a mistake many of us make – was to confuse *ritual* self-effacement with the literal kind. All human relations require us to find ways to get what we want from others without seeming to dominate them. Allowing others to feel they are doing what you want for a reason less humiliating to them fulfills this need.

Thinking of yourself as the wronged party who is victimized by a lawbreaking boor makes it harder to see the value of this method. But suppose you are the person addicted to smoking who lights up (knowingly or not) in a no-smoking zone. Would you like strangers to yell at you to stop smoking, or would you rather be allowed to save face by being asked politely to stop in order to help them out? Or imagine yourself having broken a rule inadvertently (which is not to imply rules are broken only by mistake; it is only to say that sometimes they are). Would you like some stranger to swoop down on you and begin berating you, or would you rather be asked politely to comply?

As this example shows, conflicts can sometimes be resolved without confrontational tactics, but current conventional wisdom often devalues less confrontational tactics even if they work well, favoring more aggressive strategies even if they get less favorable results. It's as if we value a fight for its own sake, not for its effectiveness in resolving disputes.

This ethic shows up in many contexts. In a review of a contentious book, for example, a reviewer wrote, 'Always provocative, sometimes infuriating, this collection reminds us that the purpose of art is not to confirm and coddle but to provoke and confront.' This false dichotomy encapsulates the belief that if you are not provoking and confronting, then you are confirming and coddling – as if there weren't myriad other ways to question and learn. What about exploring, exposing, delving, analyzing, understanding, moving, connecting, integrating, illuminating ... or any of innumerable verbs that capture other aspects of what art can do?

## THE BROADER PICTURE

The increasingly adversarial spirit of our contemporary lives is fundamentally related to a phenomenon that has been much remarked upon in recent years: the breakdown of a sense of community. In this spirit, distinguished journalist and author Orville Schell points out that in his day journalists routinely based their writing on a sense of connection to their subjects – and that this sense of connection is missing from much that is written by journalists today. Quite the contrary, a spirit of demonography often prevails that has just the opposite effect: Far from encouraging us to feel connected to the subjects, it encourages us to feel critical, superior – and, as a result, distanced. The cumulative effect is that citizens feel more and more cut off from the people in public life they read about.

The argument culture dovetails with a general disconnection and breakdown of community in another way as well. Community norms and pressures exercise a restraint on the expression of hostility and destruction. Many cultures have rituals to channel and contain aggressive impulses, especially those of adolescent males. In just this spirit, at the 1996 Republican National Convention, both Colin Powell and Bob Dole talked about growing up in small communities where everyone knew who they were. This meant that many people would look out for them, but also that if they did something wrong, it would get back to their parents. Many adults grew up in neighborhoods that worked the same way. If a young man stole something, committed vandalism, or broke a rule or law, it would be reported to his relatives, who would punish him or tell him how his actions were shaming the family. Western neighborhoods today often lack these brakes.

Community is a blend of connections and authority, and we are losing both. As Robert Bly shows in his book by that title, we now have a *Sibling Society:* Citizens are like squabbling siblings with no authority figures who can command enough respect to contain and channel their aggressive impulses. It is as if every day is a day with a substitute teacher who cannot control the class and maintain order.

The argument culture is both a product of and a contributor to this alienation, separating people, disconnecting them from each other and from those who are or might have been their leaders.

---

## WHAT OTHER WAY IS THERE?

---

Philosopher John Dewey said, on his ninetieth birthday, 'Democracy begins in conversation.' I fear that it gets derailed in polarized debate.

In conversation we form the interpersonal ties that bind individuals together in personal relationships; in public discourse, we form similar ties on a larger scale, binding individuals into a community. In conversation, we exchange the many types of information we need to live our lives as members of a community. In public discourse, we exchange the information that citizens in a democracy need in order to decide how to vote. If public discourse provides entertainment first and foremost – and if entertainment is first and foremost watching fights – then citizens do not get the information they need to make meaningful use of their right to vote.

Of course it is the responsibility of intellectuals to explore potential weaknesses in others' arguments, and of journalists to represent serious opposition when it exists. But when opposition becomes the overwhelming avenue of inquiry – a formula that *requires* another side to be found or a criticism to be voiced; when the lust for opposition privileges extreme views and obscures complexity; when our eagerness to find weaknesses blinds us to strengths; when the atmosphere of animosity precludes respect and poisons our relations with one another; then the argument culture is doing more damage than good.

I offer this book not as a frontal assault on the argument culture. That would be in the spirit of attack that I am questioning. It is an attempt to examine the argument culture – our use of attack, opposition, and debate in public discourse – to ask, What are its limits as well as its strengths? How has it served us well, but also how has it failed us? How is it related to culture and gender? What other options do we have?

I do not believe we should put aside the argument model of public discourse entirely, but we need to rethink whether this is the *only* way, or *always* the best way, to carry out our affairs. A step toward broadening our repertoires would be to pioneer reform by experimenting with metaphors other than sports and war, and with formats other than debate for framing the exchange of ideas. The change might be as simple as introducing a plural form. Instead of asking 'What's the other side?' we might ask instead, 'What are the other sides?' Instead of insisting on hearing 'both sides,' we might insist on hearing 'all sides.'

Another option is to expand our notion of 'debate' to include more dialogue. This does not mean there can be no negativity, criticism, or disagreement. It simply means we can be more creative in our ways of managing all of these, which are inevitable and useful. In dialogue, each statement that one person makes is qualified by a statement made by someone else, until the series of statements and qualifications moves everyone closer to a fuller truth. Dialogue does not preclude negativity. Even saying 'I agree' makes sense only against the background assumption that you might disagree. In dialogue, there is opposition, yes, but no head-on collision. Smashing heads does not open minds.

There are times when we need to disagree, criticize, oppose, and attack – to hold debates and view issues as polarized battles. Even cooperation, after all, is not the absence of conflict but a means of managing conflict. My goal is not a make-nice false veneer of agreement or a dangerous ignoring of true opposition. I'm questioning the *automatic* use of adversarial formats – the assumption that it's *always* best to address problems and issues by fighting over them. I'm hoping for a broader repertoire of ways to talk to each other and address issues vital to us.

## 2

# BOTH SIDES COME OUT FIGHTING: THE ARGUMENT CULTURE AND THE PRESS

'TAKE A SIDE' the advertisement blares in big block letters. In smaller print, it continues:

Join the battle as opinion leaders fire off their views about today's hot issues on two of the most dynamic shows on the air.

Photographs of the hosts appear under the logos of the two shows – *Hardball* and *Equal Time* – arrayed as if they were at war with each other. Each show occupies one side of the page, and over each logo is a photograph of an army marching into battle, one side brandishing blue flags, the other waving red.

An ad for the popular political talk show *Crossfire* has a similar theme: Four people are featured, with arms crossed, looking grim. Over each one's head is a banner headline in block letters: 'IT'S

A LEFT,' 'AND A RIGHT,' 'AND ANOTHER LEFT,' 'AND ANOTHER RIGHT' – playing on the double entendre of punches in a boxing match and the political 'left,' represented by Geraldine Ferraro and Bill Press, glaring at the political 'right,' represented by John Sununu and Robert Novak. The two 'lefts' (on the left-hand side of the page, of course) are separated from the 'right' by a crack in concrete that opens to show a brick wall background against which appears the commentary 'There's new fuel on the left. The old fire's back on the right.'

These ads, like the shows they promote, tell readers that issues can be understood as having two – and only two – diametrically opposed and warring sides, rather than having many sides that reflect complex interacting forces and interests. The two ads end: 'Watch what happens' and 'Now watch the sparks really fly,' sending another message: Politics is a spectator sport. You may root for one side or the other, but nothing else is expected of you. This is as different from participatory democracy as watching a ball game on television is from going out and playing one.

Almost any news item can be described as a fight – and often is. For example, a newsmagazine article about the Guggenheim Museum Bilbao – a joint venture of the Guggenheim Museum in New York and the city of Bilbao, Spain – implies that the architect, Frank Gehry, was picking a fight with another architect when he designed the building:

> When you think 'Guggenheim,' you think Frank Lloyd Wright, and the towering central atrium in Bilbao – at 165 feet, half again the height of Wright's New York spiral – seems to say 'Take that!' to the master.

Yet Gehry himself says his work pays homage to a film, as the article goes on to quote:

> It is full of light, soaring spaces and is criss-crossed by catwalks, with three levels of galleries spinning off it. 'The whole idea here was Fritz Lang's "Metropolis," to make a visionary city,' says Gehry.

How different to think of the new museum as a visionary city inspired by another artist rather than an aggressive assault by an upstart who beats the master by building a higher atrium.

Business news also fits easily into the fighting frame. For example, the headline 'A CLASSIC MATCHUP' is aided by the subhead, 'It's only the opening bell, but the merger battle between Hilton and ITT promises to be bloody.' Alongside is a color photograph of two boxers in red gloves punching each other in a boxing ring identified as Caesar's Palace. The photograph is captioned, 'Business brawl: Fighting over assets like ITT's Caesar's Palace.' When I was flipping pages in search of this story, I missed it the first time through because, despite knowing what page it was on, when I saw the photograph, I drew the hasty conclusion that I had reached the sports section and kept flipping.

The contested takeover bid, a recurring feature of the British business scene, is likewise regularly reported as though it were a sporting contest. The most heated bid in years was made in November 1995 by Granada, the television and leisure conglomerate, for Forte, the family-run hotel and restaurant group. 'This one will go all the rounds, and it will not be fought according to the Queensberry rules,' wrote the London *Times*. The *Sunday Times* picked up the metaphor: 'Heavyweights limber up for the Forte prize fight.' The *Sunday Express* called it 'the title fight of the decade' and the *Observer* noted: 'The target has come out of its corner fighting.' The *Independent on Sunday* extended the war metaphor, noting that the Forte camp 'risks running out of ammunition.'

In a single issue of an American newsmagazine we find a Chinese political leader who is 'well positioned to win this battle, which is why he's likely to fight it,' traditional car dealers who are 'about to become roadkill,' 'telecommunications price wars,' 'cereal wars,' the prediction that Alan Greenspan might 'launch a pre-emptive strike against inflation' and that consumers, by shopping for the lowest prices, may be 'the real anti-inflation fighters.'

All these accounts simply report events, but the way events are reported shapes our thinking about them – and can affect the events themselves. Writing in terms of opposition can actually create the opposition and all that goes with it. A magazine for college professors entitled *Lingua Franca* focuses on behind-the-scenes academic intrigue. By reporting on battles, the magazine also foments them.

Someone who was party to such a 'battle' commented, 'There is a way in which certain *Lingua Franca* accounts of academic debates needlessly polarize academic communities and generate more division than exists.'

The most extreme battle imagery, as seen in the *Crossfire* ad, is associated with television and its desire to create lively programming – often defined as provocative programming. In this view, the more extreme a statement is, the more readers or viewers will be interested. As *Washington Post* media critic Howard Kurtz put it in *Hot Air*, 'The middle ground, the sensible center, is dismissed as too squishy, too dull, too likely to send the audience channel surfing.' Getting a rise out of audiences is seen as good, regardless of what that rise consists of. Print journalists are not immune to this motivation. I once asked a magazine editor whether he and his colleagues regret publishing pieces that so anger and offend readers that a large number of them write to express disapproval. No, he replied. Anytime a piece triggers a flood of mail, the editors are happy. (An ironic result is that writing a letter to express outrage can have an effect opposite to the one intended: Rather than discouraging editors from presenting such material in the future, it may serve as encouragement.)

For the British satirical magazine *Private Eye*, to cause offence seems like a primary objective. Hardly a week goes by when the correspondence columns do not contain at least one letter from a reader who has given up their subscription because of horror and distress at a joke or an article. The magazine covers politics in exclusively personal terms. Parliament is portrayed as a seething cauldron of rivalries and vendettas. Politicians' indiscretions, real or imagined, are magnified and reported with relish.

The combative attitude spills over into the mainstream British press. 'The Clare v Liz turf war' shouted a headline in the *Independent on Sunday*, reporting a feud between Clare Short, a Cabinet minister, and Baroness Symons, a junior minister at the Foreign Office. In January 1998 the London *Evening Standard* told how 'Deputy Prime Minister John Prescott and Eurotunnel chief John Noulton were at each other's throats today.' (Note that whereas the men are referred to by first name plus surname, the women are simply 'Clare' and 'Liz' – adding trivialization to militarization, suggesting a cat fight perhaps, rather than a fist fight.)

Democracy is not only a matter of giving everyone a right to vote. People need to understand what they're voting about. Framing news as a fight between two sides often results in needed information not getting out – and even in false information getting spread. In the worst cases, our situation is comparable in this respect to that of totalitarian countries whose governments deliberately mislead their people by spreading disinformation.

---

## NO FIGHT, NO NEWS

---

Any day you open a newspaper or magazine, you can find evidence of the belief that controversy is interesting and the absence of controversy is dull. For example, a newspaper reports that at an annual meeting of the mutual fund industry 'the hallway chatter focused all week on the possibility of fireworks at the final session, when two industry titans with no love lost between them would face off,' but 'the debate turned out to be disappointingly tame.'

Almost any topic it seems can be turned into a viable news story if the notion of conflict can be sustained. Consider this opening sentence from a report in the London *Independent on Sunday* in September 1997: 'The bucolic world of TV gardening – all hearty bonhomie, twee jokes and pastoral rapture – has been riddled by the worm of dissension.' Readers were told how TV presenters were 'livid' at 'scathing attacks' made on them in a gardening magazine. The *Guardian* carries a feature every Saturday called 'Head to Head,' in which people known to have conflicting views on an issue engage in acrimonious correspondence.

Because of the belief that fights – and only fights – are interesting, any news or informational item that is not adversarial is less likely to be reported. I have talked to many heads of organizations and institutions who are frustrated because they cannot get press coverage to inform the public of what they do unless someone is protesting it – and then coverage focuses on the protesters. James Billington, director of the Library of Congress, for example, was frustrated that few people knew about a major exhibition the library mounted in 1995, 'Creating French Culture: Treasures from the Bibliothèque Nationale de France.' But everyone seemed to know about an exhibit on Freud that was not mounted that year. Billington maintains that the exhibition had to be postponed because of lack of funds – a message he was never able to communicate because news stories focused on protesters' belief that the library had cravenly caved in to political pressure from other protesters – critics of Freud. (In fact, the Freud exhibition was later rescheduled to open in fall 1998.)

I also heard from the head of a public institution who spent hours talking to a journalist preparing a story on one of their programs – a story that never ran because no one could be found who opposed the program: no fight, no story.

Few people who have experienced this are eager to talk on record because they fear offending journalists whose goodwill they need for future coverage. No one wants to step on the tail of a sleeping dragon. In order to tell a true story with all the details, I'll use my own experience, with the caveat that I have, over the years, received more than fair treatment from journalists, some of whom I count among – you should pardon the expression – my best friends. But I ran headlong into the no-fight-no-story principle when I appeared on a platform with Robert Bly, the poet, author, and leader of men's retreats. Following the trail of media coverage of this event offers a glimpse into the conviction that only fights are news.

Bly invited me to engage in a public conversation with him at New York's Open Center. Our conversation was advertised in the Open Center bulletin under the title 'Where Are Men and Women Now?' The bulletin referred to the event as a 'dialogue,' promised that we would discuss 'the differing modes of language that men and women inhabit,' and asked how understanding these differences could help 'in working toward a reconciliation of men and women.' Despite this decidedly peaceful description, notice of the dialogue appeared in the major New York newspaper under the heading of – what else? – 'Battle of the Sexes.' The column referred to our meeting as a 'face-to-face, word-to-word confrontation' and 'a debate' – the first time Bly and I would 'face off publicly.'

On the basis either of this notice or of their own curiosity, organizations that requested complimentary tickets included *The New York Times, The New York Post, The New Yorker, People* magazine, *USA Today Weekend, The Village Voice,* and *The Economist.* A *Newsweek* photographer photographed Bly and me as we sat down to dinner before the event, at which we went ahead with our plans to have a conversation rather than a fight. The media disappointment was resounding.

Most of those who had asked for complimentary tickets decided not to publish reports. *The New York Times* did cover the evening, contrasting our 'unrelenting agreement' unfavorably with the 1971 Town Hall encounter between novelist Norman Mailer and feminist author Germaine Greer. *New York Newsday*, we learned, had prepared a favorable article but decided not to run it after the *Times* piece appeared; they did not want to appear 'soft' by taking seriously an event at which the *Times* had scoffed. *The Economist* echoed the *Times*'s tone, running a one-page story under the ironic heading 'GREAT DEBATES' with a subhead 'Bill and Coo.' The disappointed reporter blamed us for not fulfilling *The New York Times*'s promise: 'It was advertised as a battle of the sexes,' he began. 'One that would revive memories of the bruising clashes between Norman Mailer, a self-confessed "Prisoner of Sex," and militant feminists in the early 1970s.' He expressed his disapproval by calling our interchange 'a throwback to the 1870s.' Continuing to use the image of us fighting as a backdrop, he wrote, 'Both contestants came out of their corners cooing.'

*Newsweek* was perhaps the most inventive, devoting most of its article to describing the fight we did not have. The audience, readers were told, 'spent the whole time wondering if he would hit her over the head with his mandolin,' which was described as 'a savage-looking instrument.' Things looked 'promising,' the account went on, 'when Bly asserted that "both men and women want to fight in a healthy way"' but turned disappointing because 'he didn't do any fighting with Tannen, healthy or otherwise.' The writer opined that the hope that Bly and I would fight was the only thing that could explain the sellout crowd. But tickets were sold out within a week of the appearance of the Open Center catalogue, long before *The New York Times* mentioned the event and reported that 'thousands of requests continue to flood the office.'

It is common to read about imagined fights if no actual ones are at hand. When Madeleine Albright was nominated for the position of secretary of state, the press was overwhelmingly favorable, but at least one account predicted potential friction with Bill Richardson, Albright's proposed replacement as U.N. ambassador:

Relations between him and Albright could grow prickly. As U.N. ambassador, Albright had a reticent boss down in Washington, Warren Christopher. Richardson will not be so lucky. 'She's very controlling,' says one Washington insider who knows them both. 'There could be sparks.' . . . Richardson . . . could also prove tough competition for Albright as a media darling. Thanks to his fluent Spanish, he's probably better liked in Latin America than she is.

The most contentious phrase in the short article was pulled out to be featured in the subhead: '"There Could Be Sparks" with Albright at State.'

---

## WHAT'S LEFT OUT

It was no great loss to the world that my public conversation with Robert Bly was less widely reported than it might have been, or that what we said was obscured by what we did not do. But the habitual preference for stories about fights often results in important news not being covered, either because it doesn't seem controversial enough to be interesting or simply because there is no space left. Airtime and column inches devoted to controversy and fights are not devoted to discussing the issues and problems that our nation faces.

During his first year in office, President Clinton inaugurated a program called AmeriCorps that allowed college students to earn tuition by working in national service projects. *U.S. News and World Report* editor James Fallows recounts how journalists' inclination to focus on conflict obscured information about the program. A number of reporters were present as Clinton explained the details of AmeriCorps to a gathering of students in Chicago, who gave him a standing ovation. But during the question period, an audience member asked a challenging question: 'Mr Clinton, how can you talk about service when you didn't go to Vietnam?' A cry went up among the television news crew – 'Roll tape! Roll tape!' – and that's the small bit that got on the news.

It is easy to appreciate the motivation behind this decision. A single person challenging the president is more dramatic than the unfocused wave of a standing ovation, let alone the details of how AmeriCorps would work. Television, being visual, has to be dramatic. But the very aspect that made this interchange stand out – it was an isolated moment, different from the tone of the rest of the event – also made it unrepresentative and therefore misleading. Although I have no doubt that those who chose this part for the evening news had no motive other than putting together an interesting show, the cumulative effect is a shower of scenes of conflict. When such seeds are sown nightly, the bitter harvest is an overwhelming mood of hopelessness and a conviction that nothing constructive can ever be accomplished, plus a corrosive attitude of contempt for public figures. And again, events are not only reported but created: Knowing that moments of conflict attract media attention, political opponents can orchestrate such moments by planting protesters or hostile questioners on occasions like these.

In analyzing why efforts toward health care reform failed utterly in the Clintons' first term – a failure they call 'one of the greatest lost opportunities of our time' – journalists Haynes Johnson and David Broder dissect a large number of interacting forces, one of which was that 'The journalistic culture – both its professional mind-set and its commercial, competitive pressures – nudges the coverage strongly to emphasize conflict and dissent rather than clarification of alternatives and the search for consensus.' Thus, 'When the opponents of change began flooding the airwaves and the mail with warnings of dire consequences and mobilizing their grassroots campaigns to frighten people, the press reported their efforts but did not try to debunk them.' The authors show that this occurred first when Republicans and one set of interest groups helped defeat the Clinton plan to provide universal health insurance, and later happened again when Democrats and another set of interest groups helped defeat the Gingrich plan to cut spending by restructuring Medicare and Medicaid. Overall, they report, 'the *politics* of the battle was reported twice as often as the *impact* of the plan on consumers.' In the same spirit, the failure to reform health care went down in history as a political loss for the administration rather than as a grievous loss for the American people.

The focus on conflict results not only in neglecting to convey needed information but also in disseminating misinformation. Howard Kurtz documents how numerous false rumors were originated by right-wing groups hoping to harm the Democratic administration, then spread by fax and right-wing talk shows. The mainstream media then pick up the ball, reporting on the false rumors as a phenomenon but, in the process, repeating them. *The New York Times Magazine*, for example, in a cover story called 'The Clinton Haters,' detailed one bizarre and unfounded belief after another about the Clintons. By reporting on a phenomenon involving only a small number of deluded individuals, it ensured that a vastly larger number of people were exposed to the groundless rumors.

Several years ago I was on a local television talk show with a representative of the men's movement. I didn't foresee any problem, since there is nothing in my work that is anti-male. But in the room where guests wait to go on, I found a man with waist-length red hair wearing a shirt and tie and a floor-length skirt. He politely introduced himself and told me that he'd read and liked my book. He also expressed surprise that we were waiting in the same room; usually, he said, producers keep fellow guests apart from him until airtime. I recalled that I had experienced this on shows that had ferreted out guests who would oppose me, like isolating boxers in their own corners. Then he added, 'When I get out there, I'm going to attack you. But don't take it personally. That's why they invite me on, so that's what I'm going to do.'

When the show began and I spoke for the first time, I got as far as a sentence or two before this man nearly jumped out of his chair, threw his arms before him in gestures of anger, and began shrieking – first attacking me, but soon moving on to rail against women. The strangest thing about his hysterical attack was what it sparked in the studio audience: They too turned vicious, attacking not me (I hadn't gotten a chance to say anything) and not him (who wants to tangle with someone who will scream at you?) but the innocent and helpless guests: unsuspecting women who had agreed to appear on the show to talk about problems they had communicating with their spouses. This is one of the most dangerous effects of the argument culture: It creates an atmosphere of animosity that spreads like a fever.

The screaming man had been invited on this show to be outrageous and pick a fight. It would be easy to dismiss this as an aberrant local show; certainly, it was an extreme, not a typical, example. But I have also been on a talk show that prides itself on offering light rather than heat and encountered a fellow panelist whose expertise was not related to this topic yet who made false statements with a great air of authority. When I later asked how the panel members had been chosen, I was told that this guest was highly opinionated and could be depended on to make the show lively. If you're looking for a fight, you will get heat, not light. The British media are driven by similar values. *Newsnight* on BBC2 is one of several programs that regularly stage discussions on current topics, with the guests deliberately chosen because they are known to hold opposing views.

The BBC Radio 4 discussion program, *The Moral Maze*, has a regular panel who interrogate 'witnesses' chosen for their strong views on a particular topic. The panelists are adept at withering put-downs of witnesses with whom they disagree. Granted, the withering put-down is a British convention with a long and venerable heritage, yet the manner adopted by Dr David Starkey, a historian, on the program has provoked the *Daily Mail* to call him 'the most obnoxious man in Britain.' Moreover, this program is not unique, the critic Cosmo Landesman, writing in the *Sunday Times*, observed: 'Controversy . . . has become a marketing tool, a PR tactic used to promote products and personalities. The idea is to turn your movie, play, book, TV series into a media event and thus something the public feels it must experience.' Underlining this ethic is the conviction that the most engaging media event is a fight.

---

## TWO SIDES TO EVERY ISSUE:
## THE SEARCH FOR BALANCE

---

Staging political discussions as fights is especially characteristic of television. But print journalists use war imagery, especially in headlines, to attract attention and make writing snappy. There is also another factor at work in print journalism: the conviction that journalists' responsibility is to provide balance, which is often understood as presenting both sides. This is a laudable and often constructive goal, but it can lay traps for well-intentioned writers.

One way television shows and print news stories try to achieve balance is to include representatives of both the left and the right. This prompts us to squeeze people with widely diverse views into the procrustean beds of left and right. Harvard Law School professor Randall Kennedy, for example, chafes at being labeled a conservative for his opposition to affirmative action (he believes that race should not matter), because he also supports many policies that are clearly liberal, such as raising taxes, spending public funds to educate inner-city youth, and redistributing power and wealth. Labeling people left or right, liberal or conservative, obscures the complexity of their views and makes it harder for people to hear what others have to say: Once we see someone as bearing a label we don't like, we stop listening.

Another trap is the belief that the work is done when the two sides have been represented – without examining their claims for accuracy. In mid-February 1997, National Public Radio reported on proposed regulation of political fund-raising. The short report ended with the dual observation that Republicans accused the president of lacking credibility on the topic and that Democrats claimed Republicans had raised more funds from foreign sources than Democrats had. With this, the segment closed and the show moved on to the next story. These two concluding comments are balanced: Republicans accuse Democrats, Democrats accuse Republicans. But with a small amount of research, a journalist could determine which party had raised more funds from foreign sources, whereas few listeners could.

A valuable service that journalists are uniquely suited to provide is to investigate charges they report and inform audiences of their truth. But because their concern is with balance – presenting both sides – and because information tends to be filtered through our two-party systems, it is easy to see how a reporter might feel the job is done when Democratic and Republican or Conservative and Labour accusations are both reported. By focusing on balancing two sides, the press moves away from the investigative role for which it is so singularly well equipped. The result is that less needed information gets out.

## WHEN LIES BECOME 'THE OTHER SIDE'

Yet another troubling trap laid by the two-sides-to-every-issue approach is that sometimes there is no other side; there is only one side: truth. Once again, a dramatic example is Holocaust denial, an example so pivotal that it bears a closer look.

That the Holocaust took place is known because of a mountain – no, a mountain range – of evidence in the form of documents, film, artifacts, buildings, and the personal experience of innumerable people who lived through or observed it. That a few individuals would wish to deny the existence of so recent and well-established a historical fact is surprising. What is more surprising is that they have received so much attention and free publicity, to the extent that some young people who did not experience World War II firsthand have begun to doubt the facts.

Emory University professor Deborah Lipstadt documents how this happened in *Denying the Holocaust*. She shows that those who deny the Holocaust – or admit it happened but vastly understate what it entailed – are driven by anti-Semitic motives. They feel that Jews derive a moral advantage from having been victims of the Holocaust, so denying the Holocaust deprives them of that advantage. (A parallel move would be to deny that Africans were ever brought forcibly to the United States as slaves in order to deprive African Americans of the moral advantage that slavery affords in, for example, making a case for affirmative action.)

If denying the Holocaust results from these evil motives, the *spreading* of Holocaust denial results from the good intentions of some who fall into the trap of blind devotion to 'the other side.' Among the deniers' most striking successes, Lipstadt shows, was a 1993 campaign to place advertisements in American college newspapers claiming (falsely, of course) that the U.S. Holocaust Memorial Museum contains no proof that gas chambers actually existed. In justifying his decision to run the ad, for example, an editor at the State University College at Buffalo student newspaper explained, 'There are two sides to every issue and both have a place on the pages of any open-minded paper's editorial page.'

Lipstadt was invited to appear on national television – in many cases if and only if she would debate deniers. She refused because there was nothing to debate: She did not want her book to become a pretext for giving a national forum to deniers trying to convince people of what the producers knew were lies. One producer, reluctant to accept Lipstadt's refusal, challenged, 'Don't you think viewers have a right to hear the other side?' Being legitimized as the other side in a debate is exactly the credibility that Holocaust deniers seek.

One television show on which Lipstadt refused to appear devoted the largest portion of airtime to deniers, then ushered on Holocaust survivors to refute their claims. The host, Montel Williams, urged viewers to stay tuned during a commercial – and return to learn whether the Holocaust is a 'myth or is it truth.' You can almost see someone slotting this topic into a familiar format: myth or reality, such a handy opposition.

Presenting known lies as the other side would be harmless if there were, as Czech poet and president Vaclav Havel put it, 'a special radioactive power of the truthful word.' Sadly, there is no evidence that there is. People are often persuaded by lies rather than by truth. The success of Holocaust deniers in exploiting our two-sides faith can be heard in the remark made by a visitor to the Holocaust museum (a New Zealander) who described the exhibits as 'one-sided Jewish propaganda.' His comment was an idiosyncratic, not a typical, one, but his choice of the word 'one-sided' is telling.

## MISREADING THE FIRST AMENDMENT

Lipstadt shows that those who help Holocaust deniers spread their lies are sometimes motivated by a misinterpretation of freedom of speech. The editor of *The Georgetown Record* explained his decision to publish the deniers' ad by saying, 'The issue of freedom of expression outweighed the issue of the offensive nature of the advertisement.' The First Amendment says that the government shall not suppress speech. Thus the government cannot forbid Holocaust deniers to express their opinions – nor would Lipstadt want them to. But this is reinterpreted to mean that those who have the power of the press are *obligated* to publish or disseminate outrageous views. This same sense of First Amendment rights is not applied to those who hold reasonable views.

Almost anyone who writes a book would love to appear on television to promote it. Many others would love to get on television simply to express their opinions. But television producers would laugh them off the phone – if the producers ever took their calls in the first place – if authors demanded that the First Amendment gives them the right to appear on *Oprah!* Producers and editors make decisions every day about what of all the potential material can be included in the limited time or space available. Since the cry 'free speech' seems to be heard only when someone wants to say something outrageous, we have to suspect that the argument culture is the culprit. The First Amendment becomes a pretext to justify the airing of just those views that make for the most entertaining fights.

Sometimes our strengths are also liabilities. Holocaust denial has had the greatest success in the United States because of our devotion to freedom of speech and balance. Contrast the reaction in Japan, for example, when a reputable magazine printed an article making exactly the same claim: The magazine's publisher publicly apologized, recalled all copies of the issue, and closed the magazine for good.

The college editors who decided to publish deniers' ads were young and inexperienced. Television producers, too, are often young and relatively unseasoned. But the laudable goal of providing balance can set a trap even for mainstream journalists – and did, according to journalist Ross Gelbspan in *The Heat Is On*, with regard to global warming.

The earth's atmosphere is heating up at an alarming rate, because of the burning of oil and coal. The disastrous consequences already upon us include record heat and record cold plus unprecedented numbers of droughts, floods, and storms. These natural disasters bring others in their wake, such as the fires that follow droughts and the homelessness, starvation, and disease that often accompany great natural disasters. Epidemics result when malaria-bearing mosquitos invade areas that previously were too cold for them, and entire island nations are threatened by rising sea levels due to the melting of the Arctic ice cap. On these facts there is virtual agreement in the international scientific community. But Gelbspan shows that public relations firms working for oil and coal companies mounted a campaign to convince Americans – both citizens and lawmakers – that the scientific community is divided and the reality of global warming is disputed. The success of their campaign hinged on the mainstream media giving a platform to a small number of dissenting scientists by presenting their discredited views as a balanced 'other side' in a scientific debate. 'In the area of climate research,' Gelbspan shows, 'virtually no news story appears that does not feature prominently one of these few industry-sponsored scientific "greenhouse skeptics."' The result has been a loss of will to avert further disaster by developing alternative energy sources, even though the technology already exists. In 1996, Congress cut off funds for the major scientific effort to monitor climate change.

A scale will balance only when the items placed on both sides are of equal weight. When journalists showcase marginal, extreme, or even thoroughly discredited views and people in order to provide balance, they give them more weight than they deserve and bestow upon them the credibility of the press.

Not only the relative weight of opinions but essential moral distinctions can be erased when ideas are pressed into the debate format. This point is made by David Gelernter, a Yale University professor who was permanently maimed, and nearly killed, when he opened a package mailed to him by the Unabomber. When the then-unidentified bomber's political manifesto was published, a newspaper columnist devised a side-by-side comparison of the bomber's opinions and those of his victim. The resulting 'debate' set the murderer on an equal footing with his victim.

---

### 'TWO SIDES' GETS IN THE WAY OF SOLVING PROBLEMS

---

Global warming is an example of how our devotion to a two-sides notion of balance has gotten in the way of solving problems we face as a society. Another problem we have failed to solve is the question of whether abortion should be legal. Here, too, the 'two-sides' approach has exacerbated the problem. Communications researcher Celeste Michelle Condit shows that presenting the abortion issue as a two-sides debate not only fails to represent the issue accurately but actually gets in the way of addressing it.

The biggest danger of the 'two-sides' approach to this issue is not discussed by Condit because she herself falls into its trap: erasing crucial moral distinctions, as in the Unabomber example. Condit points out that television typically chooses the most strident advocates to represent each side. She identifies these 'polarized extremes' as 'the ideologues who form the ranks of Operation

Rescue or of the National Abortion Rights Action League.' But these two organizations, like other activists on these two sides, engage in such different activities that they occupy very different moral landscapes. Those who form the ranks of NARAL may be ideologues, but they use legal means to achieve their ends – and those ends consist of ensuring citizens' access to medical services they are entitled to by law. Activists on the other side, however, do not simply seek to change the laws they do not like. They engage in harassment and physical obstructionism to prevent people from obtaining services they are entitled to by law – as well as terrorist tactics to stalk, harass, and murder physicians and to bomb clinics. Being legitimized as the other side in a debate glosses over and implicitly condones these tactics – and gives airtime to those who engage in or encourage them.

Condit does show, however, that our approach to the issue of abortion is needlessly polarized. Polls, she notes, became more sophisticated by giving respondents more than two options: not just 'Abortion should be legal (1) in no circumstances' or (2) 'in all circumstances' but (3) 'in some circumstances.' But Condit observed that newspaper reports of poll results often lump the middle-ground responses with one side or the other. Those who answered 'Abortion should be legal in some circumstances' could be tallied with those who checked 'Abortion should be legal' to yield a single category, 'People who oppose current law.' *The New York Times*, for example, reported such a poll under the headline 'POLL ON ABORTION FINDS THE NATION IS SHARPLY DIVIDED' and featured a graphic in which 'Legal as it is' was in a white section of a circle and both 'Legal only in certain cases' and 'Not permitted at all' appeared together in a shaded part. In this way, results of a study that shows there are more than two sides got pressed into a polarized representation. This impression is reinforced by the word 'divided' in the headline, suggesting 'divided in two.'

Condit also notes that articles and commentators not only are less likely to report nuanced views but go so far as to denigrate them. Politicians who try to find a middle ground are depicted as 'two-faced, unreliable, and acting merely to deceive potential constituents.'

At first blush, I was inclined to agree with those whom Condit cites as polarizing the debate, such as a 1985 *Newsweek* article that proclaimed, 'Abortion is one of the rare issues that inherently does not admit compromise ... it is nearly impossible to imagine the meeting point that would satisfy both.' But Condit shows that the only reason it seems impossible to imagine a meeting point or compromise is precisely because of the way the issue has been framed: as a fight between two opposing polarized sides. If the issue were framed as, on the one hand, the desire to reduce the number of abortions performed, and, on the other, the desire to give women control of their own bodies and lives, there would be feasible ways of reconciling and satisfying both.

First, it is well known that making abortion illegal does not prevent abortions from being performed. That result would more effectively be accomplished by, for example, increasing education about and availability of contraception. This would also increase women's control over their bodies and lives. Neither 'side' is getting much of what it wants anyway: Although abortion remains legal in the United States, it is becoming harder and harder for anybody to get one, both because of the legal chipping away of access (for example, by making abortion unavailable at public clinics and military bases or by instituting waiting periods and requiring parental consent) and because of de facto erosion: Most American women live too far from a provider to make the trip in a single day; it is difficult to find doctors willing to risk their lives in order to perform abortions; and medical schools rarely teach the procedure. At the same time, the steady erosion of services and chipping away at legalization, though seeming to represent triumphs of the antiabortion forces, have not changed the fact that there are more abortions performed in the United States than in any other Western nation.

In other words, Condit shows that the tendency to frame discussion of an issue as a debate between two opposing sides actually shapes policy makers' attempts to address those issues and solve problems. In the end, it makes it much harder to see viable solutions and therefore less likely that a solution will be found.

Another example of a complex phenomenon that is approached through polarized opposition is race. This subject is complex and nuanced – a full discussion would require a book, and many have been written – but I will mention only the tendency to reduce our understanding of race to a simple black/white dichotomy. This tends to obscure, first of all, the existence of many other races: Asian, American Indian, Polynesian, Semitic, Arab, East Indian, Mongolian, and so on. Even within the framework of Americans of European and Americans of African ancestry, there are many who are biracial or multiracial: They have parents and grandparents who came from white, black, and other roots. Lise Funderburg's *Black, White, Other* gives the personal stories of Americans who had one black and one white parent, many of whom found that their desire to embrace both their heritages is undermined when they are forced to choose one identity or the other. The ultimate point, for us, is that no sooner do we conceive of something as composed of two – and just two – elements than we begin to think of those elements as more different than they are, opposed to each other, and potentially in conflict.

The scourge of drug use is another problem we haven't been able to solve in part because of the way we frame it. What we've had is a war not so much on drugs but between the two sides of a debate: drug warriors versus legalizers. Once these two extremes define the issue, any proposal or statement is assigned to one side and demonized by the other. Anyone who is against current policy must be in favor of legalization, and anyone against legalization must support every detail of current policy. Those who find both extremes unacceptable are effectively locked out of the discussion, and many politicians remain silent on the issue because they know that if they open their mouths, one group or the other will jump down their throats. In this spirit, Senator Jesse Helms prevented the nomination of William Weld as ambassador to Mexico even from being considered by the Senate Foreign Relations Committee ostensibly because Weld favors allowing seriously ill people to use marijuana for medical purposes. A group of scientists, policy experts, and public officials have united to stake out a middle ground and open the field to other alternatives, such as 'smarter prohibition' by which minor offenders receive treatment for drug abuse rather than long prison sentences that cost taxpayers huge amounts of money without curbing drug use.

A journalist who experienced frustration with her own colleagues is Deborah Blum, author of a book about the use of animals in scientific research. Her point, Blum told me, was to show that there are reasonable and rational arguments on both sides. If those who oppose using animals for research and those who advocate it could only listen to each other, they would see that there is common ground, and work together to make things better. But when her book was published, Blum found it was almost impossible to get this message through. The worst was a cable talk show that invited, along with Blum, an animal rights activist and a scientist who had long been avowed public enemies. The author made a brief opening statement; then the two other guests commenced screaming at each other. When she tried to step in, they screamed at her. But her fellow print journalists also tended to sift through the interview or the book to pull out the parts that were confrontational. Being a journalist herself, she recognized the impulse: 'Let's put an edge on it.'

In writing the previous paragraph, I originally began, 'Deborah Blum, author of *The Monkey Wars* . . .' and stopped right there. Could journalists be faulted for missing the message of peace and focusing on the fight when the title of the book sent them in that direction? I called the author back and asked about the title. She told me how it came about: The book was based on a Pulitzer Prize-winning series of articles she had written for *The Sacramento Bee*; the title had been assigned by her editors, even though she had 'fought it tooth and nail.' By the time the series became a book, the title had taken on a life of its own.

---

### THE MEDIA AND ME: 'LET'S YOU AND HIM FIGHT'

---

Headlines are the most likely place to find war imagery. Because I write about communication between women and men, I have had plenty of opportunity to experience firsthand the impulse to frame gender relations as a fight – as well as the consequences. Here's just one example.

In 1996, I wrote an article for *The New York Times Magazine* about apologies. I explored both the good that apologies can do and the reasons many people resist uttering them. There is a gender dimension to this issue: In our culture, men are more likely than women to avoid apologizing. But this does not mean that all men avoid apologizing, nor that all women are quick to apologize. Furthermore, saying 'I'm sorry' is not always preferable. I gave examples showing that sometimes it's better to resist apologizing. And the gender pattern was not the main point. A large portion of my essay discussed cultural differences, such as the Japanese custom of uttering apologies more elaborately and more frequently than Americans.

When the article appeared, it was packaged to focus on the gender aspect alone, and it did so in a way that seemed designed to make men feel angry and attacked. I had called the piece 'I'm Sorry, I'm Not Apologizing,' referring to women's frequent use of 'I'm sorry' to mean 'I'm sorry that happened.' The editors changed it to 'I'm Sorry, I Won't Apologize,' referring to men's refusal to say they're sorry. By itself, this difference is subtle and minor; when the change was suggested, its impact went right by me. But the cover of the issue announced my essay as 'Why Men Don't Apologize,' and the subhead read, 'A simple statement of contrition can fix an honest mistake. So why can't men seem to do it?' The illustration also went for the stereotype: A man in the foreground is holding his head on a platter, offering it to a fuming woman standing with her arms crossed and smoke rising from her head. The illustration is more subtle than might at first appear: The man has his fingers crossed behind his back, a visual analogue to my observation that when people say 'I'm sorry I hurt your feelings' (in private) or 'I'm sorry if my words offended anyone' (in public), they may appear to apologize and yet stop short of admitting fault. In fairness, art often draws on stereotypes to achieve quick recognition. But choosing a stereotype that pits men against women aggravates the battle of the sexes at the same time that it attempts to draw on it for humor.

When I learned of the subhead, I pleaded with the editor to change it but was told it was too late and that, furthermore, the packaging of a story – headlines, subheads, and illustrations – has to attract attention. But I paid a price for this. A caller to a talk show I appeared on shortly after was typical. He said, 'I've followed Dr Tannen's work for years and always appreciated her fairness and even hand, but this article was the first time she offended me.' Generously, *The New York Times Magazine* later ran an apology explaining that the headline treatment did not accurately represent the spirit of the article. I greatly appreciated this unusual gesture. But I doubt it did much to repair the animosity stirred up in men who took the article to be one more male-bashing attack by a woman. And women feel the repercussions of men's anger against women in public and individual women in private. The harm was done. And it is done daily when the battle of the sexes is used to stir up interest but at the same time stirs up the battle.

Editors, producers, and advertisers need to stir audience interest, which means arousing emotions. Anger is one of the easiest emotions to arouse. And I'm sure it is tempting to step into existing debate frameworks, like stepping into a ready-made suit rather than spending far more time getting one fitted to size. When polarized debate is sought, those with the greatest expertise are often rejected or refuse to take part because they resist slotting complex issues into a simplified debate format. Those who are willing or eager to cloak their moderate expertise – or lack of it – in fiery capes are given the platform instead. When this happens, the entire society loses.

## NEWS AS ENTERTAINMENT

Why has talk on radio and television become more contentious – more a matter of having fights and less of making reasoned arguments? A number of interrelated forces are at work. Most people now get most of their news from television and radio rather than from reading newspapers. The technologies of television and talk radio return, in some ways, to the past. With the advent of print, Western society became less disputatious, according to cultural linguist Walter Ong: In the absence of audiences before which to stage debates, attention gradually focused on the internal argumentation of published tracts rather than the debaters' performance. The rise of contentiousness today is being fueled in part by the return of oral argument on television and radio, where, once again, the ability to dispute publicly is valued – and judged – as a performance. There are also more information sources competing for audiences – and most are, after all, commercial enterprises. To those who depend on it for profit, news has to be entertaining to keep the audience. Given the belief that watching fights is fun, the result is inevitable.

Many Americans say they listen to right-wing talk radio because they find it entertaining. But even public radio in America and the BBC in Britain are not insulated from having to entertain or from the conviction that fights are the most entertaining form of speech.

A Washington, D.C., radio talk show, *The Derek McGinty Show*, includes a weekly feature called 'The D.C. Politics Hour with Mark Plotkin.' A WAMU publication heralds the weekly feature as 'sometimes combative and always entertaining.' Host and guest 'often sound like a vaudeville act, trading jibes and insults, along with pertinent information about the goings-on in the city.' Plotkin is quoted as saying, 'Politics is theater and sport and it should be viewed that way.' This pithy statement has a ring of truth (this feature is one of the station's most popular) – but also is scary when you think that politics, unlike theater and sport, results in concrete effects on everyone's daily lives.

The assumptions that news discussion programs must be entertaining, and that it is entertaining to watch people fight, are pervasive in the UK as well. Two of the regular presenters on the early morning *Today* program on BBC Radio 4, John Humphrys and James Naughtie, have made their names by being confrontational, prompting the *Daily Telegraph* to comment that their listeners are drawn to them by their 'sheer, raucous aggression.' When interviewees lose their tempers and respond in kind or abruptly curtail the interview, newspapers report the clashes in terms of winners, losers, and gaffes.

John Birt, the director-general of the BBC, criticized the confrontational interview technique in a way that highlighted its role in inviting audiences to view political interchanges as drama or sporting events. Writing in *The Times* in February 1995, Birt commented, 'Rivalry between politicians, or differences within parties, are played out as a national soap opera. Sometimes the press, broadcasting and Parliament combine in a feeding frenzy in which it is difficult to exercise cool and measured judgment.' Describing specific interviewing techniques, he implicitly called attention to the parallel with boxing: 'the disorienting opening question, the rabbit-punch designed to knock off balance.' This article itself became a subject of contention, as newspaper reporters sought reactions from the BBC interviewers whom Birt was assumed to be targeting. A few weeks later, Simon Jenkins, a *Times* columnist, described such contests between politicians and interviewers as 'a compelling blood sport.'

One danger in staging political discussion as sport and theater – and a particular kind of theater: staging a fight – is that the quality of information can be affected. The picture of commercial radio and television talkers provided by Howard Kurtz in *Hot Air* is far more troubling: Regular commentators on national television, for example, are called upon to analyze current events with little or no preparation and must be willing to offer opinions on a wide range of topics, some of which they know little or nothing about. Kurtz quotes Jack Germond, a regular commentator on *McLaughlin*: 'We have topics that none of us knows anything about, except what's in *The New York Times*.' Yet, he says, he cannot simply admit he doesn't know. 'You can't do that on television. It drives McLaughlin crazy when I do that. He acts like it's serious information we're passing on.' Another regular commentator on the same show, Eleanor Clift, explains, 'The nature of these shows is you're forced to speak more provocatively to make a point in the short time you have before you get interrupted. People know there's an entertainment factor, but the danger is it turns us all into stereotypes, because you don't have time to express the ifs, ands or buts.' Kurtz also quotes another regular commentator, Mort Kondracke, who says, 'Is it oversimplified? Sure. You don't have much time to think.'

---

### SPORTS COMMENTARY:
### IT'S NOT HOW YOU PLAY THE GAME
### BUT WHETHER YOU WIN OR LOSE

---

If political and other current events are presented as sports, how sports are presented is also changing – in the spirit of the argument culture. The link among sports, violence, and spectatorship goes way back in time – think of the Roman gladiators. But sports are now often filtered through the media, which emphasize the violent aspects even of supposedly noncontact sports.

Taking part in sports, many believe, teaches cooperation, team spirit, and positive values. But participating in sports is one thing; watching sports is another, and watching it on television yet another. On television and radio, sports events are accompanied by running commentary that encourages and enhances the agonistic elements of sports, emphasizing the ways that sports can be like war.

'It's not whether you win or lose but how you play the game,' the saying goes. But this spirit isn't what drives coverage. Sports psychologists Jeffrey Goldstein and Brenda Bredemeier show that television sports announcers emphasize not the process of play but the outcome. In other words, the operative principle seems to be 'It's not how you play the game but whether you win or lose.' Commentators who discuss sports events after the fact concentrate less on skill, artistry, fairness, and so on, and more on why the winners were successful and the losers failed – more or less as political campaign coverage tends to focus on who's ahead and why rather than on the candidates' qualifications or positions.

This preoccupation with winning dovetails with the increase in aggressive violence in many team sports, since violence can help a team win without exercising commensurate skill. Sports researcher Jennings Bryant explores the intricate relationship among sports, violence, and media. He finds that in the popular mind 'sports and violence have become almost inseparable.' This shows up in the way people talk about ostensibly nonviolent and noncontact sports such as baseball (for example, a 'knockdown pitch' or a 'bean ball' aimed at the batter's head) and, of course, in headlines ('PLAYING FOR BLOOD,' 'A BLOODY MESS'). Personal fouls, fights, and infractions are the norm in professional sports, not the exception to the rule.

The frequent fights that break out during games seem to be the spontaneous expression of personal frustration, but Bryant quotes Cliff Fletcher, then general manager of the Calgary Flames ice hockey team, who admits that players deliberately use violence to intimidate opposing team members and that 'intimidation is probably the major factor in hockey.' According to team member Dave Brown, intimidation by physical violence is his main job – and it is a job, not a spontaneous emotional outburst: 'I don't know if I ever really get all that mad,' he says. A coach may decide that the penalty for a foul is a small price to pay for putting the opposition team's star player out of commission with a well-planned blow.

Ice hockey is particularly known for physical attacks, but televised sports, in general, like other types of media coverage, proceeds on the assumption that watching fights is entertaining. Bryant quotes former New York Knicks general manager Al Bianchi: 'Fouls are fouls, but the overall unwritten indelible code for NBA [National Basketball Association] officials is "Let Them Play! . . . Less fouls, more fun."' In other words, let the players beat each other up and don't stop them by calling fouls. And this is basketball, in principle a noncontact sport. None of this is to say that there is anything wrong with competition, conflict, a two-sides structure, or even violence in sports. What concerns the experts quoted here is the relative weight given to these aspects of many sports – a disproportionate emphasis on the display of violence and the importance of winning over all else – and the role played by media coverage in encouraging this emphasis.

In soccer, foul play is an integral part of the game. Every match has its quota of players given yellow cards (warnings that they are on probation) or being sent off the field for making unfair and dangerous tackles or indulging in other forms of violence or verbal abuse. Except in extreme cases, soccer writers praise some of the offenders for their 'commitment.' Even cricket, a comparatively gentle sport, is characterized by 'sledging' – hostile remarks exchanged between the batting and fielding sides – and with physical intimidation as fast bowlers aim to bounce the ball close to the batsman's head. Commentators describe this as being 'competitive.'

Canadian sociolinguist Jeff Deby analyzed the commentary accompanying the 1996 World Cup hockey championship, showing how the commentators, John and Mike, reinforced the impression that violence is both admirable and fun to watch. For example, after discussing an instance of particularly rough play, Mike exulted, 'It's fast! It's scintillating! It's vicious! And it's entertaining!' That players were physically hurt was emphasized: 'You can see the grimace,' 'You could hear the whack.' When a blow forced a player to sit down, John made explicit the assumption that physical injury gives the game significance, even though the rules prohibit undue force: 'Oh look at that! Think this game means something? Wow!' The commentators' admiration and excitement placed the players' ability to inflict and withstand injury – rather than their skill – at center stage.

Sports, like politics, is a matter of winning and losing, of opponents pitted against each other. But the oppositional aspects of both can be played up or played down. In our culture, on television and radio and in newspapers, the oppositional, win-lose aspect of sports as well as politics is played up. The commentary that viewers hear encourages the ethos that it's good to use violence and intentionally break the rules to intimidate or injure opponents in order to win.

Am I putting too much emphasis on the commentary rather than the action itself? Research has shown the power of commentary to shape – and even alter – how viewers perceive the action they see. Together with Paul Comisky and Dolf Zillmann, Jennings Bryant identified two segments of an ice hockey game. In one segment, the play was extremely rough, but the commentators did not mention it. In the other, the play was not particularly violent, but the commentary stressed the roughness that was there. When viewers were shown the segments without commentary, they accurately judged the rough-play segment as more action-packed, enthusiastic, rough, and violent (and, not incidentally, more entertaining and enjoyable). But when they viewed the same segments with the commentary superimposed, their judgments were reversed. They saw what was actually normal play as rougher, more action-packed, and more enjoyable. The commentary shaped what they saw, overriding what they witnessed with their own eyes.

---

## WHAT TO DO

---

The way television and radio present ideas and information does matter. Presenting everything in terms of two sides fighting may be intended simply to catch interest, but it helps shape the way people regard the world, events, and other people. Is it necessary to highlight opposition and conflict to interest audiences? There is evidence that it isn't. Oprah Winfrey, for example, made a unilateral decision to reshape her show as less sensationalist, more helpful – and is still top-rated. There is other evidence, as well.

The March 9, 1997, issue of *The New York Times Magazine*, devoted to 'The Age Boom,' offered a positive look at the subject of aging. Reader response was overwhelmingly favorable. Jack Rosenthal, the editor of the magazine, was invited to appear on *The Jim Lehrer News Hour* to talk about the topic. He also appeared on *The Diane Rehm Show*, a national radio talk show, for the same purpose. Weeks after the issue came out, it was still being discussed. The themes developed in these discussions and in the special issue were in sharp contrast to the culture of critique. Rather than taking the generation-war approach that has dominated recent coverage (old folks who are draining the economy versus young folks who are sick of working to pay old folks' bills), Rosenthal claimed that the income transfer from old to young far outstrips the flow in the opposite direction. The special issue emphasized the positive aspects of aging. And according to Rosenthal, the public response to this special issue was an all-time record high, out of perhaps twenty that had been done in the three years the magazine had been putting out special issues at the rate of eight per year.

Changes are already taking place within journalism. There is a movement in the press to provide more 'news you can use.' But these changes must not be limited to features and items that run in addition to coverage of politics and current events. Changes need to be made in the way all material is presented. We need a general truce, so television and radio stations, newspapers and magazines, do not fear falling behind if they make a unilateral retreat from covering news as battle.

In Britain, journalists themselves are suggesting change. Martyn Lewis, a BBC newsreader, pointed out, 'We are very good as journalists at analysing failure, but we are not so good at analysing success,' he told an interviewer. 'It's not true that only negative news is serious . . . In politics, balance is not simply finding someone with a different view.'

Sometimes it will be obviously appropriate to present a story as a two-sides fight. But not *all* stories fit naturally into this format. And framing everything as a fight may lose more readers and listeners in the end. When polls ask people why they dislike 'the media,' results always show the negativity of the press at the top of the list. Highlighting conflict to keep audiences may be a case of what anthropologist Gregory Bateson called 'complementary schismogenesis,' a situation in which each party's behavior eggs on the other to more and more exaggerated forms of an opposing behavior in a mutually aggravating spiral. Dwindling readership drives journalists to emphasize conflict in an effort to interest readers, but the rising level of opposition drives more readers away.

In an early draft of this book, I wrote, 'I do not believe that journalists set out to polarize citizens, incite them to anger, and undermine our respect for each other.' Someone who read that draft wrote in the margin, 'You don't? The alternative is great naïveté.' It is chilling that an educated consumer of news believes that the press is intentionally poisoning his informational food. The widespread mistrust, contempt, and even hatred that many citizens now feel against the press is as dangerous as – if less widely reported than – the mistrust, contempt, and even hatred that many citizens feel against the government.

I prefer to believe that the troubling effects I've described are the unintended result of the argument culture. If I'm right, then understanding the argument culture – and the related culture of critique – should be the first step in finding ways to communicate news that are less destructive to society and more enlightening to us all.

# 3

## From Lapdog to Attack Dog: The Aggression Culture and the Press

A joke was going around midway through Bill Clinton's first term in office: The president went on a fishing trip with members of the press corps. After their boat left shore, the president realized he had left his tackle on the dock, so he stepped off the boat, walked to shore, picked up his tackle, and walked back over the surface of the water. The next day's headline read 'CLINTON CAN'T SWIM.'

This joke more or less sums up what many people think of the press: Everything is given a negative slant, and even miraculous accomplishments are ignored to focus on failures. University of Virginia political scientist Larry Sabato used this analogy: During the Kennedy administration, the press was like a lapdog, taking government press releases at face value. During Vietnam and Watergate, it was like a watchdog, scrutinizing the public behavior of public officials. But the press today is like an attack dog, 'constantly chomping at the ankles of public officials every day about everything.'

Former Republican Senator Alan Simpson had a jolt as he chatted with the daughter of old friends, a young woman he had known all her life. Since she had just graduated from Columbia University School of Journalism, he inquired about her plans. 'I'm going to be one of the hunters,' she announced. He asked, 'What are you going to hunt?' She replied, 'People like you!' That explains how people like him – indeed, almost everyone in public life – feel today: not just scrutinized but hunted.

---

## WATERGATE: ROOT OF THE
## AGGRESSION CULTURE

---

Investigative reporting is the jewel in the crown of journalism. A role that only journalists can fulfill, it is the tradition that helped expose the scandals of Watergate and Vietnam – vast programs of illegal action and public deception that had disastrous consequences. But in the search-and-destroy culture of critique, investigative reporting has metamorphosed into prosecutorial reporting. An investigation sets out to determine the facts. Prosecutors set out to build a case against someone.

ABC White House Correspondent Brit Hume recalls that the eras of Vietnam and Watergate were

> difficult times for the country, but they were absolutely won-
> derful times to be a journalist in Washington, particularly one
> who had a piece of the story. It helped to promote a certain
> romance about the news media and its role in American
> life, and it also enhanced the prestige of the news media
> generally ... And there was a tendency then by everybody
> from the generals down to the buck privates in our trade
> to fight that last war over and over again, and to look for
> entry points into what might be the great new scandals of
> the day.

Many journalists prominent today were high school or college students at that time and were inspired to enter the profession by the example of Watergate and Vietnam: They, too, would fight government duplicity and expose government lies. *The New York*

*Times*'s Jill Abramson, formerly *The Wall Street Journal*'s deputy bureau chief in Washington, recalls being glued to the radio during the Watergate hearings while studying at Harvard. Fascinated by the inside view of goings-on at the White House, she determined to pursue a career in journalism as a public service – and cut her teeth as a reporter for the student newspaper by pursuing wrongdoing in the Harvard administration 'with Woodward and Bernstein-like zeal.' She, too, notes that journalists today are seeking another Watergate-like scandal – in her words, the way surfers lust for the perfect wave. Ambition and zeal can dovetail: You can expose evil and make a name for yourself at the same time. With the success of the film *All the President's Men*, Bob Woodward and Carl Bernstein became celebrities. Aspiring journalists could also hope to be the next Woodward or Bernstein.

In Britain too, investigative journalism was at its zenith in the sixties and seventies, especially in the *Sunday Times*. A dedicated investigative unit, known as Insight, uncovered scandals relating to profiteering landlords, the financier Robert Maxwell and thalidomide, the drug that caused deformities in children. In the nineties, the *Guardian* picked up the baton, with exposés that effectively halted the careers of two Conservative junior ministers, Jonathan Aitken and Neil Hamilton. The London tabloids, meanwhile, plowed their own distinctive furrow with a series of scandalous revelations about the sexual indiscretions of politicians, leading to more resignations.

Watergate inspired British as well as American journalists. Bernard Ingham, when he was press secretary to Margaret Thatcher, made a habit of criticizing what he thought were overzealous attempts by the press to uncover scandals in government. 'Some journalists, at least, believe passionately that another Watergate is lying just around the corner waiting to be uncovered,' he said in 1985. 'I believe that the Watergate syndrome, combined with the broadcasters' "confrontation" approach to interviews . . . seems to require that any self-respecting reporter should knock seven bells out of symbols of authority, and especially Government . . . Its effect on our democracy is, in my view, corrosive.'

Attacking those in power is also a show of independence. In an essay about *Washington Post* owner and publisher Katharine Graham, David Remnick tells how Graham brought *The Washington*

*Post* up in the world by defying the government and publishing the Pentagon Papers. The *Post*'s fearless defiance of the Nixon administration in pursuing the Watergate scandal proved the paper's mettle and Graham's courage – and established the *Post* as a major national force. It was just such courage to attack, Remnick notes, that had helped *The New York Times* earn its own reputation by going after Boss Tweed years before.

But how does a newspaper prove its mettle when there is no Watergate to expose? The need to find scandals to uncover can become a danger. According to Remnick, Graham worried about

> a newspaper's need to guard against 'the romantic tendency to picture itself in the role of a heroic and beleaguered champion, defending virtues against overwhelming odds.' Watergate, she writes, 'had been an aberration, and I felt we couldn't look everywhere for conspiracies and cover-ups.'

Yet this is exactly what happened. In the first term of the Clinton administration, scandal after scandal made headlines, many with -*gate* affixed to them: nannygate, travelgate, FBI filegate. But none of these 'scandals' has anywhere near the force of Watergate. Twenty-five years after those events, which he observed up close for CBS, journalist Daniel Schorr pointed out that the Nixon-authorized attempt to break into Democratic headquarters to plant an eavesdropping device was only the tip of the iceberg. There were other break-ins, plans to use the CIA and FBI to spy on citizens the president regarded as his enemies, even talk of firebombing the Brookings Institution and assassinating newspaper columnist Jack Anderson. When a grand jury and federal courts supported Special Prosecutor Archibald Cox's request for tapes, President Nixon refused to hand them over, ordered the attorney general to fire Cox, and sent the FBI to seal off the special prosecutor's offices. No comparable threat to constitutional democracy had ever occurred before – nor has occurred since.

What we have now is a kind of scandal inflation plus predictable cover-ups that are their inevitable by-products. A British example goes even further, not only emphasizing minor scandals but actually creating them: in 1997 the *Daily Mirror* set a trap for William Straw, the Home Secretary's son, who sold a small amount of cannabis to their reporter. The result is not only elevating commonplace indiscretions, such as having hired domestic employees without paying Social Security tax for them, but also inuring citizens to concern about serious governmental wrongdoing: Appending *-gate* to so many less serious, even trivial matters has made Watergate itself seem less significant in retrospect than it really was. Astonishingly, a June 1997 poll found that nearly half of those polled (44 percent) thought Watergate was no worse than any scandal before or since – 'just politics.'

Constantly covering relatively minor scandals also interferes with the more mundane task of the press: conveying information about daily developments in public life. Former Clinton campaign strategist Paul Begala pointed out that when the president brought together clothing manufacturers, human rights activists, trade unions, and consumer groups to combat sweatshop labor, it was not mentioned on that evening's news. 'This is a relevant problem, this matters to people's jobs,' he said. Yet there was 'no coverage of that, but lots of coverage about how five-year-old documents that were released today by the DNC [Democratic National Committee] suggested that maybe the president's supporters should get jobs when he won. Oh, boy!'

You don't have to be a Clinton partisan or even a Democrat to feel that the focus on scandal dangerously crowds out other news. Republican Bay Buchanan (sister of Pat Buchanan and cohost of *Equal Time*) made the same point: 'Bill Clinton can go all the way overseas and meet with the Russian president and get possibly a one-day story if he's lucky. The vice president of the United States – he goes all the way to China, a historic meeting, first major official since Tiananmen Square, and the story in our paper is about scandal . . . It's difficult if not virtually impossible to get another message through.'

---

## AGGRESSION WITHOUT A CAUSE

---

The problem is not that the press has become more aggressive or even more abusive. Historians can unearth examples of astounding venom and vituperation hurled against politicians and other public figures from the time journalism began. But in earlier times, those who attacked public figures did so with a purpose: They were ideologically opposed to what their opponents stood for, and they loudly proclaimed that conviction. Aggression was a weapon in a war against specific wrongs. The spirit of attack today – aggression in a culture of critique – is disinterested, aimed at whoever is in the public eye. And a show of aggression is valued for its own sake. In other words, it's agonism: automatic, knee-jerk aggression.

At the same time, the focus of attack has shifted from the domain of public policy to the vaguer notion of character in the form of personal foibles and inconsistencies. And rather than exposing specific acts of wrongdoing, the aggression often surfaces as a sneering and contemptuous tone that has been remarked – and questioned – by journalists themselves. Adam Gopnik, for example, calls it 'a kind of weird, free-form nastiness – spleen without purpose.' Kenneth Walsh describes it as 'adding opinion or "edge" – often in the form of a derisive tone or smart-ass attitude.' James Fallows calls the tone 'snarl' and notes that it is typical for articles about the president to drip condescension without bothering to provide any factual basis for the disdain. He quotes a newsmagazine writer: 'Pieces that are harsh and snide and critical and quizzical always do better and get bigger play and attract more attention.' And as with an addiction, ever-greater doses of attitude are needed: 'Yesterday's edge becomes today's tedium,' says Adam Gopnik, 'and the only way to get more attention is to continually up the ante.'

Peer pressure drives the engine, according to Walsh:

> Reporters feel pressured by their editors and colleagues to have a harder edge, to take shots at those in power, and almost never to praise anyone in public office. Journalists are simply afraid of being labeled as shills for those in authority, and with good reason.

James Fallows quotes ABC reporter Charles Peters, who agrees:

> There is nothing that the average journalist fears more than ridicule. You are really going out on a limb if you say, 'This is a good idea. This is what is good about Bill Clinton' – or Bob

Dole or Newt Gingrich. Or if you say, 'This is an important idea.' You immediately lay yourself open to people saying that you're being boring, and getting laughed at.

Republicans and Democrats, Labour and Conservative, all believe the press is out to get them and biased toward the other party. The view is especially prevalent during a British general election campaign. Newspaper editors and producers of news and discussion programs on television and radio receive daily telephone calls from spokesmen for the major parties commenting on the slant given to particular stories and alleging partisanship.

Philip Harding, the editor of *Today* on Radio 4, said that when he arrived at the office at 7.30 one morning during the election campaign, an hour after the program started, there had already been five complaints – two each from the major parties and one from the Liberal Democrats.

In reality, the aggression is bipartisan, what *Washington Post* ombudsman Geneva Overholser calls 'equal-opportunity sneering.' It is not the aggression itself that has a corrosive effect on the human spirit but the unprincipled nature of the venom. It robs the aggression of its moral underpinnings: the difference between, on one hand, fighting for your country or for a cause and, on the other, climbing up on a roof and taking potshots at passersby. It's the difference between passionate engagement and random malice.

The abstract pursuit of aggression goes with a principled conviction that journalists should not be concerned with the effects of their actions either on public policy or on the feelings of those they attack. There is a genuine philosophical divide here. Many among the press believe that journalists should take into account the effects of their writing on society. But they are dissenters. The prevailing view is that reporters should seek to convey information without regard to its consequences, not as carelessness or lack of responsibility but as adherence to a larger good: objectivity. This conviction was stated explicitly by Howell Raines, editor of *The New York Times*'s op-ed page, in an editorial criticizing James Fallows's book *Breaking the News*. Raines sees Fallows's concern with the effect of press practices on public policy as debased, the unfortunate residue of time Fallows spent as a speechwriter for

President Carter. In contrast, Raines claims that reporters should be 'agnostic as to public policy outcomes, to be dogged in the collection and delivery of information for its own sake.' In the same spirit, *U.S. News & World Report*'s Richard Folkers wrote, after the death of Diana, Princess of Wales, 'Journalists are taught to separate doing the job from worrying about the consequences of what they record. Repeatedly, they are reminded of a news-business dictum: Leave your conscience in the office.'

In this way journalism, like much of contemporary culture, is modeled on a vision of science that wears objectivity as a shining badge of honor. But many now question whether science itself can be objective; objectivity is even more elusive in journalism. Simply choosing which stories to pursue is a massive act of interpretation. So are decisions about whom to interview, whom to quote, which bits of their comments to include in the story, and how those bits are framed. Reporting includes ever-larger doses of interpretation, as audiences are told not only who did what but why they did it – the 'strategy' perspective from which political affairs are routinely reported. And taking an aggressive stance in wording and tone drenches news stories in interpretation. It is the very opposite of objectivity.

Claiming a false objectivity is arguably more dangerous than acknowledged subjectivity because it is like speeding along in a car that has no brakes. Far safer would be acknowledging that objectivity is impossible and finding ways to safeguard against inevitable bias.

## THE PRESS CORPS AS A CHARGING ARMY

Small, privately owned stores are fast disappearing, replaced by publicly held chains. Purchasing is done by a central office, so stores all over the country offer customers exactly the same stock. In a similar pattern, we have more and more news outlets – proliferating cable channels, radio stations, magazines, and newsletters – but they are all covering the same stories. As a result, subjects are pursued by a huge army of reporters. 'Army' is the correct metaphor because having a horde of reporters following your every move, staking out your house hoping to catch you if you step out, feels like a form of attack. And if those who experience this assault object, they are derided as 'whining' and attacked again – accused of having asked for it. (The verb 'whining' shows how a word can interpret; it not only trivializes the objection but turns the objector into a crybaby. Chillingly, linguist Kathryn Ruud points out that this tactic was used by Hitler, who regularly referred to 'whining Jews' and his opponents as 'whining sissies,' transforming their political viewpoints into character flaws.)

After the death of Diana, Princess of Wales, commentators saw irony if not outright hypocrisy: Diana complained about being hounded by the media yet 'was not above using the press when it suited her needs' to win public support in her divorce settlement and coverage for her charity work on behalf of people with HIV and children maimed by land mines. There is an odd assumption here that someone who wants press attention has no right to object to any form it might take. By this logic, if you have a relationship with someone, you should not object to being stalked or beaten; after all, you are in the relationship, so you asked for it.

The death of Diana, and the widespread grief that ensued, caused British editors, reporters and photographers to pause and reevaluate this philosophy in terms of the impact of their actions on their 'victims.' The suspicion that the driver of her crashed car was speeding to escape the attentions of the paparazzi, the photographers who dogged her every footstep, led some people to blame them for the tragedy. But paparazzi were not the only ones who made Diana's life miserable. When she told a French newspaper that the one thing keeping her in Britain was her children, her explanation of why she would otherwise leave was: 'The press is ferocious. It pardons nothing. It only hunts for mistakes. Every motive is twisted, every gesture criticized.' At her funeral her brother, Earl Spencer, sounded a similar note: 'I don't think she ever understood why her genuinely good intentions were sneered at by the media, why there appeared to be a permanent quest on their behalf to bring her down.'

There was an outpouring of sympathy for her sons William and Harry, who had suffered through the years by having to read sneering reports about their mother. Overcome by apparent remorse, some editors vowed that in the future they would pay more regard to the privacy and feelings of the celebrities whose lives they made a misery. However, this self-denying ordinance did not last long. By the end of the year the tabloid press was busily prying into scandals about the personal lives of politicians, sports and media stars, and their close relatives. A report that the Foreign Secretary, Robin Cook, was having an affair with ´a political aide provoked the breakup of his marriage. A week or two later the *News of the World* reported that the teenage daughter of a backbench Member of Parliament had been earning money as a call girl. On the morning after both these reports appeared, scores of reporters showed up on cue outside the houses of the principal characters in the dramas.

The explosion of numbers foments the aggression culture of the press. Many journalists believe that some of the hostile animus emanating from the White House press corps comes from the conditions of their employment. They are frustrated and resentful because here they are, having reached the top of their profession, and rather than being rewarded with cushy working conditions and respectful treatment, they are confined in what *New York Times* reporter Todd Purdum (taking part in a panel discussion on *The Diane Rehm Show*) called 'a glorified sort of dog run.' Reporters are confined to a small area, waiting for a feeding – the appearance of an aide offering a press release, which the journalists are likely to distrust (with reason) as spin. When they accompany the president on trips, they find themselves literally roped off, confined to a press plane, or, if they are among the lucky few in the 'pool,' isolated in a back section of the president's plane. James Fallows regards the press's 'snarl' as revenge for this demeaning treatment.

The White House press corps wasn't always herded around and confined like animals. David Gergen, a journalist who served for a time in the Clinton White House as well as in Republican administrations, recalls a time when reporters could roam the halls where administration officials had offices and drop in on them unannounced. At that time, 'the heart of the White House press corps was just a few dozen people at most.' But now, Gergen notes, 'you have, I think, well over sixteen or seventeen hundred people accredited to cover the White House . . . And it's changed the whole nature of the relationship.'

The so-called Parliamentary Lobby, the group of accredited correspondents who cover national politics for the British media, is smaller, but many of the same drawbacks and frustrations apply. What was, in the early years of this century, an informal system of contact between politicians and journalists, has become institutionalized. Lobby correspondents are briefed twice a day, at fixed times, by the Prime Minister's press secretary. Other ministers or their press officers call briefings when they have something to say, or occasionally when asked to do so by the journalists. Consequently, the reporters work as a pack, with very little room for individual initiative.

For members of the press, the growth in size of the press corps and the increasing institutionalization of previously informal contact, means doors being slammed shut in their faces. For public figures, it means being trailed by an anonymous pack. The situation is aggravated by the knowledge that many of these reporters are waiting for a false step, a mistake, a slip – something they can report that will make you look bad.

---

## A MUTUALLY AGGRAVATING SPIRAL

---

Resentment among members of the White House press corps at being herded around is a matter not only of bruised egos but of professional frustration. To do their jobs, they need to know more about what's going on and the public figures they cover. In a word, they need access. This subject arose during the panel discussion on *The Diane Rehm Show*. Kenneth Walsh put it this way:

> Reporters like to have the instinct where you can say, if you hear rumors or talk about the president or first lady, that . . . 'that's not the Bill Clinton I know' or 'the Hillary Clinton I know.' Very few White House reporters can say that about the Clintons. Especially Mrs Clinton.

In response, David Gergen explained that denizens of the Clinton White House have constructed barriers to the press because they believe that the press corps is 'full of piranhas,' so 'if one speaks to them they're going to do you in, tear you apart.' Walsh agreed that there was some basis for the perception that the press was out to get the Clintons: 'The first two years of the Clinton presidency, we were unrelenting in looking at Bill Clinton, and his coverage was overwhelmingly negative.'

Republicans are in exactly the same bind. In a symposium held at American University, Bay Buchanan, who managed her brother Pat's presidential campaign, commented that a campaign manager has to make sure your candidate does not speak off the cuff. Pat Buchanan, she said, loves to sit around talking to reporters. But that's just the atmosphere in which he's likely to tell a joke, and then someone – it takes just one – will seize on it and

> the next thing you know you're apologizing or explaining. You cannot have a relaxed moment with the press anymore. That is the bottom line, unfortunately. It's not that you can't trust six of them, it's the seventh one there.

Author Patricia O'Brien, a member of the White House press corps during the Reagan administration, sees the success of that administration in manipulating reporters as another source of the press's conviction that any information given should be distrusted as 'spin.' For one thing, the Reagan White House selectively fed 'news tips' to the most powerful news organizations, who gave prominent play to these exclusives attributed to an unnamed 'White House source' – only to be embarrassed, in some cases, when the tips turned out to be false. For another, reporters traveling with the president were often forced to depend on press releases handed them just before they got on the plane; in the days before every reporter had a cellular phone, this artful timing meant there were few opportunities to delve below the surface before crafting and filing stories. O'Brien recalls,

> Many of us knew we were being used, but Reagan was too popular a president for us to do anything about it. His administration showed how much the White House could both stage and control the flow of information, and how easily the media could be corralled. It was like putting all these reporters into a champagne bottle and shaking it up. The cork had to pop. What we're seeing now is that cork popping.

It's a common human inclination to see others' actions as the instigation, our own as the reaction. The press blames the White House and Downing Street for keeping them at arm's length, not giving access, and feeding them spin rather than truth. The White House and Downing Street blame the press for ignoring their accomplishments, focusing on slips and mistakes, and portraying anything they do in the worst possible light. The result is complementary schismogenesis, a mutually aggravating spiral: The press reports on public figures in ways that make them look bad, so public figures try to keep the press at bay. Being denied access and 'fed spin' – given only information that makes the administration look good – frustrates reporters and makes them more aggressive, more hostile, and more determined to uncover the unflattering underbelly of the spin. The more politicians feel their sincere efforts are being undermined by a barrage of negative images, the more they feel they must find ways to overcome these negative images – in other words, to spin. On and on it goes, the behavior of each group aggravating the behavior they dislike in the other.

---

## THE OBSERVER'S PARADOX

Researchers who study human interaction talk about the observer's paradox: We want to observe how people interact naturally. But we're not invisible and we don't have X-ray vision, so we have to observe how people talk when we are there (or a camera or video recorder is there), even though our being there changes the nature of the interaction. All we can do is work with what we've got, taking into account the effect of our presence, or the presence of the recorder, on how people behave.

The observer's paradox applies to journalism as well. The relentless criticizing of public figures inevitably affects how they behave. Reading journalists' accounts of interviews, I often get the impression that the behavior being criticized or lampooned is in part a reaction to encounters with journalists – either previous ones or the ones at hand. For example, this comment appeared in a *Time* magazine profile of Elizabeth Dole:

For such a political powerhouse, she can come across as surprisingly insecure. With strangers, her eyes seek out approval. Her charm is palpable, her graciousness as carefully applied as her glue-gun red lipstick. Yet when a journalist prepares to ask her a question, she tenses up as though waiting for a blow. Her answers are often so resolutely bland as to suggest a terror of revealing anything human.

Or perhaps of revealing anything that could be used against her. Given the culture of critique, is it necessarily a sign of pathological insecurity to tense up as though waiting for a blow when a journalist prepares to ask a question? Many journalists are aware of the effects of asking aggressive, embarrassing, and compromising questions, so they save them for the end or even apologize: 'My editor insists I ask you this.' Yet not enough attention is paid to the observer's paradox: how much of the way public figures behave is a response to being under constant attack by the press.

In Britain in the early nineties, the so called 'killer bimbo' (this moniker interestingly slanders the perpetrator with the demeaning term 'bimbo' even as it characterizes her as slaughtering her prey) interview became fashionable. Lynn Barber pioneered this aggressive technique in the *Independent on Sunday* which was copied by several other journalists, mainly women. They asked intimate, provocative, and hurtful questions typically highlighting their victims' weaknesses. For example, Richard Adams, author of the children's classic *Watership Down*, was one of the first to be 'Barbercued,' as it came to be known. 'Over and over again,' Barber wrote, 'and sometimes seemingly at random, his eyes would fill with tears and he would start talking in a broken voice, gasping between sobs, about the death of a friend or about cruelty to animals. I found myself wanting to bark "Brace up, man!" but his rabbit-like demeanour has a fox-making effect.'

Barber reported that when she met the actor Richard Harris, he spent much of the time with his hand down the front of his tracksuit bottoms. Melvyn Bragg, the novelist, refused to speak to her after she suggested that one of his novels, about the relationship between a middle-aged man and an 18-year-old woman, could be autobiographical. Barber asked the film director Ken Russell: 'Have you ever been certified insane?'

In our private lives, it is hurtful and confusing to have criticism repeated to us, especially if the source is not identified. How would you respond if someone told you, for example, 'People think you're too self-centered.' You can't confront those who said so, because you don't know who they are. And you're not supposed to be angry at the person who's telling you, because, after all, other people said it. This is just the sort of secondhand criticism that those in public life confront daily and that sparks reactions that are then used against them.

Many journalists claim that the Clintons failed to establish connections with journalists who could have been helpful to them because they brought with them to Washington a deep distrust of the press. But the public record shows where this distrust could have come from. During the 1992 presidential campaign, Mrs Clinton was widely criticized for two remarks, both of which were spoken in reaction to being confronted with criticism.

The first was a reference to Tammy Wynette. When the Clintons agreed to discuss their personal relationship on *60 Minutes*, the interviewer, Steve Kroft, suggested that their decision to remain married was an 'arrangement.' Protesting this insulting evaluation, Mr Clinton said, 'It's not an arrangement. It's a marriage.' And Mrs Clinton said, 'I'm sitting here because I love him and I respect him and I honor what he's been through and what we've been through together.' The sound bite that was picked up, however, was a phrase she used to reject the 'arrangement' idea: She said that she was not 'some little woman standing by my man like Tammy Wynette.' This phrase was repeatedly quoted as if it were the first move in a conversation, interpreted as an insult to women who stay home rather than work outside the home. The fact that the remark had been provoked by an insult to her marriage was lost.

A similar provocation triggered the other sound bite that became famous during that campaign: the 'cookies and tea' remark. The context was an accusation by presidential primary candidate Jerry Brown that Mrs Clinton had exploited her marriage to the governor of Arkansas to draw state business to the law firm at which she was a partner. Reporters repeated the accusation to Mrs Clinton and asked for her response. Her spontaneous reply touched on a number of points, including her personal struggle to combine work and family: 'I've done the best I can to lead my life but I suppose it'll be subject to attack but it's not true and I don't know what else to say except it's sad to me.' Pressing the point, reporters asked how the appearance of conflict could be avoided. Her answer was, 'I've tried very, very hard to be as careful as possible' so the only way to completely avoid the appearance of conflict would be not to have her own career at all. The way she worded this was 'I suppose I could have stayed home and baked cookies and had teas but what I decided to do was fulfill my profession which I entered before my husband was in public life.' No sooner were these words spoken than the day's sound bite was in the can. Gone was the context that had provoked her frustration. Lost were her statements about trying to be careful and about struggling to balance work and family. All that remained was 'cookies and tea,' transmogrified into another insult to women who stay home.

It is easy to see why these two sound bites were the ones chosen by reporters to highlight from these longer interviews. They fit into a popular polarization, a ready-made war: women who stay at home versus women who work. Yet surely the ironic edge in both cases came from having been asked hurtful questions. This is the spiraling effect of the culture of critique: Attack begets response, which becomes fodder for further attack. Even more important, these remarks were made during spontaneous, early interviews given to the press. The experience of trying to be honest and having a chance remark yanked out of context to become a bludgeon with which to beat them no doubt explains the later reluctance of the Clintons – and other public figures – to talk freely to the press.

Emphasis on the negative is often a stretch. Pulling out the most negative perspective can be like reaching for the ring as the merry-go-round whirls past it. The same newspapers that devoted so much attention to exploring negative responses to Mrs Clinton during the campaign reported that a *New York Times*/CBS News poll found that 29 percent of registered voters held a favorable opinion of her, whereas only 14 percent did not – twice as many. Yet far fewer column inches were devoted to exploring the basis for the 29 percent than for the 14 percent. In the culture of critique it seems more interesting to explore the reasons for negative reactions than for positive ones.

We all tend to think of ourselves as reacting to others and others' behavior as absolute. If we hear ourselves snapping at someone, we focus on what we were reacting to. We think of ourselves as nice people who were provoked. But if someone else snaps at us, we rarely wonder what we said to provoke this response. Instead, we judge the other person's personality: He is rude, she is temperamental. The same thing happens when public figures are criticized for behavior that is a reaction to provocative questions put to them. This would be less unjust if the provoked reactions really did reveal their 'true selves.' But as often as not, they simply reveal the frustration of being caught in the web of the culture of critique.

There are many ways that the press's coverage of politicians encourages some of the behavior that the press in turn deplores. Kathleen Hall Jamieson, dean of the University of Pennsylvania's Annenberg School for Communication, shows that speechwriters, knowing that speeches are reported in sound bites, try to write sound bites that will get on the news. This discourages discussing complex issues; what would be the point in preparing such speeches if no one is going to hear them? And some sound bites are juicier than others. Politicians can improve their chances of getting on the news by lashing out at opponents.

As in all matters of public life, the ultimate losers are the public. If the press has less access, citizens have less information. And this goes for all public officials, not just those in the White House and Downing Street. The logic underlying attack is the assumption that when people in power know that what they say will be scrutinized for weaknesses, they will think more carefully in advance and give more reliable information. Surely this is true in some situations. But often less, not more, information results. If public figures know from experience that anything they say will be used against them – and they cannot rely on an agreement with the press to repay access with discretion – they become more guarded. One public official (who of course requested anonymity) told me that he used to give long, freewheeling press conferences but now limits himself to reading brief prepared statements. In cases like this – and I have no doubt there are many – the culture of critique gives us less information, not more.

Given the appeal of making others look bad, technology provides a rich source of ammunition: evidence that politicians are hypocrites if not liars because they change their positions over time. Everything a politician says becomes part of an easily accessible public record, and it is just a matter of spending a few minutes with a computerized database to find a flip-flop. In the spirit of critique, having changed a position becomes the focus rather than the relative merits of the positions before and after. President Bush was mercilessly punished for breaking his 'Read my lips: no new taxes' promise, but little discussion focused on whether or not the new taxes he imposed were needed or fair. Finding things to criticize overshadows other types of investigation.

## PROVOKING – TO WHAT?

When interviewing public figures, journalists often want to get interviewees to talk about subjects they would rather not discuss. In principle, an interviewee does not have to answer anything. But refusing to answer a question can be described in a way that makes the refuser look bad. This raises questions on two levels: Is it fair to the interviewee? But also, does it always result in getting more rather than less information?

Ah, the power of the English passive voice: 'When asked,' an article tells us – as if the question fell down from heaven. So, for example, we read in an article about the actress Vanessa Redgrave about a painful topic that was 'broached':

> Although Redgrave has long been regarded as one of the world's most accomplished, fascinating actresses, her insistence on exploiting that renown for political purposes has often alienated peers and audiences; there were long periods during which the roles offered Redgrave did not reflect her stature or talent. This is not a subject she enjoys discussing, but it is broached during a late dinner.

Her voice, we are told, 'dropped to a whisper, her hint that the conversation is getting too personal, too close. "It bothered me a lot,"' she said. What else could she have replied? Could she have said, 'No, it didn't bother me at all. I loved doing crummy roles for lower pay than I deserved'? This hurtful question did not ferret out new information; it simply offered readers a titillating glimpse of a person in pain.

One rationale behind asking questions that interviewees do not want to answer is the belief that someone who has been goaded or upset will blurt out truths that would otherwise be guilefully hidden. This assumption was made explicit in a discussion on the Washington, D.C., talk show on which a commentator recalled a remark House Speaker Newt Gingrich had made as a guest on the show:

PLOTKIN:  He said to me, and to the citizens of the District of Columbia, 'You should be happy. You have more freedom than anybody in Cuba.'

If you had read only this, you might conclude that the speaker has a very haughty attitude toward the District of Columbia and a callous and flippant way of expressing it. But the host of the show added information about how this remark had emerged:

McGINTY:  But the fact was that you kept asking the same things over and over again and he just got upset and blurted that out. I don't think you can say that that really is the status of the speaker of the House's thoughts on Washington, D.C.

Plotkin agreed about the circumstances of the comment but disagreed about the light that shed:

PLOTKIN:  Oh, I think they are. Absolutely. I think I got under his skin. Exactly. And he came out with the truth. You know, like somebody wakes you up, or you're drunk, or you're in any other different state, where you speak the truth.

This is the reasoning that drives many of the challenging or even insulting questions that interviewers ask. But McGinty questions the assumption:

McGINTY:  Well, and that is the standard belief that people have. That when you say something when you're angry, when you say something when you're not calculating, that that's the truth. But how many times has that happened, Mark, when you *mis*-spoke, . . . when you said something that if you thought about it for a minute you really didn't mean it.

That is the question for us, as receivers of information: Does provoking interviewees – getting under their skin – always lead them to blurt out the truth, or does it, sometimes at least, provoke them to say something they don't really mean? Some people become inarticulate when they feel hurt, upset, or caught off guard. And some simply clam up or call the interview off.

In Britain for example in December 1997, a Labour Party spokes-man threatened to withdraw all cooperation from the BBC follow-ing an interview John Humphrys conducted with Harriet Harman, then Secretary of State for the Social Services, on the *Today* program. Harman had been criticized for the Government's decision to cut financial assistance to single parents, a group she had defended vigorously when in opposition. Humphrys asked her whether she had taken the decision willingly or whether it had been forced on her by the Cabinet and continued to repeat the question long after it was clear that Harman was not going to answer it. On another occasion he interrupted Kenneth Clarke, the Conservative Home Secretary, 32 times in the course of one interview.

Clearly there are occasions when interviewers need to confront interviewees by asking challenging questions. It is the automatic, pervasive use of such questions that I am questioning. Sometimes an interviewer can get more and better information by taking a supportive stance, encouraging interviewees to let their defenses down. For example, journalist Gitta Sereny was able to get Albert Speer to reveal his complicity in Nazi genocide, something the Nuremberg trials had failed to do. As a reporter at the trials, she saw that prosecutors' questioning often led witnesses to stonewall. As Hitler's minister of armaments, Speer had had responsibility for 14 million workers, including concentration camp inmates, yet he managed to convince the war crimes tribunal that he had not known of the genocide and hence was acquitted of complicity (though sentenced to a prison term for exploiting slave labor). When she talked with Speer, Sereny professed interest only in getting a sense of his life – and she was there, patiently listening, when he let his defenses down and revealed that he had, after all, known of the genocide.

Taking a sympathetic stance in order to coax out damaging revelations is not necessarily nicer. People particularly resent being blindsided by someone who comes on as a friend, then uses the information gleaned to make them look bad. My point is to show that taking an aggressive stance, while succeeding in making the questioner look tough, often fails to elicit more or better information. But it never fails to contribute to the atmosphere of aggression that is the culture of critique.

## THE DEATH OF AN ADMIRAL:
## A DRAGNET OF ATTACK

On May 16, 1996, Jeremy 'Mike' Boorda, the top-ranking admiral heading the U.S. Navy, left his office to go home for lunch – and shot himself in the chest. Details of events leading up to this tragedy were reported by Nick Kotz in *The Washingtonian* seven months later. Drawing on this account, the accuracy of which I have confirmed with others close to the events, I will recount some key elements, because they illustrate how the culture of critique in journalism can dovetail with similar forces in other segments of society, with tragic consequences.

Many people believe that anyone who commits suicide must have harbored within himself some underlying psychological instability. Even if this is true, those who kill themselves are often responding in an extreme way to provocation that would be deeply distressing to anyone. The events that led to Admiral Boorda's suicide provide a glimpse of the kinds of pressures that the culture of critique brings to bear on people in public life. We should look carefully at this unusual case, because it forces us to consider what is going on daily without our thinking about it.

On the morning of his suicide, Admiral Boorda thought he had a meeting scheduled with David Hackworth, a retired Army colonel who had published a best-selling autobiography, *About Face*, that had gained him a high public profile and a contributing editor position at *Newsweek*. Boorda's office had been notified that Colonel Hackworth was planning to write about the admiral. They suggested the meeting so Colonel Hackworth could get a sense of who the admiral really was. Two hours before the meeting, Admiral Boorda learned that he was to meet not with Colonel Hackworth but with two journalists from *Newsweek* who were going to question him about having worn medals that some felt he had not earned. Certain that no matter what he said, he would be publicly accused and humiliated, the admiral went home and killed himself.

Mike Boorda had been appointed chief of naval operations at a critical time: His charge was to integrate women into the Navy and to restore the Navy's credibility and integrity following the Tailhook scandal. He was unusually popular with enlisted men, from whose ranks he had risen. He also had unusually good relations with the senators and members of Congress who ultimately ruled on military matters. But he earned the resentment of officers, who saw Washington as the enemy and thought he should resist civilian demands rather than implement them. Such tensions are common in any leadership position. But in this case, as Nick Kotz documents, a confluence of critique came together with the press's power of public exposure.

The planned exposé of Admiral Boorda's medals was only the most recent of a series of public attacks. In April, James Webb, who had been secretary of the Navy under President Reagan, delivered a speech at the Naval Academy fiercely attacking Boorda for being too political. Webb did not simply disagree with Boorda's policies; he accused him of being motivated not by a desire to do what was best for the Navy and the country but by a desire to advance his own career. Boorda was devastated when he read of this speech – not because of what Webb had said (according to Kotz, Boorda told his aides this was 'Webb being Webb') but because the midshipmen, the officers-in-training attending the academy, had stood and cheered, just one day after they had cheered Boorda himself.

Ominously, the speech then entered the journalistic echo chamber by which accusations are repeated until they bounce off the walls. Webb's speech was published in *The Washington Times* and reprinted in a Pentagon publication called *Early Bird*. So when Admiral Boorda went to the Army War College in Carlisle, Pennsylvania, several days later to address a group of young officers, he was pelted with questions about how he would respond to Webb.

The reverberations continued: Another former officer, John Carey, read Webb's remarks and wanted not only to endorse them but to up the ante. He wrote a letter calling for Boorda's resignation that was published in *The Navy Times* – anonymously, making it impossible for Boorda or anyone else to gauge its significance. Robert Caldwell, an editor at *The San Diego Union-Tribune* (San Diego is a city with a significant Navy presence), played a crucial role in these events. He had encouraged Webb to deliver his speech at the Naval Academy; he had alerted Carey in advance that the speech was in the offing; and on May 5, he published a full-page excerpt from Jim Webb's speech accompanied by a cartoon caricaturing Admiral Boorda beheaded and sinking into the sea.

These events were known to Admiral Boorda, and unsettling. At the same time, unbeknownst to him, another movement was afoot: a move to expose him for having affixed to a medal he had been awarded a small 'V' for 'Valor.' The question of whether or not Admiral Boorda was entitled to wear the 'V' on his medal hinges on whether the 'V' represents heroism in a combat mission in general (there was no question that Boorda had earned this) or whether it is limited to those who have been directly fired upon (his ship had not). What seems clear is that the issue is cloudy: The Navy changed its regulations over time, and at least one other officer did receive explicit authorization to wear the 'V' for participation in the same maneuver for which Admiral Boorda had been awarded the medal. In any case, the admiral had taken the 'V' off a year earlier, as soon as he learned that questions had been raised about it.

Colonel Hackworth was the one planning to expose Admiral Boorda in *Newsweek*. According to Kotz, an Air Force public affairs officer recalls that Hackworth 'took great pride in saying that he was working on a story that would bring a Navy admiral down, and the Navy to its knees,' and *Newsweek* editor Maynard Parker recalls that Colonel Hackworth said, '"This could be a real career-ender."'

The legwork on digging up evidence that Admiral Boorda had worn the 'V' and that he might not have been entitled to was done by a man named Roger Charles, Washington correspondent for the National Security News Service. This is an organization funded by foundations whose main concern is furthering the cause of nuclear disarmament, but Charles, Kotz notes, saw his own goal as exposing the wrongdoings of military officers.

Medal inflation, Kotz shows, is a common phenomenon, as much discussed in the military as grade inflation is in academic circles. A final irony was an event reported exactly a year later. In May 1997, it emerged that Colonel Hackworth had included in his résumé two decorations he had not earned. When the error was brought to his attention, he removed them from his résumé.

If the worst was true – if Admiral Boorda had intentionally affixed a 'V' to his medal knowing he was not entitled to – why was it worthy of a major exposé in a national newsmagazine, especially since no one was claiming that he was still wearing it? If Admiral Boorda was so important that this small error was a major story, why had he not received attention from *Newsweek* for any of his accomplishments?

The answer is the culture of critique, which drove events from beginning to end: It drove military traditionalists not only to oppose Admiral Boorda's policies but to impugn his motives. It drove Bob Caldwell of *The San Diego Union-Tribune* to urge James Webb to launch his attack on Boorda, to alert Jim Carey to the attack, and to publish excerpts alongside the cartoon. It drove *The Washington Times* and the Pentagon's *Early Bird* to report the speech as news. It drove audience members at the Army War College to question the admiral about how he would respond to Webb. It drove Roger Charles of the National Security News Service, like so many independent investigative organizations, to dig up dirt to feed to major news outlets. It accounts for the appeal of the story to *Newsweek* editors. And all this without any acknowledged malice but only membership in the I'm-just-doing-my-job club. Bob Caldwell probably spoke for many of the participants when he said afterward, 'I never wanted to hurt Mike Boorda personally.'

Explaining *Newsweek*'s view of events, Jonathan Alter wrote, 'It is possible [Admiral Boorda] could have moved the story in a different direction, or talked the magazine out of publishing anything on the matter at all.' Alter may well be aware of instances in which public figures succeeded in talking journalists out of proceeding with plans to expose them, but I doubt there are many citizens who believe such an outcome is likely. Clearly Admiral Boorda did not, as he wrote in his suicide note, addressed 'To my sailors': 'I don't expect any reporters to believe I could make an honest mistake and you may or may not believe it yourselves.' His assumption reflects the spirit many perceive not only in contemporary journalism but in contemporary society: A presumption of sincerity is far less common than the presumption that those in public life are self-aggrandizing and deceptive.

In explaining why Boorda was not given more warning about the impending visit, Hackworth (quoted by Kotz) said, 'Evan [Thomas, the *Newsweek* editor] didn't want to walk into an ambush. He wanted all the ammo in place.' Yet having all the ammo in place before confronting Boorda without warning sounds rather like . . . an ambush. Kotz also quotes Thomas himself: 'If you go in too soon, the Navy can counterattack, and the opposition gets the story. The idea is to maintain an exclusive, but to allow enough time to see if it was true. Forty-eight hours is enough.' According to Kotz, although Admiral Boorda was given two days' notice about the meeting, he was not informed of its purpose until two hours before. The timing of his suicide supports this version. But whether it's two hours or two days, what seems like plenty of time to journalists concerned with preserving a scoop seems like very little time to a human being suddenly faced with the threat of public exposure.

In my research on workplace interaction I found that those in high-ranking positions are often unaware of how intimidating they appear to those who hold less power. Journalists too are sometimes unaware of their own strength. Some medical schools now require future doctors to check into hospitals as patients in order to experience a medical encounter from the patient's point of view – and discover why many patients find the experience dehumanizing. Journalists, too, could benefit from a temporary reversal of roles. One who did was Joe Klein, *Newsweek* columnist and CBS correspondent, who at first denied but eventually was revealed as being the anonymous author of *Primary Colors*, a roman à clef about the Clintons. Following his exposure, Klein became the object of media attention and criticism the intensity of which he found intolerable. Among his objections was that he was given only a few hours' notice of *New York* magazine's intention to expose him. In response to Klein's complaint, *New York* columnist Richard Turner described the magazine's timing in terms that echo almost word for word Evan Thomas's explanation of *Newsweek*'s timing in confronting Boorda:

It's common-enough journalistic practice: In an effort to

preserve the scoop, you wait till the last minute so they can't send out a press release, feed another version to someone else, whatever.

That this is 'common-enough practice' makes it more troubling, not less.

Perhaps the saddest aspect of events leading up to Admiral Boorda's suicide is that so many people played a role, so few of them operating from vicious or venal motives. Each was just playing his role in the quotidian drama of the culture of critique.

---

### WHY DOES CRITICISM SPEAK
### LOUDER THAN PRAISE?

---

Reaction to Admiral Boorda's suicide tended to focus on his 'thin skin': Why did he allow criticism to overshadow the praise he was receiving and other evidence that he was doing a good job? If this is how he responded to such a small threat, one journalist commented to me, how would he react to a military invasion? Differently, I'd say, because a military invasion is what he was trained for, and he would know who his enemies were. The culture of critique works stealthily, chipping away at the human spirit.

In a charming little book about aging, psychologist Ann Gerike encourages people to go easier on themselves, realizing that

> Unless you're a public figure and the media picks up on it, you can make a fool of yourself in public, and most people (with the probable exception of a spouse or partner!) will have forgotten what you did by the end of the day, if not by the end of the hour or minute.

Illustrating this passage is an amusing because absurd cartoon of someone reading a newspaper with a look of horror on his face: 'TODD MARTIN MAKES FOOL OF SELF IN PUBLIC,' the head-line reads.

Meant as a humorous spoof depicting a self-evidently absurd scenario, this cartoon actually offers a glimpse of what life is like for people in public life. They may indeed open the papers to find that a small misstep is reported in detail, probably distorted. It is the realization of everyone's worst fears: A small gaffe will ruin your reputation, overshadowing all the good you have done. Yet individuals who do not define themselves by their mistakes and missteps are often willing to define public figures that way. Though it is unfortunate for the public figures themselves, the real losers are the people and the nation.

---

## CYNICISM: THE BITTER HARVEST

The culture of critique undermines the spirit not only of people in public roles but of those who read about them, afraid to believe in anyone or anything because the next story, if not the next paragraph, will tell them why they shouldn't. The aggression culture makes it harder for leaders to solve problems because it encourages citizens to lose trust in their leaders. ABC News correspondent Cokie Roberts notes this danger: Not only government, but 'all public institutions – religious institutions, educational institutions, the family – all have been under attack. Who is then left to fix anything, if you're constantly running down every institution that is in a position to do so?'

The aggression culture also discourages leaders from seeking compromise or undertaking ameliorative behavior. Adam Gopnik points out that since the aggressive stance of journalists is presumably intended to temper the arrogance of those in power, the press's aggression should rise in proportion to how authoritarian the person in power is. In reality, it's the reverse. 'Temporizing, moderate figures, like Clinton – or, for that matter, George Bush or, better still, Michael Dukakis – get treated with a disdain bordering on contempt.'

Just about anyone commenting on the current state of journalism sooner or later – usually sooner – gets to the issue of cynicism. I asked Geneva Overholser what, in her role as ombudsman at *The Washington Post*, is the complaint she most often hears from readers. They complain most, she said, of news stories telling them not just what public figures did or said but what they hoped to achieve by that action or statement. We are not simply told, 'The speaker

of the House proposed ...' but rather 'In an attempt to ...,
the speaker of the House proposed ...' Readers tell Overholser,
'Just give it to me straight. Don't tell me what to think about it.'
Ironically, what these readers are complaining about is ... spin – just
what journalists deplore in information they get from politicians.
Most dangerously, press coverage becomes, in part, a self-fulfilling
prophecy. Politicians who despair of having their sincere actions
presented as such can start to think they might as well be as cynical
as everyone thinks they are.

Voter turnout for elections seems to get lower each year. Many
observers believe that covering current events from the perspective
of strategy rather than substance is a factor in creating public
cynicism, which then keeps voters away from the polls. Joseph
Cappella and Kathleen Hall Jamieson devised an ingenious way of
testing and documenting this belief. They took the actual coverage
of a mayoral race and persuaded the same journalists who covered
that race to write alternative copy and create alternative versions
of broadcast news focusing on substance rather than strategy and
assessments of who was ahead and who was behind. Voters in
different cities who knew nothing of the original mayoral race were
given one or the other type of coverage to read and watch. Then
they were tested to see how cynical they felt about the election and
what they had learned. Sure enough, those who had read and seen
the strategy-focused coverage were more cynical and had learned
less than those who received the substance-focused coverage. These
findings confirmed a study of the 1974 elections that found that
those who watched television news more frequently were more
cynical.

Clearly, journalists are not solely responsible for trends in our
society. There is a web of influence among journalists, politicians,
business leaders, and other professionals and citizens, so it is easy
for each group to blame another. One review of the Cappella
and Jamieson book exonerated journalists and blamed politicians:
'Whatever the reporting style,' the reviewer concluded, 'our current
crop of politicians can engender cynicism all by themselves.' In
pointing the finger at politicians, the review not only ignores how
styles of reporting can aggravate cynicism, but also sidesteps the role
of press attacks in influencing who decides to pursue and remain
in public office. The caliber of public officials is not only a cause

but also in part a result of the culture of critique – in journalism and other institutions – as dramatized by the case of another Navy admiral.

---

### 'A LOT HARDER AND A LOT HOTTER'

---

On January 18, 1994, retired admiral Bobby Ray Inman withdrew as nominee for secretary of defense. In an hour-long news conference, Admiral Inman, who had held high public office in both Democratic and Republican administrations, explained that he did not wish to serve again because of changes in the political climate that resulted in public figures being subjected to relentless attack. He described what he saw as a material change in the confirmation process since 1981, when he had been confirmed as deputy director of Central Intelligence following a two-hour hearing. The motivation behind his withdrawal was summed up by a senior official in the White House this way: 'This was a guy who knew how to play the game and thought he could play the game. Only he discovered that the game had gotten a lot harder and a lot hotter.'

In his remarks, Admiral Inman recounted events that made him rethink his decision to return to public life. First, he said, a *New York Times* reporter called asking questions about his tenure at the helm of a business called Tracor. Inman asked whether the article would consider all his business experience, such as his successful service on corporate boards, and was told that the reporter was going to write 'exactly the story my editors wanted.' Next, the administration felt it had to admit in advance that the admiral, like many other individuals nominated to public office, had hired a woman to help with housework and had not paid Social Security tax for her. Inman noted that anyone who had ever paid a baby-sitter more than fifty dollars in a three-month period would be in the same position. The revelation now threatened this loyal employee (who had not been reporting her income to the IRS) with loss of her home and other legal difficulties. Inman also said he was told by friends in the Republican Party that although his confirmation was not in danger, senators felt obligated to raise difficult questions during the hearings. Inman also referred to vitriolic attacks by newspaper columnists (William Safire, for example, called him a 'tax cheat'), noting that columnists have unprecedented power to make accusations without needing to support them and without those attacked having an opportunity to respond in the same frame. He said he was told by an editor, 'Bobby, you've just got to get thicker skin. We have to write a bad story about you every day. That's our job.' It was not the confirmation hearings that Inman dreaded but that media criticism would become 'the daily diet, every day going forward for three years, and that one should accept this as the cost of doing public service.' Though this was accepted in Washington, Inman said, from the rest of the country he heard, 'Why would you put up with that garbage just to do public service?'

Reports of Inman's withdrawal used words like 'bizarre,' 'mystified,' 'stunned,' 'astonishment,' 'extraordinary,' and 'puzzlement.' Everyone agreed that Inman would certainly have been confirmed. In reacting to his statements, politicians and journalists expressed exactly the view that Inman attributed to them. As one official reportedly said, 'I know he doesn't like to have people criticize him, but that's what happens when you're going to stand up for an office like that.'

What's wrong with this picture? In doing public service, a person makes a personal sacrifice to contribute to society. The notion that people must pay a high price for the privilege of making sacrifices makes no sense. But today the assumption is that people seek public office not to serve their country but to advance their careers and enhance their personal power. Looked at that way, it makes sense: You have to be willing to pay a price to enjoy the power and glory. This assumption is bound to be self-fulfilling: Those who aspire to public office in such a climate are more likely to be those who pant after the glory and power, not those who approach the task in the spirit of public service. As Admiral Inman put it, there are probably 'a good many people who have been approached about public service who have elected not to undertake it for precisely the reasons I've tried to focus on today.'

The idea that all public figures should expect to be criticized ruthlessly is evidence of the ritualized nature of such attack: It is not sparked by specific wrongdoing committed by individuals but rather is triggered automatically. In this process, politicians and journalists both play a role: Politicians want to harm their opponents to ensure success in the next election, and journalists are simply doing their job, a big part of which is seen as attacking high officials. As Geneva Overholser put it when she was editor of *The Des Moines Register*, 'After Watergate, many reporters began to feel that no journalism is worth doing unless it unseats the mighty.'

The reason Inman's withdrawal was so shocking was that reaction to his nomination had been comparatively tame. *The New York Times* summed up: 'In fact, with the exception of a few columns, ... a few editorials and one or two news stories, the selection of Mr Inman had been unusually well received in Washington.' This last evaluation dramatizes how run-of-the-mill systematic attacks have become. With a wave of the subordinate clause, 'a few columns, a few editorials, a couple of news stories' attacking someone personally and (from his point of view) distorting his record are dismissed as so insignificant as to be unworthy of notice.

---

## DON'T TAKE IT PERSONALLY

In explaining his decision, Admiral Inman described his personal reaction to criticism he considered unfair. 'I'd wake up thinking about the stories, the hostile stories, not all the friendly ones,' he told a *Washington Post* reporter. His sense of humor disappeared; he became short-tempered; he lost sleep. But rather than evoking reconsideration of the practices that Inman described, these admissions (like Admiral Boorda's suicide) evoked discussion of his thin skin. The front-page profile, for example, described Inman's 'lifelong insecurity.'

Part of the cult of objectivity is a lack of responsibility for the human suffering caused by attacking others. It's all part of the game; the attacks should not be taken personally. No matter how viciously public figures are attacked, they are expected to continue to be cordial, friendly, and open to those who have attacked them because the assaults are supposed to be ritual, not real (though they have very real consequences for those who are attacked). This can be dangerous for everyone: journalists, their subjects, and citizens watching from the sidelines.

The only way anyone could think attacks would not be taken personally is to ignore the fact that the object of attack is a human being. Those who do dreadful things to other people (like soldiers in war or civilians involved in racially or ethnically motivated assaults) always dehumanize their opponents – for example, by calling them derogatory names. But becoming inured to others' suffering is in itself dehumanizing.

Ironically, members of the press themselves are very sensitive to being criticized. Edward R. Murrow said of his own profession, 'Journalists don't have thin skins. They have no skins.' This sensitivity is not something unusual about journalists; it is something usual about people. In private life, too, the power of one or a few people who are attacking can outweigh a much larger number of people who praise. A teacher gets course evaluations and loses sleep over the one or two angry responses, no matter how enthusiastic the others were. A single critic can make someone want to quit a job or even actually quit. Words can be like weapons of destruction: It takes so much effort, and the cooperation of so many people, to build something – and so little effort of so few to tear it down. As *Washington Post* editor and *Newsweek* columnist Meg Greenfield put it, 'Thin skin is the only kind of skin human beings come with.'

The entire culture loses a measure of humanity when we deny this truth and insist that public figures are not supposed to be hurt by personal attacks. Like children who think their parents are invulnerable, we expect our leaders and other public figures to be impervious to attack. Of course, there will be times – many times – when criticizing and attacking public figures is justified or even required, just as there are times you have to criticize someone in your private life. But we know that in our private lives we must weigh our need to criticize with the effect of criticism on others and their likely response. This measure of responsibility is needed in public discourse, too, along with the acknowledgment that people in public life are still people.

Several newspapers, commenting on Inman's withdrawal, noted that his remark about the attack mode of politicians and journalists sounded a lot like the suicide note of Vincent Foster, who wrote that, in Washington, 'ruining people is considered sport.' In a letter to the president, Admiral Inman wrote, 'I sense elements in the media and the political leadership of the country who would rather disparage or destroy reputations than work to effectively govern the country.' Professor Lani Guinier, whose nomination as assistant attorney general for civil rights was withdrawn by the administration because of wide-spread attacks, distinguished between responsible debate of policy and ideas, on the one hand, and what has become the norm: 'We attack people's reputations or we dismiss them, sound bite style.' She herself was 'sound-bitten to death by the phrase "quota queen."'

---

## REPEAT AFTER ME

---

Because sound bites are catchy, they are easy to pick up. Language is not something static that we learn as children once and for all but a constantly evolving organism. New expressions, new usages come into the language daily. At first they sound odd, but before long they start to sound catchy and then they just sound right, until we hear ourselves using expressions that not long before we had never heard or thought odd. When I returned to the United States after several years abroad, I heard the expression 'off the wall' for the first time and had to ask what it meant. Then I found it nifty and started using it myself. And I am old enough to remember when the expression was 'I couldn't care less,' not the 'I could care less' that we all understand to mean the opposite of what it actually says. A major component of the language we hear around us is what we hear and read in newspapers, on the radio, and on television. Citizens pick up not only the ideas they read and hear but the attitude, the tone, the very wording. The writer of a snappy headline or a jazzy story is suggesting to citizens how they should regard their government, the world, and one another.

Public discourse creeps into private conversations, private minds. I recall asking a friend why she was voting for Ronald Reagan when he was running against Walter Mondale. She replied, 'Mondale is boring.' Never before had whether or not a candidate was boring seemed a reasonable judgment of his qualifications. But this phrasing caught on that year and seemed to make sense because it was heard so often.

Kathryn Ruud studied the manipulation of language by Nazis in the years leading up to the Holocaust. She cites a book by Victor Klemperer, a German Jewish professor who meticulously recorded distortions of language – new uses and misuses – that became part of private conversations after they were introduced by Hitler and other Nazi speakers and writers. When she listened to right-wing talk radio in the United States, Ruud was stunned to hear phrases that were similar to verbal manipulations employed by propagandists in the Nazi era. And she also noticed with alarm that some usages coined and repeated on those shows began to turn up in daily discourse. It is commonplace to hear ordinary citizens, including many who would never listen to right-wing talk radio, talk in disparaging, contemptuous ways about the president and other politicians and leaders. The public discourse we hear around us is part of our upbringing as citizens. Public discourse provides a model for private talk: People pick up phrases, ideas, and attitudes from what they hear and repeat them as if they were their own – repeat them because they have *become* their own.

---

## JOURNALISTS' AGGRESSIVE STANCE IS RITUAL – BUT TAKEN LITERALLY

---

Just as politicians and journalists may maintain an aggressive stance in public while exhibiting a conciliatory persona in private, journalists are not personally as cynical as they seem from their writing. Making this point, James Fallows cites a Times Mirror study which found that a majority (53 percent) of journalists 'thought public officials as a class were more honest and more honorable than the general public was!' Journalists, in other words, know that the stories they write are not the whole story. But the public, judging from this survey, tends to think that it is: 'Four-fifths of the public believed that politicians' morals were worse than those of the average citizen. Four-fifths thought that political authorities could "never" be trusted to do the right thing. (In the early 1960s, 70 percent of Americans thought the government *could* be trusted to do the right thing.)'

Throughout my writing on language, I emphasize that talk has a ritual aspect. People say things in particular ways because they have learned that this is the way to say them. Tone of voice, choice of words, what type of comment is appropriate to make – all are culturally relative. Most Britons, for example, can tell the difference between a ritual 'We should get together for lunch sometime' and a literal invitation to dine, but many visitors to the United Kingdom are confused – and feel misled – when a literal invitation never follows a ritual one. An American tourist in Greece may overhear a conversation in which voices are raised and arms fly and assume the conversationalists are having a fight, while the Greeks know they are just having a lively conversation. Something similar seems to go on with the cynical tone of much current coverage of politicians. The tendency to sneer and deride that so many press critics, including many from within, have described has a ritual nature. Reporters and columnists write with an edge because that is how editors expect them to write and that is how their respected peers write. But they may have no personal animosity toward the public figures they deride. Readers and listeners, on the other hand, take literally the implication of ubiquitous insincerity and Machiavellian motives. The result – probably unintended but no less damaging – is widespread public cynicism.

---

### THE PEOPLE'S FAULT

---

Journalists writing about their own trade are acutely aware of many of the pitfalls they confront. Many blame the public for demanding debased forms of discourse. For example, in a Media Studies Center forum one broadcaster claimed, 'The viewers are responsible to a large degree, and if they prefer to see entertainment news instead of NAFTA, what are you going to do about it?'

In Greece, when a guest declines an offer of food by saying 'I'm not hungry,' the host typically responds, 'Eating opens the appetite,' implying that even if you aren't aware of feeling hungry, you should eat anyway, and you'll discover a hunger you didn't know you had. This is the logic by which companies offer free samples. Free information broadcast over public airwaves can work the same way. Newspapers, radio, and television have whetted the appetite for scandal by serving it up. People who would not have missed knowing about murders, court cases, or scandals, once informed, are caught up and eager to learn the outcome, like sitting glued to a television set to see the ending of a drama you didn't want to watch in the first place.

## THE AGGRESSION CULTURE BOOMERANGS

A woman commented to me, 'I used to follow politics, but now when I turn on the television and hear all that yak, yak, yak, I just turn it off.' She thought it was something about her: 'I guess I'm just getting older and my time seems more precious.' But a March 1997 Pew Research Center survey found that she is not alone: The number of people who say they enjoy reading or watching the news has gone way down since the same questions were asked in 1985.

In Britain, sales of national daily newspapers have been steadily declining for years. At the end of 1997 the total market was just over 14 million a day, compared with more than 15 million a decade earlier. The popular end of the market has seen the sharpest fall, with sales of the tabloids down to 11 million, from 12.5 million in 1987.

I'd be willing to bet that part of the reason is that what people come away with after listening or reading is less pleasant. First of all, they have less of the satisfaction that comes from having been informed, and having engaged with important events and ideas. But in addition, I would wager that they feel vaguely sullied by what many refer to as 'all that negativity.' A woman who spent a year living abroad wrote to me,

> I have always been a compulsive newspaper reader – New York Times *every* day, then the Jerusalem Post daily in Jerusalem. I have not been able to read a paper since I returned – I am totally turned off by the focus on violence and crime and the tone of the writing. I've tried a few times and hate it!

Sometimes moving from one culture to another brings into focus what otherwise would not draw attention.

Many journalists are raising questions about developments in their profession. The books by Fallows, Walsh, and Johnson and Broder are only a few examples. Walsh, for example, notes that the press is losing credibility, readership, and market share. Worst of all, 'We're losing a whole generation of news interest. The most troubling is people twenty-one years of age and older aren't developing the habit of following the news.' When Jill Abramson recalled how she chose a career in journalism, she began, 'I was a newly minted high school graduate, interested in the news.' How many high school graduates today would say that? And the threat is not only to the journalism profession and industry but to the country. How can citizens make meaningful use of the right to vote if they don't have basic information about public affairs?

Public regard for the press has plummeted, and some journalists see this as the harvest of a crop they helped to plant. Journalists are now public figures, so engendering an attitude of contempt and distrust for public figures has contributed to an attitude of contempt for and distrust of journalists themselves. The Pew Research Center found that a majority of those surveyed believed that news reports are inaccurate and unfair, and that the media are too intrusive and actually get in the way of society solving its problems. *U.S. News & World Report* White House correspondent Ken Walsh presents the same view from personal experience:

> When I first started covering the White House, ten years ago, you'd go around and people would say to you, 'Well, you have such an interesting job, you meet such interesting people, you have such an interesting life.' Now people say . . . 'What's *wrong* with you people in the media?'

Public anger at the press is dangerous, because it interferes with the press's crucial watchdog role. There is a boy-who-cried-wolf aspect to attacks and exposés. Readers just figure it's the scandal of the week and pay no attention. The Pew Center survey found that appreciation for the press's watchdog role is weakening. In 1985, 67 percent of respondents said that press criticism of political leaders is worth it because it keeps them honest; in 1997 this majority was only 56 percent, and the number of those who felt that press criticism interferes with leaders doing their jobs had almost doubled, from 17 percent in 1985 to 32 percent in 1997.

Journalism professor Maxwell McCombs is convinced that declining newspaper circulation and network television audiences are evidence of a public backlash against the press's negativity. Although it is a truism that only bad events are news, McCombs notes that now journalists actively seek out bad news. Larry Sabato comments that the press's attack dog mode is 'one of the reasons why the press is losing the respect of the American people, and why their support scores are lower on virtually every measure.'

Public animosity toward the press is also evident in recent jury awards against major news organizations. In October 1993, *The Wall Street Journal* was sued for publishing an article criticizing a small brokerage firm for improper practices; a federal jury in Houston, Texas, awarded the plaintiff a stunning $222.7 million in damages – $200 million of which were punitive damages, a sum larger than the $190 million that Dow Jones & Company, the newspaper's owner, had earned the previous year. The judgment came shortly after another highly publicized jury award: $5.5 million to Food Lion in a suit against ABC News in connection with a story using undercover reporters to expose unsafe and unhealthy practices. The jury award in the Food Lion case indicated that jurors cared less about the dangers posed by the food chain's practices than about what they saw as the dishonest practices of the undercover reporters.

---

## THE GREATEST LOSS

---

In an interview following his appointment as dean of the Journalism School at the University of California, Berkeley, Orville Schell discussed the transformations he has seen in journalism. He received his own training, he said, by writing for *The New Yorker*, where he learned

> a basic presumption that you'll find some fundamental empathy with your subject. You could be critical, but to write from a perspective of mockery, disdain, or overblown cynicism is dangerous . . . The whole point was to try and find where you connected to your topic and cared about it. That's certainly not the predominant sentiment behind much of what gets written nowadays, which is very flip, even savage, and often contemptuous. This tends to create a climate where everybody, writers included, feels very vulnerable, very attacked and insecure.

It is not criticizing that is bad; what's corrosive is the tone of contempt, the flippant air, the savagery. These make citizens feel more and more cut off from people in public life – and from the larger community we all live in.

By a boomerang effect, journalists themselves, according to Schell, suffer from this loss as well:

> I have a lot of friends in all forms of media, and there's not very many of them who seem to be entirely content where they are ... Most people have this gnawing sense of being forced to do things they wouldn't do otherwise ... There's something about people being forced to write and run newspapers and TV networks and magazines in a way which violates their better principles that is awkward and really, really painful.

---

## WHAT WE NEED: MORE OPPOSITION

---

With our tendency to think in polarized opposites, it may seem that calling off the attack dog mode would relegate the press to becoming lapdogs. But there's another alternative: the watchdog role. It is the press's job to expose governmental wrongdoing and subject leaders to public scrutiny. This is the essence of a free press and a free country. Ironically, the aggression culture has resulted in less real scrutiny. A dog that is busy attacking is not watching.

Take, for example, the practice of always asking follow-up questions – not because a particular question raises doubts but as a matter of course. Fallows claims that this practice cuts in half the number of questions asked at a White House press conference. In the end, he shows, 'The hostile tone of press briefings and the "attitude" of political coverage coexist with the media's willingness to give politicians a free pass on many issues of substance.'

Continual attacks on leaders distract both the leaders and the citizens of the nation from problems that need to be solved. According to the Pew Center survey, a whopping 65 percent of the public said that press coverage of the personal and ethical behavior of political leaders is excessive. But fewer than half thought that press criticism of the policies and proposals of political leaders is excessive. In other words, the problem is not too much aggression but misplaced aggression.

Many people feel that serious government wrongdoing goes

uncovered and unpunished while relatively trivial indiscretions are relentlessly pursued. The most significant post-Watergate scandal occurred when the Reagan administration sold arms to Iran and diverted the profits to the Nicaraguan contras, both in direct defiance of laws passed by Congress. Yet press coverage of Iran-contra was far less extensive than the coverage of, say, Whitewater events that occurred years before Clinton was elected president. In a National Public Radio discussion about Watergate twenty-five years later, *Los Angeles Times* reporter Ronald Ostrow remarked, 'I've never quite understood why Iran-contra didn't catch on more than it did because there were some real abuses of power there. There was some of the same disregard for constitutional guarantees' as there had been in Watergate. Similarly, veteran journalist Studs Terkel accused fellow journalists of taking at face value misinformation put out by the Pentagon during the Gulf War. And the savings and loan debacle, which cost taxpayers billions of dollars, went largely unnoticed by the press until the damage was done.

The British press for their part, did not investigate Robert Maxwell's practices in his control of the Mirror Group of newspapers. Only after his death was it disclosed that he had been raiding the company's pension fund to keep his disparate empire afloat.

*Washington Post* ombudsman Geneva Overholser points out that the press is less oppositional today than it was in the past, as journalists are less distinct from public figures than they used to be. 'We have become players,' she says. 'We get on TV and debate politicians. Rather than vigorous criticism, we're bringing a general sense that no one can be trusted. We contribute to apathy and despair.' Less of this general suspicion and distrust could leave the way clear for more pointed criticism of specific behaviors. And specific errors can be corrected, whereas a general sense of cynicism leaves people feeling hopeless.

Overholser believes that journalists should do more sniffing out of wrongdoing, less presupposing malfeasance in every move made by those in power. She has other recommendations to her colleagues as well. First, she says, reporters should refuse to let people make negative comments anonymously. It poisons the atmosphere while making it impossible to gauge the significance of the criticism. Second, editorial judgment and opinion should be separated from straight reporting of news and labeled for what they are. *What*

Clinton or Gingrich said or did is fact; *why* they said or did it is interpretation. And why the journalist thinks it is important is yet another level of interpretation. All these levels are needed, but they should not be mixed up. Finally, she says, sometimes the press needs to step out of the way and allow public figures access to the public. *The New York Times* and *The Washington Post* often publish verbatim texts of speeches; we need more.

Overholser's job as ombudsman at *The Washington Post* entails reading her own newspaper critically as well as conveying public complaints to her peers. This invaluable service could be duplicated at all newspapers, and at radio and television stations, too.

In his *Newsweek* article following the suicide of Admiral Boorda, Jonathan Alter also made a suggestion to his colleagues: 'We can insist that the picture of public life be textured enough to prevent the exposure of human foibles from destroying everything that a person like Admiral Boorda has built.' If coverage focuses only on criticism, it is not being accurate, because errors and mistakes are not the whole story. Perhaps my own experience is relevant here. Before I got a doctorate in linguistics, I taught English as a second language and remedial writing. Grading papers in these classes was easy: I looked for grammatical errors and corrected them. But then I began teaching freshman composition to nonremedial students as well. When I got my first set of papers from a freshman English class, I panicked. Some of the papers had no grammatical errors, and I was at a loss as to what to do with my red pen. After my initial panic, I figured out that there was still a lot I could offer the students, but I had to step back and regard their papers from a more holistic perspective, thinking about what they were trying to do in the paper and how well they succeeded in doing it. And I took that perspective back to the papers written by remedial students and nonnative speakers. They, too, could benefit more from having me comment on their papers as a whole rather than just picking out grammatical errors. And it made my job of reading their papers much more interesting. Perhaps a similar readjustment could be made by journalists, even though they, too, might feel a moment (or more) of panic at first. Freed of the task of looking for errors, not only readers but writers and commentators could step back and take a more holistic view, which would, in the end, be a more accurate one.

Another way of getting a more accurate view of public life would be for journalists to hold meetings where they agree not to use what they hear against the politicians, but just to get a better understanding of who they are and what they're up to. Not likely, you might think. Yet in just this spirit, when Ken Auletta agreed to cover communications for *The New Yorker*, he began by spending four months 'interviewing sources solely on a background basis about their vision of where their businesses were headed. Without the threat of being exposed in print, sources opened up.' And they later gave Auletta access to their companies that would otherwise have been unthinkable.

Journalists are concerned. The American Society of Newspaper Editors has undertaken a major initiative to identify and address the causes of their profession's dwindling credibility. And a group of prominent journalists signed a statement calling for a 'period of national reflection' about the direction of the profession. The death of Diana, Princess of Wales sparked a similar resurgence of concern in the British press. The British Press Complaints Commission, a voluntary body funded by the newspaper industry to police its behavior, has long had a code of practice which begins by stating that 'all members of the press have a duty to maintain the highest professional and ethical standards.' Specific articles in the code cover accuracy, the right to reply, privacy, harassment, intrusion into grief, reporting of children, the use of listening devices, behavior in hospitals, treatment of innocent relatives and friends and the victims of sexual assault, discrimination, misrepresentation, payment for articles, and the protection of sources. Following Diana's death, some of these clauses were made more rigorous. The time is ripe, I think, on both sides of the Atlantic, to look deeper into why journalists are still largely distrusted, and in particular to question how the argument culture has affected the press and the society it serves. Freed from the need to attack unremittingly, the press could assume its crucial watchdog role. The aggression would still be there, only channeled to more constructive ends.

# 4

## 'A PLAGUE ON BOTH YOUR HOUSES!': OPPOSITION IN OUR POLITICAL LIVES

Following the close of the 104th Congress in 1996, a startling event occurred: Fourteen incumbent senators decided not to seek reelection. Such an exodus was unprecedented in U.S. history. In contrast, the average was five and a half per session for the years 1946 to 1994. Even more distressing, the voluntarily retiring senators were a particularly distinguished and respected group, widely agreed to be exceptionally thoughtful, fair, and moderate. In his introduction to a collection of farewell essays by thirteen of them, Norman Ornstein singles out a theme running through their remarks that also caught my attention: Many of the outgoing senators 'lament the increasing level of vituperation and partisanship.'

Politics is partisan and oppositional by nature. Political parties vie for power and votes. Legislation is proposed and either supported or opposed. Bills, like candidates, are either voted in or voted down. But these outgoing senators, and other members of the Senate and the House of Representatives who decided to step down in recent years, along with others who have remained, make it clear that congressional combativeness has increased exponentially. With politics as with law, the American and British systems are inherently adversarial in their structure, the British more so. The very shape of the House of Commons, with the two main parties arrayed on either side of the chamber separated by a narrow gangway, encourages head-to-head conflict. On nearly every issue debated and voted upon, the House divides on strict partisan lines. Cross-party alliances are seldom formed. Every week, a half hour is set aside for the Prime Minister to be questioned by MPs – a session that invariably degenerates into a raucous shouting match, despite the efforts of the Speaker to enforce a semblance of order.

In recent years, in both Washington and Westminster, a kind of agonistic inflation has set in whereby opposition has become more extreme, and the adversarial nature of the system is being routinely abused. The effect on the legislative process differs in detail between the two countries, but in both cases it's getting in the way of governing. The American senators who decided not to seek reelection are in a position to observe the increased level of rancor and partisanship.

Senator Howell Heflin of Alabama points out that a certain amount of 'gridlock' – action prevented by countervailing forces 'between the two houses of Congress, between the political parties, and between the Congress and White House' – is 'built into the system.' But, he says, the *degree* of gridlock that has developed in recent years is not built in – and not beneficial. Senator Heflin, like other outgoing senators, notes that work gets done only when members of different parties work together and that this practice has fallen not just into disuse but into disrepute:

> The bipartisanship that is so crucial to the operation of Congress, especially the Senate, has been abandoned for quick fixes, sound bites, and, most harmfully, the frequent demonization of those with whom we disagree.

Senator Paul Simon of Illinois blames political parties: 'There is much more partisanship than when I came to Washington two decades ago, and most of it serves the nation poorly. Both political parties share the guilt.' Senator J. James Exon of Nebraska fingers the more general atmosphere of contention:

What I have called the 'ever-increasing vicious polarization of the electorate, the us-against-them mentality,' has all but swept aside the former preponderance of reasonable discussion of the pros and cons of many legitimate issues.

Also in a position to know that things have changed is Senator Robert Byrd of West Virginia. He made a dramatic statement included in the *Congressional Record* for December 20, 1995, in which he too notes that his colleagues' departures are related to an increase in vituperative opposition:

> In my 37 years in the United States Senate, this has been a different year . . . The decorum in the Senate has deteriorated and political partisanship has run rife . . . When we accuse our colleagues of lying and deliver ourselves of reckless imprecations and vengeful maledictions against the President of the United States, and against other senators, it is no wonder – no wonder – that good men and women who have served honorably and long in this body are saying they have had enough!

The words – and actions – of these senators are testament that the argument culture has affected our political lives as deeply as it has the press. The pattern I see is the argument culture: The constructive opposition of our two-party system – our system of checks and balances, and the balance of power between political parties and interest groups – has deteriorated to become obstructionist. An aspect of the argument culture is the culture of critique: Relentless attack is interfering with our leaders' abilities to do the work of government and with citizens' sense of connection to their government and consequently their country. Many of these attacks are aimed at those who hold the highest offices in the executive branch. As a result, many – though by no means all – of my examples are of President Clinton and his administration. Some readers may perceive this as a partisan defense of Clinton and me as an 'apologist' for him. Granted, I am a Democrat, but I do not agree with all of President Clinton's policies. The reason many of my examples come from Clinton is that he is the president holding office as I write this book. (The very fact that defending our nation's elected leader makes one suspect – an 'apologist' – is in itself evidence of the culture of critique by which only criticizing seems like worthy intellectual work.)

---

## COMPROMISE: FOR BETTER OR FOR WORSE

---

The term 'compromise' has two senses. It can mean 'weaken, undermine, destroy,' as in 'the body's immune system was compromised by the virus.' It can also mean 'give in for the purpose of reaching agreement.' The first sense of the word is decidedly negative, but the second sense could well be positive. In recent years, even this sense of the word has taken on negative connotations.

Both senses of the word 'compromise' appear in a book called (the war metaphor again) *Combat* by Senator Warren Rudman, who voluntarily retired in 1994, two years before the mass exodus of his colleagues. Senator Rudman illustrates the negative sense of the word when he writes, 'People often ask me about political compromise. Aren't politicians always selling their souls – or at least their votes – for some political or financial reward?' Here 'compromise' means 'cheapen yourself,' 'sell your soul.' The very word 'politician' in English has a faint scent of this sense of the word, suggesting – at the very least – insincerity. (The corresponding French phrase, *un homme politique*, does not have that unsavory connotation; it refers to someone whose profession is *affaires d'état* – doing the business of the state, not just doing politics.) Senator Rudman uses the word in its positive sense when he writes, 'The system thrives on compromise.' He explains: 'Liberals want $20 billion for a social program, conservatives think $10 billion is enough, so you split the difference and no one thinks he's sold his soul.' This sense of compromise protects against the first. In other cases, according to Rudman, compromise is just a matter of 'accepting reality,' as when he agreed to exclude entitlements from the automatic cuts required by the Gramm-Rudman bill, even though he believed it was crucial to cut back on entitlements to balance the budget. He agreed to do this because he believed that a bill that cut back entitlements would not pass.

There was a time when the ability to compromise was considered a great strength. Henry Clay, an immensely influential nineteenth-century senator and presidential contender, was called the 'Great Compromiser' – and this was said with admiration. It is hard to imagine a contemporary president being labeled in this way: The word 'great' would not easily be appended to 'compromise' without irony. (The spirit of our times is better captured in the phrase applied to Ronald Reagan: 'Great Communicator.') *The New York Times*, in an article about the decline of compromise as a respected mode, notes journalists' role: 'Mr Clinton also fears attacks from the press, which cannot believe that Mr Clinton can give ground to help the country, but only because he is wishy-washy.'

Yet compromise, in the positive sense, is exactly what the retiring senators agree is needed. Senator Heflin makes an appeal:

> The extreme elements of our government must realize that compromise is not bad, that we can be compassionate and responsible at the same time by being moderate in our approach to public policy ... If compromise is abandoned for rigid ideology, the system cannot work as it was intended.

Senator Exon concurs: 'Unfortunately, the traditional art of work-able compromise for the ultimate good of the nation, heretofore the essence of democracy, is demonstrably eroded.' And Senator Rudman gives this as the reason for his departure: 'I thought the essence of good government was reconciling divergent views with compromises that served the country's interests ... The spirit of civility and compromise was drying up.' In their place, he says, 'partisanship' and 'ideology' had risen.

## THE CONFIRMATION PROCESS

Nowhere is the rise of partisanship and ideology clearer than in the increasingly rancorous process by which people are appointed to high public office. The first surgeon general in the Clinton administration, Dr M. Joycelyn Elders, was asked, 'Dr Everett Koop once said that his confirmation for Surgeon General was one of the worst single experiences of his life. Was that true for you too?' Dr Elders replied:

> Yes. The confirmation process had very little to do with what kind of Surgeon General I would be. I felt it was more a mechanism to try to destroy me than anything else. Had I not decided that I was not going to let other people keep me from doing what I felt was important, I would have dropped out. But I was not going to let other people make that decision for me. They might win, but that there was no way, *no way* they were going to do it without a battle. [Laughs] When it was all over I remember thinking, 'I came to Washington, D.C., like prime steak and after being here awhile, I feel like poor-grade hamburger.'

Not only is this cruelly unfair to the honorable people who agree to commit a portion of their lives to public service, but it is unfair to the society and its citizens who are thereafter served by individuals who have been publicly humiliated: It is as if citizens ordered prime steak but had it ground to hamburger before it was served to them.

C. Everett Koop was confirmed as surgeon general in 1981. If he found his confirmation hearings a devastating experience, the destructiveness of the process is not brand-new, but the intensity of attacks on disputed nominees has increased in recent years. According to historian Michael Beschloss,

> We have much higher standards for public officials than we did even thirty or forty years ago. You have to disclose a lot more of your financial history, your personal history, sexual history in some cases, and the result is that many candidates that were easily nominated and confirmed as recently as the late 1960's probably would not get into this today.

'NOMINEES NOW FACE "TRIAL BY FIRE": SENATE CONFIRMATION PROCESS HAS EVOLVED INTO POLITICAL WARFARE,' a *Washington Post* headline declared after Anthony Lake, nominated to head the CIA, withdrew under fire in 1997. Demanding a nominee's FBI files – unthinkable not long before – has become almost routine, the article said. In the words of Democratic Senator Patrick Leahy of Vermont, 'Advice and consent has become harass and maim.' His Republican colleague Senator John McCain of Arizona agreed: 'When it gets nasty these days, it really gets nasty.' Confirmation hearings are focusing on more and more personal attacks, reflecting a widespread tendency that has infected all arenas of political activity. Wisconsin Republican and experienced House member Steve Gunderson speaks to this point as well: 'It's the politics of personal destruction . . . I don't think democracy can survive if we abandon political debate for personal attacks.'

## THE NEW INTENSITY: SINCE WHEN?

Senator Rudman (like many other commentators) traces the 'new intensity' in partisan opposition to 'the liberal campaign that defeated the nomination of Robert Bork to the Supreme Court in 1987.' While Democrats hold that their campaign to oppose the nomination of Judge Bork to the Supreme Court was motivated by a concern for Bork's judicial positions and was waged on that level, Republicans claim that his record was distorted and he was personally demonized. Rudman also points to the watershed use by George Bush's presidential campaign of the now infamous 'Willie Horton' ads, which implied that the Democratic candidate, Massachusetts Governor Michael Dukakis, was responsible for a convicted criminal committing rape while on furlough from prison. The ads, in Rudman's words, implied that Dukakis was 'soft on black rapists.' In reality, the furlough program under which William Horton (he never went by the sinister-sounding name 'Willie') was released from prison had been put in place under Dukakis's Republican predecessor.

Senator Rudman goes on, 'The brass-knuckles trend continued after Bush became president, when the far-right activist Paul Weyrich used unconfirmed charges of drunkenness and womanizing to defeat former senator John Tower's nomination to be secretary of defense.' The net result was a 'new mood in Washington' that 'was no fun for those of us who were more concerned with national defense and the deficit than with the demonizing of those who disagreed with us.'

---

## BRINGING THE HOUSE DOWN

---

A unique perspective on the rise of destructive partisanship is provided by a congressman who also decided not to run for reelection in 1996. Former Congressman Steve Gunderson provides an invaluable perspective on the breakdown of bipartisan action within the House in his book *House and Home*. He gives many examples of how the rules that made working together possible have broken down. For example, there was an unwritten agreement that members of Congress would not campaign against sitting members from their own state. But this rule was broken in Gunderson's last campaign, when the senior Democratic congressman from Wisconsin wrote a widely circulated letter soliciting financial support for Gunderson's Democratic opponent. Gunderson was reelected nonetheless. But it is easy to see that working with someone who campaigned against him would be harder than working with those who observed an agreement not to do so.

Gunderson also recounts an attack made on him by a fellow congressman from his own party that would have been unthinkable in the not distant past. After Representative Gunderson spoke in favor of a bill, Representative Robert Dornan of southern California spoke in opposition, accusing Representative Gunderson of supporting the legislation because he is homosexual: 'The gentleman from Wisconsin didn't tell you when he was debating this amendment that he has a revolving door on his closet. He's in, he's out, he's in.' Then Representative Dornan addressed his colleague directly: 'I guess you're out, because you went up and spoke to a huge homosexual dinner, Mr Gunderson.' Gunderson explains that Dornan violated the 'rigorous rules of decorum and respect' by addressing Gunderson directly, questioning his motives, and attacking him personally. Though Representative Dornan was pressured to 'take down' his remarks – strike them from the official record – he immediately left the House floor and went right to the press corps, to whom he repeated and intensified his remarks. Gunderson's account continues:

'We've got a homo in our midst in the Republican party,' he told a reporter from one of my state's most influential newspapers, the Milwaukee *Sentinel*. 'And they're destroying the country, to say nothing about the party, and we have a moral obligation to expose them and destroy them.' . . . How, Dornan demanded, could I call myself a Christian when all Christians denounce homosexuality?

Representative Gunderson was raised in a devoutly Christian family and remains a devout practicing Christian.

One of the most stunning insights Representative Gunderson's experience affords is how closely the behavior of Representative Dornan and other representatives of the radical right was paralleled by attacks launched against him by extremists with very different views: militant gay rights activists identified with an organization called ACT UP who were enraged at Gunderson for failing to 'come out' publicly. Gunderson was puzzled by this rage, since from his point of view, he was out: He was living openly with Rob Morris, his life partner, taking him to public events such as the presidential inauguration and White House dinners. Nonetheless, a radical gay activist confronted Gunderson in a gay bar, where he had gone for dinner with Rob Morris, and began screaming at him, 'When are you going to come out?,' then dumped a drink on his head. In a scenario reminiscent of the Dornan incident, the activist then issued a press release describing his own behavior. Even after Gunderson came out completely – stating in print that he was gay, releasing photographs of himself and his partner to the press – the radical gay activists continued to portray him as an enemy, and the face-screaming, drink-dumping incident was repeated. This suggests that some of those who are given to dramatic acts of public attack enjoy the attacks themselves as much as – or more than – they seek a particular outcome.

Gunderson notes that his Democratic opponents never knowingly misrepresented his record as a congressman, but both the Christian-right school board member who opposed him in the Republican primary and the radical gay rights activists who vilified him in their publications habitually misrepresented facts about his record and his life. The gay activists presented him as having opposed legislation for AIDS funding and gay rights, when the opposite was the case, and the radical right represented him as supporting gun control and abortion rights, whereas in fact he opposed both.

---

## PROGRESS IN REVERSE

---

The rise of radical factions that eschew compromise and flamboyantly attack those they see as opponents, both in the other party and in their own, is a development that has a surprising corollary, a cautionary tale of sorts, in Japanese history. Japan had a democratic government imposed on it following World War II. Historian Ellis Krauss provides a history of conflict in the Diet, the Japanese equivalent of our Congress, showing how its members had to learn by experience to make this form of government work. Reading Krauss's account, I kept getting the uncomfortable feeling that the United States is going through a comparable process, but in reverse! We seem to be *unlearning* how democracy can work.

Krauss shows that in the early days of Japanese democracy, partisan oppositionism prevented the Diet from getting anything done, but eventually procedures were developed for working together – just the sorts of long-standing procedures that are being undermined in our own Congress. According to Krauss, in the early period of the Diet (from 1958 through the 1960s) there was extreme polarization between the majority and minority parties. For example, the majority party, which had enough votes to pass legislation, would call for a 'snap vote' and declare the motion passed, but the minority party would then boycott sessions and bring everything to a screeching halt. These early disasters were evidence that majority rule by itself is not only ineffective but actually dangerous 'because it can create permanent alienated minorities and overbearing majorities who have little motivation to engage in conflict regulation and accommodation.' This description calls to mind Senator Rudman's account of changes in the U.S. Senate:

> More and more Republicans were arriving who had previously served in the House, such as Trent Lott of Mississippi, Dan Coats of Indiana and Bob Smith of New Hampshire. In the House they had been part of a bitter, frustrated minority, fighting a guerrilla war against the Democrats. The confrontational,

take-no-prisoners attitude they brought to the Senate was not one with which I was completely comfortable.

One of the major causes of debilitating conflict between the parties in the early years of the Japanese Diet was the simple fact that members of the two parties never talked to each other. A crucial development in learning how to make democracy work was establishing a bipartisan House Management Committee, whose members got to know each other through not just working but also socializing together. As one representative put it, 'They have become friends and they can't be unreasonable with each other.' This is just the sort of friendship and communication across party lines that outgoing U.S. senators complain is decreasing. Senator Heflin recalls that cross-party friendships 'have led to more openness and willingness to discuss issues on a cordial basis. They promote the identification of common ground.' He calls for more opportunities for 'informal togetherness among members of opposite parties.' How ironic that we are developing less and less of what the Japanese Diet had to learn over time to have more of. An article about House Speaker Newt Gingrich begins:

Once they were friends. Newt Gingrich and Dick Gephardt both came to Congress in the 1970's. They worked together, socialized with their spouses, traveled abroad together. But in the past year, as Gingrich reigned as speaker and Gephardt toiled as minority leader, the two have spoken at length only once – at a matter-of-fact working breakfast.

Finally, Krauss claims that the new effectiveness of the Japanese Diet was made possible because of the arrival of new members 'who had not been socialized into the conflictual patterns of the past.' Sadly this is the exact opposite of what has happened recently in the United States, where new members are arriving who have not been socialized into the bipartisan spirit by which members of different parties maintained mutual respect and worked together. This development dovetails with another troubling aspect of the argument culture: a widespread view of government as the enemy, even when the government is the source of the bounty that citizens want the government to leave alone. (One constituent said to Senator Nancy Kassebaum, 'Tell the government to keep its hands off my Medicare!') One result of this tendency to see the government as the enemy is the election of candidates who have no government experience and consequently no familiarity with the traditional norms and rules by which government has been run. In some cases, this has resulted in extreme forms of opposition, such as those described by Congressman Gunderson and Senator Byrd.

## THE POWER OF CONCILIATION

Like Senator Rudman, Representative Gunderson shows that conciliation can be more powerful than vocal opposition. He recalls an incident in which Congressman Dick Armey was videotaped referring to fellow Congressman Barney Frank as Barney Fag, substituting a derisive term for homosexuals in place of the congressman's last name. Gunderson came to Armey's defense, publicly accepting his somewhat implausible explanation that the slur had been a slip of the tongue, and declaring that he had never heard Armey utter a bigoted statement. A gay person's public defense of someone who had publicly uttered an antigay slur might seem to be an obvious lapse in integrity and conviction. Yet Gunderson shows how this investment of goodwill paid off. When the Health Subcommittee called a hearing on reauthorization of the 'Ryan White CARE Act,' a bill providing funding for AIDS research, Gunderson used the political capital he had gained:

> Worried that the Ryan White bill would either be held up or modified by amendments from hostile elements within my party, I went to Dick Armey, the House majority leader, and pleaded with him to suspend the usual process and send the bill through without procedural interruptions . . . He remembered my support. In an action that was unprecedented for a bill of such financial magnitude, he put the reauthorization on the Suspension Calendar, meaning that no amendments could be offered. Committee leaders from both sides of the aisle were shocked and delighted. The bill breezed through the House without hateful, homophobic amendments and was sent to conference with the Senate.

Another lesson that this dramatizes is a dramatic and perhaps cautionary one about the benefit of limiting debate on an issue that is known to be inflammatory, like a couple who learn over time to avoid discussing issues that they know will lead to rancorous confrontation with no resolution.

## THE POLITICS OF OBSTRUCTION

If his account of the Ryan White CARE Act shows the usefulness of ideologically opposed representatives working together, Representative Gunderson also provides a chilling first-person account of the politics of obstruction. He organized a weekly lunch meeting of 'House Republicans who resisted the takeover of the party by confrontational conservatives who sought to exclude us.' He calls his group 'governing Republicans' rather than 'moderates,' 'because we want to work through government to get something accomplished.' After an election, governing Republicans believe, 'We should put party labels on the shelf and sit down and govern in a bipartisan way, working together constructively, not destructively.'

This might sound tautological: Obviously, anyone elected to public office wants to 'work through government to get something accomplished.' Not so, says Gunderson. Increasingly, the leadership of the Republican Party was dominated by those 'who believe that unless you're in the majority, you have no role in government except to try to bring down the other party.' Since the party they are trying to bring down is the democratically elected administration that is trying to run the government, the opposition party then functions as a kind of internal third column, working from within to prevent the government from working. When the Republican House members elected their leadership in December 1992, he says, 'every one of the moderate candidates – including those ... who were clearly more qualified than their conservative opponents – went down to defeat.'

Gunderson shows that you don't have to be 'moderate' to believe in governing. Pat Roberts, for example, 'is hardly a moderate' but he is 'very clearly a governing Republican who believes that you've got to get things done.' Throughout his book, Gunderson restates his conviction that in order to govern, the two parties must work together. Republicans Reagan and Bush, he notes, accomplished their goals by enlisting the aid of conservative Democrats. He faults the Clinton administration for failing to enlist the aid of moderate Republicans as much as he faults his Republican colleagues who saw the need to destroy the Clintons as a greater mandate than the need to govern the country.

A cartoon published in 1996 shows a young boy eagerly announcing, 'When I grow up, I hope to spoil someone's bid for the Presidency.' This is the cruelest harvest of the culture of critique, as embodied in the politics of obstructionism. It creates an atmosphere easily mimicked by citizens in which creating roadblocks to others' accomplishments is more appealing than actually accomplishing something yourself.

The defeat of the Clinton administration's attempt to provide universal health care coverage is a dramatic example of the politics of obstruction (as well as the failure to seek compromise). Journalists Haynes Johnson and David Broder, in *The System*, detail the constellation of factors that led to the tragic demise of health care reform, despite a broad bipartisan and public consensus that it was desperately needed. The United States is the only advanced industrialized country in the world that has not found a way of providing health care to all its citizens: At the time there were 40 million uninsured Americans; at the time of this writing the number has risen by another 3 million. As Johnson and Broder document, there was tremendous coordination, effort, and money brought to bear by Republicans working closely with interest groups such as the Christian Coalition and the National Restaurant Association, to prevent the Clinton administration's health care reform, while interest groups whose members would have benefited did not expend effort to support the plan. (Some later told the authors that they were sure some kind of reform would pass and were holding out to get the best deal they could.) The citizens who would have benefited most – middle-class working people who were uninsured – had no group to represent their interests.

For their part, journalists, Johnson and Broder show, did not help the public understand the Clinton plan or the alternatives because of their inclination to emphasize conflict. When opponents of change predicted dire and outlandish consequences, both to the Clintons' plan and later to the Gingrich-led plan to restructure

Medicare, the press reported the accusations but did not examine and expose them as false. The authors tell a heartbreaking tale of public opposition manufactured by misinformation. When *The Wall Street Journal* asked members of a focus group for their opinions of the Clinton plan, they expressed hatred for it – based entirely on misconceptions. When asked what they would like in a health care plan, what they described were the elements of the Clinton plan. They didn't know that what they were so emphatically opposing would have given them just what they said they wanted.

A similar story is told by Eleanor Clift and Tom Brazaitis in their book, tellingly titled *War Without Bloodshed: The Art of Politics*. They stress that Bob Dole and other Republicans had initially been willing to support a modified plan but that the Clintons did not want to compromise their goal of universal coverage and 'feared a trap.' By the time the Clintons were ready to compromise, the Republicans had closed ranks behind Speaker Newt Gingrich, who had been convinced since before Clinton was elected that if the Democrats succeeded in reforming the health care system they would then be unbeatable. Representative Gunderson sees a parallel motivation on the part of the Clinton administration: He believes that they wanted to ensure universal health care for Americans, yes, but they also wanted it to be clearly a Democratic accomplishment, like the institution of Social Security by the Roosevelt administration.

In the opinion of Johnson and Broder, representatives of both parties approached the health care legislation in the spirit of a political campaign. And this was one more factor in a web of forces that resulted in a battle in which the biggest losers were the American people.

The British people, for their part, lose out when the argument culture results in the trivialization of political argument to the extent that it becomes no more than a battle of personalities, of demonizing and scoring debating points over the other side. Consider for example, Prime Minister's Question Time every Wednesday afternoon in the Commons. The format of the occasion dictates that the topic for the main exchanges – those destined to appear on the evening news bulletins – is decided by the Leader of the Opposition, who will usually choose not the most vital issue of the day but the one on which it is easiest to score points over the Prime Minister.

Thus on January 28, 1998, when the prospect of an allied bombing attack on Iraq was growing graver by the day, William Hague, the Conservative leader, chose to question Tony Blair about the private life of the Foreign Secretary, Robin Cook. Mr Cook was alleged to have dismissed his diary secretary with the intention of replacing her with Gaynor Regan, exposed not long before as his mistress. In fact, Ms Regan was not given the job, but that did not deter Mr Hague from asking a string of questions about the matter. Mr Blair became exasperated: 'The very fact that you engage in that type of question shows how completely useless and pathetic the Conservative opposition is.'

The following week the Cook affair was the subject of a Parliamentary debate. The Conservative MP who opened it was unable to complete his speech because he was persistently shouted down by Labour members. The *Daily Telegraph*'s reporter wrote: 'A Government licensed lynch mob hijacked the House of Commons yesterday.' Later, just before Prime Minister's Question Time, the Speaker had to chastize members of both main parties for the growing habit of cheering their leaders when they entered the chamber, as though they were prize fighters entering the ring. Her admonitions went largely unheeded.

---

## A CAMPAIGN FOR ALL SEASONS

---

This is the ideal model of a democratically elected government: Two (or more) parties offer candidates for an elected position. There ensues a campaign, during which candidates try to convince citizens to vote for them. The election is held; citizens cast their votes. The candidate with the majority of votes wins and assumes the duties of heading the government until the next election rolls around, preceded by another campaign.

This is what we have now: The next campaign begins the day after an election.

The campaign spirit accounts for the situation Representative Gunderson described by which some of his colleagues believe that their best hope for future election is to prevent the party in power from achieving anything. We also have a campaign for all seasons in the protracted primary process by which the Republican and Democratic Parties now choose presidential candidates.

Thomas Patterson makes a convincing and deeply troubling case for the devastating effect of the 1968 change in the primary process. The task of selecting presidential candidates, once fulfilled by political parties behind closed doors, was turned over to the electorate: Presidential candidates are now chosen by a series of statewide primary elections, held at different times, in which voters choose among an array of candidates, most of whom they know little about. Patterson enumerates the many problems with this system: Candidates must decide whether or not to seek nomination so long before the election that they cannot make an informed decision about the wisdom of running. (In 1992, for example, prime contenders for the Democratic nomination, Dick Gephardt and Al Gore, decided to sit out that election because President George Bush seemed unbeatable; when the flagging economy rendered Bush vulnerable, it was too late for them to change their minds.) The grueling primary system also makes it almost impossible for someone holding public office to consider a run, giving the edge to currently unemployed former officeholders as Jimmy Carter and Ronald Reagan were when they ran. And the new decision makers – the voters – have neither time nor expertise to evaluate the candidates adequately from the most relevant perspective: their past performance in office. With political parties no longer fulfilling the role of mediators between the public and politicians, this mediating role passed to the press – with disastrous consequences. For one thing, the press is ill suited to this job: By definition, their goal is the pursuit of stories of current interest, not the painstaking analysis of policy options, their long-term prognosis, and individuals' capabilities to fulfill them. Furthermore, forcing the press to take the mediator role in the election process interferes with its ability to fulfill its true and truly essential role of watchdog.

Having candidates chosen directly by voters rather than by political parties irreparably weakens parties and forces prospective candidates to raise huge amounts of money on their own, with the result that they are beholden not to the party but to those who gave them the money to get elected. In this sense, part of our problem is not too much partisanship, but too little.

## INTRAPARTY PARTISANSHIP

The prolonged and public primary process creates another deficiency in partisanship: When parties chose presidential candidates in private, they could offer up to the country a unified front once the decision was made. What the primary process now offers is prolonged public battles among party members, battles that can do as much damage to the ultimate candidate as the other party's candidate does during the campaign. Once again, the infamous Willie Horton ads provide an example: The Horton case was originally found by fellow Democrat Al Gore's campaign workers while scanning newspapers for articles that could link the Massachusetts governor with any unsavory characters or events that could be placed on his watch. By setting party members against one another in public, primaries provide the winner's future opponent with ammunition to use in the presidential campaigns. For example, Democrats quoted negative statements that conominees Bob Dole and Jack Kemp had made about each other when they were both campaigning for the Republican presidential nomination.

The public opposition of same-party members in primary campaigns is just one form of destructive internecine battles within the political parties. Another is described by Ronald Radosh in his book *Divided They Fell*. Radosh shows that the Democratic Party was irreparably weakened in the years between 1964 and 1972 by a struggle between party officials and a radical wing that attacked the party's liberal leadership more ferociously than Republican opponents. He believes that appeasing the radicals was a fatal mistake. A comparable split is now occurring in the Republican Party. Many of the outgoing Republican senators and congressmen discuss the struggle for control of the Republican Party between those who consider themselves true conservatives because they believe government should interfere as little as possible in individuals' lives and those who Gunderson describes as 'the big-government social right, as exemplified by the leaders of the Christian Coalition.' There are many within the Republican Party (including Rep. Gunderson) who believe that appeasing the Christian right will have a similarly destructive effect on the Republican Party.

The failure of within-party unity is also seen in the role played by

Democrats in preventing President Clinton from passing health care reform, which led, as Speaker Gingrich correctly predicted, to the Republican takeover of the Congress. Many Democrats' refusal to back their president's plan contrasts sharply with Senator Rudman's account of his role in passing President Reagan's package of tax cuts and increased military spending in 1981. Senator Rudman was convinced that the country desperately needed to balance the budget even if it meant higher taxes and spending cuts. Yet he voted to support President Reagan's plan to do just the opposite.

Rudman's decision to support his party's president is the kind of partisanship that makes action possible. Such partisanship is required by the structure of the American government, by which the president is elected separately from the Congress. This means that the president can be, and in recent years typically has been, from a different political party than the majority in Congress – a setup for obstructionism and adversarialism. Yet when considering the form of partisanship by which members of a minority party can prevent the majority party from achieving anything, it is easy to forget that during the first two years of President Clinton's administration, the period during which his attempt to provide health insurance for all Americans failed, his own party held a majority in both the Senate and the House of Representatives. He did not have enough partisan support to enact his plan.

Under the British parliamentary system, in contrast, the Prime Minister is not elected separately but is automatically installed by the party that wins a majority. In this system, the Prime Minister and parliamentary majority always come from the same party, making it much easier for that party to accomplish its goals. However, all political parties are coalitions of people with a range of views on specific issues, and some of the most bitter conflicts occur between politicians of the same party. Although they can usually be counted on to toe the party line in Commons votes, they argue constantly among themselves.

One reason for the heavy defeat of the Conservative Party in the 1997 election was its lack of unity on the issue of how far Britain should be integrated into a united Europe, and in particular whether it was advisable to subscribe to the European Monetary Union, with the ultimate loss of distinct national currencies. Politicians on both sides of the argument held passionately to their views.

Those against integration, led by the former Cabinet Minister John Redwood, presented it as an unacceptable loss of national identity. The Chancellor of the Exchequer, Kenneth Clarke, was equally adamant that the possibility of a single European currency should not be ruled out. It was left to the Prime Minister, John Major, to cobble together a form of words that would allow the party to enter the election with the semblance of unity; but the electorate was not convinced.

Labour, too, has its doctrinal differences. Its long period out of office, from 1979 to 1997, was marked by a series of vicious conflicts between the left wing of the party and the moderate center. In the end the moderates carried the day, persuading the party to drop its traditional commitment to wholesale nationalization of industry, and to reduce the power of the trades unions in the decision-making process. Only when these 'New Labour' policies were established beyond doubt were voters prepared to put Labour back into office, but even then disputes within the party did not entirely die down. When the Government proposed measures that seemed to go against Labour's traditional principles – such as reducing welfare benefits for single mothers – many party members vociferously expressed their displeasure and a few refused to support the measure in Parliament.

## NOT TOO MUCH PARTISANSHIP
## BUT TOO LITTLE

There is yet another sense in which action has been prevented not by too much partisanship, but too little. Haynes Johnson and David Broder explain that until recently, there was a beneficial balance of power between political parties and interest groups. Political parties often want to make changes to solve problems; interest groups, on the other hand, represent people who are benefiting from the status quo, so they typically oppose changes that would limit those benefits. In the past, a political party could offer some measure of protection to lawmakers: Stick with the party, and we'll get the votes out to put you back in office come election time. But since political parties no longer control the nomination and election of candidates, they now lack that grassroots power, so the power of interest groups has swelled out of proportion. With advances in technology such as faxes, phone campaigns, and mass mailing, lobbyists can marshal what appears to be a groundswell of public opinion to sway an officeholder. Even if they want to defy a powerful interest group in order to support legislation of benefit to a majority of citizens, officeholders can no longer afford to do so because the interest groups can mount an effective campaign to defeat those who vote in ways they don't like on the issues of concern to them. Since every attempt to make a change will limit the benefits of some group, officeholders end up unable to make any changes at all, like rats in a maze that bump up against a wall no matter which direction they run.

Johnson and Broder show how this worked to prevent the passage of health care reform – both the universal health insurance that the Clinton administration wanted to enact and the Gingrich-led Republican attempt to limit Medicare costs. The Clintons' attempts at reform were scuttled by one set of interest groups; the Republicans' by another. In this regard, 'gridlock' is as much the result of too little partisanship – the political parties' loss of power – rather than too much.

## WHEN DOES A POLITICIAN
## GET TO BE A LEADER?

If rancorous opposition is the campaign spirit, there is another sense in which our political campaigns go on forever: We are never permitted to think of our president as a president first and a representative of a political party second; he is presented to us as a party member first and always. Nothing the president does is regarded as the work of our leader; every move he makes is regarded as the work of a representative of a political party, or a potential candidate in the next election (or, if he is in a second term, of someone who is not a potential candidate – a 'lame duck').

First Lady Eleanor Roosevelt wrote a newspaper column, and every major paper in the country carried it. Few major newspapers carry Hillary Rodham Clinton's column, because they feel it would be too partisan. The editors are viewing her not as the first lady but as a Democratic politician.

When Franklin Delano Roosevelt delivered his famed fireside chats, people throughout the country gathered around their radios – symbolically gathering together – to listen. President Clinton, too, has tried to speak directly to the people by delivering weekly remarks on the radio on Saturday mornings, but few major radio stations carry the broadcasts. Granted, President Clinton's weekly addresses are far more frequent (as well as briefer) than President Roosevelt's fireside chats ever were; no doubt the infrequency of those early radio broadcasts, along with the relative novelty of the medium, contributed to their drama. Nonetheless, the most significant difference between the radio broadcasts of Presidents Roosevelt and Clinton is that each of President Clinton's radio addresses is followed immediately by a Republican response. The practice of presenting an opposition response to presidential addresses provides a small but powerful example of how the tendency to cast everything in debate format aggravates agonism and weakens the public's ability to see leaders as leaders, with all that entails for a nation.

---

## THE STATE OF POLITICS IN THE
## STATE OF THE UNION

---

Once each year, the president of the United States delivers a State of the Union Address to the Congress. This address is one of the few that is televised in full, and it is followed immediately by a response delivered by a member of the opposing political party. I thought I was the only one who questioned this practice, but following the 1997 State of the Union Address, I listened to two national radio talk shows on which the address was discussed, and on both shows callers expressed the same concern. Considering how few callers actually get through to a national talk show, it seems fair to assume that many other citizens share their reaction.

*Talk of the Nation* featured guest historian Wayne Fields, author of a book about presidential addresses. The caller asked, 'When and why was the Republican response added to the State of the Union Address?' Fields answered that the practice was related to the advent of television and its concept of equal access. The notion that 'equal access' should apply to the State of the Union Address makes sense only if the president is regarded as a politician representing a political party rather than as an elected official representing the country. But providing an opposition response creates a self-fulfilling prophecy: It makes the event more partisan.

Exactly the same question was asked on a *Diane Rehm Show* panel devoted to the State of the Union Address with four journalist commentators, only this time the caller made clear her view of the practice. She asked, 'When did this ridiculous idea of having the other party respond to the president of the United States' State of the Union Address start, and why?' Two journalist commentators provided more specifics in their responses. Susan Page of *USA Today* explained that in the early Reagan years, when the president gave a speech, the networks would invite various members of the opposition party to respond. The 'opposition party,' she explained, 'thought that if there's a formal party presentation by the president, the Democrats should have the same opportunity, so it evolved that way out of a sense of trying to be evenhanded.' The most telling piece of information in this statement is not stated but assumed: the notion that the State of the Union Address is 'a formal party presentation' rather than a formal presentation by the nation's leader.

Page's statement provides a fascinating example of how politics and media intertwine and affect each other. It is easy to see how seeking out spokespeople from the opposition party would seem an admirable and natural way to be evenhanded. It is also easy to see how the opposition party would conclude that it would be better to have a single, unified response rather than a variety of spokespeople responding in a scattershot way. It is very easy, moreover, to see that no one involved in creating this practice foresaw the unfortunate result: Assuming that the president's speech is 'a formal party presentation' results in the systematic infusion of partisanship into even the most formal and ceremonial aspects of governing. Another unintended and probably unforeseen consequence is a reduction of respect for the presidency as a result of the face-off in which the nation's elected leader is 'balanced' by a spokesperson from the opposition party who holds a significantly lower office – in 1997, J. C. Watts of Oklahoma, who had been a congressman for only two years.

Many of the other remarks made during this panel discussion provide a glimpse of how the culture of critique shapes our responses to political figures and processes. And bear in mind that this is an example not of the fringe talk-show culture but of the uniquely thoughtful National Public Radio with mainstream print journalists as panelists.

Another panelist, Gerry Seib, made an early comment: 'These speeches tend to be seamless mush,' he began, setting the tone of critique and derision. The same tone suffused the opening remarks made by David Corn: 'It's classic Clinton, although classic Clinton does seem to change from month to month.' After accusing the president of issuing big talk but modest proposals, Corn summed up his evaluation with a metaphor: 'He thinks he's conducting an orchestra, but he's really giving us two guys on a flute and a banjo.' Whereas Seib is associated with the politically conservative *Wall Street Journal*, Corn writes for the ostensibly liberal *The Nation*. But the culture of critique unites apparently opposite spokespeople, presumably chosen to provide balance, in their derisive attitude toward the president and the address.

Seib also noted that this address was interesting because it had a theme: education. 'Overall,' he said, 'it really was a statement of how in touch Bill Clinton is with the public mood, because education is the theme to pick up if you look at public polling over the last two-three years.' By viewing the address through a lens of political strategy, praise for the president's choice of an issue voters care about comes across as an accusation of political manipulation and insincerity. It's like children who say something nice while crossing fingers behind their backs.

Bill Kristol of *The Weekly Standard* then reminded the group that Clinton had tried tackling a 'big issue': health care. Then he asked, 'Are there any issues of any moment left? The president of the United States is going to devote himself to improving the reading scores of fourth-graders?' Another fascinating and subtle form of critique is at play here. Kristol used a rhetorical device called 'synecdoche' – substituting the part for the whole: By substituting a seemingly trivial part of education – 'the reading scores of fourth-graders' – for the important issue of education, he made the entire issue seem trivial.

As discussion continued on why the president did not address 'big issues,' Kristol commented, 'If you look in the past . . . Teddy Roosevelt went after the trusts himself, Eisenhower built the high-way system, even Reagan doubled the military. Great presidents do big things.' The show's host, Diane Rehm, pointed out that such measures require spending large amounts of money, a move that is precluded by the current need to balance the budget. Kristol replied:

> Well, there are plenty of big debates that aren't budget debates. But I agree, this is – Bill Clinton wants to be in the center, what he calls the vital center and what might turn out to be the . . . boring center [*laugh*] of American politics. I don't criticize him for that. It certainly is a smart reelection strategy, and it's where most Americans *are* obviously by definition. But it means you're *not* going to be bold. He did not pick any big fights in this State of the Union. Great presidents fight big fights. Clinton's entitled not to . . . He shouldn't go out of his way to pick big fights if they don't exist.

This short statement, spoken (we should bear in mind) off the cuff and as part of a freewheeling discussion, reveals many of the assumptions that underlie our current approach to politics. On one hand, Kristol acknowledges that the 'center' is 'where most Americans are,' yet he dismisses it as 'boring.' When is policy judged by whether or not it is boring – as opposed to, say, whether or not it is beneficial to the country? When news is regarded as entertainment and politics as spectator sport.

Even more fascinating is the assumption underlying the observation that the president didn't 'fight any big fights' in his State of the Union Address. Kristol noted that the president could have made statements about abortion, race, or affirmative action but didn't:

> Apart from a very vague statement about racial healing, he didn't take that on. Again, I'm not really criticizing him; it's just striking that he did not take on the big divisive issues in America today.

If the State of the Union Address is an opportunity for the president to connect with all the people in the country, these comments are very odd. That the president mentioned the issue of race from the perspective of *healing* a hurtful divide would seem appropriate, even admirable. Instead, it is compared unfavorably to 'taking on' 'the big divisive issues,' implying that stirring up divisiveness is more admirable than healing. Most interesting is the phrase 'big divisive issues.' The two adjectives are paired as if they were naturally linked. But do 'big' issues have to be 'divisive' ones? To complain that mentioning race only in a spirit of healing is a failure to 'take on' race as a 'big divisive issue' implies that trying to *heal* the divide is not taking the issue on.

Kristol's complaint that President Clinton did not bring up 'big divisive issues' reflects a development that Senator Howell Heflin decried: 'The focus on divisive issues has increased the alienation and driven us farther and farther apart,' Heflin wrote, making it harder and harder to achieve the bipartisanship that is needed to run the country. Kristol's remarks make sense only in the context of the argument culture, whereby polarized opposition is a measure of importance.

In an effort, perhaps, to be evenhanded, Seib pointed out, 'Republicans aren't really picking fights either,' and the host agreed, 'Everybody is looking for quiet and nice.' Kristol reinforced the point: 'All platitudes.' Kristol's rephrasing implied that the alternative to picking fights is not compromise in the constructive sense but 'platitudes' – empty words with no substance.

Now look at what Bill Kristol said next:

> Let me just throw out an example. You could have had an interesting argument last night on the partial birth abortion ban issue, which is an emotional issue that clearly divides the two parties. President Clinton obviously had nothing to say about it, but J. C. Watts on behalf of the Republicans didn't have anything to say about it either.

While it is balanced in criticizing both the president and the Republican respondent, this comment is staggering in the assumptions it reveals. In the preceding discussion, a 'big fight' seemed to mean a 'fight about a big issue.' Now Kristol is suggesting that a big fight could have been picked about the ban on 'partial birth abortions' (a misnomer referring to what are actually very-late-term abortions). In what sense is this a 'big issue'? Surely not in the sense of a major problem facing the country. Such 'big issues' might be the budget deficit, the health care crisis, the future of Social Security and other 'entitlements,' issues of world trade or world terrorism, or the widening gap between rich and poor. One might even argue that the abortion issue is a big issue because it is important to the lives of many individuals. But so-called partial birth abortions account for only a tiny fraction of abortions performed or sought. It is, in other words, a 'big divisive issue' not because it is very important but because it is very divisive. It is a 'big fight' not in the sense of being a highly significant fight but only in the sense of being a highly rancorous and emotional one.

Think about it: How in the world could the late-term abortion controversy be regarded as an appropriate topic for the president's State of the Union Address? The only answer is that it is 'an emotional issue that clearly divides the two parties.' When Kristol said, 'You could have had an interesting argument last night,' he clearly meant 'argument' in the sense of *having* an argument, not in the sense of *making* one – and 'interesting' in the sense of a good show, not in the sense of shedding light or affording insight and certainly not in the sense of moving the country closer to solving its problems.

That the president focused on elements that were vague enough to appeal to the widest number of citizens from both parties, to bring the people together rather than divide them, is, as the show's host pointed out, what the country seemed to want, and good for the country. This point was also made by one of the journalists, Susan Page:

> PAGE: From a news point of view it's not great to have everyone be friendly, but from the point of view of actually passing some legislation—
>
> REHM: And the point of view of the public generally—
>
> PAGE: It may be what the public wants to see and it may actually contribute to getting a balanced budget deal and maybe doing some fixes on welfare reform and doing some of the things that are on Congress's plate.

With the comments of these professional journalists in mind, let's return to the *Talk of the Nation* discussion devoted to the State of the Union Address. The caller made clear that she was disturbed not only by the existence of the opposition response but also by the general tenor of commentary that follows such public addresses:

> I just want to point out that what I find wrong with all these speeches today, which I've been watching for well over fifty years, or listening to, is that we're not allowed to feel inspired, or appreciate, and it doesn't matter which party's in power, because before the applause even dies away, we are told what was wrong with it and what – that it was dull, or too long, or not inspiring or it didn't really say anything . . . And I think this is really detracting from the respect that these things deserve.

The caller identifies an unintended but troubling effect of the culture of critique: discouraging if not precluding a respectful response to ceremonial events and the cumulative effect of eroding respect for public office.

The next caller spoke in the same spirit:

> The reason why I'm calling is because I notice a tone of skepticism in the way the program is laid out. As a citizen, I look forward to every single word that the president will say, especially because this is one of the most powerful men in the world. I believe that the full breadth of the whole speech is something that is so important to the whole country . . . And the president – the elected official – his term in the White House is of extreme importance. In other parts of the world, when somebody makes a speech of this nature, usually it takes much much longer and it is a tedious harangue . . .
>
> I imagine that, because so many institutions in the country have been put into question, either by the media or by public opinion, there is this impression that one should put into question the substance of whatever the president is going to be saying. What I propose is, let's hear what the guy has to say, without the prejudgment or the postjudgment of the words in a partisan mode or taking sides in any way. To see what the full breadth, the full concept, is and take it from there as the united country that we are.

What comes through in these comments is the desire of citizens to be allowed to regard their president as their president, not as a politician, a campaigner, a spokesperson for a party to be opposed at every turn by a spokesperson for another party. These callers are pleading for a respite from the argument culture.

What form could that respite take? It would be pointless to ask that television and radio stations not provide instant responses to public addresses, but they might provide more varied responses. Rather than, or in addition to, opposition response and critique by journalists, they could provide commentary and analysis by historians, political scientists, and other experts to expand, explain, and provide context for the remarks from their various perspectives.

This is not to say that there is no place for the other party to critique the State of the Union address, or any other public statement by an elected leader. The British context offers examples of appropriate debate. Britain has no exact equivalent to the State of the Union address, but the Queen's speech at the beginning of the Parliamentary session is written for her by the Government and outlines its legislative program. It is then debated (and predictably denounced) by the Leader of the Opposition – in the House of Commons. The procedures for announcing the annual Finance Bill or Budget offer another example of appropriately enacted conflict. After announcing his proposals to the Commons, the Chancellor of the Exchequer is allowed time on national television to explain them to the nation. The next night the Opposition spokesman is given equal time to criticize the measures. The interval of a day, and the prescribed roles of both spokespersons, distinguish this ritual from the American State of the Union address, in which the president's ceremonial speech was followed immediately by an opposition response delivered by a first-term member of Congress.

## OPPOSITION GONE WILD: DIRTY TRICKS

The American and British two-party structure – and elections in general – are adversarial by nature. But opposition needs to have rules to play by, or things get out of hand. Political scientist Larry Sabato and journalist Glenn Simpson have looked carefully at American politics. They conclude – and document in their book

*Dirty Little Secrets* – that political corruption in America is worse now than it has been since Watergate.

According to Sabato and Simpson, lawmakers routinely vote in ways that benefit groups that have contributed significant amounts of money to their campaigns. Voter fraud is rampant, with mail-in ballots being cast by dead people and pets. 'Street money' is paid to religious and civic leaders in minority communities to encourage them to support Democratic candidates. And there is also the reverse pressure: Political consultant Ed Rollins first boasted, then retracted, and in his memoir reinforced the claim that the campaign for New Jersey Republican gubernatorial candidate Christine Todd Whitman paid Black ministers *not* to encourage their congregations to vote.

Misnamed push-polls (they are actually fake polls) employ banks of callers to pretend to be polling but in fact to spread innuendos or outright lies about an opponent. For example, phony 'pollsters' in Maine called voters at home and, buried within a series of questions that sounded very much like authentic polls, asked whether it would affect their vote if they knew that GOP nominee Rick Bennett had defaulted on his student loans. (He had not.) In Alaska, phony pollsters called voters at home and told them that Tony Knowles, Democratic candidate for governor, supported gay marriages and adoptions. (He didn't.) 'Knowing this,' they were then asked, 'does this make you more or less likely to vote for Tony Knowles?' Candidates found that simply being accused was damaging, even if the accusation could be proven false. If they held a press conference to refute the charge, they would simply plant the accusation in the minds of more voters who firmly believe 'where there's smoke, there's fire.' Furthermore, many of the push-poll efforts take place just before an election, limiting the time falsely accused candidates have to respond, even if they want to.

Since the rise in popularity of 'wedge issues' – issues that will sway voters because of their emotional appeal, regardless of their significance or whether elected officials have any control over them – a great number of push-polls funded by the far right involve accusations not only of supporting homosexuality but of practicing it. Sabato and Simpson report that in 1994 on election eve voters in Minnesota were bombarded by callers asking, with reference to a Democratic Senate contender, 'Would it make a difference if you knew that Anne Wynia is a lesbian?' They say the same tactic was used against incumbent Ohio Democratic Congressman Eric Fingerhut. Both candidates were heterosexual. Both candidates lost.

The use of wedge issues is inflammatory, unfair, and, in cases like these, based on lies. But perhaps their most destructive aspect is distraction: Attention paid to wedge issues is attention not paid to real problems and potential solutions. Brookings Institute authors E. J. Dionne, Jr., Stephen Hess, and Thomas E. Mann quote a Gingrich aide and Republican consultant named Joseph Gaylord who advised candidates to avoid voters' main concerns on the grounds that 'important issues can be of limited value.' In support of this view, he too cites the Willie Horton ads 'to demonstrate the usefulness of a "minor detail" against an opponent.' The Brookings authors conclude, 'Gaylord's compendium of campaign tips suggests that the things so often bemoaned about the political process are not simply the product of a few evil geniuses, but *systematic* characteristics of the modern political campaign.'

Sabato and Simpson show that although there is nothing new about spreading rumors about an opponent and using any available negative information, what has developed in the 1990s is a concerted, tireless, and well-funded effort to dig up ever more personal, recondite, and irrelevant information that can make an opponent look bad. The justification for this practice is a concern with character, the importance of which is self-evident. But just about anything can be lumped into the category of 'character,' and in recent years the concept has come to focus almost exclusively on personal frailties, to the exclusion of aspects of character directly related to governing. As Dionne, Hess, and Mann put it, 'We focus more and more on sex and money, and less and less on a constancy of belief, a commitment to public purposes, a capacity to lead.' In pursuit of character, supposedly private credit reports are acquired, as well as school records, traffic violations, and past addresses that enable investigators to approach former neighbors, seeking anything that might make an opponent look bad.

Sabato and Simpson identify three reasons for the exponential increase in this sort of opposition research. First, the technology is there: Thanks to computerized databases, a researcher can dig up reams of information without leaving the computer screen. Second, the money is there: The cost of campaigning has ballooned, and candidates feel they might as well use the large amounts they have had to raise. Third is a snowball effect: Each side is convinced the other side will use these tactics, so if they don't, they'll lose. Finally, the authors fault what they identify as 'the increasing meanness of American politics.' And this may be key. For it is not just meanness in politics but an increasing meanness of spirit and practice in our public discourse in general – what I am calling the argument culture – that creates both the will to generate this new dirty product and the market for it.

One more example that Sabato and Simpson describe shows how the argument culture in different institutions weaves tangled webs in which public figures are snared. When Republican millionaire Bruce Benson was running for governor of Colorado, a local television station sued for access to documents related to his divorce settlement, which had been sealed. One of the most damaging bits in the records was the allegation made by his former wife that he had threatened to kill her. The *Rocky Mountain News* eventually concluded, 'In hindsight, that [threat] claim appears to be a hard-ball legal tactic by Nancy Benson's attorney, who himself insists there had been no abuse at any time during [a] long marriage.' In other words, in a divorce battle, especially one involving millions of dollars, spouses may make extreme accusations in order to have a position from which to retreat in the process of securing the most advantageous settlement. The accusations become part of a public record that can be retrieved and used against potential candidates. (Sympathy for Benson is tempered, incidentally, by Sabato and Simpson's account of dirty tricks used in his campaign against his Democratic opponent.) This example shows how increasing agonism in one domain of public life feeds into and exacerbates the escalation of opposition in another.

Not only can material generated by lawsuits be used in dirty tricks; lawsuits themselves can be provoked as a way to weaken an opponent. It was political activists eager to damage President Clinton who encouraged Paula Jones to sue him and financed her efforts. Since the Supreme Court has allowed this suit to go forward while President Clinton is in office, the temptation will be enormous for opposition parties to foment civil suits against the president or other elected officials of the other party.

## SCANDALS, LAWSUITS, AND INVESTIGATIONS

The dirty tricks I just described may seem aimed primarily at the state level, but everyone has been touched by political dirty tricks in the form of Whitewater. In a book devoted to laying bare the underpinnings of this scandal, Gene Lyons shows that the Whitewater investigation was 'the result of the nastiest and most successful political "dirty tricks" campaign in recent American history.'

Writing in the *Columbia Journalism Review*, Trudy Lieberman shows that the mainstream media – newspapers, network news, and CNN – got most of their Whitewater tips directly from an organization misleadingly called 'Citizens United,' actually a Republican operation headed by a full-time director named David Bossie, a former official of the 1988 and 1992 Republican presidential campaigns. Intriguingly, Lieberman notes that 'His boss, Floyd Brown, worked as Dole's Midwest political director during the 1988 campaign, but is best known for producing the Willie Horton commercial that helped sink the presidential ambitions of Democrat Michael Dukakis.' Why so intriguing? Just as William Horton was made more repellant by changing his name to 'Willie,' the moniker 'Slick Willie,' used to impugn the character of William Jefferson Clinton, was first devised by Brown as the title of a book he wrote and released during the 1992 presidential campaign.

The subject of Whitewater leads inevitably to the independent counsel – a legacy (like the spirit of critique) of Watergate and Vietnam, watershed events that convinced both journalists and citizens that people in government are likely to conceal, mislead, and lie. Passed in the wake of Watergate, the independent counsel statute requires the attorney general to appoint an independent prosecutor when there is evidence of criminal behavior on the part of those high up in the executive branch of government. The first special prosecutor was appointed in 1972 to investigate the Watergate cover-up. This unusual step was deemed necessary because it was suspected (and later confirmed) that members of the Justice Department – including the attorney general, who was eventually indicted – were directly involved in the events to be investigated. But like so many other Watergate legacies, the practice has multiplied and gone out of control in sorcerer's apprentice fashion.

Describing 'the special-counsel madness' that had 'run amuck,' Kim Isaac Eisler, writing in *Washingtonian* magazine, noted in April 1997 that we had had no fewer than seventeen independent counsel investigations up to that point, of which ten had produced no indictments. Shortly thereafter, a nearly three-year independent counsel investigation of former Secretary of Agriculture Mike Espy ended in an indictment that accused Espy of having accepted $35,458 worth of inappropriate gifts, including such items as tickets to a basketball game priced at $90. (The investigation, in contrast, cost taxpayers nearly $9,000,000.) With no natural limits, these investigations tend to stretch like Rubber Man into unforeseen directions and stretch out over time – like the investigation of former HUD Secretary Samuel Pierce, which Eisler noted was 'still going on ten years later,' when hardly anyone remembers what the allegations were in the first place.

One of these independent counsel investigations has focused on Whitewater. Writing in *The New York Times Magazine*, Jeffrey Rosen observes that Kenneth Starr's Whitewater investigation has borne out the fears expressed by Supreme Court Justice Antonin Scalia that such 'investigations have a hydraulic tendency to expand far beyond the scope of their original mandate,' and if they turn out to be overzealous, unfair, and wrongheaded, there is no accountability. As of June 1997, the independent counsel investigation (run by someone who is independent of the Democratic administration, yes, but a prominent Republican known for his animosity toward the president) had cost taxpayers $28 million to investigate a $300,000 loan made years before the president took office.

Larry Sabato has called scandals the 'elevator music of American politics.' This aptly captures the ubiquity of scandals and the public indifference to them. But it is far too benign an image. Behind the scenes, scandals and their attendant investigations and lawsuits drain public funds, public energy, and the time and attention of both journalists and elected leaders (not to mention their bank accounts; according to Rosen, the Clintons owe their lawyers more than $2.5 million as a result of this investigation). There is little public interest in Whitewater, but the investigation hurtles ahead, keeping twenty-five lawyers busily at work, at the public's expense.

And whereas elevator music remains in the background, scandals hog center stage. Every Whitewater story bumped another more substantive news item off the front page and perhaps out of the news. (In 1994, James Fallows observed, twice as many stories were published about Whitewater as about the Clintons' health care proposals.) On May 27, 1997, President Clinton took part in a historic meeting attended by all the European heads of state to sign the Founding Act on Mutual Relations Cooperation and Security between Russia and NATO. The front pages of all the major European newspapers showed photographs of the gathered heads of state. The front pages of American newspapers showed photographs of Paula Jones. The citizens of Europe got to contemplate the meaning of global realignment and their countries' place in the family of nations. You can surmise what the citizens of the United States got to contemplate.

Watergate came to public awareness because a security guard discovered a criminal break-in by chance. Most of our current scandals and attendant investigations resulted from a combination of concerted opposition research on the part of political operatives and journalists' conviction that scandals are of more interest to the public than are other current events. Polls of television viewership bear out this assumption. But scandals have a paradoxical effect on voter interest: Though people may be drawn to scandal stories, the nonstop bombardment has dulled their responses. Bill Clinton was easily reelected despite Whitewater and other scandals, and polls repeatedly find his approval rating to be high. But this is not to say that scandals have no effect. They contribute to a general cynicism that lowers voter turnout. Citizens see politicians from both parties as equally venal, throw up their hands, mutter, 'A plague on both your houses!' – and stay home on election day.

Political commentator and *Washington Post* editor Meg Greenfield suggested, tongue in cheek (well, maybe not entirely), that among the seminars offered to first-term members of Congress should be training in how to deal with investigations, since the chances are great that members will confront one at some point – if not outright 'cops' in the guise of 'FBI agents, prosecutors, and other representatives of criminal-law enforcement,' then 'congressional investigators, departmental ethics officers, media scourges and deposition-taking, civil-suit lawyers who represent the aggravated, the oppressed and the merely litigious,' thanks to 'an era in which opposition politicians and investigative journalists are increasingly on the prowl.' The question that comes to mind is: If this trend intensifies, who is going to run for office?

Another cost to the public is more nebulous, but equally unfortunate. With the likelihood of investigations so widespread, many public figures no longer dare keep diaries or even detailed notes for fear they will be subpoenaed. It is troubling to contemplate the prospect of historians trying to understand an era in which no one dared write down what happened to them, what they observed, or what they were thinking.

## GOVERNING UNDER FIRE

In the culture of critique, any misstep is reportable – and who can walk through a day without stumbling at some point? A journalist who became the object of intense media criticism had the opportunity to glimpse – from the inside – what politicians now experience on a daily basis. When *Newsweek* columnist and CBS commentator Joe Klein admitted to being 'Anonymous,' the author of *Primary Colors*, a novel about characters everyone recognized as based on the Clintons, he became the focus of intense media attention, including vociferous criticism by colleagues for having repeatedly and forcefully denied that he had written the book. Klein called the media coverage that followed his admission 'a vicious, witless, disproportionate assault,' an 'overzealous, bloodthirsty, witless pursuit over a very trivial matter,' 'rude and ugly,' 'an inquisition.' This experience gave him an inkling of what it feels like to be the focus of press scrutiny and assault. In a column that he wrote following his exposure, Klein described his experience:

> The ensuing maelstrom was unbelievable. Not just the zoological press conference – that was to be expected. But also the endless chattering and battering and pontificating on the air about what I did. The requests for interviews. The need to spend time with all the responsible journalists doing 'think' pieces, to defend myself on 'Larry King,' to strategies

about what to do next. I couldn't sleep. I couldn't eat. I kept drinking water, but felt dehydrated. It was, I realized, probably a pretty typical campaign day for Bill Clinton or Bob Dole.

. . . I've also learned this: what it's like to live as a politician . . . And it is impossible. It is impossible to think straight. It is very easy to screw up, and it is unrelenting. *They* do it every day, and that is no way for a civilized nation to choose its leaders . . . Now that I've lived it, I hope I'll show a little more mercy on this page for the brave, frail fools and heroes who live our public lives. I hope you will, too.

Few of Klein's colleagues seemed to be moved by his remarks. Rather than experiencing new compassion for politicians, many journalists dismissed Klein's objections by pointing out that in issuing them, he sounded like a politician.

---

## NOT ALL NEGATIVITY IS BAD

---

Like Klein, I hope everyone will show more mercy for people in public life. But objecting to relentless, random attack – putting a negative interpretation on every move – is not to suggest that no one should ever question, oppose, or argue. The difference between constructive opposition – skepticism – and knee-jerk opposition – cynicism – is described by outgoing Republican Senator Alan Simpson of Wyoming:

> Cynicism is a cop-out. It takes no virtue – or brains – to be a critic. Anyone can qualify. It serves no one – certainly not the children of America – to carp, snipe, and complain, and to leave national challenges unmet.
>
> Skepticism, on the other hand, is essential to the functioning of a representative democracy.

Not all negativity is inappropriate in politics or in campaigns. Indeed, I disagree with some characterizations of opposition as overly negative.

An article about a San Francisco congressional campaign

began, 'With two months to go before the election, Rep. Frank Riggs and Democratic opponent Michela Alioto began the fall campaign season Wednesday on the attack.' The attack consisted of challenger Alioto 'blasting' incumbent Riggs's voting record. Criticizing an opponent's voting record is negative, yes. But surely it is also fair – and a necessary source of information to voters. Distorting or misrepresenting an opponent's voting record is unfair and destructive because it spreads disinformation, not because it is negative.

As I think I've made clear, I also do not object to partisanship in any form. Again, Senator Byrd of West Virginia:

> Political partisanship is to be expected in a legislative body –
> we all engage in it – but bitter personal attacks go beyond the
> pale of respectable propriety. And let us all be scrupulously
> mindful of the role that vitriolic public statements can play in
> the stirring of the dark cauldron of violent passions which are
> far too evident in our land today.

Once again, I am not calling for a make-nice world in which no one should criticize anyone else. Criticism is necessary when people perceive wrongs that they believe must be set right. But it is neither necessary nor helpful when criticism derives only from a ritualized devotion to criticizing for its own sake or the concerted efforts of people dedicated to destroying their opponents. And vituperative, mean-spirited, personal attacks are almost always destructive, as they confuse and distract from real issues, undermine citizens' respect for and connection to our leaders and the nation, and stir up animosities that make it harder for people to work together to solve problems and accomplish goals.

I am not against criticism and opposition. After all, this book criticizes patterns I find dangerous and troubling. I object only when criticism and opposition become automatic and exaggerated, and fly out of control – as they are doing in our political lives today.

# 5

## 'LITIGATION IS WAR'

'You be the judge.'

'He thinks he's both judge and jury.'

'The jury is still out on that one.'

We sometimes talk as if the world were one big courtroom, our lives a series of trials. We look to courts to reveal the truth, and often they do. But our legal system isn't designed to uncover truth – at least not directly. It's about winning, even if it means coloring, distorting, or hiding facts in order to win. The American legal system is a prime example of trying to solve problems by pitting two sides against each other and letting them slug it out in public. It reflects and reinforces our assumption that truth emerges when two polarized, warring extremes are set against each other.

The United States has a long and proud tradition of using law to bring about social change. Lawyers have played heroic roles in combating injustice (in the civil rights movement, for example) and exposing wrongdoing (for example, that tobacco companies knew about and concealed the link between smoking and lung cancer).

My father practiced workers' compensation law; I have always taken pride in his efforts to help workers win benefits due them when they were injured on the job. We regard the law as a cherished route to truth and justice, and it often leads us there.

But just as some journalists are expressing concern about developments in their profession, some lawyers are expressing concern about theirs. The District of Columbia Bar and the New York State Court of Appeals have recommended or adopted codes to curb what are referred to as 'Rambo,' 'pit bull,' or 'scorched earth' tactics. Many complaints are addressed to abuses of the system. And some are questioning the system itself, especially its adversary character. Lawsuits are adversarial by nature. But the American system of law is more adversarial than others, and some in the legal profession believe that its adversary structure causes problems at the same time that it attempts to solve them.

## THE ADVERSARY SYSTEM:
## THE PEOPLE V. THE LAW

We were sitting around a nighttime campfire in August in the Canadian lake region north of Michigan. Our six-person camping group included one young lawyer. The rest of us were saying that it is wrong for lawyers to defend clients they know to be guilty. The lawyer found this claim offensive. Everyone is entitled to the best possible defense, she argued. Those rights would mean nothing if lawyers refused to take cases just because they believed the accused to be guilty. This is the basis of the adversary system of law: Justice lies in having advocates of the two sides make their best case. If no one will advocate for one of the sides, there can be no justice.

Nothing is more partisan than our legal system in which facts are uncovered and revealed by lawyers who are advocates for the two parties to the dispute. How else could it be? In the German and French systems, fact gathering is controlled by a judge, not by attorneys. The judge does most of the questioning of witnesses, and the judge's goal is to determine what happened, as nearly as possible. Such a system surely has its own liabilities, but it provides an illuminating contrast to the goal of attorneys in the adversary system: to manipulate facts to the advantage of their side.

This was one aspect of the O.J. Simpson trial that aggravated many Americans' misgivings about their legal system. Despite overwhelming physical evidence that Simpson had murdered his wife, Nicole Brown Simpson, and her friend Ron Goldman (evidence that included Simpson's blood at the crime scene, Goldman's blood in Simpson's car, Nicole's blood on Simpson's sock, and Simpson's hair on Goldman's shirt), attorneys were able to convince jurors that the police had planted all the evidence in an elaborate scheme to frame Simpson – a scenario for which there was no evidence and which, as Jeffrey Toobin shows in his book *The Run of His Life*, was physically impossible. The Simpson trial was an anomaly, given the unique constellation of the defendant's wealth, celebrity, and race; the judge's markedly lenient style; and the role played by television. But the trial dramatized the possibilities inherent in the American adversary system, driven not by a search for truth but by a search for the best defense.

A leading critic of the adversary system is Carrie Menkel-Meadow, professor of law at Georgetown University. She shows many ways that the adversary system fails to serve us well even if there is no miscarriage of justice. For one thing, it encourages lawyers to overstate claims, puffing up their side to persuade. This gets in the way of the truth coming out. For another, there has been a rash of complaints against attorneys who suppress evidence. This, Menkel-Meadow maintains, is the inevitable result of requiring lawyers to do everything they can to win for their client. Yet another weakness goes to the heart of the system: In many civil disputes there is some right on both sides. In those cases, a winner-take-all result cannot be fair, yet that is the type of resolution the system is designed to seek.

Menkel-Meadow also illustrates another way the adversary system can obstruct justice. A Japanese immigrant discovered, after he had retired, that he had been paid far less than his white colleagues doing the same job. His American-born son wanted him to sue his former employer, but he said no, his reputation and the preservation of harmony were more important. In this way, those who recoil from open conflict – whether because of cultural experience, individual temperament, or simply a realistic appreciation of the toll it takes to be involved in a lawsuit – do not get relief for injustice. Perhaps most important, Menkel-Meadow says, many people who pass through our legal system emerge bitter and angry, and this is dangerous for society, which depends upon the trust of its citizens for the institutions making up that society to work.

---

## THE LITIGATION BEAST

'I remember back in 1971,' said attorney John McGuckin on a *U.S. Business Litigation* panel, 'the senior partner of the law firm where I practiced said to me, "Litigation is war."' Panelist Laureen DeBuono agreed: 'There is this push to kill your adversary at all costs. It's definitely part of the litigation beast.'

The litigation beast stalks more than just the litigation forest. According to Georgetown University law professor David Luban, most lawyers' work is done outside of court, but out-of-court work is often regarded as of a piece with litigation. The British, he points out, distinguish between barristers, who are trial lawyers, and solicitors, who do the many other tasks that law requires. But to Americans, a lawyer is a lawyer is a lawyer. As a result, the warlike stance associated with litigation can be carried over to other contexts in which lawyers do their work.

Sociolinguist Yoshiko Nakano worked for a Japanese television station and served as an interpreter in negotiations with an American professor they hired as a consultant on a documentary. One morning her fax machine began spitting out an outraged message from her Japanese employers. They had received a draft contract from the station's American attorney detailing exactly what each party should provide and what should be done in the case of potential disputes. 'What is going on here?' the Japanese executives wanted to know. 'We cannot work together without trust. It is wrong to spell out minor matters like these in a contract.' Nakano assured them it was a difference between Japanese and American assumptions about contracts. Americans believe that spelling everything out in advance lays the foundation for trust by ensuring there will be no misunderstanding down the line. To the Japanese, trust is a prerequisite for working together; if there is trust, details will be worked out as they arise. Trying to specify everything in advance shows that there is no trust – and no basis for a working relationship.

The Japanese approach may seem quaint and naïve to Americans accustomed to detailed contracts, yet the Japanese approach can shed light for Americans as well. My own experience shows how the adversary approach to contract negotiations can turn negotiating parties into enemies by assuming that's what they are.

For my book *Talking from 9 to 5*, I spent time in companies observing people, interviewing them, and having individuals tape-record their conversations when I wasn't there. The companies with which I worked were all happy to proceed on the basis of our verbal agreement on certain ground rules: The individuals would control the taping, any identifying names would be changed, and I would show them what I wrote about conversations that had taken place in their company and change or take out anything they did not approve. In some cases I also signed a confidentiality agreement, promising not to reveal anything I learned about the company's business. In several other companies, however, the people with whom I came to a verbal agreement turned the matter over to attorneys to draw up a contract stating what we had agreed to. In no case where the matter was referred to attorneys were we able to come up with an agreement to work together.

Negotiations with one company stand out. They had approached me to help them figure out why women were not advancing to the highest levels of management. I explained that to answer this question I would need to examine closely what was really going on in day-to-day business and that I would like to use my findings in my book. After a number of informal meetings and negotiations, we agreed on the procedures and safeguards and expected to have a contract drawn and signed in a matter of weeks. But six months later, after thousands of dollars in legal fees and untold hours of everyone's time, the company's lawyers called the negotiations a bust, advising the company that the risk was too great.

Since the company had a lawyer representing them, I needed a lawyer to represent me. The points on which negotiations between the lawyers broke down were these: The company's lawyer was demanding approval and veto power over my entire book. I could not agree to that; it meant I might write a three-hundred-page book in which a half-dozen examples came from this company and then have the company decide they didn't like one example and tell me I could not publish the book. My lawyer was demanding for me total rights to the videotapes of conversations to use any way I wanted. The company could not agree to that; it meant I could put videotapes of the company's employees on national television, make them look bad, reveal company secrets, and open the company up to being sued by its employees. Yet the people I was working with at the company had no desire to pass judgment on any part of my book that did not involve them, and I had no intention of using the videotapes except for analysis. The lawyers apparently figured they ought to ask for everything and back off if they had to. But this impasse came after a long string of such maneuvers that had used up everyone's patience (as well as the time I had to conduct the research). Rather than focusing on what the company and I had agreed to do to help each other, the lawyers tried to foresee and forfend everything we could do to hurt each other. We thought we were working together toward a common goal; the lawyers were constructing a world in which we were enemies.

When these negotiations broke down, this company and I parted ways and I found other companies to work with. But often parties to legal disputes must continue to deal with each other. Even those who defend the adversary system, such as DePaul University law professor Stephan Landsman, acknowledge that in such situations, it might not be the best hope for resolving disputes. Requiring people to behave like enemies can stir up animosity that remains long after the case has been settled or tried and the lawyers have moved on to other cases.

---

## IT'S LIKE BEING RAPED ALL OVER AGAIN

---

Even when litigation succeeds in convicting the guilty or awarding damages to the aggrieved, it can take a toll on those who put their trust in the system by taking part in it. Though fewer than 1 percent of civil cases are heard by juries, in our culture, most people regard a trial by jury as the quintessential legal proceeding. And those who participate in trials often find the experience deeply distressing. Having your day in court should be a positive experience: You get to tell your story. Why should it be a nightmare? One reason is cross-examination – the opposing attorney's opportunity to destroy your testimony or, if it is impossible to refute your story, then to destroy you: discredit you, confuse you about what you know, make you appear like an unreliable person, a liar, or worse. Lawyers do not have to be scoundrels to do this; they just have to be doing their job.

A rape trial is a stunning illustration of the difference between an investigation that attempts to determine what happened and a fight between two sides determined to discredit the other side in order to win. Many women who have brought charges of rape have said later that going through the trial was like being raped again – only the rape was over in a relatively short time, whereas the trial went on and on. Reading the transcript of a cross-examination at a rape trial makes it clear why this would be: Given the nature of human sexual encounters, it is easy to distort events so that a rape can appear to be consensual sex. This is precisely the task of the defense attorney in cross-examination. Sociolinguist Keller Magenau studied the transcript of a rape trial and documented how the cross-examining attorney tried to make the rape appear to have been consensual sex. The following account is based on her analysis.

A young woman was gang-raped by four men. What happened, according to the woman, was this: She and a friend were walking home at night when a car containing four young men they knew slightly from the neighborhood drove by and invited them 'to party.' They refused, and the car drove away. Then another car with two strangers in it drove up, and these men also tried to pick the two women up. To get rid of them, the victim gave them a false name and phone number. Meanwhile, the car with the four young men she knew from the neighborhood returned, and one of them called out to her and her friend. She left her friend and the two strangers and walked over to the car containing the men she knew, who again asked her to come with them. When she again refused, two of the men jumped out of the car, grabbed her, and hauled her into the car; one of them showed her that he had a gun. They drove to an alley, where each raped her in turn. After the rapes, the men let her go. She found her pants on the ground and set out to find a pay phone but was assaulted a second time by the man with a gun who dragged her into another alley and forced her to perform oral sex on him. As she was leaving the alley she accused him (or his friends) of having taken her money from the pocket of her pants.

He gave her some money and said he would give her more the next day if she kept quiet about what happened. The victim's account was corroborated by her friend, the two strangers, the police report taken shortly after the rapes, and physical evidence collected from a police rape kit.

Magenau shows that in cross-examining the young woman, the defense attorney tried to confuse her so it would appear that she was mixing up facts – giving the impression that she was unreliable or even making things up – and tried to make it appear that she had willingly had sex with the men for money. Listening to him do this, you see how easily your grasp of your own life can be undermined, reflected in a house of horrors mirror: The elements of what happened are there, but they are re-formed into an image that is completely distorted.

Women are instructed not to fight back when a man tries to rape them. If you fight, women are told, you are more likely to get hurt. But if a woman did not fight back, it is easier for a defense attorney to reframe the rape as consensual sex, as the defense attorney in this case tried to do:

ATTORNEY: But you did not resist him or push him or pick up those available sticks and objects and resist him before the alleged oral sex, did you?

WOMAN: No.

By admitting she did not fight – a reasonable course of action, since one of her attackers had a gun – the woman supports the interpretation the attorney is constructing. By detailing all the ways she could have fought off the young men, he gives the impression that she was well aware of her options but simply was not interested in using them.

The attorney makes the woman's story seem all the more implausible when he juxtaposes her not resisting before the assaults with her alleged behavior after:

ATTORNEY: Is it your testimony that as a result of forcing him and pushing him, that you managed to get out of that shed and up the alley?

WOMAN: Yes.

Yet it is logical that the men would allow her to leave after they had raped her, but not before. Now watch how the attorney constructs an alternate scenario, that she voluntarily exchanged sex for money:

ATTORNEY: But not before, according to you, he took two ten-dollar bills out of his pocket and handed them to you, true?

'According to you' implies 'even you admitted this.' 'But not before he gave you money' implies she made sure to get paid before being on her way.

In her response, the woman tries to answer truthfully yet make clear that the way he was making it look was not the truth:

WOMAN: True. Which were probably mine, yes.

The attorney implies she is answering improperly:

ATTORNEY: Ma'am, whether that was yours or not, he had it according to you, did he not?

Her next response sounds deflated, as if she has given up trying to resist his distortion of her experience, just like a victim giving up resisting being raped:

WOMAN: Yes.

The attorney then repeats the same facts he just established, reinforcing his version of them:

ATTORNEY: Now you are telling us that after this forced oral sex and after you pushed him, he produces cash and gives it to you?
WOMAN: Yes.

In this last question, the attorney switches to the present tense: 'He produces cash and gives it to you.' This is different from the way he asked the same question just before: 'He *took* two ten-dollar bills out of his pocket and hand*ed* them to you.' Although it might not have been consciously thought out, this switch in tense could imply that the exchange of cash is habitual, rather than a onetime event. As Magenau shows, he is building an image of the woman as a prostitute.

Shortly thereafter, the woman explains why the man gave her money:

> WOMAN: I was looking and I asked, 'Did you all take my money? I have no money. Why did you take my money?' And he pulls the money out of his pocket and he says, 'Take this. I'll give you fifty dollars tomorrow if you don't say anything.'

The attorney restates what she said to give a different impression:

> ATTORNEY: So he not only gave you cash on the barrelhead then, plus – but he promised you an additional fifty dollars the next day, true?

'Cash on the barrelhead,' Magenau notes, describes the payment of money for goods, not the return of stolen money. The attorney also, by his wording, transforms the man's offer of $50 from hush money (the promise of which is an admission of wrongdoing) to a promise of future payment for goods or a service. Through skillful word choice, the lawyer is trying to plant his version of events in the jury's mind. This can be very effective, because language often does its work stealthily, through the power of metaphor to shape thinking.

The cross-examining attorney also tries to reshape how the jury regards the young woman's encounter with the strangers. She has testified that she gave them a false name and phone number to get rid of them. In questioning her, he tries to create a compromising image of her as the kind of woman who would be walking down the street talking to strange men driving by in a car – in a word, a streetwalker:

> ATTORNEY: The passenger spoke to you and, without telling

us the words, what was the general nature of the conversation?

By referring to the verbal exchange as 'a conversation,' the attorney is creating the impression of a social exchange in which all parties participate willingly. The young woman tries to deny this impression:

WOMAN: He was just trying to pick me up.
ATTORNEY: And on that occasion, you didn't ignore him, did you?
WOMAN: Yes, I did.
ATTORNEY: Well, I thought you told us you stopped, you talked to him, and you even gave him a name and phone number.
WOMAN: No, he just got the name and I walked off.
ATTORNEY: Well, I'm asking as an immediate matter, when two strange men drove up to you whom you said you had never seen before in your life trying to pick you up, you did not ignore them and simply continue walking. You did not say, 'Get lost.' You stopped and talked to them, true?
WOMAN: No.
ATTORNEY: Ma'am.
WOMAN: That's not true.
ATTORNEY: What's not true, you didn't stop or you didn't talk to them?
WOMAN: I didn't stop.
ATTORNEY: But you did talk to them.
WOMAN: If you call that conversation, yes.

You can hear the woman trying to get out her version: Giving a false name and number was a way to avoid a conversation, not have one. Yet by the rules of cross-examination, she is compelled to answer in the terms he sets, so she ends up saying 'yes' to a question she has just answered 'no.' By saying 'If you call that conversation,' she implies that though she changed her answer to 'yes,' the spirit of her answer was still 'no' – the words exchanged were not conversation.

Having gotten the woman to change her answer from 'no' to 'yes,' the attorney then criticizes her wording:

ATTORNEY: Well, I'm not asking you to elaborate on conversation. Did you exchange communication with them?

She is hamstrung:

WOMAN: Yes.

He then gets her to say what she has been trying to resist saying, because it does not describe her view of what happened:

ATTORNEY: Again you didn't ignore them, true?
WOMAN: Yes.
ATTORNEY: You didn't tell them to get lost or drop dead or anything of that nature. You gave them the name, right?
WOMAN: Yes.

In his skillful cross-examination, the defense attorney not only suggests his own version of events but also repeatedly gets the young woman to change her answers from 'no' to 'yes,' making her appear unreliable. Watch how he makes her seem confused – or duplicitous – by asking confusing questions. About the strangers he asks:

ATTORNEY: Had you seen either of those two men earlier that night in the nightclub?
WOMAN: No.
ATTORNEY: Have you seen either of them since?
WOMAN: Just here, no.
ATTORNEY: Well, have you seen them here?
WOMAN: Yes.

Again, she ends up changing her answer from 'no' to 'yes,' making her seem confused, unreliable, or worse.

It is chilling to read this transcript because it shows how easily details can be distorted to make events appear other than what you know they were. I believe this young woman's version of events was the truth and that the attorney was attempting to distort the truth in order to get his clients off – exactly what his job is under the adversarial system. This is what the jury concluded, too: The men were found guilty. But the outcome does not undo the woman's experience under cross-examination. In any case, it is not necessary to believe this individual woman for my point to be made. Even if this individual woman were lying and events were as the attorney presented them – she willingly engaged in sex for pay and then decided to bring charges against the innocent young men – the transcript shows how easily (and how commonly) an attorney can distort the truth in defense of a client. The point for us is that in our system, attorneys are not only permitted but required to do so. That they are often successful is clear: The percentage of reported rapes that end in conviction is tiny.

Reading this transcript and Magenau's analysis of it makes one yearn for a system of justice that is investigative rather than adversarial: a system in which experts could set out to discover what really happened, as nearly as they can. In a case of rape, it is obvious that a defense attorney's best bet will be to try to show that the act could have been consensual rather than forced. But the nature of rape also makes it particularly clear how cruel this approach is to the individual involved. David Luban illustrates another type of case that dramatizes the potential cruelty of cross-examination in an example he attributes to Stephan Landsman:

> In an infamous Canadian trial of a Holocaust denier who was prosecuted for violating Canada's prohibition on ethnic hate speech, the defense lawyer cross-examined witnesses who had survived concentration camps where their parents had perished. He challenged them with utmost brutality, asking whether they had actually watched their parents be gassed to death (of course, they hadn't, since they were survivors), and – when they admitted they had not – went on to suggest that for all they knew their parents were alive but simply didn't want to see them again.

As Luban comments, 'The lawyer was offering the only arguments he could to discredit the witnesses,' which it was his job to do.

A system that requires attorneys to do all in their power to manipulate facts and distort impressions if necessary to make the best case for their clients undermines our society in many ways. It contributes to the contempt in which many citizens hold lawyers and consequently our justice system. It can make those who have gone through the justice system feel abused and undermine their sense of the world as a safe and right sort of place. This is why participating in a legal proceeding can make someone cynical and bitter. And all that intentional distortion pumped into proceedings makes it harder (though luckily not impossible) for the truth to come out.

---

## JUDGING PERFORMANCE

---

Just as journalists judge each other by whether they ask tough questions, trial lawyers judge each other by how tough their cross-examination is. And media coverage often takes the same perspective. When the prosecution rested its case against Timothy McVeigh, who was ultimately convicted of blowing up the federal building in Oklahoma City, coverage turned to the next phase of the trial – and the performance of defense attorney Stephen Jones. *Newsweek*, for example, reported that Jones's 'lackluster performance inside the courtroom has contrasted sharply with his somewhat more successful pre-trial efforts to present McVeigh as an intelligent, even affable boy next door through a series of "exclusive" interviews, including a *Newsweek* cover story, and carefully timed leaks.' The magazine quoted legal experts not to comment on the case but to critique the defense attorney's performance:

> 'Out of the 125 witnesses we've heard, there have been around 10 substantive cross-examinations,' says Denver lawyer Andrew Cohen. 'Out of those 10, maybe one or two cross-examinations have actually been successful . . . I expected a little more from Stephen Jones.'

The word 'successful' does not refer here to success in getting at the facts or understanding what happened or bringing the miscreant to justice. 'Success' here refers to undermining and discrediting witnesses, even those who are telling the truth. The article reinforces this definition:

> To be fair, Jones has had some successes. On May 8, he unveiled a blistering cross-examination of Eric McGown, a young Kansas motel worker whom Jones forced to contradict himself several times, leaving jurors with the impression that McVeigh might have had two Ryder trucks.

The effect of this 'blistering cross-examination' must surely have been upsetting to the motel worker, but what did it have to do with finding out whether or not McVeigh was guilty? Not much; according to the same article, 'the overall point – that there may have been two trucks – does not exonerate McVeigh.' Why bother, then? The purpose of the cross-examination was, no doubt, the purpose of most cross-examinations: not to establish facts but to discredit the witness.

---

## MANIPULATING FACTS TO WIN

Seeing attorneys deliberately attempting to discredit a rape victim, Holocaust survivor, or hapless witness makes you wonder how any decent person could find it in his heart to treat someone so cruelly. The answer is the concept of zealous advocacy – the tenet that a lawyer must do everything possible to serve a client's case, short of breaking the law. Monroe Freedman, former dean and professor of legal ethics at Hofstra University Law School, quotes sources from as far back as the 1908 Canons of Professional Ethics that require a lawyer to give 'entire devotion to the interests of the client [and] warm zeal in the maintenance and defense of his rights,' and as recently as the 1983 Model Rules of Professional Conduct, which require 'zeal in advocacy' as 'the fundamental principle of the law of lawyering.'

Freedman cautions that the current concern for civility can violate a lawyer's primary obligation to provide zealous advocacy. He tells of a young lawyer who discovered that the firm's client could win a case summarily because the opposing lawyer had missed a statute of limitations in filing a key document. But the partner in charge of the case declined to use this as a basis for winning. 'We don't practice law like that in this office,' the partner said – as recalled by the young lawyer, now a judge lamenting the loss of civility. Freedman, however, sees this not as a triumph of civility but as a failure of zealous advocacy: The firm sacrificed its client's interests to a misguided notion of courtesy to a fellow lawyer (though it could also be understood, I would add, as respect for justice: If the case cannot be won on its merits, it should not be won on a technicality).

Putting yourself in the role of the client brings Freedman's point into focus: You expect your own lawyer, whom you are paying to represent you, not to pass up a chance to win your case quickly and legally. From the point of view of clients, lawyers watching out for each other rather than their clients is as offensive a prospect as doctors sticking together to hide errors and make sure that incompetent surgeons have as much opportunity to operate on unwitting patients as skilled ones. But from the point of view of society at large, many now question the ethics of the adversary system in general and the principle of zealous advocacy in particular – because it often serves to obscure the truth rather than reveal it, because it is inhumane to the victims of cross-examination, and because of what it does to those who practice within the system, requiring them to put aside their consciences and natural inclination toward human compassion. Just as Orville Schell is troubled that fellow journalists feel required to do things in the course of their work that they would not deem right in their private lives, David Luban feels that something is amiss when lawyers are required to do things in their professional roles that they would consider morally wrong to do in their personal lives.

And this, Luban feels, is what results from the principle of zealous advocacy. Except in criminal cases, where the power of the state is usually vastly disproportionate to the power of the accused, he believes that zealous advocacy is morally indefensible, especially when it goes along with another principle, moral nonaccountability. According to this principle, lawyers do not have to believe what they say on their clients' behalf and are not accountable for harm done as a result of their advocacy. Luban quotes a famous statement of this principle: 'An advocate, in the discharge of his duty, knows but one person in all the world, and that person is his client,' said

Lord Henry Brougham in 1820. In 'performing this duty, he must not regard the alarm, the torments, the destruction which he may bring upon others.' The perspective of society at large is closer to Luban's view, if popular culture is an indicator. In the film *The Devil's Advocate*, an attorney who skillfully manipulates witnesses to win acquittal for guilty defendants is literally selling his soul to the devil.

Defenders of the adversary system compare it to the scientific method, by which, in Luban's words, 'every thesis is subjected to raking criticism aiming to probe for weaknesses, unearth contrary evidence, and ensure that no proposition enters the corpus of scientific doctrine based on wishful thinking.' But the scientific method, he notes, does not require researchers to exclude evidence on technicalities, delay in hopes that key witnesses will move away or forget, try to move their labs to locations more favorable to their hypotheses, or abuse regulations to exhaust or harass opponents – all tactics countenanced by the adversary system. We might add, moreover, that the goal of science, at least in principle, is to ferret out truth, whereas the goal of attorneys is to win the case.

If the O.J. Simpson trial was anomalous in many ways, there was one way in which it was typical. Almost all criminal defendants are guilty, says Harvard law professor Alan Dershowitz in his book *The Best Defense*, so most of his efforts, like those of most defense attorneys, are aimed at trying to set guilty people free. 'I do not apologize for (or feel guilty about) helping to let a murderer go free,' he writes, because his job is not to serve justice but to serve his client. The adversary system, as Stephan Landsman reminds us, was designed not to uncover truth (which, Landsman points out, would be an elusive goal anyway) but to protect individuals' rights. Monroe Freedman explains the distinction this way:

> Before we will permit the state to deprive any person of life, liberty, or property, we require that certain processes be duly followed which ensure regard for the dignity of the individual, irrespective of the impact of those processes upon the determination of truth.

It is not, Freedman explains, that the system does not value truth, but that it holds the dignity of the individual to be a higher value.

## THE COST IN HUMAN SPIRIT

Though guilt or innocence – and the search for truth – may not be the point of the adversary system, it is very much the point for most citizens. The requirement to ignore guilt, innocence, and truth for the sake of the law is deeply upsetting to many.

Let's say you're driving along ever so slowly in the parking lot of a mall, scanning the storefronts for the shop you are looking for, when you feel a bump, hear a noise, and look up to see that you have run into another car. Because you were looking at the storefronts rather than the road, you didn't notice that you had moved beyond the lane of parked cars and entered the cross lane of traffic. You know it's your fault; you feel like getting out of the car and apologizing to the driver of the other car, but you know you shouldn't. You have been told many times, 'If you're in a traffic accident, never admit fault.' This is one of the costs of the adversary system and perhaps one of the most damaging ones: It disrupts human impulses toward honesty and corrupts human relationships. This is hurtful to the human spirit.

Apologies are deeply important to many people. I have written about this, yet even I was astounded at the following evidence of the power apologies can hold for those who feel they have been wronged. A woman stood to collect damages in a class action suit: As a result of having worn the contraceptive device known as the Dalkon Shield, she underwent a hysterectomy, lost the chance to have children she desperately wanted, and continued to live with relentless pain. Yet she was more interested in an apology than money. According to Ronald Bacigal, author of a book describing this litigation, 'She wants the Robins officials "to apologize to me. That would be worth millions."'

Anthropologist Susan Philips studied legal proceedings in magistrate's court on the Polynesian island of Tonga. Consider these facts about Tongan court proceedings that Philips mentions as background to a case she analyzed: The overwhelming majority of defendants plead guilty. Of those who plead innocent, most are found guilty. When cases are dismissed, it is usually because the plaintiff withdrew the complaint before the case went to court. This can happen because the defendant offered a formal apology to the victim or compensated the victim for the loss. 'There is rarely contestation of these cases,' Philips notes, 'and when there is, there is usually no disagreement over "what happened," or the facts of the case.' In the case Philips studied, a man had hit his wife. He did not deny that he had hit her, but he pleaded innocent because she was his wife. The magistrate accepted this as a reason to dismiss the case – but also warned the man that if he did it again, he would go to jail.

Most striking to me in Philips's account is that Tongan defendants nearly always plead guilty and do not contest what happened, only how those events should be judged. This contrasts with our system, in which defendants plead innocent if they think they can beat the rap or plead guilty to a lesser charge in what is called plea bargaining. (Former Vice President Spiro Agnew, for example, accepted a criminal sentence for income tax evasion to avoid almost certain conviction on extortion and bribery charges.) It also contrasts with attorneys' attempts to discredit witnesses' accounts of what happened or suggest events that did not happen. Those who have taken part in legal proceedings often find it extremely upsetting to have others dispute or distort what they know to be true. People seem to have a profound desire for wrongdoers to acknowledge their guilt. Following the civil trial of O.J. Simpson, in which the jury awarded a large sum of money to the family of Ron Goldman, Goldman's father announced that he would renounce the entire amount if Simpson would admit that he had committed the murders.

In ordinary human relations, acknowledging guilt or taking responsibility is the first step in setting things right. In our criminal justice system, whether accused parties plead guilty is less a matter of whether or not they are guilty than of what their chances are of winning in court.

By the ethics of lawyer-client privilege, lawyers to whom clients confess could be sued for malpractice if they reveal the truth (though they cannot allow testimony they know to be false). A case that dramatized the gulf between this requirement of the adversary system and what most citizens feel is right occurred in upstate New York and is retold by one of the lawyers involved in a 1984 book entitled *Privileged Information*. The guilt of the accused, Robert Garrow, was not in question because there were three eyewitnesses.

Garrow had come upon four teenagers, three boys and a girl, on a camping trip. He tied each one to a tree, intending to kill the boys first so he could rape and torment the girl at his leisure before killing her too. But while he was torturing and killing the first boy, another boy escaped and returned with help.

While awaiting trial, Garrow revealed to his court-appointed lawyers that he had raped, tortured, and murdered two other girls – and told them where he had buried the bodies. The lawyers confirmed his story by locating and photographing the bodies, with the goal not of alerting authorities or the victims' families but of improving their client's chances to plea-bargain. (They offered to help police solve the other murders in exchange for allowing their client to serve his sentence in a mental hospital rather than a jail; the prosecutor rejected the offer.) Unaware of this information, police continued to investigate the other murders, and the other victims' parents continued to search for their missing children. One set of parents even went to see Garrow's lawyer, asking whether he or his client knew anything of their daughter's death; he told them he knew nothing.

When these facts emerged (the murderer confessed on the witness stand, and one of the lawyers later revealed their prior knowledge to reporters), there was a general expression of outrage. The lawyers were bombarded with hate mail and death threats. But they had done what the legal code of ethics required. Monroe Freedman explains, 'Not only did the two lawyers behave properly, but they would have committed a serious breach of professional responsibility if they had divulged the information contrary to their client's interest.'

---

## TODAY, IT'S 'ALL-OUT WAR'

---

These troubling aspects are built into the adversary system. But many in the legal profession believe that the practice of law in the United States is becoming even more adversarial and rancorous than it used to be. When a *U.S. Business Litigation* panelist observed that litigation is war, another panelist, attorney Joseph Cotchett, added that now it is 'all-out war.'

There are rigorous rules meant to keep partisanship from getting out of hand. But in practice and belief, David Luban points out,

American lawyers sometimes get around, abuse, ignore, or discount the rules intended to limit the adversary nature of the system. For example, Model Rule 3.3(a)(3) says that a lawyer who knows of applicable law that would benefit the other side is legally obligated to inform opposing attorneys of it. Luban finds that students in his law classes refuse to believe that the rule exists. When he shows it to them in black and white, they don't believe it is meant. They object, 'It's contrary to the adversary system' – and this objection is so damning that it nullifies the rule in their minds.

Abuses do not define a system. But they can shed light on problems inherent in the system. I will cite some examples of abuses that lawyers have given not to suggest that the abuses are typical but to show that things have gotten worse and, perhaps more important, to claim that those who commit abuses are falling into traps laid by the adversary nature of the system.

One litigation battleground is a process called 'discovery,' the procedure by which lawyers representing one side can ask the other side to provide relevant information and allow them to question ('depose') potential witnesses before a case goes to trial. Discovery is crucial so each side can gauge the other's case and prepare to respond. But, as one judge put it, 'attorneys ... routinely twist the discovery rules into some of the most powerful weapons in the arsenal of those who abuse the adversary system.'

A case between Philip Morris and ABC gives an idea of the type of 'warfare' that discovery can involve. The Philip Morris corporation filed a $10 billion lawsuit against ABC for claiming on its *Day One* television show that the tobacco company deliberately added nicotine to its cigarettes to make sure smokers got hooked and stayed that way. ABC's lawyers complained to the judge that the tobacco company delivered to them twenty-five boxes of requested documents – on dark red paper that made them hard to read and impossible to copy or scan into a computer. When you're dealing with over a million pages, if they can't be scanned, they can't be mined for information at all. What's more, ABC claimed that the paper gave off a noxious chemical vapor that made people who handled the documents sick.

This seems like an obvious attempt to appear to fulfill a discovery order without really doing so. But it was just the latest maneuver in what *Legal Times* called a 'protracted discovery battle.' When ABC's lawyers first requested the documents, Philip Morris's lawyers fought the request on the grounds that the documents contained trade secrets. A judge imposed safeguards and ordered Philip Morris to produce the documents.

Fie on Philip Morris! you say. But according to the tobacco company, the request was 'overbroad and burdensome' – which is to say that the ABC lawyers were asking for more documents than they really needed in order to harass their opponents. Philip Morris's lawyers claimed that their client had already given ABC a million pages of the most relevant documents and that this latest order was for 'the most peripheral documents imaginable.' Nonetheless, they said they were really trying to comply: They had thirty lawyers and paralegals working round the clock, separated from their families, trying to dig the documents out of their archives.

Fie on ABC, you say. And indeed, a later court decision ruled that though the documents printed on 'specially treated red paper with a distinctive background' were not as 'comfortable' to read as the usual black on white, they were 'reasonably usable.' Nor did the court observe the noxious odor of which ABC complained. Nonetheless, the case took on symbolic meaning, and was discussed by Charles Yablon, a law professor at Benjamin N. Cardozo School of Law, in an article entitled 'Stupid Lawyer Tricks.' According to Yablon, some litigators explained what he calls 'the stinky paper ploy' as 'an inevitable result of the current litigation climate, where overaggressiveness is equated with zealous advocacy, and attorneys are expected to win at all costs.' Others 'just wanted to know where they could get some of that smelly paper.'

There are many ways the legal process can be abused – and sometimes is. As Philip Morris accused, lawyers can request reams of documents – far more than are really needed – as a form of harassment. On the other hand, when asked to provide documents, they can send so many that the other side will have to spend enormous amounts of time and money to get through them or be unable to get through them at all. The law provides means to dispute a discovery request that is deemed illegitimate, but lawyers can also harass and delay by disputing every discovery request, legitimate or not. Other tactics include scheduling depositions on Christmas Eve or Jewish holidays or outright lying to a judge about having informed opposing attorneys of a date without really having done so.

Here's another example told by attorney Susan Popik: One side in a lawsuit requested tax returns from the other side, which objected on privacy grounds. There followed a year and a half of costly motions, hearings, requests approved, denied, appealed, going all the way up to the California Supreme Court and back. In the end, the lawyer was compelled to produce the tax records, at which time he revealed what he had known all along: The records did not exist; tax returns had not been filed that year. Yet rather than say this from the start, he preferred to force the other side (and the public, who pay for the courts) to spend time and money tilting at the windmill of the nonexistent forms.

Such tactics take a toll on attorneys. Michael Gottesman was a senior partner in one of America's leading labor law firms, but he decided to leave private practice to join the faculty of Georgetown University's law school. Like the experienced, talented senators who voluntarily retired from office, Gottesman gave as one reason for his decision that the practice of law had become so adversarial that it just wasn't fun anymore. I talked to Gottesman about how he saw things changing. The following is based on our conversation.

In the past, the assumption among lawyers was that their clients were adversaries, but the lawyers were not; lawyers generally cooperated with each other. For example, lawyers who asked for extensions did so because they really had made their best efforts and, for reasons beyond their control, needed more time. They could pretty much count on opposing lawyers to accommodate their requests. Now the game has changed. Lawyers often try to score points against opposing lawyers as part of the process. A lawyer may ask for an extension ostensibly for a good reason but in reality simply to stall or frustrate opponents. And opposing lawyers may deny the extension for the same reason. Lawyers themselves are now opponents, sometimes going so far as to exchange insults and threats.

Laws designed to protect the disadvantaged side are now used to harass the poorer opponent. For example, an attorney may insist on deposing a huge number of witnesses not because their testimony is vital but because doing so takes time and costs money. Rules and procedures designed to protect rights are abused to delay and generally make life miserable for the opposing side. The effect of all these tactics is to make the process so frustrating, costly, and distressing as to badger the opposing party into settling prematurely for as little as possible. (Jonathan Harr, for example, writes in his book *A Civil Action* about a real-life lawyer who was handling a class action suit to prove that the children of Woburn, Massachusetts, had contracted childhood leukemia as a result of toxic waste dumped by local chemical factories. Determined to pursue the suit, he became destitute, lost his home, and ended up sleeping in his office.) In the end, the richer side often wears out the poorer side.

There is a rule – Rule 11 – that requires lawyers to have some basis for their proceedings and motions; the rule can be invoked if one side feels the other is instituting procedures and filing motions as a form of harassment. But Rule 11 itself can be used to harass: Some attorneys file Rule 11 motions on a regular basis, forcing their opponents to respond, costing time and money they may not be able to afford. This has led to yet another layer of protection-or-harassment: filing Rule 11 on the filing of Rule 11!

In deposing the other side's witnesses, attorneys sometimes ask the most disturbing questions possible. The Dalkon Shield class action suit provides an example. Attorneys for the manufacturer had the right to depose women who had developed pelvic inflammatory disease after having the contraceptive device inserted in their wombs. Questions put to these women included: At what age did you first become sexually active? Did you have any problem achieving orgasm prior to having the Dalkon Shield inserted? Do you engage in oral or anal intercourse, and with what frequency? Do you use marital aids such as vibrators and artificial penises? What are the names of your sexual partners, besides your husband? When you go to the bathroom, do you wipe from front to back or back to front? The ostensible justification for asking these questions was the company's contention that pelvic inflammatory disease could be caused by sexual and hygienic practices; the real reason was to humiliate potential witnesses and dissuade them from testifying.

According to Gottesman, just about any run-of-the-mill interaction between lawyers can be abused to harass. Let's say attorneys Smith and Winston have a telephone conversation that ends in agreement on a number of issues. Smith follows up with a letter intentionally misstating what Winston agreed to. If Winston does not catch it and immediately correct the record in writing, Smith's letter can be used to misrepresent Winston's position later on: Score

1 for Smith. At the very least, Winston has to invest time and the client's money writing a follow-up letter correcting the errors.

All these tactics result in expense and delay, which in themselves can be powerful weapons, since the person who is suing may well need the money and be unable to wait indefinitely for the case to come to trial or reach a fair settlement. But the cost to those who are seeking satisfaction through the courts goes beyond money. Often the greatest cost is psychological: Gottesman points out that people are inclined not to get on with their lives until a pending lawsuit is resolved. As so often happens with the argument culture, the ultimate price is paid by human beings in personal suffering.

## FIRING RHETORIC ACROSS ENEMY LINES

Are things really worse, or is technology just making possible more sophisticated forms of age-old behavior? If people's complaints about lawyers are an indication of lawyer behavior, then the behavior is not new: Public hostility toward lawyers goes as far back as the profession itself. So finds Arizona State University College of Law professor Jonathan Rose, who searched documents dating back to the thirteenth century and found the same complaints about lawyers that are heard today: There is too much litigation that is harmful to society, there are too many badly trained or dishonest lawyers – and there are too many lawyers, period; their sheer numbers create demands for excessive and specious litigation. (Recall Charles Dickens's *Bleak House*, in which a lawsuit drags on for decades, until all the money in dispute has been depleted by legal fees.)

Rose also reminds us that hostility is not the only attitude toward lawyers, then or now; it's just one part. Nor is it to say that the *level* of hostility is the same; that has not been addressed. But it does show that the problems are not new. Nonetheless, some members of the legal profession feel that the incidence of abuses and levels of rancor are rising.

Arthur Gilbert, an associate justice of the California Court of Appeals, writes that judges' opinions and attorneys' briefs have become nastier, trading more in mutual insult than in arguments from fact. Capturing the spirit of the times with war imagery, he writes,

In the Ninth Circuit, two able appellate judges who reside at opposite ends of the philosophical and political spectrum have launched multiple warheads at one another. In one recent case, verbal explosions scar and devastate the terrain for miles around. Deadly projectiles like 'preposterous,' 'laughable,' 'dangerous,' and 'activist' are fired across enemy lines.

Judge Gilbert explains that while judges may enjoy indulging in such rhetorical excess and others may enjoy watching the display, it is harmful when observers focus on the fight rather than the issues: 'The meticulous inspection of the mud splattered on the wall evokes more interest than the substance of the opinion, which may affect millions of people.'

Judge Gilbert is not alone in his concern. According to Roger Abrams, the dean of Rutgers Law School, 'The lack of civility and courtesy among lawyers has corroded the practice of law.' The president of the American Bar Association, N. Lee Cooper, 'surveyed the presidents-elect of state and local bar associations across the country.' He reports that an overwhelming 'ninety percent of those who responded believed civility was a problem in their jurisdiction.'

The behavior lumped under the rubric of civility is often far more serious than the term suggests. It goes from rudeness to harassment of opposing lawyers to breaking the law, as in this example given by Cooper:

A lawyer holding a deposition in his office failed to produce requested documents, violated Rule 30(c) of the Federal Rules of Civil Procedure, ignored a court order, and then threatened opposing counsel with violence if he tried to use the phone to call the judge, though there was an agreed procedure to call the judge in discovery disputes.

Cooper's essay was titled 'Courtesy Call,' but the word 'courtesy' seems an understatement to describe such behavior.

If you are arguing with someone who hurls insults at you, you usually end up focusing on the insults rather than trying to understand whatever else is being said – so it is less rather than more likely you will settle the argument. In the same way, aggressive tactics can make it harder to settle a legal dispute. On the *U.S. Business Litigation* panel, John McGuckin, an in-house attorney for a bank, recalled a case that he was ready to settle, until he received opposing attorneys' demands that he himself and the company's CEO submit to deposition. 'At that point,' he said, 'I started clenching up.' Panelist Jerome Falk remarked, 'It's hard to handle when you get around to settlement conversation and the lawyers aren't speaking to each other.' In some situations, he said, the level of animosity between lawyers reached such heights that other lawyers in the firm had to be called in for a 'cooler heads' chat.

---

### 'OUR CLIENTS MAKE US DO IT'

---

Why is our legal system getting more adversarial? It is subject to some of the same forces that are shaping every aspect of public life: larger and larger organizations replacing smaller ones, the broken connections that result, and the infusion of greater amounts of money, like highly flammable material, into the system.

When large institutions replace small ones, anonymity creates fertile ground for aggressive displays. Attorney Susan Popik points out, 'You don't come up against the same people all the time. That encouraged you to get along with them because you knew that in six months, you would be across the table from them again. You don't get in front of the same judges so often now.' A similar opinion is expressed by Arthur Garwin of the American Bar Association: 'Behavior seems better in small towns, where attorneys must deal with each other all the time. In Chicago, an attorney is more likely to be rude to a lawyer he or she probably won't see again.'

Professor Menkel-Meadow recalls that when she graduated from the University of Pennsylvania Law School in 1974, companies tended to stick with their law firms for life, and law firms tended to keep attorneys until they retired. Now companies shop around for law firms and do not hesitate to switch if they are dissatisfied; law firms cut loose attorneys who are not bringing in enough business; and attorneys move around among law firms, sometimes taking whole divisions with them to establish competing firms.

The result is more competition and less collegiality. According to attorney Joseph Cotchett, questionable tactics are 'expanding exponentially' and young people are feeling pressured to compete more viciously.

Another form of economic pressure is the rising cost of education: New lawyers often emerge from law school wobbling under the weight of enormous student loan debt, making it harder for them to make ethical statements that might risk their jobs. Cotchett recalls receiving a phone call from a friend whose daughter faced what father and daughter regarded as a dilemma: The daughter, a recent law school graduate who had landed an excellent position at a major Los Angeles law firm, had come across documents that implicated her own client. According to law, it was her obligation to disclose this evidence, but her boss had told her to bury it under the rock of attorney-client privilege – in her view, to commit fraud. Cotchett says he expressed shock that his friend had any question about what to advise his daughter, but the friend 'started telling me about all of the student loans she had and what a wonderful job this was. And it was clear if she did anything she was going to lose that job.' Professor Joan Williams of American University's Washington College of Law points out that law school debt also exerts pressure on graduates to shop for the highest salaries and, once hired, to work the longest possible hours, creating a physical exhaustion that in itself can make them edgy.

Just as journalists blame the public for demanding scandal, lawyers blame clients for demanding 'pit bull' or 'Rambo' tactics – words that lamentably have favorable connotations, according to the moderator of the *U.S. Business Litigation* panel. Bank attorney John McGuckin quotes litigators who say, 'It's our clients who want Rambo litigation. It's our clients who order scorched earth litigation. We're just delivering what they asked for.' But he is skeptical: 'None of us in a group of eighty-five general counsel here in San Francisco admit to hiring Rambo litigators.' Of course, admitting it and doing it are two different things. But even if clients do demand such tactics, do lawyers have to give them what they want?

Yes, many believe, if the stakes are very high. And that is another frequent explanation for the rise in extreme tactics: the huge amounts of money involved in corporate lawsuits, the battleground for many of the abuses I've mentioned. This also means that huge amounts of money are made available for litigation, just as dirty tricks in politics result in part from the large amounts of money available in political campaigns.

These are forces by which the rich are getting richer; there are also forces by which the poor are getting poorer. Since justice depends on both parties being represented, says David Luban, providing advocates to people who have no money is a requisite for justice. But we are seeing drastic cutbacks in funding for legal aid and public defenders. This means less justice for anyone who isn't rich enough to hire a good lawyer. Luban points out that the situation is worsened by the enormously costly defenses of high-profile defendants such as Timothy McVeigh and Theodore Kaczynski, which will come out of the hides of innumerable indigent defendants, since the budgets for public defenders have not been increased to reflect the extra costs. (As of May 1997, McVeigh's defense had reportedly already cost taxpayers $10 million.)

## WHY CHANGE? AND HOW?

Rutgers Law School dean Roger Abrams has noticed a nationwide reduction in applications to law school. He believes this reflects not only the diminishing job market but also that 'people might be finding a career in the law less attractive because, for many, it is no longer much fun. For many, it is not a joy to practice law.'

An attorney with the American Bar Association, Cornelia Honchar, agrees: 'Lawyers as a group are stressed out and unhappy with the nature of their work,' she said. 'It's hard to get up every day and fight.' With the anecdotal exception of litigators who thrill to the excitement of battle (Marcia Clark, for example, the lead prosecutor in the O.J. Simpson trial, had requested demotion from a higher-paying management job because she missed the adrenaline high of her work as a prosecutor), there is a high rate of job dissatisfaction among lawyers – and it is getting higher. According to Mary Ann Glendon, 'in all branches of the profession lawyers reported that their levels of satisfaction with their work plummeted by 20 percent in the six years between 1984 and 1990' and 'nearly one lawyer in four says he would not become an attorney if he had it to do over again.'

Lawyers' dissatisfaction alone is unlikely to lead to change. If pit bull or Rambo tactics work and are valued, why should anyone give them up? There is evidence that they are valued, but less that they work. Attorney Bartlett McGuire claims that Rambo litigation often backfires. There can be a backlash from judges and juries, and entire firms' reputations can be tarnished. Tactics intended to harass opponents into caving in can fire them up with vengeful determination to retaliate in kind. Since most cases are settled out of court, the buildup of animosity threatens the settlement process. McGuire points out that 'courtesy and decency, often mistaken for weakness, can provide a competitive advantage.' Opponents are on their toes when they know they're dealing with an aggressive attorney but may let their defenses down if they think they're dealing with a lax one.

That they do is documented by Mona Harrington. She interviewed women lawyers who told her they best represent clients not by being as aggressive and confrontational as possible but by listening, observing, and 'reading' opponents. In taking depositions, they get better results by adopting a 'quiet, sympathetic approach,' charming witnesses into forgetting that the attorney deposing them is their adversary, than by grilling and attacking witnesses. Attorney Falk agrees: 'Seldom does uncivil, obstreperous, obnoxious behaviour further the goal of winning. It's just the opposite. It certainly doesn't further the goal of settling or resolving a case in a cost-effective way.'

Roger Abrams believes the marketplace will provide the solution to the problem it has in part created: 'There is no question that civility and courtesy save time and money for clients,' because it is clients who pay the costs of all the time lawyers spend throwing roadblocks in each other's way – and struggling to remove the roadblocks erected by others. 'Unprofessional conduct wastes money,' Abrams says. As corporations become more cost-conscious and less willing to spend gobs of money on litigation, the economic pressure to cut back on costly tactics should increase.

The value placed on aggressive tactics is a matter more of display than of results. Charles Yablon believes that young litigators learn the Rambo stance from listening to established litigators' war stories about 'the heroic deeds they performed and the smashing victories they obtained during pretrial discovery in cases which ultimately were settled.' But this does not mean the tactics helped – or even were as tough as they become in the retelling. Many experienced litigators, Yablon says,

> derive job satisfaction by recasting minor discovery disputes as titanic struggles. Younger lawyers, convinced that their future careers may hinge on how tough they *seem* while conducting discovery, may conclude that it is more important to look and sound ferocious than to act cooperatively, even if all that huffing and puffing does not help (and sometimes harms) their cases.

By implication, elder-statesmen litigators could play a major role in recasting values for younger ones.

Seeing law through the war metaphor makes everyone battle-weary and even – perhaps especially – harms those who glory in the battle, says law professor Elizabeth Thornburg. She suggests new metaphors that might broaden and humanize the practice of law and use conflict in more constructive ways. Rather than seeing lawyers only as jousting gladiators, she suggests thinking of lawyers as builders creating a structure, teachers in an educational process, guides on a journey, cooks preparing a meal, or – not surprisingly, my favorite – speakers in a conversation rather than an argument.

Charles Yablon notes that only the worst cases of unethical behavior are punished and suggests that improvement would be more likely if judges quickly sanctioned even minor infractions. 'These days,' he writes,

> only the most disgusting and despicable litigation conduct tends to get sanctioned. By letting the little stuff slide, judges eventually are confronted with conduct so abusive, it requires a really big, dramatic, atomic bomb of a response . . .
>
> Because only the worst abuses get sanctioned, lawyers assume (generally correctly) that they can get away with conduct that is boorish and wasteful as long as it is less repulsive than the stuff they read about in the sanctions opinions.

This sounds an awful lot like the approach of William Bratton, former New York City police commissioner, who oversaw a 60 percent reduction in murders and shootings in that city. His policies included cracking down on such minor but highly visible infractions as graffiti painting, panhandling, and what New Yorkers call 'squeegee men' who approached drivers at traffic lights and offered to wash their windshields for a tip – but sometimes became abusive if the drivers turned them down. Though many question whether these policies are responsible for the decrease in crime, others are convinced that ignoring such minor infractions creates an atmosphere of lawlessness that encourages major crimes. The British Labour politician Jack Straw was impressed by Bratton's 'zero tolerance' approach and became a powerful advocate of such measures when he was appointed Home Secretary in 1997.

Yale law professor John Langbein believes that American lawyers and judges should pay more attention to the Continental legal system, in particular, its giving judges rather than attorneys the task of establishing the facts of a case. Following the arrest of photographers pursuing Princess Diana's car before it crashed, *USA Today* noted how differently the case would be handled in France than it would have been in the United States. Some of these differences will strike Americans as exceedingly dangerous, but others will have a commonsense appeal: The photographers were held for two days without charges being filed and without being allowed to confer with lawyers. Investigation into whether or not the photographers committed a crime was being led by a judge. If the case goes to court, it will be decided by a panel of judges, not a jury, and cameras are not permitted in court. The judges do most of the questioning; though lawyers can also ask questions, they cannot cross-examine witnesses. Guilt, in the end, need not be established 'beyond a reasonable doubt' but simply by the *conviction intime du juge* – the judge's intimate belief, or deeply held sense, of what happened.

Legal ethicist Paul Spiegelman is concerned that the adversary system emphasizes the competitive aspect of human nature and suppresses cooperative impulses. As a result, legal training encourages 'ethically and emotionally insensitive, amoral, and often cynical' perspectives on interpersonal relations. Derek Bok, who was dean of Harvard Law School before he became president of Harvard

University, sees hope for change. 'I predict,' he says, 'that society's greatest opportunities will lie in tapping human inclinations toward collaboration and compromise rather than stirring our proclivities for competition and rivalry.' He calls on lawyers to take the lead in 'marshaling cooperation and designing mechanisms which allow it to flourish.'

Years ago, another prominent lawyer admonished his colleagues to pay primary attention to their role as peacemakers. The year was 1850, and the lawyer was Abraham Lincoln:

> Discourage litigation. Persuade your neighbors to compromise whenever you can. Point out to them how the nominal winner is often a real loser – in fees, expenses and waste of time. As a peacemaker the lawyer has a superior opportunity of being a good man. There will still be business enough.

This may sound surprising to us today. Yet my father recalls being taught in law school in the late 1920s that a lawyer's first obligation is to discourage litigation. (He took this advice to heart; when a relative sought his help in securing a divorce, my father convinced him to reconcile with his wife – and the relative blamed my father each time his troubled marriage caused him further pain.) Lawyers' peacemaking role is less frequently stressed in law schools today. Professor Adrienne Davis of American University's Washington College of Law tells me, 'I try to train my students to learn negotiation skills that encompass advocacy and mediation and reconciliation,' but she finds that the students resist.

With the complexity of these issues in mind, law schools might emphasize – as many already do – the reading of published legal articles discussing whether lawyers should adhere to the neutral partisanship of zealous advocacy or take into account how their actions affect individuals other than their client as well as society as a whole. Legal ethicist Rob Atkinson, for example, discusses these two competing ethical visions by analogy to Kazuo Ishiguro's novel *The Remains of the Day*. Ordered by his British employer to fire two devoted and capable maids simply because they are Jewish, the butler sees his role as carrying out those orders even if he believes them to be morally reprehensible; the head housekeeper believes she is sullied by doing so. Atkinson suggests the butler would have served his employer better by showing him the error in his wishes rather than implementing them.

## A PROBLEM-SOLVING APPROACH

Some lawyers are trying to move their profession toward greater use of cooperative approaches such as alternative dispute resolution. Even corporations are looking to ADR as a way to cut costs.

Professor Carrie Menkel-Meadow believes that the best hope is moving away from the adversary system and toward a problem-solving approach that takes into account disputants' underlying needs and how strongly they feel about them. For example, she shows, if two children are arguing over a piece of cake, it may seem self-evident that the way to resolve the conflict is to cut the cake and give each child half. But this is not the best solution if one child likes the cake and the other likes the icing. In that case, they would do better with a Jack Sprat solution by which both could get all of the part he or she likes best.

The key to the success of such an approach is giving up the adversarial stance, which assumes that there is a single resource at issue, so either party's gain is the other party's loss. Menkel-Meadow points out that this understanding of compromise is fundamentally adversarial, based on the assumption that both parties will start out by demanding more than they really need of the disputed resource and then split the difference. In this spirit, a basic principle of negotiation is that lawyers should not reveal what their clients really want, because that is perceived as giving the other side too much power.

Even in negotiation, Menkel-Meadow shows, an adversarial stance can create problems by forcing the parties into 'attack and defensive postures which then may inhibit creativity in finding solutions.' If one side caves in, it may be in a spirit of resentment that results in either not following through on the agreement or seeking revenge at the first opportunity. Menkel-Meadow points out that handbooks for negotiators are full of 'advice to overpower and take advantage of the other side.' But these tactics are useless if negotiators on both sides have learned the same tricks – for example, never to make the first offer and always to draft the final agreement.

In this view, eradicating abuses would not fix the system. Even when everyone is civil and no one is abusive, Menkel-Meadow stresses, the win-lose, two-sides structure of the adversary system leads to bad solutions. Adversarialism, she shows, reduces complex human problems to just two sides: Everyone must align with plaintiff or defendant. A problem-solving or mediation approach overcomes these drawbacks by providing for participation of more than two sides.

Many attorneys feel they have to engage in scorched earth tactics because the other side does it, just as journalists feel they have to cover a sensational story because the competition is doing it. This is what Gregory Bateson called 'symmetrical schismogenesis' – each person does more and more of the same thing in reaction to the other. An illustration in a book by communication theorists shows two people in a small sailboat, holding on to opposite ends of a rope attached to the mast, leaning in opposite directions. As one pulls toward one side of the boat, the other has to lean toward the other side to prevent the boat from capsizing. This prompts the first to lean farther out, and so on, until they are hanging dangerously over opposite edges of the boat. How much better, the authors suggest, for one to let up slightly. To keep the boat balanced, the other person will have to let up, too, until both are sitting comfortably in the boat instead of hanging over its sides. This image can be a model for change in settling legal disputes. Someone can start letting up a little, instead of everyone getting more and more aggressive. How much safer we all will feel – and be – if we can sit comfortably in the legal boat instead of hanging precariously over its sides.

In a brief history of the adversary method, Stephan Landsman explains that in Northern Europe during the early Middle Ages 'trial by battle' was standard legal procedure: The disputing parties, or 'champions' they hired, did literal battle; the victor was then found to be right, since divine intervention was believed to determine the outcome of the battle. We have come a long way since trial by battle, but the adversary system retains traces of this ethic. When the goal is winning a fight, truth and justice are sometimes lost. Moving away from, or mitigating, the adversary system might take us closer to those goals. It might also restore citizens' faith and trust in our legal system.

# 6

# BOYS WILL BE BOYS:
# GENDER AND OPPOSITION

What is the connection between gender and agonism? Are men more likely to engage in ritual opposition, nonliteral attack? Are they more likely to take an oppositional stance toward other people and the world? Are they more likely to find opposition entertaining – to enjoy watching a good fight, or having one?

The short answer is, Yes.

The long question is, Why?

Before I explore that question by showing how fighting plays different roles in the social lives of boys and girls and, later, of women and men, I want to say a few words of caution.

*Caution One:* What I just said can sound like an accusation, but it isn't. For those who believe that fighting is bad, saying boys and men fight more than girls and women sounds like a slur against males. But fighting and aggression are not bad in themselves. Showing the purposes they serve for boys and men is meant not to denounce this association but to make sense of it.

*Caution Two:* People can read patterns as norms. It's a short step from 'men and boys tend to be more aggressive' to 'any little boy or grown man who isn't aggressive isn't normal, isn't masculine enough,' and from 'women and girls tend to be less aggressive' to 'any little girl or grown woman who is aggressive isn't normal, isn't feminine enough.' It's a short step – but a false one. The range of normal is very wide; it isn't defined by the average.

*Caution Three:* The female-male polarity, though real, is more like ends of a continuum than a discrete dualism. Think of the men and women you know, and you will find a vast range of behaviors, personalities, and habits. Yet readers of *You Just Don't Understand* tell me they are amazed and relieved to learn that behavior they attributed to their partners' personal failings – or a failure of love – is behavior common among the other sex. Readers also tell me that in some ways they (or their partners) have characteristics more common among the other sex than their own. The forces of gender are far more complex than a simple male-female dichotomy suggests. Many variations exist, shaped by culture, geography, class, sexual orientation, and individual personality. Since one of the goals of this book is to limit our tendency to think in dualistic polarities, you may wonder whether it is worth describing gendered patterns at all.

It is worth it because the patterns exist and are relevant even to those who do not fit the pattern. Women and men who behave in ways associated with the other gender are often judged harshly as a result. The very word 'aggressive' has different connotations when applied to a man or a woman.

Of the many dynamics that tend to distinguish males and females, the uses of and attitudes toward opposition and fighting are among the most significant. So in order to understand the argument culture, to fully grasp the forces driving agonism in our public and private lives, we have to take into account the role played by gender.

## 'YOU BE THE MONSTER AND CHASE ME': CHILDREN AT PLAY

A mother bought a toy for her three-year-old son that she remembered liking when she was a child. Called 'A Barrel of Monkeys,' it was a yellow plastic barrel containing bright red plastic monkeys with long arms shaped to hook into each other. The mother assumed her son would play with this toy as she had: looping the arms together to make a long strand of monkeys. But he had a different idea about how to play with this toy. He grabbed a bunch of monkeys in each hand, stood them up facing each other, announced, 'These are the nice ones and these are the mean ones' – and set them upon each other in mock battle.

Watch small children at play. First of all, you'll see that girls and boys tend to play with other children of the same sex if they have a choice. And the way they play tends to be different. The girls spend a fair amount of time sitting together, and talking is a big part of their play: 'Let's pretend,' you hear. And 'Wanna know a secret?' Most boys spend a lot of time roughhousing, grappling for toys, threatening or clobbering each other with toy weapons. These different ways of playing explain, in part, why they prefer to play with other children of the same sex. The boys find the girls' way of playing boring; the girls think the boys play too rough. And sometimes, so do the boys' mothers.

Few girls use their toys to set up battles between monsters and heroes. This is not to imply that little girls don't fight; of course they do. They struggle over rights to toys and have power struggles over who's in and who's out. But their disputes are more likely to be primarily (though certainly not exclusively) verbal, less likely to be primarily physical, all-out grappling to get what they want. Most important, girls don't tend to play-fight for fun. They are less likely to pick up whatever is at hand and turn it into a weapon. As the mother who bought her son A Barrel of Monkeys put it, 'My friend has a little girl the same age as my son. When her little girl wants to play, she says, "You be the baby and I'll be the mommy." When my little boy wants to play he says, "You be the monster and chase me!"'

Go into a kindergarten classroom, and you're likely to see this classic scene: A pair or group of little girls builds a structure in the block corner; then a pair or group of boys descends upon them and destroys it. The boys think it's hilarious; the girls are genuinely upset, even incensed. The girls think the boys are mean for having destroyed their creation. But the boys may be trying to include the girls in their play, setting up a mock attack.

When I teach a course on gender and language, I ask the students in the class to keep a log of their experiences that relate to the course. One young man, Anthony Marchese, wrote about playing 'Jenga,' a game of blocks, with two friends:

> We played about three or four games and then we started building things with the blocks. It was really fun because we felt like little kids again. There were three of us building our own little structures, two guys and one girl, Alicia. We had each built a unique design, when suddenly the other guy threw a block at my structure to knock it over. It only glanced my building, and for the most part it stayed up. I then threw a block at his building, which prompted him to throw a block at Alicia's. She put her arms around her building to shield it from the flying blocks. While my friend and I destroyed each other's buildings, we couldn't get hers because we did not want to hit her with the blocks. Another guy in the room said to her, 'Why didn't you throw blocks at them?' She said she did not like to play that way and she did not find our play very amusing. Honestly, it has been over ten years since I built anything with blocks, and I am sure it has been just as long for my male friend. But I can recall that when I played with blocks with my brothers, we would destroy each others' designs. Last Friday, I was just playing the way I used to play ... I did not want my building ruined, but I had a lot of fun throwing blocks at my friend's and destroying his.

Anthony's perspective sheds light on the kindergarten scene. It's not that the little boys are necessarily destructive, insensitive, and mean, though the girls may think so. It's a kind of game – it's fun. But they end up looking like bullies because of the way the girls react. This is not to say that boys are never mean: Both boys and girls can be exceedingly cruel to other children. But sometimes what is taken as being mean is simply an attempt to play in a way another child does not understand or appreciate – and this dynamic is especially likely between boys and girls.

I saw this contrast one spring afternoon – and got a glimpse of the joyful spirit that can underlie what comes across as aggressive behavior. My husband and I were eating lunch at an outdoor table behind a fast-food restaurant adjoining a large picnic area beside the ocean. It was Sunday, one of the first warm days of spring, and families had brought children who were running and playing as their parents ate. A little girl who looked about four or five was standing alone, absorbed in eating an ice cream cone, surrounded by a horde of boys of varying ages. One little boy, littler than she, was especially exuberant; he was skipping and running, waving his arms around: His joy was palpable. At one point he ran over to the little girl, whom he obviously knew, and clamped his hands on her hips. It wasn't even a shove, just a grab. Startled, she took a second or two to respond – by dropping her jaw, starting to cry, and heading straight for her father, who was sitting not far away. The girl soon stopped crying and went back to her ice cream cone. The boy continued to run around with the same look of excitement and pleasure on his face. Before long he ran up to an older boy and grabbed him in exactly the same way. The older boy at first ignored him but then allowed him to tumble into play. Soon they were roughhousing, pulling each others' jackets, pushing, shoving, and having a ball. It was clear as the warm spring day that by running up to the little girl and grabbing her, the boy was just trying to engage her in play – in a way she interpreted not as play but as an attack.

---

## 'LET'S PRETEND IT'S ANOTHER DAY': CHILDREN IN CONFLICT

---

If boys are more likely than girls to roughhouse and play-fight, girls are as likely as boys to have conflicts over toys, territory, or getting their own way. Comparing how very young boys and girls tend to work out conflicts has been the focus of research by linguist Amy Sheldon. The next two examples, and my discussion of them, come from Sheldon's study of three-year-olds at a day care center. Both the boys and the girls are struggling over possession of toys, and in both cases the child who starts out with the toy loses it in the end. But whereas the boys' struggle is short and physically as well as verbally aggressive, easily recognizable as a fight, the girls engage in a protracted negotiation apparently designed to get what they want while *avoiding* a fight. The section that follows is my paraphrase of Sheldon's analysis.

## THE BOYS' FIGHT

Tony is sitting on a large foam chair dialing a toy telephone. While he holds the base of the phone on his lap, he has left the receiver to rest unattended beside him. Charlie seizes the opportunity to take possession of the receiver, claiming, 'No, that's my phone!' In an effort to hold on to the telephone, Tony grabs the cord and tries to pull the receiver away from Charlie. Tony protests:

> TONY: No, that – uh, it's on MY couch. It's on MY couch,
> Charlie. It's on MY couch. It's on MY couch.

Tony's claim is territorial: the phone is his because it's on 'his' chair (which he calls a 'couch') – and the chair is his because he's sitting on it. Tony does not construct a complex argument but simply restates his claim as he attempts to pull the telephone receiver back. Though his argument sounds simplistic and repetitious ('It's on MY couch') to adult ears, bear in mind that it is accompanied by physical force. Charlie is on the same wavelength: He doesn't argue with Tony's reasoning. Ignoring what Tony says, Charlie keeps holding on to the receiver and talking into it while Tony keeps the base in his lap.

Still talking on the phone, Charlie then walks behind Tony's chair. Tony gets up, sets the phone base on the floor, and tries to keep possession of the phone by overturning the chair on top of it. He explains what he's doing: 'I'll rock the couch like this.' Charlie tries to reach for the phone under the chair. Again, Tony protests: 'Don't! That's my phone!' Still ignoring him, Charlie pushes the chair off the telephone and pulls it away from Tony, justifying, 'I needa use it.' Charlie has won. As Sheldon describes, Tony kneels, then 'sits back on his heels and watches Charlie playing with the phone. In this conflict,' she shows, 'each child tries physically to overpower the other in order to use the telephone.'

## THE GIRLS' 'FIGHT'

Look how different the girls' conflict is. They, too, are struggling for possession and control of toys. But whereas the boys were clearly fighting – struggling physically for the telephone – and their short fight ended when one of them won, the girls engage in lengthy negotiations.

Elaine is playing with an array of toy medical instruments; Arlene wants them – and gets them. But Arlene doesn't begin by grabbing what she wants; she starts by asking for a toy thermometer: 'Can I have that – that thing? I'm going to take my baby's temperature.' Elaine doesn't refuse; she gives in, but with qualifications that maintain her control. She says, 'You can use it – you can use my temperature. Just make sure you can't use anything else unless you can ask.'

Next Arlene wants the toy syringe. She begins by asking, 'May I?' Elaine resists complying but gives a reason: 'No, I'm gonna need to use the shot in a couple of minutes.' Arlene doesn't accept the refusal. She does what Charlie did: takes the object. But in doing so, she adopts a beseeching tone to which Elaine accedes, while also reasserting her control:

ARLENE: [*beseeching*] But I – I need this though.
ELAINE: [*firmly*] Okay, just use it once.

Arlene takes the toy syringe but resists the control, asserting her right to use it more than once. Elaine again tries to reassert her superior rights to the toys:

ARLENE: No, I'm gonna give her a shot on the—
ELAINE: Hey, I'm the nurse. I'm the nurse. Arlene, remember, I'm the nurse, and the nurses getta do shots, remember?
ARLENE: But I get to do some.

Elaine concedes permission for Arlene to use the toy syringe more than the one time she initially allowed: 'Just a couple, okay?' Having succeeded thus far in her demands, Arlene gets bolder:

ARLENE: I get to do some more things too. Now, don't forget – Now, don't touch the baby until I get back, because it IS MY BABY!

The power dynamic is shifting; now it is Arlene who is issuing orders. She goes on to take yet another instrument, but again she explains why she needs it and ends by seeming to ask for agreement: 'I'll check her ears, okay?' Arlene puts down the syringe and picks up the ear scope. Elaine picks up the syringe that Arlene has put down and announces her intention to use it. Now it is Arlene who tries to limit what Elaine can do. She says, 'There can only be ONE thing that you – that – NO, she only needs one SHOT.' Elaine's rejoinder is a triumph of compromise: 'Well, let's pretend it's another day that we have to look in her ears together.' But this is not acceptable to Arlene:

> ARLENE: No, no, yeah but I do the ear-looking. Now don't SHOT [*lowering her voice but still insisting*] DON'T SHOT HER! I'm the one who does all the shots, 'cause this is my baby!

In these lines, Arlene insists on keeping control, but note two things that Sheldon emphasizes: She shows her insistence not by shouting but by *lowering* her voice. And she gives a reason for her rights: It's her baby. Still resisting Arlene's encroachment, Elaine protests – but she does so *in a whisper* and also gives a reason: 'Well – I'm the nurse and nurses get to do the shots.'

What comes next is rather odd but seems to be Arlene's way of rubbing in her ascendance:

> ARLENE: [*spoken very intensely*] An' me' – and men – well, then men get to do the shots too even 'cause men can be nurses. [*taunting, slightly sing-song*] But you can't shot her.

Elaine does not concede her right to give shots, but her response allows Arlene a certain priority:

> ELAINE: I'll have to shot her after – after – after you listen – after you look in the ears.

Arlene is recalcitrant, commanding, 'Now don't shot her at all!' In response, Elaine lowers her voice – lower than Arlene's but equally intense – and demands, 'Stop saying that!' After a pause comes the coup de grâce, which will sound familiar to anyone who has ever been around little girls – or been one: 'Well, then, you can't come to my birthday!' Familiar, too, will be Arlene's rejoinder: 'I don't want to come to your birthday.'

In many ways, these two examples show how similar boys and girls are. In both cases, a child wanted what the other child had, and got it. Both could be called conflicts. But the examples also show that they conducted the conflicts very differently. Charlie and Tony struggled physically to determine who got the toy telephone. In contrast, as Sheldon points out, Elaine and Arlene engaged in complex verbal negotiations. At each step, Elaine tried to keep control of the toys while conceding something to Arlene. Sheldon calls this 'double-voice discourse,' because the girls (as she found common among girls in her study) use language to get what they want while attempting to accommodate the needs of others. In contrast, the boys (as boys in her study often did) use what she calls 'single-voice discourse' because they have 'the single orientation of pursuing their own self-interest without orienting to the perspective of their partner.' When Arlene persists in telling Elaine that she can't 'shot' her 'baby,' Elaine issues a threat that illustrates what for girls is a tough punishment: cutting her out of the social group.

Sheldon points out that previous researchers have described differences like this by saying the boys are more 'forceful' – and they conclude that girls have to learn to be more assertive. She shows that the girls appear less forceful only if you take the boys' behaviour as the norm. If you look at the girls on their own terms, they are forceful and assertive in a different way. They use the force of their wills to balance their needs with the needs of others.

---

## GIRLS AND BOYS AT PLAY

---

If you watch girls and boys at play, you can see interactions like this any day of the week. Students in my class found many similar examples. Here are just a few.

Maria Kalogredis was baby-sitting for her four-year-old cousin, Rebecca. Rebecca wanted to play her favorite game, 'house.' Maria decided to test what we had been reading about. Knowing Rebecca always wanted to be the mommy, Maria said *she* wanted to be mommy this time. Here is how Rebecca reacted:

Rebecca seemed rather upset. She said, 'But . . . but . . .,' and sat down in a chair. She did not want to start a fight, but she

> wanted to win. She then said, 'Are you sure you want to be
> mommy because it's more fun to be baby.'

Like the little girls in Sheldon's studies, Rebecca argued from the
point of view of what was good for Maria, not what she wanted for
herself.

Another student observed a similar pattern. Elizabeth Cooper
spent some time in a toy store:

> I overheard one girl tell her mother that she needed the Hello
> Kitty markers because the colors were much prettier than the
> ones they had at school. And further that she had wanted to
> draw her mother a picture during free time but she didn't
> think her mother would like the colors they had in her class. In
> contrast to the girl, the boys I watched would tell their parent
> that they had to have a certain toy because one of their friends
> had it or because they wanted to bring it to school to show
> their friends.

The boys in the toy store argued from the point of view of what was
good for them, either to have what another boy had or to display
something no one else had (after which their friends might pester
their parents to buy one). This girl (and, according to the student
observer, other girls) tried to convince her mother that giving her
what she wanted would also be good for her mother: She could
draw a prettier picture for her mother with the new markers.

Another example shows similar dynamics in a very different
situation. Igor Orlovsky had worked at Discovery Zone, a public
entertainment center for children:

> One Saturday, I decided to organize a conga line. I brought out
> maracas, tambourines, hats, and other fun toys. The children
> rummaged through the toys and found one to use in the
> conga line. The maracas were the first to go and they were
> the most problem causing. The older boys who did not get
> maracas decided to take them from other children ... They
> used physical strength/intimidation to get what they wanted,
> maracas. The girls who did not get maracas, but still wanted
> them, used a different tactic to get what they wanted. The girls

would find a different toy, usually a tambourine, and would try
to explain why their toy was better. They would try to convince
the maraca holders to trade their maracas for tambourines.

Although the boys' tactics were more likely to be effective in gaining
the maracas, they were not necessarily more successful in the long
run, at least not in this situation: If Igor saw a boy using physical
force to take another boy's toy, he would make him give it back
– an interesting reflection of adults' inclination to condone verbal
manipulation but not physical force.

In all these examples, the girls are as intent as the boys on getting
what they want, but they find ways of *making* an argument for what
they want while avoiding *having* one. Yet sometimes girls do fight
physically. One student observed a girl physically attacking another
girl – though the girl who was attacked responded not by fighting
back but by placating her attacker. What provoked the attack was
characteristic of girls' social world: anger at being left out.

At a family party, Laura Dunphy watched her little cousin
Alexandra and two friends, Alice and Emily, who were meeting
each other for the first time. All of them were just under three years
old. Alice was jealous because Emily and Alexandra were leaving her
out: Emily was playing with Alex's hair bow, and Alex was playing
with Emily's necklace. So Alice got revenge: She 'grabbed Emily
by the legs and sent her flat on her back on the ground.' This led
to crying, recuperating, and then playing together again, only this
time Emily was careful to placate Alice:

> Alice commented on a four-foot-tall Mickey Mouse balloon,
> saying, 'That Mickey is bigger than me!' Emily, quite preco-
> cious, said in an adult voice, 'Yes, you're right. You're right,
> it is!' She included Alice in the games she wanted to play with
> Alex, as well, saying, 'Alex and I are going to play harmonicas
> now. Are you going to play with us?'

Emily prevented future attacks by agreeing with Alice's statement
about the balloon and inviting her to join their play. But by doing
the inviting, Emily maintained her position as the dominant friend,
giving Alice something while keeping something for herself.

One last example from my students' observations shows similar patterns among older boys and girls who attended a co-ed party (but kept apart from each other). Aiyana Hoffman took several other class members with her to attend her twelve-year-old cousin's birthday party. There was a lot of commotion at the party because one girl (I'll call her Mary) said something that hurt the feelings of another girl (I'll call her Sue). Sue felt so bad, she went into the bathroom, crying. The other girls started going in and out of the bathroom to check on Sue, find out what was wrong, and try to comfort her. Sue's best friend, Kate, seemed to be in charge, speaking privately with all the other girls, reporting on Sue's feelings, and even talking privately with Mary, the girl who had hurt Sue's feelings.

At the same time that the girls were caught up in this drama, the boys were playing video games and (as another student observer, Cortney Howard, put it) 'goofing off.' One boy (I'll call him Jason) was giving another boy (Joe) a hard time, and two other boys joined in. Their conversation, as Cortney wrote it down, went like this:

> JASON: So what's up with Karen? She's got you all whooped.
>   JOE: No, dude, she's just some girl, nothin' special. I ain't whooped.
> JASON: Yeah, you've been calling her, I saw you talking to her on the playground after school last week, too.
>   JOE: What are you talking about? I was just getting the math homework, that's all.
> JASON: Horse crap! You like her!
>   SAM: Look, man, he's turning red! You're turning red! Haha!
> BOBBY: You wimp, you're red all over that ugly face of yours!

This conversation differed from the girls' in many ways. First of all, Jason insulted Joe openly. When Mary said something to make Sue feel bad, she said it in private, and the other girls had to find out later what it was. Second, when the other boys (Sam and Bobby) heard Jason insulting Joe, they joined in. How different this is from the girls who were trying to console Sue.

Another difference is how the boys and girls react when their friends show their feelings. Sue didn't try to hide the fact that she was upset: Crying in the bathroom gave her a kind of power; in a way, she became the most important person at the party, and the bathroom became her headquarters. When Joe reacted to the teasing by turning red, this show of emotion gave the other boys another way to put him down. They called him a 'wimp.' And when he tried to get even with Jason by hurling a matching accusation, Jason dodged the attack – and used Joe's blushing as ammunition against him:

> JOE: Well . . . well, I saw you talking to Sally last week. Huh? Huh? Got anything to say about that?
> JASON: Yeah, she likes me. She won't leave my good-lookin' bod alone. What can you do? At least I ain't all red.

From the transcript, it is impossible to tell whether the boys were genuinely hostile, just teasing, or both. Whichever it was, this example, along with the others that precede it, shows that conflict is played out very differently by boys and girls, and plays a very different role in their interactional lives.

---

## A TICK BOMB BLOWING UP:
## LITTLE BOYS' FANTASY PLAY

---

Some years ago I conducted an experiment: I invited children of varying ages to sit in a room and talk to their best friends while a video camera recorded their conversations. I sat with the camera crew outside the room, watching what was recorded on a remote monitor.

One of the most dramatic differences that leapt out at me from the start was the girls' relative comfort with what they were asked to do: They pretty much sat down in the chairs and began talking. But at each age, the boys seemed very uncomfortable being asked to just sit and talk. The littlest boys jumped up and down in their seats and kicked the chairs with their feet until they leapt out of their chairs and started running around the room. The older boys had an opposite but related response: They sat very stiff and still, as if they had learned not to jump around but were still uncomfortable sitting. Perhaps it was because of this discomfort that the boys were more likely to express hostility to the experimenter, the person who had told them what to do. But their opposition to the researchers was only one type of opposition among a whole range of types that characterized the boys' conversations, but not the girls'.

The littlest boys, five-year-olds, plotted to escape the room – and to bomb it. Ryan produced a small imaginary 'bomb' and proceeded to play with the 'timer' on it. Rick went one better:

> RICK: You know, Ryan, I wish we had a real bomb so we could blow this whole house up.

Ryan, though, was more practical; there was one thing in the house he liked to play with:

> RYAN: Not this house. It has a Nintendo.

Rick wanted to make a distinction: The Nintendo was downstairs, but the room where I had made them sit and talk was upstairs:

> RICK: No, not downstairs, the upstairs.

But Ryan delivered the disappointing news that this wouldn't work:

> RYAN: If a tick bomb blows up the downstairs, it will blow up the upstairs.

Rick could see the logic in this:

> RICK: Yeah, 'cause then it makes a hole and then everything falls right downstairs.

Continuing the fantasy of blowing up the room, Ryan worried that Rick's plan would not work:

> RYAN: And we will, too.
> RICK: Right.
> RYAN: That's why we don't want to have a real tick bomb.
> RICK: What if we bomb someone . . .
> RYAN: And then if we fall from here we die.

RICK: Okay.

RYAN: Nah.

RICK: I don't wanna die.

RYAN: Quick, quiet, I'm gonna do something. Let's go under the rug.

RICK: We can't.

RYAN: There, the tick bomb's going to blow up all everything downstairs.

RICK: It's going to blow up us.

RYAN: No, it won't.

[*Ryan places the bomb under the carpet.*]

It's ticking, we've got to get out of here.

RICK: How do we . . .

RYAN: Jump out the window.

RICK: We can't do it.

RYAN: Let's see how high it is.

RICK: Let's see how high it is from this one. It's real high. I mean it.

RYAN: Too high.

RICK: Look at that one . . .

RYAN: Holy heck, this is stupid. We have to get back downstairs. Okay, let's go.

RICK: How do we . . .

RYAN: Now the tick bomb has stopped ticking. The building won't blow up. We can go now.

The ten-year-old boys, David and Allen, also filled their conversation with opposition. They created a sense of commotion by making action noises:

ALLEN: Yeah, remember that flying guy YYYEEEEEER-RRRRRR.

DAVID: Yeeeer then he went pffft body slam agggh shot splat.

ALLEN: Aggggh splat ouch um pancake.

They too talked of the researchers as enemies, calling us Russian spies. (Perhaps the video camera reminded them of spy movies they had seen.) At one point, they began to talk about whether we could hear them and conferred on how they might arm themselves against us:

> DAVID:  I wonder if they can hear us.
> ALLEN:  Who, them?
> DAVID:  Them!
> ALLEN:  [Twilight Zone *theme*] Da da da da da da.
> DAVID:  [Twilight Zone *theme*] Da da da da da da aggghh.
> ALLEN:  Arm yourself with what?
> DAVID:  Hehe a duh a chair.
> ALLEN:  A window shade.
> DAVID:  He he eh aha.
> ALLEN:  Aha, the chairs!

Nothing comparable appears in the conversation of the girls. Two little girls (aged six and five) talked about how exciting it was to be videotaped. This led them to a type of opposition that typifies girls' conversations: They banded together to discuss why they don't like someone else – in this case, one of their teachers:

> STEPH:  I've been on videotape, see my . . . Mrs Smith was taping us on TV.
> LIZA:  Mrs Smith.
> STEPH:  That's my crafts teacher. I hate her.
> LIZA:  I've met her. I hate her.
> STEPH:  Why?
> LIZA:  I don't know. I hate her attitude.
> STEPH:  Well, I like her.
> LIZA:  It's just her attitude. I like her, but it's just her attitude, uugghh.

This short interchange is funny because the girls seem to do flip-flops in order to agree with each other. Stephanie says she hates Mrs Smith, so Liza says she hates her too. But then Stephanie says she likes her. Liza then comes up with a way to agree but still maintain her prior position: 'I like her, but it's just her attitude, uugghh.' What is most striking about the girls' talk is how starkly it contrasts with the boys'; whereas they chose to sit and talk about themselves and other people they knew, the boys created an elaborate fantasy about planting bombs and blowing things up.

Why would boys choose to fight as a form of fun? For one thing, they seem to enjoy the rough-and-tumble physical action that goes along with it. One mother commented that her husband gets down on the floor and rolls around with their four-year-old. She doesn't do that. Instead, she tries to engage him in conversation – for example, by asking what happened at his play group. Play fighting is fun because it flirts with danger but is not real. For boys, starting a fight can be a way to get into interaction with other boys – interaction that can then be rekeyed as play. This is what may be going on when a little boy likes a little girl, and shows this by pulling her pigtails and giving her a shove. Rather than fighting back and then staying to play, the little girl runs away, leaving the boy to wonder why his gambit didn't work.

A three-year-old is telling his mother what happened at play group today: 'Bobby hit me! I got a boo-boo!' This is not a complaint but a report on the fun he had. 'I hit him back!' he announces cheerfully. She checks it out: 'But you still love him?' 'Yes, I still love him!' 'Do you want to play with him again?' 'Yes!' When one boy pushes another, they may end up chasing each other, having fun together. Sometimes the different assumptions about what's fun arise between mother and son. This mother told me she had to explain to her little boy that hitting her and laughing 'doesn't work for me.'

---

### 'WHAT THE *#!% DO YOU KNOW?': PLAYFUL INSULTS

---

You don't typically see adolescent boys roughhousing and play fighting (though some affectionately take each other's heads in a neck hold or affectionately punch each other's arms and chests). But that does not mean the pattern has changed completely. For teenage boys, physical rough-and-tumble play is replaced by verbal banter, exchanges of good-natured insults – a form of verbal mock attack. Because this is the kind of fun you can have only with good friends, it can be a way to show that you are close.

Girls are often surprised by boys' playful insults, since girls are more likely to take them literally and mistake them for real fights. Again, a student's observation captures just such a misreading.

Rachel Grant was riding on a bus, sitting across from 'two college-aged boys' who were congenially talking about sports and women. One moment they were trading statistics and other information about baseball; the next there was a 'sudden outburst':

> One guy exclaimed, 'It was all Strawberry! Without him the Mets would've gotten as bad as they are now a long time ago!' The other guy, leaning over the seat, growled back, 'What the *#!% do you know coming from Cleveland?' The first guy, now thoroughly incensed, leans further over his seat proclaiming, 'Before the strike the Indians—' Before the first guy could finish his sentence both of them had somehow managed to start wrestling with each other, on the bus, with the back of the seat between them. After a few moments of pandemonium the guys settled back into their seats and several minutes of silence ensued. I thought that perhaps they were really angry with each other, but then the first guy turned to the other and said, 'Check out that babe in the blue car down there!' As the two guys leered out the window together ... I was amazed that the guys were not angry after their bus ride brawl.

Exchanging insults was part of these young men's friendly conversation, an analogue to the physical wrestling: It's a play fight. Because the young woman would be unlikely to fight for fun, she mistook it for a truly rancorous altercation. (Another aspect of this example is that the young men reestablished their friendly rapport by banding together to look at a woman – a way of reaffirming their sameness in opposition to the other sex.)

For some men, insulting as a sign of affection continues into adulthood. The youngest of three brothers, Steve was planning his wedding to Marian, who was in the room when he made telephone calls. First he called his brother Bill, to ask him to 'stand up with' him at his wedding (in other words, take part in the ceremony):

> STEVE: I'd like you and Rob to stand up with me.
> BILL: Well, you see, I've got this cocktail party leg.
> STEVE: Ahh, shut up!

The 'cocktail party leg' was not just a humorous way of pretending to say no; it also referred to a family joke. Their mother had coined the term 'cocktail party leg' to refer to their father's excuse for wanting to sit down or leave when forced to stand at a cocktail party – but not, she noticed, when he had to stand to play golf.

Steve then called his second brother, Rob:

> STEVE: I just spoke to Bill a few minutes ago, and I want both of you guys to stand up with me.
> ROB: What if I refuse?
> STEVE: Fuck you!

At this they both cracked up. Savoring the glow of having two brothers with whom he felt close, Steve turned to Marian and translated: 'He said he'd love to.'

This kind of male joshing is at the heart of the popular British television sitcom 'Men Behaving Badly'.

## WOMEN CAN INSULT FOR FUN, TOO – WITH CAUTION

This is not to say that no women playfully insult their sisters or friends as a sign of closeness. There are individual differences here, and cultural and class differences too. It is more common among working-class girls and women to playfully insult each other, according to the research of sociologist Donna Eder and of sociolinguist Kristine Hasund. Eder, for example, studied the talk of junior high school girls and found that middle-class girls often teased each other about boys, while girls from lower- or working-class backgrounds often exchanged insults. For the girls, these were ways of communicating what kinds of behavior were acceptable and which were not.

It is easy to find examples of girls and women who use insults or arguments to create and display closeness, but they risk alienating other girls and women who do not share their habit. This risk can come as a surprise to those who move to a new country, change geographic regions, or simply grow up in a family whose style differs from that of their neighbors or friends.

Sandra Petronio, a sociologist who grew up on Long Island,

recalls that in her extended Italian-American family, exchanging putdowns and comebacks was an essential part of friendly conversation. If you didn't take part, someone would ask, 'Are you feeling okay?' But when she moved to the Midwest, she found that others didn't share her sense that hostility could be friendly: 'In Minnesota,' she says, 'if I did that, I was forever explaining that I was only joking.'

A Greek woman who came to the United States to study noticed that as she began to feel friendlier with the other women in her dorm, she began to tease them with playful insults – and was surprised when they genuinely took offense. The same occurred with a Japanese college student, since what sociolinguist Haru Yamada calls 'personal teasing' among close friends is typical of Japanese culture as well. In a book comparing Japanese and American communication styles, Yamada quotes an American woman who lamented what she saw as a threat to friendship: 'We used to be good friends,' she said of her Japanese roommate, 'but now she's always cutting me down.' Yamada felt sure that it was precisely because they were becoming good friends that the Japanese woman was 'cutting her down' – probably playfully insulting her friend in a teasing spirit, as a sign of growing intimacy.

Several students in my class told similar tales. Jackie Dinella, for example, wrote, 'I believe/have found that I can only argue/disagree with people that I am comfortable with, for example my parents, my twin sister and my closest friends. My sister and I often fight very heatedly about the most trivial things, yet of all the people in the whole world she is my best friend.' But Jackie recognized the risk:

> Doing so with another would seem inappropriate with others because we lack the closeness that arguing entails. Additionally, if they don't know me well, I fear that they would begin to dislike me. Therefore among acquaintances a (kind of) nonconfrontational atmosphere must be maintained.

Another student, Julie Sweetland, also discovered that although arguing connotes closeness to her, it can alienate other young women:

> I grew up in a very confrontational family (my mother *refuses*

to agree with anything!) and I also lived several years in a predominantly African-American neighborhood. Between the two, I guess I've turned out pretty argumentative, but only among close friends. I've found that using this style with (mostly white) students at Georgetown creates problems. For example, a girl got assigned to our apartment and left after a semester. Although I had tried my best to make friends with her, that often entailed disagreeing with her. When she left, she said she had often felt intimidated by me. I said, 'I'm 5'2" and weigh 100 pounds! How could I possibly intimidate you?' She said, 'Just like that!'

It seems that Julie's way of trying to make friends with her new roommate meant not only expressing disagreements that arose but actively seeking things to disagree about, because in her style being able to disagree shows – and creates – friendship. As often happens when conversational styles differ, what she was doing to make friends was just what drove the new roommate away.

A third young woman, Memy Hwang, expressed a view similar to Julie's:

I do believe conflict is necessary in order to get to know each other. One good one a week is enough to get closer.

But Memy also learned that others may not share this view:

In high school I liked to argue a lot ... Each day I would get in an argument with a different friend. To me I guess I didn't realize I was being weird or different because I argue a lot at home with siblings. But my friends would get annoyed and upset. I would argue, rant and rave, and then when I would realize how ridiculous I was I would laugh it off at the end. However, sometimes my friends got offended, the conversation would take a serious turn and I would feel bad. Some friends would just agree with everything I said to avoid confrontation. Since then I have toned down.

These anecdotes show that women as well as men can believe fighting is a sign of closeness. But many of these women ran into trouble when they used this style with other women. So their experiences also illustrate that those who do not conform to expectations for their gender can meet with negative responses.

Many men and some women regard being able to fight, argue, or insult each other as a sign of closeness precisely because it is generally unacceptable to behave this way. It's a kind of rule of breaking rules: The fact that people agree to break the standard rules of polite behavior shows that they have a special relationship, a fine rapport. This is just one of many functions that disagreement, fighting, and opposition can serve in human relations. (Sports, games, and all types of competition are examples of ritualized opposition that can have useful results, from learning skills to improving productivity and creativity, as well as establishing camaraderie.) Banter that is apparently hostile can be not only friendly but flirtatious – and often is, in life as in art. A stock scene in films has a woman and man begin by play fighting – whacking each other with pillows or tussling – and end up making love, as their playful fight gradually mutates into serious kissing and hugging. Fighting brings people into intimate contact, which can then be recalibrated as intimacy. This is one plot line of Shakespeare's *Much Ado About Nothing* in which Beatrice and Benedick appear at first to be enemies who trade barbed insults and end up getting married. Their exchange of insults was the first evidence of their intense interest in each other.

---

## RITUAL, HABITUAL ATTACKS ON THE PLEDGES: NEGOTIATING STATUS AND FORGING BONDS

Linguist Scott Kiesling was a member of a fraternity in college. As a graduate student, he used his connection to his old fraternity to get permission to tape-record conversations among the current members. Kiesling's transcripts of the fraternity brothers talking to each other show how insults can function in young men's social order.

A pervasive pattern is apparent in the way more senior fraternity brothers insult each other as well as the 'pledges,' young men who are seeking admission to the fraternity. One conversation about pledges is particularly telling because a female friend of one of the members happened to be there, and her reaction prompted the young men to verbalize what they were doing. Walt, one of the older members, was telling about something that happened involving several pledges. This is the conversation that followed:

LARS: Stupid pledges!

WALT: I mean, they're morons!

TINA: That's not nice.

LARS: Why?

SCOTT: Why?

WALT: Why?

[*Scott laughs.*]

LARS: We've been doing this for years.

TINA: I like – Some of those pledges are really nice guys.

LARS: Absolutely. I agree completely.

SCOTT: We didn't say they're not nice.

LARS: They're just stupid.

WALT: Nooo. They stink.

[*Scott laughs again.*]

WALT: They're so nice they can suck [*inaudible*].

SCOTT: I don't think she understands.

LARS: This is ritual, habitual, bitching about the pledges.

The older fraternity members obviously enjoy joining together in bad-mouthing the pledges. The girl, Tina, just doesn't get it. To her, insults are insults – hostile and not nice. She's taking them literally: Because the pledges are nice guys, they shouldn't be put down. When Scott (the researcher) articulates the obvious ('I don't think she understands') Lars explains in plain English that the insults are 'ritual' – the 'habitual' bad-mouthing of pledges.

This conversation is a mild, verbal example of 'hazing,' the practice common among college fraternity brothers of inflicting humiliation – and, potentially, harm – on pledges. Women's sororities also require potential new members to subject themselves to humiliation by current members, but the practices seem to be typically tamer than those to which young men are subjected. Finding no research or books on hazing among women students (nor on the parallel initiation ritual called 'rushing'), I sent out an informal e-mail query and received recollections of such humiliations as 'memorizing the Greek alphabet, our motto, learning the secret handshake,' wearing certain colors on certain days, having to carry around bags of candy (or condoms or cigarettes) that sorority members could request at any time, memorizing information about sorority members, offering to do the bidding of sorority members (but if the order seemed out of line, pledges could complain to the president). None of these seemed to match the intensity of fraternity hazing.

The extreme practices that fraternities subject pledges to are a constant concern to university administrators and parents. Periodically, hazing rituals turn up in the news when young men are seriously hurt or even killed. Some of the tamer hazing rituals – activities that pledges are forced to engage in if they wish to enter the fraternity – described in an article by journalist Anne Matthews are 'duck-walking across campus, eating raw hot dogs dredged in tobacco, rubbing testicles with Ben-Gay ointment.' These are tame in comparison to the dangerous ones: 'Campus infirmaries and paramedics dread the season, when naked pledges are tied to trees, locked in car trunks, tossed into rivers, sent running through flaming gasoline.'

In a memoir, Christopher Darden describes the hazing he endured as a freshman at San Jose State University, ranging from being forced to keep sphinx heads that the older 'brothers' tried to steal and memorizing frat history as well as the personal history of brothers, through 'constant beatings and harassment,' pushing, and threatening from older members, until the final 'Hell Week,' when he almost drowned – thrown into a swimming pool blindfolded with his hands tied behind his back, which was more humiliating than dangerous to the other pledges; only Darden sank to the bottom and stayed there because he couldn't swim. The climactic initiation came when 'they drove us out of town, stripped us to our underwear, and poured molasses, syrup, oatmeal, flour, rice, and spaghetti sauce all over our bodies. Then they covered us with manure and made us eat whole, raw onions. And then they drove away,' leaving the pledges naked, stinking, and penniless twenty-five miles from town.

To outsiders (men as well as women) this all seems cruel and pointless. But Darden writes, 'In some ways, the entire purpose of pledging a fraternity is the initiation.' He explains, 'I needed to subjugate myself, to learn discipline, and to be thrown together with other young men, to open myself up to other people.' This last point is perhaps the hardest but also the most important to grasp. Fraternity life, Darden says, forced him to 'socialize and compromise. But the best thing I got out of the fraternity was a group of lifetime friends.' Having gone through these ordeals together was the basis for the friendship: These were 'the kind of friends I'd never had before, friends who see you at your weakest and most vulnerable.' Looked at this way, the goal of hazing is in a way not unlike the goal of troubles talk by which girls and women expose their weaknesses to each other in order to become closer.

Not all those who have experienced hazing are as approving of it as Darden. At least one college fraternity member who survived Hell Week is less sanguine about it. Anne Matthews quotes a former pledge: 'Hazing is very educational about human nature. The nicest, politest, most churchgoing people turn out to be so mean and angry. And cruel, if you give them a little power.' There is plenty of evidence that hazing can have a sinister side. Had Darden's friends not noticed soon enough that he was not bobbing to the surface of the swimming pool like the others, he would not have lived to become a prosecutor – or to write his memoir. Journalist Susan Faludi describes horrific examples of hazing that took place at the Citadel, the all-male military-style academy that entered the spotlight when courts forced it to admit women. Here is just one of many examples she describes:

> A leader of the Junior Sword Drill, a unit of cadet sword-bearers, leaped off a five-foot dresser onto the head of a prostrate cadet, then left him in a pool of blood in a barracks hall. According to one cadet, a lacrosse-team member return-ing from an away game at three in the morning stumbled upon the victim's unconscious body, his face split open, jaw and nose broken, mouth a jack-o'-lantern of missing teeth.

Faludi shows that during World War II hazing all but disappeared at the Citadel, since it interfered with preparing cadets to serve in the military. But it was reborn, with renewed strength, during the Vietnam War (that ever-resurfacing watershed) and was described by a 1979 Citadel president as 'mean and out of control.' Faludi provides ample evidence that it has reached a peak in recent years. In this sense, hazing is an example of what this book is about – a form of ritual opposition that has a long history, has its own logic, can work well, but in recent years has gone too far and gotten out of control.

Hazing is a form of agonism – mock battle – driven by the same fundamental logic as playfully insulting real-life brothers. In Darden's words, 'It's just a chance to engage in the most natural of activities: tormenting someone you like.' (Again, what seems 'natural' to members of one group may seem nothing of the sort to those of another.)

Darden also recounts an incident at his first job that was a reduced form of hazing practiced by a group of grown men – young district attorneys assigned to a rough Los Angeles neighborhood. Darden and his colleagues devised a way for a new member of their group to prove himself: They drove him to a porn shop, made him cross six lanes of traffic to buy the biggest dildo he could find, then drove off and left him standing there, holding the giant dildo in public (though they quickly circled back and picked him up). Darden describes the atmosphere among this group as being 'like soldiers at war.' This comment may hold a truth: The military-like hazing of fraternities, and of military-style all-male institutions like the Citadel, is designed to approximate the shared suffering and resultant bonding of men at war.

The basic training of the military is a form of hazing in which new recruits are subjected to extreme stress and humiliation. Such practices, however, are not limited to basic training. A recent exposé revealed a practice called 'blood pinning' in which Marine paratroopers who successfully complete ten jumps are rewarded with a gold pin – pinned directly into their flesh. This recognition crowns their achievement with yet another ritual of shared pain.

The most intense form of bonding through opposition, perhaps, is the bond among men forged in actual war.

---

## BONDING THROUGH WAR

---

In June 1996, I drove my Uncle Norman to the fifty-third reunion of his World War II battalion: the 563rd Anti-Aircraft Artillery

Veterans' Association. My uncle was eighty-seven and not in good health. (Having been drafted at age thirty, he was one of the oldest in his battalion, most of whom had been drafted at eighteen, right out of high school.) He wanted me to pick him up at National Airport outside Washington, D.C., and drive him to the reunion in Williamsburg, Virginia. I knew that if I didn't do this, he wouldn't go. And I knew that he had hardly missed a reunion since the end of the war. I said I'd be glad to do it – partly so he could go, but also so I could go. I wanted to understand what could keep a group of men coming from different parts of the country to meet with each other yearly for over half a century.

When I talked to my uncle about the reunion and asked him how many men would be there, he said, 'There are fewer each year. We lost six boys this year.' I marveled at the words he chose: I loved the poignancy of 'lost,' the group identity of 'we,' and the leap backward in time of 'boys' – coming from a man of eighty-seven. He also talked about his friendships with the 'boys.' He complained about one who had borrowed $1,000 from him after the war and paid it back in dribs and drabs over a period of years. 'I had some time getting that money back,' he said. 'That guy was never any good.' 'Then why did you lend him money?' I asked. 'What could I do?' he answered. 'We served together for three years.'

The men in the 563rd AAA battalion were not in the line of fire; they were not in immediate danger of death. But the bond created by the time they spent together had endured over decades among men of vastly different backgrounds. (The young men in the battalion had come from rural North Carolina and New York City.)

We arrived at the reunion in time for the first event: a dinner barbecue. The men identified themselves by battery: 'I was "C,"' one would say; 'I was "A,"' another would respond, to explain why they didn't remember each other all that well. As we walked past the line of gray-haired men waiting to fill their plates with barbecued chicken, pulled pork, and corn on the cob, a former New York cop called out, 'Hey, Rosey! Medic! Gimme a shot!' He bent forward at the waist and rubbed his backside. He was addressing my uncle by the nickname they had used for him – Rosey, from his last name, Rosen. Just as they were still 'boys' to him, he was still Rosey the medic to them.

An Israeli documentary film entitled *Ever Shot Anyone?* follows a group of Israeli men taking part in an annual retraining of their Army reserve unit. The film was made by a woman, Michal Aviad, who says at the start that she wanted to know what goes on among men in the military because her son, a little boy, is interested only in war and battles – an interest she felt she could not understand. She succeeds in capturing what it is that makes this activity so appealing to the middle-aged men who leave their jobs and their families to come together with their reserve unit for a month each year. The answer provided by the film is the bonding that the men feel with each other in this context, which for some is stronger than those of other friendships and even of family.

One of the men in the unit tells her, 'You can't understand how close we feel after battle.' Another says, 'This is all about friendship, about being together.' Yet another: 'My real friends are from the troop.' In one sequence, Aviad discusses with a member of the troop why he chose to come to the reserve training even though his wife was having serious surgery and needed him at home. His presence is evidence, he admits, that he puts the needs of his Army buddies ahead of the needs of his wife.

Aviad also learns, in the process of making the documentary, that 'friendship' to these men is different from what that word would mean to her. The men show their affection for one another by exchanging insults – for example, about their cooking abilities. They also compete – for example, about whose wife's cooking is better. Aviad says she looked in vain for the kinds of conversations that would entail friendship to her – the self-revealing, intimate talk that I described in *You Just Don't Understand* as fundamental to most women's friendship. In a voice-over, she says, 'After twenty days I'm still looking for conversations' about family, wives, children, feelings. 'Is there anything but jokes and nostalgia?' (The men continually remind each other of shared past experience: 'Remember when . . .') She does find what one man calls 'islands of intimacy,' but she discovers, again in the words of a member of the group, that 'Intimacy is not what this friendship is about.' It's about shared experience, the pleasure in each other's company, and the fierce loyalty that brings them all back each year, despite their differences.

Bonding through fighting, war, or structured opposition may be a facet of boys' and men's bonding through activity – doing things together – in contrast to girls' and women's typical bonding through talk. For many women it is unthinkable to consider others friends if you know little about their personal lives – details revealed in the intimate conversations that filmmaker Aviad sought in vain among the Israeli reservists. In a short story, David Margolis describes how doing things together can create a friendship between two men who are ostensibly very different: 'Maybe when you work with another man day after day you get to know him in a deep way, the rhythms of the labor merge with the personal rhythms to make you friends.'

Margolis's reference to 'the rhythms' of physical labor that create a sense of friendship captures another aspect of the bonding that occurs among men in war – the connection that emerges from synchronized movement. Why is military training so focused on repeated drilling and marching? Of course soldiers need to be able to follow orders and move as a unit. But there is another level, too, according to historian William H. McNeill, who shows that coordinated rhythmic movement creates a sense of community, 'arouses warm emotions of collective solidarity,' a sense of 'pervasive well-being,' a 'sort of swelling out' that comes from being part of something larger than oneself, 'the euphoric fellow-feeling' that he calls 'muscular bonding.' Marching together in itself creates a bond, just as dancing together can create a sense of connection among people in private life.

## THE PARADOX OF MALE
## AND FEMALE FIGHTING

Anthropologist Melvin Konner points out that males' tendency toward more aggressive behavior is one of the few clearly attested universals in human behavior that cut across all known cultures. Anthropologists Alice Schlegel and Herbert Barry, comparing studies of adolescents in 175 cultures around the world, concluded that boys tend to exhibit more aggressiveness in peer groups (and spend more time in peer groups) than girls, and that their aggressiveness far more often results in fighting to assert their masculinity. What interests me here is the greater likelihood of males to engage in agonism – nonliteral fighting. For example, anthropologists working in widely disparate parts of the world have found that men in completely unrelated cultures engage in what can truly be called a war of words: contests in which they vie with one another to devise clever insults, topping each other both in the intensity of the insult and the skill of the insulter. Just a few cultures where this genre has been found include Turkey, Crete, Cypress, Mexico, Indonesia – and American high schools. Men who take part in these games of competitive verbal display typically boast of their sexual prowess and impugn the sexual purity of the opponents' mother.

It is not unheard of for women to participate in such rituals, but it is regarded as unusual when they do. (Typically, there are different verbal rituals – such as ritual laments – through which women demonstrate their creativity and skill in making up verses.) Michael Herzfeld, for example, gives an example of an exchange of insulting rhymes in the dialect of Crete between a woman and a man, but the reason the man told Herzfeld about this exchange was precisely because it was unusual that his opponent was a woman.

Again, it is agonism – ceremonial combat – that females are less likely to engage in. This is not to say that females never do, and certainly not to imply that women will not fight if they feel it is necessary. In fact, if men are more likely than women to use opposition or fighting in their daily lives, why are women often the ones who provoke verbal altercations with husbands or boyfriends about problems or dissatisfactions in the relationship – to the stereotypic distress of those men?

A cartoon showed a stressed-out man telling a friend, 'I dreamt I had a harem – and they all wanted to talk about the relationship!' This reflects many men's resistance not only to discussion but also to open conflict about 'the relationship' – confrontations they sometimes feel women seek. The apparent contradiction is solved by paying attention to the nature of the argument. The theory of agonism does not claim that women avoid all conflicts; it claims only that they are less likely to enjoy fighting for its own sake, as a kind of game. But if they are genuinely upset about something, they are quite willing to fight about it. This explains the apparent paradox that women often seek to confront problems in a relationship with men who seem eager to avoid the confrontation. One study, for example, of fifty-four Dutch couples found that wives were more likely than husbands to spark conflicts

– typically, when the wife felt she was doing more than her fair share of household labor.

## 'HOW CAN YOU PRETEND THAT FIGHT NEVER HAPPENED?': CONFLICT ON THE JOB

Attitudes toward, and habits involving, opposition are among the styles common among men that often puzzle women. Women at work frequently express puzzlement at how men can argue with each other and then continue as if nothing happened. In a parallel way, men at work are often surprised when women are deeply upset by a verbal attack – taking personally what the men feel is simply part of getting the job done. It's like the young man who thought it was part of the game to try to destroy his friends' block creations, while his young woman friend thought others' handiwork should be left alone.

It is common to hear men using ritual opposition to accomplish a whole range of goals that have nothing to do with literal fighting, such as teasing, playfully insulting each other, or exploring ideas by playing 'devil's advocate.' It is far less common to hear women do this; many women will avoid overt disagreement when they really do disagree. Deborah Kolb studied how conflicts are settled at work and discovered that women often were behind-the-scenes peacemakers, talking privately to the parties to a dispute in order to help settle it without the dispute ever coming into the open at all. Women explained their behavior to her by saying how much they dislike conflict. Because of these different predilections, women and men may tend to react differently to jobs that require them to engage in confrontation or conflict.

I was once interviewed by a journalist for an article about a woman in public life who is often characterized as being too aggressive, too tough. She told me she had asked the public figure herself how she responds to this criticism and had received the reply that there are many men in comparable positions of public power who speak as she does, but no one thinks to call them 'too tough,' because no one notices their behavior as unusual. I took the opportunity to interview the journalist. I asked her whether posing that question to the prominent woman was an example of the journalistic practice of challenging interviewees by repeating criticism to them. She said it was, and then she added that it was the hardest part of her job, something she intensely dislikes. 'It makes me uncomfortable,' she said. 'I tell myself I'm someone else and force myself to do it.' In contrast, she volunteered, she had been talking about this to a male colleague who said, 'I love it! That's my favorite part!' She remarked that she thought her colleague's delight in confronting others with negative things said about them by others is 'a power thing,' with the journalist wielding power. I wondered, though, if it might not also be the thrill of breaking a social rule and the sheer pleasure of being aggressive toward someone as part of doing your job.

I asked the journalist what kind of reaction she gets when she does this, and she said, 'Good. I do it in a sympathetic way.' She also added that she did not at all mind challenging interviewees when she felt they were really guilty of behavior she considered wrong and gave as an example someone she felt was guilty of 'not condemning racism.' In that instance, she said, 'I had no trouble being combative. It was heartfelt.' This is precisely the distinction between agonism – conventionalized aggression, being combative for the sake of it – and literal aggression, fighting for something you truly believe in. According to Walter Ong, women are just as likely as men to fight when they mean it; they just don't get pleasure out of fighting for its own sake. I do not for a moment doubt that there are many men who are made uncomfortable by conflict, too, including many who are journalists and also dislike challenging or repeating criticism to those they are interviewing, and many women who are journalists and enjoy it. But it is *more likely* that women will find this intensely uncomfortable, 'the worst thing' about their job.

Whereas middle-class American girls learn to avoid open verbal arguments and tend to avoid physical fighting, there are many cultures where real physical fights break out among women. Working-class American girls provide one example. Another is a culture that is exceedingly peaceful: the island of Bali in Indonesia, where there are strong cultural constraints against aggressive behavior. Yet linguist A. L. Becker recalls asking a Balinese woman, a dancer and teacher, how she had come to marry her husband. She said she had had to fight four or five other women for him. Surprised, he asked, 'How?' In reply, he says, 'She swung at me like a boxer.' Getting to marry the man she wanted was serious – and worth fighting for.

## WATCHING FIGHTS FOR FUN

Journalism, we saw, proceeds on the assumption that watching fights is fun. This assumption reflects a worldview that is more common among men than women.

In January 1995, *The New York Times Book Review* published a letter from a reader asking the editors to stop publishing letters from authors unhappy with reviews of their books and reviewers' responses. A few weeks later, the *Book Review* published three letters disagreeing with this request. Each gave a different reason for wanting the *Times* to continue publishing such letter exchanges. One of the three, from Judy Seigel, said she valued letters from authors to set the record straight. She finds them

> a fascinating balance to the smart-aleck, lazy, mistaken, dumb, partisan or otherwise wrongheaded reviewer – sometimes, we suspect, callow youth dismissing years of labor with a smooth sentence or two. If there's a reviewer reply, we have an actual exchange of ideas, or at least opinions.

The other two letters defending the practice did so on the basis of entertainment value. One of these referred to the letter exchanges as 'comic relief' and explained, 'It is always delightful to watch pompous authors and equally pompous reviewers airing their intellectual dirty linen in public.' The other letter expressed appreciation of what he called 'the wonderful fights' and begged that the *Book Review* not 'close the wrestling pit.' He went on:

> Cool facades of expertise crumble in the authors' desperate defense against being caught out in some howler despite years of research on a topic, and in the reviewer's scramble to maintain an entirely unearned magisterial detachment. Ideally, allies are roused and a tagteam bout ensues.

These last two letters expressed the view of the letter exchanges as spectator sport.

I couldn't help noticing that the letter writer who valued these reviewer-author exchanges to set the record straight was a woman, while the two writers who regard it as entertainment – the fun of watching a fight – were men.

Wherever you look, there is evidence that women are less likely than men to find fighting entertaining to watch. This, too, goes back to childhood. In a conversation I tape-recorded many years ago, the topic of cartoons arose. As one of the women present, I commented that as a child, I did not like cartoons in which characters got hit, hurt, and squashed; they upset me. The other woman present agreed: She could never stand that aspect of cartoons either. But the four men present (three of whom, incidentally, were gay and had not gone in for fighting when they were kids) were surprised. 'I thought it was funny!' one of them said. 'I knew it wasn't real.' The other woman and I obviously knew it wasn't real, too. But that didn't make it funny to us.

Just as cartoons were made with the 'typical' child in mind – a boy child – computer games too have until recently been designed with boys in mind. According to Justine Cassell of the Massachusetts Institute of Technology's media laboratory, children's computer games are predominantly action-oriented and fantasy world-oriented – and overwhelmingly used by boys. Only recently have a small number of entrepreneurs started devising computer games that are more likely to appeal to girls. Early attempts removed the violence, made the protagonists female, and added pink or purple boxes. These strategies didn't work, says Cassell, because they still didn't fit with girls' reality-based, social interaction-oriented, goal/problem-solving play. Current games do. The biggest hit has been Barbie Fashion Designer (it sold more than 500,000 copies in its first two months on the market), which allows girls to design clothing on the computer, then print it out and put it on their dolls. Girls seem to enjoy using the computer as a tool in their play rather than the fight-focused action of most computer games.

There is plenty of evidence that not only boys but also grown men are more likely than women to regard displays of opposition as entertaining to watch. Sports psychologists have documented this experimentally. Jennings Bryant and Dolf Zillman showed test audiences hockey games that were more or less violent and discovered that audiences indeed enjoyed watching the more violent games more (that is, if the perpetrators were their own team) – but this finding held for men, not women, in the audience.

The greater tendency for men to enjoy watching a good fight explains many phenomena in our culture. During the 1996 presidential campaign, there was a lot of talk about the 'gender gap' and 'soccer moms.' Among the differences between male and female voters, polls showed, was that women were more likely to be turned off by attack ads and negative campaigning. This didn't surprise me. Several years before, during the Persian Gulf War, I had taken part in radio discussions of women's and men's reactions to television coverage of the war. I wasn't the only one to notice that men more often got a thrill from watching television coverage of the bombing, which showed the crosshatched sights taking aim, followed by the bomb dropping and the ensuing explosion. Several men called in to say they had to remind themselves this was war with real people getting killed, not an entertaining video game. Several women called in to say they were appalled to see their husbands reacting as if they were cheering their team engaged in a game.

It also explains the increasing violence of television and films and the proliferation of movies in which everything explodes, blows up, or crashes. Boys often talk of things blowing up and exploding and find it fun, like the little boys in my experiment who planned to bomb the room in which I made them sit and talk. A study of children's television by Amy Jordan found that industry experts believe they can attract the largest audiences by offering entertainment for six- to eleven-year-old boys: action- and adventure-oriented programs featuring male superheroes engaging in plenty of violence. They have concluded that girls will watch shows designed for boys, but boys will not watch shows designed for girls.

The same is true for adults attending movies, which no doubt helps explain the preponderance of action-oriented, explosion-filled films. When a couple is deciding what movie to attend, women often go along to movies they don't like, and men are more likely to refuse to go to movies they aren't interested in. It isn't even necessary for them to refuse. Many women back off, not wanting to impose their preferences on husbands, boyfriends, or friends. If he says he doesn't want to see a certain film, she's more likely to drop the point. But if she says, 'I don't like movies like that, but

I'll go if you really want to,' he's more likely to say, 'Okay, then, let's go.'

---

## TALKING IN PUBLIC: A REACH
### FOR THE BREECHES

---

If ritual opposition appeals to more men than women, it is not surprising that public discourse tends to be oppositional – in other words, to follow a pattern that is more commonly associated with men in our culture. The very act of talking in public is an activity that for a very long time was the exclusive domain of men, closed to women.

Not so long ago, the very thought of a woman standing up in public and facing an audience to speak was unthinkable. According to David Noble, women in sixteenth-century England were not even permitted to read the Bible aloud at home to their own families. A 1573 Act of Parliament drew strict divisions by gender and class:

> Aristocratic men and women were still allowed to read the Bible in private, but only men were permitted to read from it aloud to the assembled household. Men of the merchant class remained free to read the Scriptures in private, but their wives and daughters could no longer share that privilege. Among the lower ranks of society, both men and women alike were denied the right to read the Bible.

This was a long time ago and far away. But it was not quite so long ago that women in the United States were also barred from speaking in public in both religious and political settings.

Among the first women to speak in public were antislavery activists such as the Grimké sisters, Angelina and Sarah. At first they addressed other women in homes (this was in 1836), but then they moved to churches, which were public places, where men could attend their lectures as well. Communications researchers Karlyn Korrs Campbell and E. Claire Jerry quote a Pastoral Letter from the time decrying this development:

> The appropriate duties of women, as stated in the New Testament, are 'unobtrusive and private . . . [W]hen she assumes the

place and tone of man as a public reformer, . . . her character becomes unnatural. If the vine, whose strength and beauty is to lean upon the trellis-work and half conceal its clusters thinks to assume the independence . . . of the elm, it will not only cease to bear fruit, but fall in shame and dishonor into dust.'

Early suffragists and antislavery activists outraged society not only by the policies they were advocating but by the very fact that they were speaking in public.

In 1852, a woman named Clarina Howard Nichols became the first woman to address the Vermont state legislature. Her request to speak in favor of a bill allowing women to vote in school district meetings was called, at the time, a 'scramble for the breeches'; this clues us in to why it so upset people when women spoke in public: They wanted to 'wear the pants.'

This historical fact is cited by Madeleine Kunin, the first woman governor of Vermont (later assistant secretary of education and then ambassador to Switzerland) in her book *Living a Political Life*. Governor Kunin writes that the most important element in her transformation from private citizen to public person – and the hardest for her to accomplish – was learning to speak in public. She is eloquent in explaining why this was so hard:

> The fearful idea that by speaking out I would no longer be a good girl, that my words might antagonize those who heard me, was deeply rooted. If I said the wrong thing at the wrong time, I risked punishment: I might not be liked. Worse yet, I would not be loved.

Governor Kunin articulates the interweaving threads: the expectation that a good girl does not speak up and the fear of an agonistic response. In the minds of many women, these two forces are inseparable.

In describing how she became accustomed to public speaking, Governor Kunin explains that she had to learn to deal with conflict: 'No matter how politically skilled one became, controversy could not be avoided . . . Speaking out always carried a price.' What finally motivated her to face down her fear and speak out was a passionate belief in what she had to say: 'What a surprise to discover that when fired up by conviction, I could speak spontaneously.' Once again, she was motivated not by the adrenaline that flows in the heat of battle, not by the competitive urge to triumph over rivals but by a deep commitment to what she had to say.

Governor Kunin's early reluctance to speak in public is shared by many women (and, of course, many men). The social lives of children hold some clues to how this develops. Recall the junior high school party that my students observed, where the girls were comforting one girl who had been hurt by another, and the boys were ridiculing one boy who had been embarrassed by another. My students noticed another difference between the boys and the girls at the party. When they came upon Kate and Mary whispering in the laundry room, the girls immediately stopped talking. But when they were listening in on the boys' conversation, the boys (in Cortney Howard's words) 'kind of acted up their emotions as if they were playing in front of an important audience.' These differing reactions to being observed were extensions of the ways the conflicts were played out: the girls' in a series of private conversations, the boys' as a form of public display.

Because the boys are used to playing out their rivalries publicly, opposing someone at a meeting is probably less uncomfortable and unacceptable to more men than women. And Governor Kunin's experience is testimony to the usefulness of such early practice.

These different patterns – the girls' inclination to hide their conflict, the boys' to make it into a kind of performance – might explain why many middle-class girls are reluctant to talk in front of others – for example, in school – and why many adult women find it hard to speak up at meetings. In school, many boys compete aggressively to be called on in class, stretching out their arms and even waving them or calling out. They want to be called on, quite apart from knowing the answer. My nine-year-old nephew tipped me off to this when he said, 'You know, it's like in class. You wave your hand to be called on, and then when you are, you have to think fast what to say.' Most girls, it seems, don't raise their hands unless they've already thought of what they want to say.

Once again, we have to remember that there are cultural and class differences. Anthropologist Marjorie Harness Goodwin found that Latina girls (primarily second-generation Central Americans) playing hopscotch often engaged in open disputes. She shows, in fact, that the girls sometimes intentionally broke the rules to spark a lively altercation that they all enjoyed. She also observed African-American girls in a Philadelphia neighborhood who engaged in elaborate disputes called 'He-said-she-said' where one girl confronts another who was talking about her behind her back. Nonetheless, this ritual differs from those of the boys, whose disputes typically arise and are confronted on the spot. These early experiences dealing with conflict openly may have something to do with the tendency of some women to engage in open confrontation as adults, with the result that they risk being judged – by some others, in some contexts – as being too aggressive.

## A SOCIETY OF ADOLESCENT MEN

Public agonism is getting more and more dangerous. Two men who engage in an angry shouting match may or may not come to blows, but if they express their anger while driving down a public highway, the risks to themselves and others soar. This happened on a roadway outside Washington, D.C., in April 1996 – and the result was a crash that killed not only one of the combatants but also innocent victims who happened to be driving on the same highway at the time: in one car, a man who left a wife and two sons behind, in another a woman who only two days before had returned to work, following several years off to raise three small children. According to Dr Ricardo Martinez, head of the National Highway Traffic Safety Administration, an estimated one third of all car crashes and two thirds of all fatal crashes are caused by aggressive driving: tailgating, weaving in and out, cutting others off, and other threatening behavior behind the wheel. In Britain as in the US, such behavior is so institutionalized that a phrase has been coined to describe it – 'road rage.' Newspapers carry almost daily reports of death or injury caused by one driver's uncontrollable outrage at the perceived driving offenses of another. When weapons of destruction such as cars and trucks are in the hands of most citizens, public displays of anger threaten human lives.

All human beings sometimes engage in aggressive behavior – fighting each other – for literal reasons: to get what they want or to ward off incursions by others. But aggressive behavior serves another purpose, too; it negotiates an individual's status. Adolescent boys and young men are more likely to engage in ritual opposition because struggles for status are a larger part of their lives as they try to find their footing in the world and have to defend themselves against the aggressive behavior of their peers.

Evidence that our cultural ethos has been unduly influenced by the standards of aggressive young men appeared in an interview with the great basketball player Kareem Abdul-Jabbar when his book *Black Profiles in Courage* was published. At the age of forty-nine, Abdul-Jabbar had a different view of admirable behavior than he had when he was younger. When he was a youth, he recalled, only the most aggressive public figures appealed to him; those who preached compassion rather than aggression and had a mild personal manner had struck him as weak. For example, about meeting the tennis player Arthur Ashe, he says, 'Arthur was very polite and he would not show his anger. And I thought less of him for it – until I got to know him.' A similar motive explains why he used to prefer Malcolm X to Martin Luther King, who 'was defiant, but he wasn't trying to get anybody killed . . . I thought that Dr Martin Luther King was too accommodating. I was about 35 years old before I could view Dr King with appreciation.'

This age, thirty-five, strikes a chord. Dr Ricardo Martinez notes that dangerously aggressive drivers are generally male, between the ages of eighteen and thirty-five.

Many cultures of the world have initiation rites that take young men out of day-to-day society and require them to prove themselves by personal trials and exploits. In addition to providing an outlet for their aggressive impulses, such initiation rites also serve to get them away from the rest of society at a time of their lives when their aggressive impulses could be dangerous. What we have done in our culture, in contrast, is to put young men at the center of our society: More and more value is placed on youth in hiring and in publicly visible positions. The move to institute term limits for elected officials is also evidence of this impulse: Get the old guys out and make way for younger ones (though in the Senate they must be over thirty). It's downright scary to think of a country run by aggressive young men without the tempering effect of elders.

## NATURE AND NURTURE

Any discussion of patterns that tend to distinguish men and women raises the question: What are the sources of these patterns? Surely a biological component plays a part in the greater use of agonism among men, but cultural influence can override biological inheritance. Anthropologists Beatrice and John Whiting compared children playing in six vastly different parts of the world. One of their most consistent findings, across all these cultures, was that boys, at all ages, were significantly more aggressive than girls. This seems to support the biological basis for males' aggressive behavior. But they also note that in all six cultures, girls were more often given responsibility to care for younger siblings, spent more time at home with their mothers, and did more housekeeping and cooking chores. In Kenya, boys who had to perform household chores because they had no sisters who could do them turned out to be less aggressive than other boys. This supports the argument that conditioning accounts for aggressive behavior. For our concerns, it hardly matters what percentage of influence is cultural versus biological; what matters is that the patterns exist and we have to understand them and then decide whether we want to encourage or attempt to modify them.

Parents and caretakers play a major role in determining which impulses children learn to develop and which to avoid. Imagine an American child reporting to his parents, 'Billy keeps hitting me.' It is not uncommon for parents to respond, 'Then hit him back.' It is even common to hear of parents taking their young sons for karate or boxing lessons so they can improve their chances of prevailing in fights. According to Margery Wolf, Chinese parents would never encourage their children to be aggressive; in fact, she says, a child could retaliate against another child simply by informing the other child's parents of the aggressive behavior. The parents could then be counted on to punish their child. Another study had similar results. University students from five different cultures were asked if they would permit aggressive behavior in their children. The highest percentage of affirmative responses came from Americans (61 percent) compared with the lowest from Chinese from Taiwan (19 percent) and Thais (5 percent). When asked if they would ever actually encourage aggressive behavior, the American percentage went down to a still considerable 29 percent, compared to 6 percent for the Chinese and 5 percent for Thais.

These studies report only what people say they would do, not what they actually do. Another study asked Taiwanese and American mothers to keep track of actual incidents involving their children's aggressive behavior. In keeping with the assumption that what differs from culture to culture is not so much the children's impulses but the parents' responses, Niem and Collard found that the parents reported roughly the same number of aggressive episodes, but according to the parents' reports only two of the Chinese children were spanked, compared to eleven of the Americans. In other words, it appears that not only are American parents more likely to permit or encourage physical aggression, they are also more likely to model it by spanking their children. (That Chinese children are *discouraged* from *physical* aggression attests that they do engage in it – else there would be nothing to discourage – and is not meant to imply that they do not engage in *verbal* aggression.)

So the patterns that typify women's and men's styles of opposition and conflict are the result of both biology and culture. Pulling these influences apart is impossible. What matters for us is that the pattern is there. Like parents faced with children's unavoidable conflicts, we have to decide whether or not we want to encourage, discourage, or channel aggressive responses, and under which circumstances. Do we always want to tell each other, in effect, 'Hit him back!' or do we sometimes want to look for other, more constructive ways of dealing with conflicts?

# 7

# What Other Ways Are There?:
# Listening to Other Cultures

We tend to feel that the way we do things, say things, think about things is only logical – common sense, human nature. The level of aggression that seems appropriate, and ways of expressing agreement or disagreement, come to seem natural – the obvious way to communicate emotions and intentions. But people growing up in different cultures have very different ideas about what is natural and very different assumptions about human nature. Observing how people in other cultures deal with conflict, disagreement, and aggression can give new perspectives in our attempts to manage conflict and use opposition in constructive rather than destructive ways. The cross-cultural view provides a glimpse of possibilities – how similar ends can be achieved with different means. It can help answer the question, If there are problems with the argument culture, what other ways are there? It can also deepen our understanding of the positive functions of agonism, or ceremonial fighting.

## HOW MUCH CONFRONTATION IS
## CONFRONTATIONAL?

An American woman of European descent (her mother was Italian, her father Jewish Hungarian) who grew up in New York City went to live for a time in the Netherlands. She was dismayed to discover that the Dutch often saw her as far too confrontational. At times she felt they regarded her as something of a monster. But the same style earned her opposite reactions in Israel, where people felt she was too much of a lady. They complained, 'We don't know where you stand.' Her style hadn't changed; it just looked very different in comparison to the contrasting norms of Dutch and Israeli culture. The level of confrontation considered normal by the Dutch was lower than what she had grown up with; the level considered appropriate by the Israelis was higher.

Jewish tradition requires people to speak up and protest when they disagree, and many individuals of Eastern European background (like those of Mediterranean, Armenian, African, South American, and many other backgrounds as well) enjoy friendly contentiousness, lively argument, and bantering opposition. In India and Sri Lanka, people are often expected to be confrontational; in Bali, they are generally not allowed to be. A linguist who spent many years in Bali commented that emotional arguments are almost unheard of there, so Balinese who come to the United States are frightened when they experience one. Yet Americans, for their part, can be if not frightened, then certainly put off, by the level of confrontation they encounter in some European countries – or in the homes of other Americans.

### 'IF WE CAN FIGHT, WE'RE CLOSE'

People in many cultures feel that arguing is a sign of closeness. This can be startling to Americans who go to such countries in Europe as Germany, France, Italy, or Greece. For example, many American students who have spent time in France comment on their French families' and friends' bluntness and taste for dynamic argument. In France, as in many other countries, agreement is deemed boring; to keep things interesting, you have to disagree – preferably with great animation. Students in my classes provided many accounts from their own experience. Joanna Repczynski, for example, recalled her year in France:

> During one dinner my host mother ran through a litany of subjects, changing them every time I agreed or when there was general agreement. She would bring up one controversial topic after another, looking to start a heated intellectual debate over dinner.

Another country in which lively argument is valued is Germany. An American student majoring in political science with a special focus on Central America spent his junior year abroad in Germany. Years later, he still recalled with frustration conversations with German students who, early in their acquaintance, regaled him with their conviction that American foreign policy in Central America was self-serving, destructive, and generally venal, made worse by the hypocritical American claims to high-minded motives. The American student disagreed with his German verbal attackers and knew of numerous specific facts to counter their claims, but he found himself unable to respond – not for lack of language (his German was fluent) but because he was so taken aback by their manner: Their aggressive approach seemed hostile and rude. In order to counter their charges he would have had to respond in kind, something he did not want to do, since he did not want to be like them.

German-born linguist Heidi Byrnes relates this tale in explaining why Americans and Germans have negative stereotypes about each other. Germans tend to assume that intelligence and knowledge should be displayed through aggressive argumentation and forceful disputation of others' arguments. This behavior results in American students' impressions that German students are self-aggrandizing, pigheaded, given to facile right/wrong dichotomies, and generally inclined to put people on the defensive and humiliate them publicly. Conversely, Americans' refusal to engage in arguments in this way leads Germans to conclude that American students are superficial, uncommitted, ignorant, and unwilling (or, more likely, unable) to take a stand.

An Israeli professor visiting the United States had the opposite experience. When she met an American scholar prominent in her field, she almost immediately launched into a rundown of the points on which she disagreed. She hoped thereby to show the American how carefully she had read her work – and begin a fruitful exchange of ideas. But the American professor was offended by the assault: She did not consider it appropriate to begin an acquaintance by criticizing. Not eager to let herself in for more of the same, the American professor assiduously avoided the Israeli visitor for the remainder of her stay, exactly the opposite of what the visitor had hoped to accomplish.

You do not have to go to a foreign country to experience these cultural differences. Americans of different ethnic backgrounds can experience them just by making friends. After my class discussed these issues, Andrea Talarico wrote:

> I find it amusing how the last girl to raise her hand in class today discussed how in the Italian family voices would be raised and objects would be thrown in an intense discussion over which television show to watch, whereas in the British household a serious disagreement could be undertaken without any apparent show of emotion or distress. My Italian-American family is much the same as the Italian family. My friends have often crept up to my room in fear when the screaming begins and don't understand or believe me when I stress that what's going on is no big deal.

Andrea sees advantages to her Italian-American family's style: 'We always know how each other feels at all times.'

A Japanese woman who is happily married to a Frenchman recalls that she spent much of the first two years of their relationship in tears. He frequently started arguments with her, which she found so upsetting that she did her best to agree and be conciliatory. This only led him to seek another point on which to argue. Finally, she lost her self-control and began to yell back. Rather than being angered, he was overjoyed. Provoking arguments was his way of showing interest in her, letting her know how much he respected her intelligence. To him, being able to engage in spirited disagreement was a sign of a good relationship.

It is not simply the idea of arguing but the form it takes – the level of opposition and the way it is expressed – that accounts for surprise, confusion, or alarm when people of one cultural background encounter those of another expressing disagreement or conflict. I doubt there is any culture in which there isn't some form of opposition that can be a sign of intimacy.

Even in Japan, for example, the ability to argue can be taken as evidence of intimacy. Kimberly Jones observed that the Japanese sometimes refer to conflict as positive, even though references to harmony are more frequent. One example she gives illustrates how conflict can create solidarity among those who take the same side. Two men, Nakamura and Watanabe, were discussing the graduate program each had attended at different times. Nakamura mentioned two students who had quit before finishing. When asked why that happened, he explained that they had never really become part of the group. They had not joined the others in encouraging each other or in bad-mouthing their teachers, so they could not take advantage of the group support as the other students did. In other words, bad-mouthing the teachers was necessary to build solidarity with the other students.

Talking against teachers is very different from arguing with someone who is actually there, but positive conflict was not limited to the kind directed at absent parties. As the conversation continued, Nakamura asked whether things had been any different when Watanabe was in the program. Watanabe replied, No, the students in his time did not form factions but were a cohesive unit. Nakamura then asked, 'Did everyone get along?' Humorously, Watanabe replied, 'No one got along!' and added, 'Everyone arguing and stuff.' Here, Jones explains, the ability to argue openly was a sign of intimacy: The students in the program were a cohesive unit *because* they could argue with each other openly.

These examples all show that arguing can be a way of establishing intimacy, though the level, type, and context by which it does so can differ from one culture to another.

---

## AGGRESSION IN A CULTURE OF HARMONY

Asian cultures, such as Japanese, Chinese, Thai, and Vietnamese, place great value on avoiding open expression of disagreement and conflict because they emphasize harmony. It might at first seem incongruous to Americans that Asian cultures are also extremely hierarchical. Americans tend to associate peaceful relations with equal relations and hierarchical ones with animosity. The assumption is that those lower on the hierarchy necessarily resent those who are higher up. But Asian culture is based on different assumptions. Far from threatening harmony, Asians believe, strict hierarchy ensures it: Power relations are fixed, and fixed relations ensure inclusion in the group, that in turn promotes intimacy.

Every culture has means of expressing disagreement and conflict. Cultures that emphasize harmony have ways that may be surprising – and enlightening – to those that emphasize opposition. Again, Japan offers an example.

In 1992, there was a political scandal in Japan. The former prime minister, Noboru Takeshita, was accused of enlisting the aid of organized crime to stop a public harassment campaign against him that had been mounted by an opposing political party. This 'harassment campaign,' according to Japanese sociolinguist Haru Yamada, depicted the then prime minister 'as a great leader with integrity and honor matched by no other.'

Huh? How can praise be a form of harassment? Yamada explains that the answer lies in contrasting American and Japanese customs with regard to giving praise. It is common for Americans to offer extravagant praise both publicly (in award and recognition ceremonies) and privately (with expressions like 'Great!,' 'Good job!,' and 'Terrific!'). Self-evidently good as this may seem to Americans (we tend to assume that praise is a natural motivator – and my own research suggests that for most Americans it is), Japanese tend to regard such displays as inappropriate and embarrassing. According to Yamada, the minimal human unit in Japan is not the individual but the group, so praising someone who is close to you in your personal or professional life comes off sounding like praising yourself – in other words, boasting. (This difference contributes to the Japanese stereotype of Americans as immature braggarts: Not only our greater inclination to mention our own accomplishments but also our habit of heaping praise on friends, relatives, and coworkers gives this impression.)

Because Japanese are not expected to pile on praise, when they do so, it is interpreted as sarcasm. Also, since everyone knows that criticism will not be expressed directly, they are attuned to indirect means of expressing it. An example Yamada gives is a comment like 'What a healthy, well-built young girl you are!' – said to a child who is obviously overweight. In this spirit, making exalting comments about a public figure leads everyone to conclude that the opposite is true. That is the logic by which piling on inflated praise can amount to a harassment campaign that the Japanese press dubbed *homegoroshi*, 'to kill with praise.' The opposition party tried to praise their opponent to death.

Praising someone to death is not an isolated verbal strategy. The meaning of words comes not from their dictionary definitions but from how people in a community use them. Given the Japanese emphasis on harmony, it is not surprising that Japanese insults are often ironic variants of literally positive utterances. Nicholas Kristof, the Tokyo bureau chief for *The New York Times*, was surprised to hear the English word 'jerk' in the midst of a Japanese conversation. He asked about the Japanese word for 'jerk' – and was told there isn't any. He then considered the literal meanings of some vicious Japanese insults. One of the words translates as 'your honorable self'; one for a woman translates as 'nun.' He comments that women would probably rather be called nuns than female dogs, but I suspect this depends on which culture they grew up in. Words carry the emotional freight of the way they are used.

This is not to imply that there is no direct expression of aggression in Asian cultures. The Taiwanese Parliament, for example, is known to be so conflict-ridden that physical fights have broken out between members. The American evening news once showed a brief clip of two members of the Chinese Parliament – a woman and a man – swinging wildly at each other while their colleagues struggled to pull them apart. Linguist Sai-hua Kuo, who has studied disagreements in the Taiwanese Parliament, believes that because the Chinese have no tradition of direct expression of political disagreement in public, the parliamentary system, with its requirement for open opposition, strikes them as a no-holds-barred situation. In other words, opposition is most likely to get out of control when there are no culturally agreed upon rules or rituals in place for expressing and negotiating it.

---

### LETTING IT ALL OUT: RITUAL VITUPERATION

---

Many traditional societies have developed and maintained ways of managing conflict by ritualized genres that provide outlets so aggression can be expressed without erupting in violence. One such ritualized genre has been observed in a traditional Chinese village. Michael Bond and Wang Sung-Hsing found that a practice reported in 1900 was still widespread in 1983: 'reviling the street' – a verbal genre that allows individuals to express hostile emotions. Its ritual nature is key. This is how the practice was described in 1900:

> The moment that a quarrel begins abusive words . . . are poured forth in a filthy stream to which nothing in the English language offers any parallel . . . Women use even viler language than men, and continue it longer . . . The practice of 'reviling the street' is often indulged in by women, who mount the flat roof of the house and shriek away for hours at a time . . . If the day is a hot one the reviler bawls as long as he (or she) has breath, then proceeds to refresh himself by a session of fanning, and afterwards returns to the attack with renewed fury.

This description of 'reviling the street' has much in common with a similar practice in a very different culture: Anthropologist Don Kulick observed that women in Gapun, Papua New Guinea, when angered by husbands, relatives, or fellow villagers, can erupt in a *kros*, shouting insults and obscenities loudly enough to be heard all around. Villagers stop what they are doing to listen or get closer. The screaming woman stays near or (preferably) inside her house and often waits until the offender is at some distance or even gone from the village. Were she to venture from the house or engage the offender in direct dialogue, she would risk escalation to actual violence. Though there is a ritual aspect to the display (it follows rules and structures that Kulick describes), it is provoked by genuine anger.

Widely disparate cultures often have comparable verbal rituals. Nigerian anthropologist Tope Omoniyi describes 'song-lashing,' which has much in common with the New Guinea *kros* and Chinese 'reviling the street,' though it is very different in some ways.

Performed primarily (but not exclusively) by teenage girls living in rural, traditional Nigerian villages, song-lashing can consist of familiar proverbs or original verses. In either case, they heap insults on a listener or overhearer. Like the *kros*, song-lashing seems at first to be a very aggressive verbal genre to be practiced by girls, but in stark contrast to the *kros*, the target is usually not named but referred to obliquely. That's why it is considered too weak to be used by men, who are supposed to confront their opponents directly. The song-lashing is not obscene; songs that include taboo words are usually sung by boys. Here, too, onlookers play a crucial role. They enjoy the display as a form of entertainment (effective song-lashers are admired for their verbal skill) while providing a safety valve: If real violence threatens to break out, onlookers intervene to stop it.

All these monologue types – reviling the street, the *kros*, and song-lashing – are effective precisely because they are culturally enshrined, ritualized genres for expressing anger and opposition. They all have their own contexts, structures, and rules, as well as culturally agreed-upon ways for other community members to take part. An audience gives the speaker the satisfaction of being listened to, but it also serves as a precaution: Onlookers prevent the verbal expression from leading to physical violence.

---

## MODULATING OPPOSITIONS

---

The Japanese woman who married a Frenchman was telling me about their wedding. When she mentioned that the ceremony was conducted by a Catholic priest, I asked how their respective families felt about their marrying outside their religions. They did not marry outside their religions, she said. They were both raised Catholic; their Catholicism was a point of shared heritage. I was surprised. 'I thought most Japanese were Buddhist or Shinto,' I said. 'Well, yes,' she said. 'I was raised that, too.' After the Second World War, her mother was schooled by American Catholic nuns who instilled their religion along with education. Her mother converted, but the family did not abandon Buddhist and Shinto practices. My friend recalls that in addition to worshiping Jesus, she prayed at a Buddhist shrine to her grandfather and periodically gave him gifts, such as his favorite cigarettes. (When it became widely known that tobacco was harmful, however, family members stopped including cigarettes in their offerings.)

It is almost self-evident to Americans that people can observe only one religion: If you adopt a new one, you abandon the old. But Shinto and Buddhism are more inclusive – and therefore less polarizing. Western culture is suffused with oppositions where Asian cultures are not.

---

## THE SELF VERSUS SOCIETY

Perhaps most fundamental is the Western assumption that the individual self is in ongoing opposition to society. You can hear this in everyday conversations, as people talk about learning to be true to themselves by resisting society's expectations. Donal Carbaugh listened to hours of talk on the Phil Donahue show and found that a conflict between society and the individual self was a pervasive theme running through the comments of guests and audience members. For example, one guest expressed the hope that women would learn to 'make a decision all by themselves without regard to what society or somebody else says.' Society is seen as the individual's enemy, imposing demands that conflict with actualizing your own self. The concept of the individual self in opposition to society is foreign to most Asians as well as members of many (if not most) other world cultures, such as Africans, for whom the self exists only in relation to others – family members, clan members, covillagers, and so on. In this view, you are who you are because of your place in a social network.

The American inclination to regard the self as an individual rather than a social phenomenon shows up in our Declaration of Independence. I was a lucky member of a behind-the-scenes tour at the Library of Congress that included a visit to the Conservation Laboratory, where technicians labor to preserve old and decaying books of historic value. Our guide called our attention to a book open upon a table. This book, he told us, was where Thomas Jefferson found the phrase 'pursuit of happiness.' Fascinated, I hung back to read the context in which the phrase appeared and was astounded to see that it was used not in the sense in which it appears in the Declaration of Independence – the individual's right to pursue personal happiness – but rather in the phrase, 'an equal pursuit of the happiness of all.'

The author of the 1751 volume, Henry Home, is claiming that only 'principles of action' that are 'adapted to our nature' can move people to action. 'Our nature,' he writes, 'so far as it concerns action, is made up of appetites, passions and affections.' The 'moral sense' or 'conscience' can serve as a brake, restraining us from acting on our impulses, but it cannot be the prime mover to action. The phrase 'pursuit of happiness' appears in the example Home offers to illustrate this point:

> For example, if it be laid down as a primary law of nature, that we are strictly bound to advance the good of all, regarding our own interest no further than as it makes a part of the general happiness, we may safely reject such a law as inconsistent with our nature, unless it be made to appear, that there is a principle of benevolence in man which prompts him to an equal pursuit of the happiness of all.

In other words, Home is saying it would be useless to require people to look out for themselves only insofar as their desires are also good for society as a whole, unless it turns out that it is in our nature to put others' happiness on a par with our own. Home does not say here whether he believes this impulse is in our nature or not, but the phrase 'pursuit of happiness' is used in the sense of the good of all. Jefferson transposed it to apply to the individual's right to pursue his or her own happiness. This, it seems to me, reflects the American view of the world as an aggregation of individuals whose personal rights are central, in contrast to the sense of self in many other cultures, which see the individual self only in relation to others and where responsibilities to family members trump the individual's rights to pursue personal happiness.

## DUALISMS AND NONDUALITY

We can learn from other cultures without unrealistically romanticizing them. Writing about traditional Chinese thought, Derk Bodde tried to capture, without idealizing, the significant implications of a culture that values harmony where Western culture values opposition. The Chinese have engaged in wars. What is different, he wrote in 1953, is that they never glorified war as Western culture has. Chinese philosophy certainly deals in dualisms such as human beings/the natural world, 'quiescence and movement,' the often-heard-about yin and yang. But they regard these polarities 'as complementary and necessary partners, interacting to form a higher synthesis, rather than as irreconcilable and eternally warring opposites.' Similarly, sociolinguist Linda Young notes that the yin-yang figure is 'constantly revolving,' and 'the dark patch and light patch . . . each contains a smaller patch of the other.' This aspect of Chinese philosophy has been called 'nonduality,' because it contrasts with the Western tendency to think in polarized dualisms.

One problem with polarized dualisms is that areas of overlap or similarity are obscured as we look only for points of contrast. Aspects of an issue – or of a person – that do not fit easily into one or the other polarity are rendered invisible or unacceptable. A dramatic example is the way Americans deal with 'intersex' babies – a small but significant percentage of births – who are not clearly male or female. Some children are born with ambiguous genitalia (for example, a phallus that is larger than the average clitoris but shorter than the average penis); others have sex chromosomes or internal reproductive organs that do not match their genital appearance.

Cheryl Chase, who founded the Intersex Society of North America, notes that all species – not just humans – that have male and female forms also have in-between forms. But in American culture, there can be only two. And our determination to keep it that way has led us to drastic measures: Since the late 1950s, the standard approach in the United States has been to 'fix' intersex children, to press them into the mold of one sex or the other through surgery, begun as early as possible after birth and typically involving multiple procedures. Most are transformed into girls – though often girls without sexual function, since their small penises (or large clitorises) are removed, usually for surgical convenience. As one surgeon put it, 'You can dig a hole, but you can't build a pole.'

The wisdom of this approach has recently been questioned by adults who underwent such surgery as children and now attest that the devastating problems they have faced in their lives resulted not from their intersexuality but from the torments and complications of surgery combined with the secrecy and shame surrounding what was done to them.

The wide acceptance of this surgical approach is evidence of our culture's devotion to a dualistic notion of sexual identity. Other cultures provide an alternative view: Anthropologists have observed cultures that accept and in some cases place special value on inter-sexed people. Gilbert Herdt describes Native American cultures that recognize a 'third sex.' Will Roscoe found that among the Zuni, a native North American tribe, the death of a 'Zuni man-woman' was met with 'universal regret and distress.' In Navaho tradition, those who were not clearly male or female, called *berdache*, were believed to be divinely blessed individuals who brought luck and blessings to others. A Navaho told anthropologist W. W. Hill in 1935, 'They are leaders, just like President Roosevelt' – and without them, Navahos would be lost.

If a stark male-female polarity, one of the bedrocks of our Western devotion to dualism, is a reflection more of our cultural view than of the natural world, how many other phenomena that we polarize can be understood in less dualistic ways?

## VICTORS WITHOUT VANQUISHED

Asian culture offers an alternative to the Western tendency to regard many situations as win-lose propositions: If you don't win, you lose, and losing is so complete that it is to be avoided at all costs. But in Japanese tradition, winners and losers both have their place and are expected to coexist, the losers retaining a large measure of respect. An anthropologist who studies Japanese culture, Ben-Ami Shillony, calls this a system of 'victors without vanquished' – a system that he says has helped Japan avoid disastrous internecine ethnic and religious strife.

How can there be a victor without a vanquished? According to Shillony, the history and nature of conflict and struggle in Japan, starting with the first known great political and religious struggles several thousand years ago and continuing through feudal, imperial, and postwar Japan, present a pattern by which one group in each major historical struggle 'won' but the other did not lose – that is, it did not lose everything but was allowed to remain in existence. For example, in a large revolution in 1868, reforms were made after a Western rather than Chinese model, yet the people who had fought for the old regime were not punished but invited to join the new government (and most did). Shillony believes this pattern reflects a long tradition of accommodation in internal affairs, though, importantly, this approach to conflict was not carried over into foreign relations or colonial policies.

This pattern of accommodation is also the reason that Japan has avoided widespread religious conflict, according to Michael Ashkenazi. Just as my Japanese friend was raised Catholic but also prayed at Buddhist shrines, Ashkenazi shows how potential conflict in the religious sphere is 'avoided, mitigated, muted, or resolved' in a Japanese town. Two religions – Buddhism and Shinto – coexist in the town. Priests from each religion are at times required to take part in the other religion's ceremonies. Because religion is regarded as private rather than public, people may attend a public religious ritual they do not subscribe to, then return home to conduct the ritual in their own way. In a spirit similar to 'victor without vanquished,' a consolidation of Shinto churches resulted in one church losing its rank – but, to make up for this, it was later given some economic advantages.

In all these ways, Asian philosophy and culture suggest alternatives to the polarization that typifies Western culture: accommodating more than one religion, avoiding rigid dualisms, and subscribing to an ethic of victor without vanquished rather than winner take all. These are also ways of putting into practice an emphasis on harmony, in contrast to the Western emphasis on polarized opposition.

The concept of harmony goes back to Confucius and is pervasive in Chinese culture, which is not to say that conflicts do not arise. Quite the contrary; social pressure to maintain harmony can actually cause conflict. There are two major dynamics in human relations: the power dimension (Who has the ability to force others to comply?) and the connection dimension (How close or distant are you?). These two dimensions are inextricably intertwined: Being in a power relation with someone entails a kind of closeness; it is someone with whom you have no relationship at all from whom you are most distant. And being close to someone entails power, because people close to you can make demands on you that could never be made by others. The resulting demands cause conflict.

In just this way, Japanese anthropologist Takie Sugiyama Lebra points out that those who place more value on social interdependence, cooperation, and harmony are more likely to interfere with one another's actions – and this interference leads to more rather than less conflict. She quotes Ronald Dore's observation that 'competition within a group which is in theory harmoniously united tends to become fiercer and more emotionally involved than in one where competition is accepted as normal.' (This may help explain why conflict is often more prolonged and more upsetting to women friends than to men friends in the American context.) The people who can hurt you the most are often those closest to you, and it is in the closest relationships that deep hostilities and tensions often develop over time.

---

## 'MIND MY OWN BUSINESS!': IT TAKES A VILLAGE TO SETTLE DISPUTES

---

It is almost an article of faith for many Americans that disputes should be settled by the disputing parties without outside interference. Parents often send their children back to the playroom or playground with instructions to settle fights for themselves. Relatives and friends can be heard to say, 'It's between the two of you. I'm not getting in the middle.' The Western view of intermediaries is reflected in the fate of Mercutio in Shakespeare's *Romeo and Juliet:* When he tries to break up a sword fight between his friend Romeo and Romeo's enemy Tybalt, Mercutio is accidentally speared and killed, living just long enough to utter the now-famous curse 'A plague on both your houses!' Even psychologists tend to regard it as a sign of maturity when someone settles disputes without third parties, whose intervention may be regarded as unhealthy and inappropriate enmeshment.

Yet many peoples of the world expect conflicts to be resolved by intermediaries. This reflects an emphasis on harmony and interdependence: the tendency to see individuals as located inextricably in a social network, in contrast to Americans' tendency to glorify independence and see the individual as the fundamental human unit. To manage disputes ranging from private family matters to public conflicts between villages, cultures develop habitual ethics and formal proceedings, just as we have assumptions about how to fight fair as well as legal trials. Some cultures have ways of settling private disputes that involve the participation of others; these can be formally ritualized events or informal ways of involving the community in settling disputes. We cannot simply adopt the rituals of another culture, but thinking about them can give us pause and perhaps even ideas for devising our own new ways to manage conflict.

Japanese culture provides an example. Agnes Niyekawa examined conflicts in a popular Japanese television series. The basic plot of the series revolved around generational conflicts between a father – a retired Navy officer with outdated views – and his two sons. In these family dramas, conflicts were always solved through the intervention of friends and relatives.

In one episode, for example, the father objects to his son's choice of a bride because she works as a bar hostess. To prevent the marriage, he pretends to be dying, calls his friends (two couples) to his side, and makes a deathbed request that they make sure his son does not marry a woman who works in a food service job. But the son soon arrives with Mariko, his intended, and the wife of one friend reveals that she too worked as a bar hostess before her marriage, because, like Mariko, she had no other way to fulfill her obligation to support her family. This forces the father to rethink his intransigence, which melts entirely when he learns that Mariko has quit her job – at the behest of her own friends and relatives. The father's friends then offer her a job at their restaurant. All the action in this episode is motivated by the social network rather than individual will: not only in the father's attempts to rope his friends into preventing his son's marriage but also in Mariko's decision first to take a job as a bar hostess and then to give it up, because of her family. The ultimate solution comes in the form of a job offer by the father's friends.

Takie Sugiyama Lebra explains the many benefits that Japanese see in using intermediaries to settle disputes. For one thing, intermediaries provide a motivation to settle the conflict: to save face for them. A go-between can also offer the needed apology without the principal losing face and can absorb rejections without taking them personally. This benefit is particularly clear in the use of matchmakers or marriage brokers, a practice common in many cultures of the world: It avoids the risk of a potential bride (or her family) rejecting a suitor to his face. Finally, intermediaries can put pressure on someone to act properly without risking the direct conflict that can ensue when people make demands for their own benefit, as when neighbors pressure a son or daughter-in-law to stop neglecting a parent or parent-in-law. In other words, community pressure takes the place of a humiliating one-on-one confrontation: 'You never call me!'

Using third parties to settle disputes is not limited to Asian societies. Many cultures of the Pacific also make habitual use of this practice, often in the form of rituals in the sense that they are formalized enough to have names and standard structures or rules. As in Asian culture, they typically draw on hierarchical relations to maintain harmony.

In native Hawaiian culture, for example, there is a word, *ho'-oponopono* ('to set things right'), for a ceremony in which family members invite an elder or other high-ranking mediator to oversee the resolution of a dispute. As described by Stephen Boggs and Malcolm Naea Chun, the leader invites disputants to air their feelings and encourages them to apologize and forgive each other. The leader calls on a higher power – God and Church – to offer forgiveness, too. Hierarchical social relations play a major role, as they do in another ritual, *ho-opapa*, a verbal contest of wits and insults that can be played either for fun or in earnest combat, to establish superiority between rivals. But in the case of the dispute resolution ritual, there is no competition for superiority among the disputants, who are equal in their subordination to the elder who brokers the truce.

Karen Watson-Gegeo and David Gegeo describe a similar ritual among the Kwara'ae of the Solomon Islands. *Fa'amanata'anga* is held at home, in private, within a family, often after a meal. Here, too, hierarchical social relations are key: The ritual is presided over by a senior family member, who brings the weight of his standing to the peace-making mission and also emphasizes both his own stature and the seriousness of the event by speaking in a formal, high rhetoric to exhort the disputants to end their conflict.

One of the most intriguing accounts of how disputes are settled in this part of the world, described by Lamont Lindstrom, is found on the island of Tanna in the South Pacific. Conflicts among villagers or between villages are discussed publicly by groups of adult men at special meetings that last all day. These meetings differ strikingly from our idea of conflict resolution in that they are not designed to reconcile the individual accounts of disputing parties and elicit the truth of what happened. Instead, all the people present, disputants as well as others, come to a public agreement about what happened and how the conflict should be settled. They speak of these events not as competitions or warfare among opposing interests but as voyages through space in which they all take part – joint journeys in which all travelers reach the same destination. They perceive the conclusion not as a balancing of competing individual interests or even a compromise but of a consensus flowing from the interaction of all. Here, too, hierarchy plays a role, as the ones who begin to articulate the sense of the group tend to be those with greater social standing. These meetings do not always settle disputes once and for all, but the very participation of the disputants overcomes a degree of antagonism and displays a willingness to come to some meeting of minds.

A Fijian Indian community offers yet another contrast. According to Donald Brenneis, it is not common in this culture for outsiders to get involved in settling disputes. But there are times when disputes arise among men that others feel are serious enough to require intervention. A committee is formed that interviews disputants and witnesses beforehand, in order to compare accounts and to formulate questions to ask at the formal proceeding, called a *pancayat*. Like *nemawashi*, the Japanese custom of consulting individuals in private prior to a meeting, this seems a much better way of gathering information than forcing people to speak in a high-pressure public event. Typically, one party is not blamed; instead it is shown that both parties are guilty of minor errors and no one is seriously at fault. A common comment on the process is 'There were two wrongs and now it is right,' an interesting variation on our 'Two wrongs don't make a right.'

All these examples show that the intervention of others can be effective in settling disputes, especially when the intervention is part of culturally ritualized proceedings.

## RITUAL FIGHTING

Just as rituals for settlings disputes are invaluable cultural resources, so the benefits of ritual fighting – as compared to the real thing – stand out in relief when viewed against the backdrop of an unfamiliar culture. Seeing the elaboration of these rituals in different forms helps us understand the role that ritual opposition can play: not only to reinforce, display, achieve, and challenge status, but also to reinforce social bonds and alliances and as a safety valve for the expression of opposition.

Bali and Crete offer insights into how culturally sanctioned and structured opposition – ritual fighting – can reinforce and forge alliances. Clifford Geertz's description of cockfighting in Bali and Michael Herzfeld's of sheep rustling in Crete have much in common. In both cases, a formal agonistic system exists that has a long cultural history and is fundamental to the fabric of the society. In both cases, the practice has been outlawed by a larger political entity.

The island of Bali is now part of Indonesia, and the Indonesian government (like the Dutch colonialists before it) has outlawed cockfighting because, according to Geertz, the elite regard it as unbecoming and embarrassing. But Geertz and his anthropologist wife, Hildred, were not long in the Balinese village they had chosen to study before they found themselves in the midst of a large cockfight organized by the village chief in the public square – an event that was summarily broken up by a surprise police raid. After extensive fieldwork in the village, Geertz learned that participating in cockfights is inextricably interwoven with the Balinese social fabric.

Men (this is one of the few areas of Balinese culture that is limited to men) raise cocks, which they lovingly tend and periodically pit against others' cocks in the public arena of the cockfight. (The Balinese word for 'cock' has the same double meaning that the English word has.) At the cockfight, people bet in complicated and formally structured ways. But the betting is not simply a matter of trying to pick the winner for financial gain, like gambling at a racetrack. On Bali, betting on cocks is a way of reinforcing or challenging status hierarchies and kinship alliances in the village.

(Once again, what for us is a matter of individual choice and consequence, in other cultures is inseparable from a complex social network.)

People are expected to bet on the cocks of their kin against the cocks of their enemies. But if a cockfight is held in a different village, everyone is expected to bet on the cock from his own village – and this is one way that solidarity can be created among former enemies. If feuding families patch up their differences, betting on each other's cocks is a way of formally demonstrating their rapprochement. And refusal to take part in this enterprise is not the mark of a prudent and refined citizen. Far from it; it is taken as a show of arrogance, evidence that a man thinks himself too good for the likes of his covillagers. In other words, betting on a cock is a requisite public display of support for and alliance with the man whose cock you bet on.

The Balinese cockfight does not reflect a highly agonistic society but just the opposite. Balinese obsessively avoid confrontational behavior in their everyday lives. And the cockfight is kept to highly co-operative rules. Geertz notes that he never heard anyone question the umpire's decision, either during a cockfight or after, although men certainly talked a lot about other aspects of the fights after they were over. How strikingly this contrasts with Western sports events, at which players and spectators loudly deride the umpires and referees, and commentators and conversationalists rehash their anger at what they saw as wrong calls long after the event.

The Balinese avoidance of confrontation in everyday life also contrasts with the expressively confrontational culture of Greece, yet Michael Herzfeld found on the island of Crete a situation in some ways comparable to what Geertz encountered on Bali many years before. When he arrived in the village, Herzfeld was told that sheep rustling did not go on there. For one thing, it was illegal, outlawed by the government of Greece, the nation of which Crete is a part. Greek law aside, the villagers told Herzfeld that they would not participate in such a primitive, unbecoming activity. However, just as the Geertzes found themselves suddenly treated as in-group members because they behaved like the local Balinese when caught in a raid on a cockfight, Herzfeld discovered that when he learned to speak the local dialect, he was accepted as an in-group member and began hearing tales of sheep rustling (always and only told in dialect) until he became aware that not only was this practice still very much alive among these villagers, but it was, like the cockfight for the Balinese, highly ritualized and fundamental to the social fabric of village society.

On Crete, Herzfeld found, stealing sheep (and vengeance killing) regularly led to the forging of alliances – and even marriages. When families were caught up in a spiral of reciprocal attacks, one way of ending the feud was for heads of the warring households to marry off their children to each other as a sign of peace, as if the Capulets and Montagues had forced Romeo and Juliet to marry in order to bring the families' feud to an end. Herzfeld writes of a novelist from the region, Andreas Nenedakis, whose parents married in just this way: Nenedakis's father's family had been engaged in a reciprocal raiding relationship with his mother's family – and his parents were married to each other in order to end the feud.

Both cockfighting on Bali and sheep rustling on Crete are agonistic rituals that bind the members of a community rather than separate them. It is especially interesting that this is so for both Bali and Greece, since the two cultures are so different in their attitudes toward verbal aggression. On Bali, conflict and open confrontation are rare; on Crete, as in the rest of Greece and throughout the Mediterranean, contentiousness is expected and valued in social interaction. Yet these two vastly different cultures have agonistic rituals that function in many parallel ways to structure and negotiate alliances and hostilities among their members.

In both these cases, the ritual nature of the conflicts is key. This means that there are culturally prescribed ways of conducting and containing the opposition they enact. These two examples also show the futility, and even the danger, of trying to prevent ritual fighting that is fundamental to the culture in which it serves so many purposes. The Indonesian authorities on Bali, and the Greek authorities on Crete, succeeded in driving the disapproved customs underground but not in eradicating them. Sometimes when ritual fighting is disrupted, real fighting takes its place.

## 'HOLD ME COAT!':
### RITUAL FIGHTING IN IRELAND

Fights do not have to involve animals or birds to be ritual. Fights between humans can also be ritual – not only in a boxing or wrestling ring but on the streets of a neighborhood or on the small, isolated Gaelic-speaking island of Tory in Ireland, as described by Robin Fox. Whereas the Balinese allow cocks to fight in their place, and the Greeks steal each other's sheep, the Tory islanders fight each other – but their fights are no less ritualized. Living on Tory Island, Fox observed that fights among men were frequent, yet it was rare for anyone to get hurt. Although they seemed at first to break out at random, Fox figured out that the fights erupted when certain circumstances prevailed, and that they followed certain rules – not rules in the sense that the players could recount them but rules in the sense that an anthropologist could discern them. And on Tory Island, as on the islands of Bali and Crete, the fights were a way of displaying and negotiating kinship alliances and feuds.

Fights broke out only when there was a critical mass of onlookers, some of whom were kin of each individual involved in the fight and some of whom were kin to both (not difficult, I surmise, on an island of three hundred inhabitants). Under these circumstances, one man could loudly curse and threaten another, who could loudly curse and threaten back, and both could rely on their kin to restrain them, preventing them from hurting each other. Everything about the fight was structured so that the two men could seem eager to exchange blows without ever landing one. This paradox is embodied in a gesture that Fox describes: One man who threatens to hit another makes a display of taking off his coat, as he announces to his supporters, 'Hold me coat!' On the surface, this is a prelude to physical assault. But in reality, a man would get only as far as pulling his jacket off his back and down his arms, stopping at a point where his half-removed jacket effectively pinned his arms behind him. At that moment, the very gesture that symbolically announced his intention to fight immobilized his arms. His supporters would take it from there, struggling with him to push his jacket back on as they admonished him to keep his cool.

The fights would end when the mother of one combatant (or

another female relative if a mother could not be found) was brought into the fray, and the audience parted to make room for her. She would implore the fighter to come home and stop fighting. This gave the man the pretext to end the fight on the grounds that he could not deny his mother, who, he could aver, had saved his opponent from certain damage. As one fighter put it, 'I'd have had yer blood if me mother hadn't come. Ye can thank her that you're not in pieces on the road, ye scum.'

Since blows were never actually exchanged, one might well question whether what happened was really a fight. But Tory Islanders do not doubt that that's what it was. Indeed, as one such incident ended, a man turned to Fox and said, 'Well, and wasn't that the great fight, for sure?'

An outsider might ask, If no one is ever hurt and blows are not actually exchanged, why bother? Fox explains that, first, these fights were a form of entertainment, providing excitement for both participants and onlookers. Second, they became fodder for talk: Townspeople would discuss the details long after, and in the talking, the fight took on more violence and drama. Fights also provided a means for the participants to display their masculine prowess. The men who had taken part in a fight were regarded with increased respect for a time after, and they comported themselves with a bit more swagger and verbal aggression. Furthermore, they provided role models for boys. This comes clear in Fox's description of how the children behaved during these fights. Whereas 'Most of the little girls stood some way off with their mothers, who had banded together to deplore the episode – quietly,'

> all around milled little boys imitating their elders, cursing, fluffing, swaggering, threatening. It was particularly fascinating to see how the children learned the whole sequence of behavior. Anything that the men did, they would imitate, shouting the same things, strutting and swaggering.

Reading this, I recalled my own amusement, when I lived in Greece, at seeing little boys arguing with each other and adopting the same hand gestures, facial expressions, and ritualized imprecations that I had seen so often used by adult Greek men when they argued.

When the conditions for ritual fighting break down, an altercation can turn into the real thing, and people can be hurt. According to Fox, there were situations in which Tory Islanders became involved in literal fights and were badly hurt. This happened when they were in London bars, where the network of kin was not available to intervene.

All these examples of ritual fighting – cockfighting in Bali, sheep rustling in Crete, public fighting on Tory Island – are activities that only men take part in. Fox comments on this aspect: 'The whole thing is a peculiarly male affair. Women fight, but not over honor; their fighting is fierce and destructive, and almost inevitably ends in serious hurt to one of the partners.' Once again, it is not that women do not fight but that they do not tend to engage in ceremonial combat to negotiate status and display their prowess. It is not fighting per se that is more often associated with men but agonism – ceremonial combat.

## RITUAL STRIKES

It is not only in the world of sports that ritual opposition can avoid truly destructive rancor. The same is true for many important affairs of business and state. Yet again, Japan offers an instructive example.

There is a stereotype in the United States of idealized harmony between Japanese corporations or businesses and their employees. It might come as a surprise that periodic strikes are staged by Japanese workers, during which representatives of unions and management, in the words of anthropologist Eyal Ben-Ari, display 'militant posturing, present very rigid demands, and vow not to capitulate.' Union spokespersons 'castigate big business, the United States and the ruling elite' and 'emphasize the country-wide solidarity and militancy of the workers.' The answer to the puzzle is that these periodic strikes are ritual. The highly aggressive displays of hostility to management are part of the ritual: Even as they are going on, union leaders and management are working cooperatively behind the scenes to reach agreement. The strike simply ends when the negotiated agreement is announced.

Ben-Ari explains that preparations for the 'spring offensive' begin in October, when the unions combine to appoint a 'struggle committee,' which publishes a 'White Paper' listing scheduled offensive actions (which have been agreed upon by management), wage demands (which are based on consideration of economic information provided by management), and other aims of the strike (such as social programs). By February, workers are presented with a detailed timetable for strike action: not all-out work stoppage but a combination of half-day, full-day, and two-day strikes interspersed with workdays through the months of March through May. Before long one large company is chosen to announce an agreement, other companies follow suit, the workers abandon the strike, and union and management leaders resume playing golf together.

Another kind of staged strike is called a 'designated strike.' In this ritual, the striking workers never actually leave the workplace, so what occurs is more like a 'walk-in' than a 'walk-out.' At designated times, workers gather and display their opposition:

> General meetings are accompanied by a succession of aggress-
> ive postures and rolling cries precisely in the stereotype of the
> union image presented in the Japanese national press. Brave
> slogans, colorful banners, everyone in shirtsleeves, and poses
> before the camera with locked arms . . . are strictly observed.

During these strikes, too, highly cooperative negotiations are being conducted behind the scenes:

> Rather than viewing the bargaining process as a zero-sum
> game, both unions and management tend to see it as one which
> is guided by mutual contributions to the success of a joint ven-
> ture. Accordingly, union leaders are not averse to fraternizing
> with management (as, for instance, in the custom of drinking
> together), or to sharing information with them. Indeed, in
> recent years, managements have increasingly provided their
> employees' representatives with detailed and often confidential
> information on management policies and objectives.

Once agreement is reached, the strike is called off. This description is reminiscent of the way members of the Japanese Diet learned to deal with opposition between political parties: Though they continued to oppose each other in loud, rancorous terms, they gradually began working together behind the scenes to accomplish the goals of running the country, just as unions and management jointly found ways to run a profitable business while enacting the opposition between them – in a ritual way.

Ritual opposition provides a way of expressing polarity without letting it destroy one or both parties. Because these strikes have a ritual character, people can behave in ways they otherwise would not, including aggressive displays that Japanese culture generally discourages. Like Balinese, who can express open confrontation only while in a trance, or the tendency in many cultures (including Japanese and in some cases American) to discount behavior because someone was drunk, striking workers are free to behave in ways they otherwise would not because while striking they are in a sense not themselves. This is signaled by their signs, their slogans, and their very behavior: banding together to publicly display opposition to the company's management. In other words, having ritualized forms of opposition at their disposal can be like a safety valve for venting aggression without shedding blood. This is one of the most important functions of ritual opposition.

## RITUAL SLAYING OF THE KING

Politics is a domain that necessarily entails conflict and opposition. Anthropologists observing African cultures have written about agonistic rituals involving political leaders that can offer an instructive model for us as well.

Years ago, among the Zulu, a ritual was observed in which people attack their king. As anthropologist Edward Norbeck describes:

> Ordinary warriors may leap from the ranks, denouncing the king, blaming his actions, calling them base and cowardly, obliging him to explain, questioning his explanations, and finally threatening and expressing contempt for him.

This sounds very much like the way we treat our political leaders – except that for the Zulu, this is a defined ceremony that is perceived as ritual, not an ongoing, ceaseless, literal barrage of attack. The ritual provides a guaranteed but also contained opportunity to express hostility against leaders.

Another African group with a similar practice are the Yao, who ritually attack their headman in installing him. He is symbolically struck on the head, passes out, is given a funeral, and is reborn. Norbeck regards this as a symbolic death and rebirth, a theme which recurs in African rituals that mark changes in social status. By first killing off the citizen who used to be, the Yao can welcome the new headman in his higher-status role. And this is just what they do. The ceremony ends with a ritual display of support for the headman.

These rituals of attacking a leader are reminiscent in some ways of our culture's automatic inclination to oppose, criticize, and verbally assault our leaders. (What would political cartoonists and comedians do without politicians as the butt of their hostile humor?) These African rituals bring to mind, for example, the incessant accusations and investigations that have been heaped on every administration since Watergate, with increasing intensity in the Clinton administration (including on those who were associated with President Clinton before he took office). None of these assaults prevented Clinton from being reborn – that is, reelected – for a second term. But there are significant differences: The 'ritual' attacks on our leaders are constant, not limited to a particular ceremony. And they are more literal than ritual: They cost huge amounts of public funds in investigation and huger amounts of public attention and energy. And they do not end with a display of support. Instead, they either never end (like the Whitewater investigations) or they simply give way to the next special prosecutor/congressional investigation.

---

## ALTERNATIVES TO WAR METAPHORS:
## THE BODY POLITIC

---

If the argument culture is seen in – and reinforced by – our tendency to talk about everything in terms of war, perhaps other cultures can suggest new metaphors and alternative ways of handling information and dealing with conflict. Kimberly Jones set out to learn how a culture that emphasizes harmony and discourages confrontation accomplishes conflict. She found that in some settings, such as among coworkers in offices, the Japanese tend to avoid open conflict, but in others, such as televised political debates, conflict is common. But it is carried out in ways that would strike most Americans and Britons as 'soft'; for example, opponents quickly reach consensus on minor issues so they can save their stronger rhetoric for more important ones. Also, the terms in which they express their opposition may be different from those we take for granted.

Listening to the ways other languages express ideas offers glimpses of how different a world of words can be. In American and British English we talk about so many matters in terms of war and sports metaphors that it is hard to think how else these ideas could be expressed. Whereas we frequently talk of illness as if the human body were a battleground, Japanese experts can speak of the economy as if it were a human body – the 'body politic.'

For example, in a televised talk show analyzed by Japanese linguist Atsuko Honda, two guests differed in their assessment of Japan's economic situation: Suzuki was optimistic about the economy, and Takahashi was pessimistic. The moderator posed the medical metaphor; when asking Suzuki what had caused the recession, he used the word *yamu*, 'ailing' (a verb meaning 'to suffer from a disease') and asked for Suzuki's *shindan*, 'diagnosis.' Suzuki said he thought the problem was digestive: 'Because of overeating and overdrinking, the digestive organs went wrong. So it needs to rest quietly for a while.' This implies a condition no more serious than a little indigestion following a large meal. He elaborated: 'It's not something constitutional, like internal organs such as the liver or kidney, where the patient is no good for a while and has to be in the hospital.'

Takahashi accepted the overeating metaphor but used it to explain why the condition was more serious: 'So the muscles have quite, so to speak, been exhausted. In other words, because the excess weight has been put on, its function has very much deteriorated.' This describes a situation that warrants more concern and more strenuous efforts toward recovery. According to Takahashi, 'the circulatory organs are afflicted.' He continued the medical metaphor, using it to do something quite surprising for Americans in another way – to admit he does not have a solution: 'As for what we should do so that we could invigorate business activities, we don't have a good prescription.'

Neither do we. None of the examples in this chapter provides a prescription for curing the ills of the argument culture. They do show, though, that aggression, conflict, and opposition can be used creatively to accomplish a wide range of human goals, including building solidarity in relationships. In some cases we do not have enough agonism – that is, not enough *ritual* means of displaying opposition, not enough routinized and culturally controlled ways to manage and contain inevitable conflict. The dangers of the argument culture and the culture of critique lie not in the open expression of opposition but in an overapplication of agonism: using opposition as a required and ubiquitous way to approach issues, rather than as one of many possible ways of getting things done by talk. The examples of other cultures suggest possibilities we might not otherwise consider – not only new metaphors but also using intermediaries, modulating opposition by avoiding polarities, and creatively using culturally established and conventionalized genres that have clear rules and limits. We will have to cure the circulatory and digestive problems of our body politic in ways that are consonant with our own cultural heritage. Glimpsing through the corner of our eye how other cultures handle conflict and opposition, we can proceed with our eyes focused on that goal.

# 8

# FAST FORWARD: TECHNOLOGICALLY ENHANCED AGGRESSION

I was the second person in my department to get a computer. The first was my colleague Ralph. The year was 1980. Ralph got a Radio Shack TRS 80; I got a used Apple 2-Plus. He helped me get started and before long helped me get on e-mail, the precursor of the Internet. Though his office was next to mine, we rarely had extended conversations except about department business. Shy and soft-spoken, Ralph mumbled so, I could barely tell he was speaking. But when we both were using e-mail, we started communicating daily in this (then) leisurely medium. We could send each other messages without fear of imposing, since the receiver determines when to log on and read and respond. Soon I was getting long, self-revealing messages from Ralph. We moved effortlessly among discussions of department business, our work, and our lives. Through e-mail Ralph and I became friends.

Ralph recently forwarded to me a message he had received from his niece, a college freshman. 'How nice,' I commented, 'that you have such a close relationship with your niece. Do you think you'd be in touch with her if it weren't for e-mail?' 'No,' he replied. 'I can't imagine we'd write each other letters regularly or call on the phone. No way.' E-mail makes possible connections with relatives, acquaintances, or strangers that would not otherwise exist. And it enables more and different communication with people you are already close to. One woman discovered that e-mail brought her closer to her father. He would never talk much on the phone (as her mother would), but they have become close since they both got on line.

Everywhere e-mail is enhancing or even transforming relationships. Parents keep in regular touch with children in college who would not be caught dead telephoning home every day. When I spent a year and a half in Greece in the late 1960s, I was out of touch with my family except for the mail – letters that took hours to compose and weeks to arrive. When my sister spent a year in Israel in the mid-1990s, we kept in touch nearly every day – and not only she and I. Prodded by her absence, within a month of her departure our third sister and my sisters' daughters all started using e-mail. Though she was so far away, my sister was in some ways in closer touch with the family than she would have been had she stayed home.

And another surprise: My other sister, who generally is not eager to talk about her feelings, opened up on e-mail. One time I called her and we spoke on the phone; after we hung up, I checked my e-mail and found she had revealed information there that she hadn't mentioned when we spoke. I asked her about it (on e-mail), and she explained, 'The telephone is so impersonal.' At first this seemed absurd: How could the actual voice of a person right there be impersonal and the on-screen little letters detached from the writer be more personal? When I asked her about this, she explained: 'The big advantage to e-mail is that you can do it at your time and pace; there is never the feeling that the phone is ringing and interrupting whatever it is you are doing.' Writing e-mail is like writing in a journal; you're alone with your thoughts and your words, safe from the intrusive presence of another person.

## E-MAIL AGGRAVATES AGGRESSION

E-mail, and now the Internet and the World Wide Web, are creating networks of human connection unthinkable even a few years ago. But at the same time that technologically enhanced communication enables previously impossible loving contact, it also enhances hostile and distressing communication. Along with the voices of family members and friends, telephone lines bring into our homes the annoying voices of people who want to sell something – generally at dinnertime. (My father-in-law startles a telephone solicitor by saying, 'We're eating dinner, but I'll call you back. What's your home phone number?' To the nonplussed caller, he explains, 'Well, you're calling me at home; I thought I'd call you at home, too.') Even more unnerving, in the middle of the night may come frightening obscene calls and stalkers. From time to time the public is horrified to learn that even the most respected citizens can succumb to the temptation of anonymity that the telephone seems to offer – like the New York State Supreme Court chief justice who was harassing a former lover by mail and phone and the president of American University in Washington, D.C., who was found to be the source of obscene telephone calls to a woman he didn't even know.

But telephone lines can be traced (as President Richard Berendzen learned) and voices can be recognized (as Judge Sol Wachtler discovered). The Internet ratchets up anonymity by homogenizing all messages into identical-appearing print and making it almost impossible to trace messages back to the computer that sent them. As the ease of using the Internet has resulted in more and more people logging on and sending messages to more and more others with whom they have a connection, it has also led to increased communication with strangers – and this has resulted in 'flaming': vituperative messages that verbally attack. Flaming results from the anonymity not only of the sender but also of the receiver. It is easier to feel and express hostility against someone far removed whom you do not know personally, like the rage that some drivers feel toward an anonymous car that cuts them off. If the anonymous driver to whom you've flipped the finger turns out to be someone you know, the rush of shame you experience is evidence that anonymity was essential for your expression – and experience – of rage.

One of the most effective ways to defuse antagonism between two groups is to provide a forum for individuals from those groups to get to know each other personally. This is the logic behind programs that bring together, for example, African-American and

Jewish youths or Israeli and Palestinian women. It was the means by which a troubled Vietnam veteran finally achieved healing: through a friendship with a man who had been the enemy he was trying to kill – a retired Vietnamese officer whose diary the American had found during the war and managed to return to its owner nearly twenty-five years later. When you get to know members of an 'enemy' group personally, it is hard to demonize them, to see them as less than human.

What is happening in our lives is just the opposite: More and more of our communication is not face to face, and not with people we know. The proliferation and increasing portability of technology isolate people in a bubble. When I was a child, my family got the first television on our block, and the neighborhood children gathered in our dining room to watch Howdy Doody. Before long, every family had its own TV – but each had just one, so, in order to watch it, families came together. Now it is common for families to have more than one television, so the adults can watch what they like in one room and the children can watch their choice in another – or maybe each child has a private TV to watch alone. The spread of radio has followed the same pattern. Early radios were like a piece of furniture around which a family had to gather in order to listen. Now radio listeners may have a radio in every room, one in the car, and yet another, equipped with headphones, for walking or jogging. Radio and television began as sources of information that drew people together physically, even if their attention was not on each other. Now these technologies are exerting a centrifugal force, pulling people apart – and, as a result, increasing the likelihood that their encounters will be agonistic.

## ONE-WAY COMMUNICATION BREEDS CONTEMPT

The head of a small business had a reputation among his employees as being a Jekyll-and-Hyde personality. In person he was always mild-mannered and polite. But when his employees saw a memo from him in their mail, their backs stiffened. The boss was famous for composing angry, even vicious memos that he often had to temper and apologize for later. It seemed that the presence of a living, breathing person in front of him was a brake on his hostility. But seated before a faceless typewriter or computer screen, his anger built and overflowed. A woman who had worked as a dean at a small liberal arts college commented that all the major problems she encountered with faculty or other administrators resulted from written memos, not face-to-face communication.

Answering machines are also a form of one-way communication. A piano teacher named Craig was president of a piano teachers' association that sponsored a yearly competition. Craig had nothing to do with the competition – someone else had organized and overseen it. So he felt helpless and caught off guard when he came home to a message that laid out in detail the caller's grievances about how the competition had been handled, and ended, 'That's no way to run an organization!' Slam! When he heard the message, Craig thought, 'Here I am, being the president as a service to keep things together, and I'm being attacked for something I had no control over. It made me wonder,' he commented, 'why I was doing it at all.' Craig refused a second term in large part because of attacks like this – even though they were infrequent, while he frequently received lavish praise. Being attacked is perhaps unavoidable for those in authority, but in this case the technology played a role as well. It is highly unlikely the caller would have worked herself up into quite this frenzy, or concluded the conversation by hanging up on Craig, if she had gotten Craig himself and not his answering machine, let alone if she had talked to him in person.

In the heat of anger, it is easy to pick up a phone and make a call. But when talking directly to someone, most people feel an impulse to tone down what they say. Even if they do not, the person they are attacking will respond after the first initial blast – by explaining, apologizing, or counterattacking. Whatever the response, it will redirect the attacker's speech, perhaps aggravating the anger but also perhaps deflating it. If you write an angry letter, you might decide later not to send it or to tone it down. But if you make a call and reach voice mail or an answering machine, it's the worst of both worlds: You spout off in the heat of anger, there is no way to take back what you said or correct misinterpretations, and there is no response to act as a brake. In my research on workplace communication, I found that a large percentage of serious conflicts had been sparked by one-way communication such as memos, voice mail, and e-mail.

An experienced reporter at a newspaper heard that one of his colleagues, a feature writer, was working on a story about a topic he knew well. He had done extensive research on a related topic in the course of his own reporting. So he thought he'd be helpful: He sent her a long e-mail message warning her of potential pitfalls and pointing out aspects she should bear in mind. Rather than thanks, he received a testy reply informing him that she was quite capable of watching out for these pitfalls without his expert guidance, and that she too was a seasoned reporter, even though she had been at the paper a shorter time than he. Reading her angry reply, he gulped and sent an apology.

An advantage of e-mail is its efficiency: The reporter was able to send his ideas without taking the time to walk to another floor and talk face to face with his colleague. But had he done so, he would probably have presented his ideas differently, and she would have seen the spirit in which the advice was given. If not, it is unlikely he would have gotten so far in his advice giving before picking up that he was not coming across the way he intended, that she was taking offense. He then could have backtracked and changed the tone of his communication rather than laying it on thicker and thicker, continuing and expanding in a vein that was making her angrier by the second. What's more, if people meet regularly face to face, friendships begin to build that lay the foundation for future communication. It's harder for e-mail and memos to do that.

---

## NOT SO FAST!

---

The potential for misunderstandings and mishaps with electronic communication expands in proportion to the potential for positive exchanges. For example, two workers exchanged e-mail about a report that had to be submitted. One of them wrote that a portion could better be handled by a third person – but added an unflattering remark about her. The recipient received the message at a busy time, noticed that it called for Person 3 to do something – and quickly and efficiently forwarded it to her, disparaging remark and all. E-mail makes it too easy to forward messages, too easy to reply before your temper cools, too easy to broadcast messages to large numbers of people without thinking about how every sentence will strike every recipient. And there's plenty of opportunity for error: sending a message to the wrong person or having a message mysteriously appear on the screen of an unintended recipient.

Every improvement in technology makes possible new and scarier kinds of errors. In one company, a manager set up an e-mail user-group list, so his messages would go to everyone in the department at once and their replies would also get distributed to everyone on the list. But several people sent him replies that they thought were private, not realizing everyone in the office would see them. Like a private conversation overheard, these 'overread' messages to the manager came across to colleagues as kissing up, since people tend to use a more deferential tone in addressing a boss than a peer. It was embarrassing, but not as bad as the job applicant who mistakenly sent a message including his uncensored judgment about the person who interviewed him to that person.

---

## STOP THAT LAW!

---

Technology also plays a role in many of the problems troubling our political process. Journalist Robert Wright explains that 'cyber-democracy' makes it impossible for lawmakers to make decisions based on their judgment of what's best for the country. Any attempt to pass a law that would materially change the status quo provokes an onslaught generated by interest groups representing the citizens who stand to lose. For example, in 1986 Congress tried to find ways to stem the rising budget deficit by eliminating tax breaks. Wright quotes political scientist James Thurber, who said that no sooner was a particular tax break brought up for scrutiny than lobbyists watching the hearings pulled out their cellular phones and alerted the group that would be affected – who promptly let loose an avalanche of protest by fax, phone, or mail. (Today it would also include e-mail.)

The existence of technology means that what seems like a groundswell of popular protest is often the technologically enhanced protest of a few. Wright explains, for example, how one entrepreneur works. When he gets wind of pending legislation that would repeal or cut back benefits for a particular group, he identifies the swing-vote members of Congress, then scans a computer database to locate voters in their districts who are likely to oppose the cut. Those voters receive phone calls describing the 'looming peril' and offering to put them through to the congressional office, so they can spontaneously voice their protest.

Such manufactured protests give disproportionate representation to these groups. And the speed with which they are unleashed robs the lawmakers of time to deliberate. The speed of technology affects politicians in another way, too. With television and radio stations offering round-the-clock news, public figures are expected to have instant responses to national and international events. In the spirit of critique, if they wait to get more information or think carefully about an appropriate response, they are likely to be accused of waffling or dissembling.

---

### THROUGH THE MAGNIFYING GLASS

---

Technology also exacerbates the culture of critique by making it much easier for politicians or journalists to ferret out inconsistencies in a public person's statements over time. With every word captured and archived on Nexis/Lexis, a speech made to one group one year can be compared to statements made to another years later. It is as if someone followed you around with a tape recorder ready to compare how you told about your vacation to your mother, your best friend, and your boss. Inevitably, they would find enough differences to make you look unreliable or dishonest.

Then there was the red paper, a technologically facilitated countertactic to the request for millions of pages of documents, itself facilitated by the technological advancement of computer scanning. As with politicians' burgeoning dirty tricks, lawyers' 'tricks' (the word is used in the title of Charles Yablon's essay) are merely the use of advanced technology for things that were done in the past in a more pedestrian way. Thanks to word processors, says Yablon, law firms can now store up lengthy 'boilerplate interrogatories' (written questions requiring written responses to gather information from the other side before a case goes to trial) in word processors that can 'spit them out quickly in case after case.' In the past, attorneys' eagerness to produce interrogatories was limited by the human limitation on their ability to compose them – and they were more likely to be tailored to the case at hand.

A continuing source of contention between a couple, Joe and John, was John's habit of driving too close to the car ahead. 'You have to leave more room,' Joe would warn, 'in case he stops suddenly.' John, who was younger, would defend himself: 'Brakes are better now than when you learned to drive. Cars can stop much faster.' This sort of thinking led Edward Tenner to observe, in *Why Things Bite Back*, that technology aggravates aggressive driving: With antilock brakes and improved steering, many drivers become overconfident of their ability to avoid crashing.

---

### 'WHO IS THIS? WHY ARE YOU CALLING HERE?'

---

When technology provides both speed and anonymity, it produces a concoction that can spark hostility and attack. Aggressive driving is one example; another is new telephone technology. Just as drivers can be angered – or enraged – when someone cuts them off or otherwise threatens the integrity of their personal space (our cars and the space around them take on a sense of personal territory), it is common to feel a rush of anger against an intrusive phone call. New technology makes it easier to act on that anger. If you subscribe to caller ID service, for example, the number and sometimes the name of the party calling appears on an electronic unit attached to your phone. So people who telephone your home and hang up (or call without leaving messages on your answering machine) can be identified by their phone number and in many cases by their name as well. If you don't subscribe to caller ID service, you can use a feature called 'return call': When you dial *69, a call is automatically placed to the number from which the previous call originated. These features enable angry recipients to get revenge on intruding callers.

An article in *The Washington Post* tells of a woman, Alexis Henderson, who says her husband is obsessed with the return-call feature, which she regards as 'a vent for his hostilities.' When people call and hang up, her husband uses the feature to call them back and challenge them as to why they called. According to the article,

Henderson called a colleague on her way out the door. The colleague didn't answer, and Henderson hung up rather than leave a message, then left her house. The colleague, who was home, used return call to call back, and Henderson's husband picked up.

'My husband answers the phone, and [the colleague] says, "Who's this?"' Henderson recalled. 'And that immediately incensed him, and he said, "Well, who's this?" So she hangs up. So he uses star 69 to call her back.'

Finally, Henderson said, they recognized each others' voices and had a good laugh.

Anonymity was key to the escalating anger. This incident had a happy, and amusing, ending precisely because the callers recognized each other. But when the caller does not turn out to be a friend, ire can rise rather than dissipate. A woman who dialed a wrong number realized what she had done before anyone answered, so she hung up. But her name and number had registered on the recipient's caller ID unit. He called her right back and shouted, 'Who the fuck are you, and why are you calling here, you bitch?' – and continued to harass her by phone for several weeks after.

Our lives are populated more and more by strangers, less and less by people we know. This surely plays a role in the increasing level of aggression and hostility we experience, just as advances in technology enable new ways to express that hostility.

---

## TRAINING OUR CHILDREN TO KILL

---

Perhaps the most troubling aspect of the role of anonymity in electronic media is the effect of video war games on the children who play with them – and the consequent effect on society. Lieutenant Colonel Dave Grossman, a former Army Ranger and paratrooper who is now a professor of military science at Arkansas State University, explains that there is a natural human resistance to killing other human beings. An extensive survey of soldiers in World War II found that only 15 to 20 percent of the American riflemen in combat actually fired at the enemy. The rest were not cowards: They would stand, face fire, and risk their lives 'to rescue comrades, get ammunition, or run messages.' But they did not want to kill other human beings. According to Grossman, 'Throughout history the majority of men on the battlefield would *not* attempt to kill the enemy, even to save their own lives or the lives of their friends.'

This changed in the Vietnam War, where 90 to 95 percent fired to kill. Grossman shows that the military accomplished this transformation through scientific methods called 'operant conditioning' and 'desensitization,' designed to overcome the innate resistance that most humans feel against killing their own kind. First, soldiers bound for Vietnam were systematically desensitized by being taught to regard the enemy as nonhuman and to suppress their natural impulse to feel sympathy when seeing another person suffer. A particularly chilling example comes from a report of techniques developed by a Navy psychiatrist to train military assassins: They would be forced to watch 'films specially designed to show people being killed or injured in violent ways. By being acclimatized through these films, the men were eventually supposed to become able to disassociate their emotions from such a situation.' Although Grossman does not make clear whether or not this specific technique was implemented (though he describes many others that were), he concludes, to his horror, that just this desensitization technique is being used on the young people of our nation, in the form of movies and television:

> In a kind of reverse *Clockwork Orange* classical conditioning, adolescents in movie theaters across the nation, and watching television at home, are seeing the detailed, horrible suffering and killing of human beings, and they are learning to associate this killing and suffering with entertainment, pleasure, their favorite soft drink, their favorite candy bar, and the close, intimate contact of their date.

In Grossman's words, 'We, as a society, have become systematically desensitized to the pain and suffering of others.' This certainly seems like a factor contributing to the increasing number of senseless and cruel murders committed by younger and younger children of privileged as well as disadvantaged backgrounds.

While movies and television desensitize people against the natural human resistance to inflicting suffering on other human beings, video games work just like the operant conditioning used by modern armies to train soldiers, Grossman points out. Whereas soldiers in

World War II were taught to shoot (calmly, at stationary targets), soldiers sent to Vietnam were taught to kill – as a conditioned response. They were trained, in full combat garb, to shoot instantly at human-shaped figures that suddenly popped up in front of them. This is very much like the training many children receive playing video games in which life-like figures pop up and the player has to respond automatically by aiming and pulling a trigger – and gets an instant reward if the target is hit. But this training of young people is even more dangerous, says Grossman, because it lacks two elements essential to military training: Soldiers are taught to shoot only at the enemy and to fire only when ordered to do so by an established authority. The training of video games and violent entertainment includes no such safeguards: There is no sanction for firing at the wrong target, and no authority figure is required or involved – so the aggressive impulses instilled are virtually unchecked.

Police training has also adopted modern methods, according to Grossman. He cites law enforcement expert Bill Jordan who says police officers are trained to overcome their resistance to kill by being systematically trained not to think of their opponents as human beings. Jordan calls this process 'manufactured contempt.' It is hard to read this (in Dave Grossman's book) without thinking of how journalism today trains average citizens to adopt an attitude of contempt toward public figures and how some academics learn to adopt an attitude of contempt toward scholars who work in a different theoretical framework. I am not suggesting that 'attitude' journalism or critique scholarship actually incites us to murder. I am suggesting that the rise of the culture of critique in all these areas of our public lives is related to forces that are causing increased violence among citizens. Both entail systematically inculcating an attitude of contempt toward others and an inclination to see them as not quite human.

## WHO'S TO JUDGE?

One of the great contributions of the Internet is that it enables ordinary people to put out information that previously would have been limited by such gatekeepers as newspaper editors and book publishers, or that would have required enormous amounts of time and money to publish and disseminate independently. In a few moments, anyone with the equipment and expertise can post information on the World Wide Web, and anyone else with the equipment and expertise can read it. This can be invaluable – for example, when individuals who have unusual medical conditions and their families exchange information and personal experience through specialized user groups. But there is a danger here as well. Editors, publishers, and other gatekeepers impose their judgment – for better or worse – on the accuracy of the material they publish. Those who download information from the Internet may be unable to judge the veracity and reliability of information.

A professor at a public university was assigned a student assistant who had excellent computer skills. The assistant offered to help her make reading materials available to her class by placing them on a class Web site. He began by putting on the site readings and secondary sources that the professor had assigned or recommended. But he did not stop there. He went on to scour the Internet for anything related to the course topic and import it into the class Web site, too. When the professor discovered what he had done, she told him to remove these materials, since she did not have time to read everything he had imported to determine whether it was appropriate for the students to read. Some of it might have been irrelevant to the class and would distract them from the material she felt they should read. And some of it might be factually wrong. The idea that the professor thought she should read the material she was making available to her students in order to judge its accuracy and suitability was foreign to the student assistant – and offensive. He argued that she was trying to infringe on the students' First Amendment right to have access to any kind of information at all.

This is a danger inherent in the Internet: At the same time that the ease of posting makes available enormous amounts of useful information, it also makes possible the dissemination of useless, false, or dangerous information – and makes it more difficult to distinguish between the two. To be sure, publishers and editors often make mistakes in publishing material they should not and rejecting material they should accept (as any author whose work has been rejected can tell you – and as evidenced by the many successful books that were rejected by dozens of editors before finally finding a home). Yet readers of reputable newspapers and magazines or books published by established presses know that what they are reading has been deemed reliable by professional editors. The Internet makes it more difficult for consumers to distinguish the veracity and reliability of information they come across.

The Internet can function as a giant and unstoppable rumor mill or as a conduit for such dangerous information as how to build a bomb. It can also facilitate aggressive behavior, as author Elaine Showalter discovered when she published a book, *Hystories*, in which she included chronic fatigue syndrome among a list of phenomena, such as alien abduction and satanic ritual abuse, that she identified as hysterical epidemics. Sufferers from chronic fatigue syndrome who were angered by the label 'hysterical' used the Internet to share information about the author's public appearances, so they could turn out in force to harass and even threaten her. Law enforcement authorities have been unable to identify members of the Animal Liberation Front, who use violence and terrorism in their efforts to halt what they see as cruelty to animals, because their communication with one another takes place for the most part on the Internet rather than at face-to-face meetings.

---

## GENDER ON THE INTERNET

---

The combination of anonymity and speed that results in flaming on the Internet provides a unique opportunity to compare how women and men communicate. And nowhere is evidence of men's greater inclination to engage in dynamic opposition and nonliteral attack more stark. Study after study concludes what anyone who frequently engages in communication on the Internet observes: Flaming or verbal attack is almost exclusively practiced by men, rarely by women. This is not to say that most men engage in flaming – not at all. But of the small number of e-mailers who engage in flaming, the vast majority are men. This is the conclusion of linguist Susan Herring, who has carried out numerous studies of how women and men communicate in cyberspace.

In one study, Herring compared e-mail messages exchanged on two interest group 'lists' – groups of people who share an interest in a topic and therefore subscribe to the list. (Anyone who wants to can subscribe for free.) Subscribers receive all the messages sent (in

Internet jargon, 'posted') by those on the list and have the right to contribute to the conversation by posting their own messages. One of the lists was made up of linguists. Although men accounted for 64 percent of subscribers, they regularly accounted for 85 percent or more of the postings. The other list Herring considered was a women's studies list, in which women accounted for 88 percent of subscribers and the same percentage of messages posted.

Herring examined messages and found that on both lists men were more likely to take a stance in opposition to a previously posted message. On the linguist list, fully 68 percent of messages posted by men were adversarial: 'The poster distanced himself from, criticized, and/or ridiculed other participants.' Women on the women's studies list often 'represented themselves as aligned with other participants, even when their views differed.' For example, a woman on the women's studies list opposed a position taken by those who wrote before:

> I am somewhat puzzled by the seemingly unanimous view that it is dangerous/reprehensible to even consider the possibility that some sex differences are biologically-based. This seems to take for granted that if there are, this would be a compelling argument for an anti-feminist, anti-woman, anti-gay agenda. I would argue that this is not the case, and that taking this link for granted strengthens the anti-feminist, etc . . . case.
>
> I propose that instead, we attack the link, while keeping an open mind as to the biological facts until more is known one way or the other. [continues for three more paragraphs]
>
> Sorry for the length. But does anyone else on this list feel that the lengthiest messages are usually the most interesting? . . .
>
> If this is not the right place for this kind of discussion, can someone indicate to me where the right place would be? Thanks.

Herring points out that this writer states her disagreement in an attenuated tone ('I am somewhat puzzled') and aligns herself with those she opposes by apologizing, thanking, using 'we' ('I propose . . . we attack the link'), and explicitly asking if they feel the way she does.

Herring suspected that maybe the reason the postings on the linguists' list were more oppositional than the ones on the women's studies list was that the topic discussed there was more controversial. But consider what those topics were. The linguists were debating the use of the term 'cognitive linguistics,' whereas the women's studies subscribers were discussing whether differences between women and men are biological or cultural in origin. In the general scheme of things, the latter is a more controversial topic, but it did not appear controversial in this discussion because those who took part all expressed similar views – that gender differences are cultural in origin. No one chose to play devil's advocate or stir things up by claiming that the source of gender differences is genetic or biological; even the questioner quoted above made a pitch only for keeping an open mind. Herring's observations also dispel the misconception that men are more interested than women in information: She found that 'female users are more interested in the exchange of pure information, while male users are more interested in debating their views, regardless of the topic being discussed.'

At one point, Herring noticed that when a rancorous, polarized debate broke out on the linguist list, women did not take part. Her curiosity piqued, she sent a questionnaire to list subscribers, asking their views of the debate and why they did not contribute, if they didn't. She found that 73 percent of respondents, both men and women, who did not take part in the debate gave intimidation as the reason. As one person put it, those who participated were 'ripping each other's lungs out.' But men and women expressed very different reactions to watching from the sidelines:

Men seemed to accept such behavior as a normal feature of academic life, making comments to the effect that 'Actually, the barbs and arrows were entertaining, because of course they weren't aimed at me.'

Although Herring doesn't remark on this aspect of the comment, we can recognize the watching-fights-is-fun perspective that is so much more typical of American men than women. 'In contrast,' Herring found, 'many women responded with profound aversion.' As one woman put it:

This is precisely the kind of human interaction I committedly avoid . . . I am dismayed that human beings treat each other this way. It makes the world a dangerous place to be. I dislike such people and I want to give them a WIDE berth.

What comes through loud and clear is that the man Herring quotes is not taking the flaming literally; this explains why he could see it as fun to watch. The woman regards it as real – literal personal attacks on colleagues.

Since individuals' actual identities can be hidden in this form of communication, it is easy for people to present themselves as members of the other sex. This offers a fascinating opportunity to observe whether assumptions about gender and behavior are descriptions of patterns based on experience or just stereotypes – generalizations with no basis in observation. Herring's research provides evidence that users' expectations about how women and men use language reflect both stereotypes and real patterns.

Herring gives an example of a man pretending to be a woman whose ruse was detected because of his attitude toward agonistic debate: Using a woman's name, he criticized feminist philosophers for 'pretending' to agree with each other, and he expressed the view that open disagreement was good because 'There's nothing like a healthy denunciation by one's colleagues every once in a while to get one's blood flowing, and spur one to greater subtlety and exactness of thought' and stimulate 'vigorous debate.' In response, a female questioned whether the message was really written by a woman. It wasn't. This man was able to take a female name, but his attitude toward agonism – his belief that strongly expressing disagreement is good and sparks a useful adrenaline rush ('get the blood flowing') rather than dampening the enthusiasm of participants – was a giveaway that he was actually a man.

On another list, a woman who pretended to be a man 'sent a message expressing concern for others and appreciation for the list, and others questioned whether "he" was really a male.' Once again, the doubters were right. But Herring also cautions that such generalizations do not always hold:

In another instance, a self-identified woman on a women-only list was accused of being male on the basis of her confrontational style. However, somebody else posted a message saying they had met her in real life, and 'even though she was obnoxious, she was female.'

These examples are evidence not only that the pattern described has some basis in fact but also that patterns are not absolutes. Although men are *more likely* than women to view open disagreement in a favorable way, there are still many individual women and men who do not fit this pattern because of cultural, regional, or class differences or simply individual personality. Those who do not conform can get mixed responses; some women who are bold and aggressive and some men who are diffident and nonconfrontational can get unusually positive responses, seen more favorably than someone of the other sex with the same characteristics would be. But at times those who do not conform to expectations for their gender will be judged harshly. Though another woman confirmed that the confrontational speaker was female, she also confirmed that she regarded her behavior as unacceptable, calling her 'obnoxious.'

---

## LIKE PEAS OUT OF A POD

Flaming is only one aspect of electronic communication. E-mail makes possible extended interaction among people who are physically distant from each other. But it also makes possible anonymity and in some cases – as with young people (mostly boys) who become computer 'nerds' – begins to substitute for human interaction. Following a tragic incident in which a fifteen-year-old boy sexually assaulted and then murdered an eleven-year-old boy who happened to ring his doorbell selling candy and wrapping paper to raise money for his school, many people felt that the Internet shared a portion of the blame, because the murderer had himself been sexually abused by a pedophile he had met through the Internet. An aspect of this harrowing and bizarre event which received less comment was that as the older boy had become obsessed with the Internet, he had gradually withdrawn from social interaction with his peers.

Advances in technology are part of a larger complex of forces moving people away from face-to-face interaction and away from actual experience – from hearing music performed, to hearing recordings of performances, to hearing digital re-creations of performances that some believe bear little resemblance to music as performed. From live dramatic performances in theaters, to silent movies shown in theaters with the accompaniment of live orchestras, to sound movies, to videos watched in the isolation of one's home. From local stores privately owned and owner-operated to chains owned by huge corporations based far away and staffed by minimum-wage employees who know little about the merchandise and have much less stake in whether customers leave the store happy or offended.

All of these trends have complex implications – many positive, but many troubling. Each new advance makes possible not only new levels of connection but also new levels of hostility and enhanced means of expressing it. People who would not dream of cutting in front of others waiting in a line think nothing of speeding along an empty traffic lane to cut ahead of others waiting in a line of cars. It is easy to forget that inside the car, or facing a computer screen, is a living, feeling person.

The rising level of public aggression in our society seems directly related to the increasing isolation in our lives, which is helped along by advances in technology. This isolation – and the technology that enhances it – is an ingredient in the argument culture. We seem to be better at developing technological means of communication than at finding ways to temper the hostility that sometimes accompanies them. We have to work harder at finding those ways. That is the challenge we now face.

# 9

# THE ROOTS OF DEBATE IN EDUCATION AND THE HOPE OF DIALOGUE

The teacher sits at the head of the classroom, feeling pleased with herself and her class. The students are engaged in a heated debate. The very noise level reassures the teacher that the students are participating, taking responsibility for their own learning. Education is going on. The class is a success.

But look again, cautions Patricia Rosof, a high school history teacher who admits to having experienced that wave of satisfaction with herself and the job she is doing. On closer inspection, you notice that only a few students are participating in the debate; the majority of the class is sitting silently, maybe attentive but perhaps either indifferent or actively turned off. And the students who are arguing are not addressing the subtleties, nuances, or complexities of the points they are making or disputing. They do not have that luxury because they want to win the argument – so they must go for the most gross and dramatic statements they can muster. They will not concede an opponent's point, even if they can see its validity, because that would weaken their position. Anyone tempted to synthesize the varying views would not dare to do so because it would look like a 'cop-out,' an inability to take a stand.

One reason so many teachers use the debate format to promote student involvement is that it is relatively easy to set up and the rewards are quick and obvious: the decibel level of noise, the excitement of those who are taking part. Showing students how to integrate ideas and explore subtleties and complexities is much harder. And the rewards are quieter – but more lasting.

Our schools and universities, our ways of doing science and approaching knowledge, are deeply agonistic. We all pass through our country's educational system, and it is there that the seeds of our adversarial culture are planted. Seeing how these seeds develop, and where they came from, is a key to understanding the argument culture and a necessary foundation for determining what changes we would like to make.

## ROOTS OF THE ADVERSARIAL
## APPROACH TO KNOWLEDGE

The argument culture, with its tendency to approach issues as a polarized debate, and the culture of critique, with its inclination to regard criticism and attack as the best if not the only type of rigorous thinking, are deeply rooted in Western tradition, going back to the ancient Greeks. This point is made by Walter Ong, a Jesuit professor at Saint Louis University, in his book *Fighting for Life*. Ong credits the ancient Greeks with a fascination with adversativeness in language and thought. He also connects the adversarial tradition of educational institutions to their all-male character. To attend the earliest universities, in the Middle Ages, young men were torn from their families and deposited in cloistered environments where corporal, even brutal, punishment was rampant. Their suffering drove them to bond with each other in opposition to their keepers – the teachers who were their symbolic enemies. Similar in many ways to puberty rites in traditional cultures, this secret society to which young men were confined also had a private language, Latin, in which students read about military exploits. Knowledge was gleaned through public oral disputation and tested by combative oral performance, which carried with it the risk of public humiliation. Students at these institutions were trained not to discover the truth but to argue either side of an argument – in other words, to debate. Ong points out that the Latin term for school, *ludus*, also referred to play or games, but it derived from the military sense of the word – training exercises for war.

If debate seems self-evidently the appropriate or even the only path to insight and knowledge, says Ong, consider the Chinese approach. Disputation was rejected in ancient China as 'incompatible with the decorum and harmony cultivated by the true sage.' During the Classical periods in both China and India, according to Robert T. Oliver, the preferred mode of rhetoric was exposition rather than argument. The aim was to 'enlighten an inquirer,' not to 'overwhelm an opponent.' And the preferred style reflected 'the earnestness of investigation' rather than 'the fervor of conviction.' In contrast to Aristotle's trust of logic and mistrust of emotion, in ancient Asia intuitive insight was considered the superior means of perceiving truth. Asian rhetoric was devoted not to devising logical arguments but to explicating widely accepted propositions. Furthermore, the search for abstract truth that we assume is the goal of philosophy, while taken for granted in the West, was not found in the East, where philosophy was concerned with observation and experience.

If Aristotelian philosophy, with its emphasis on formal logic, was based on the assumption that truth is gained by opposition, Chinese philosophy offers an alternative view. With its emphasis on harmony, says anthropologist Linda Young, Chinese philosophy sees a diverse universe in precarious balance that is maintained by talk. This translates into methods of investigation that focus more on integrating ideas and exploring relations among them than on opposing ideas and fighting over them.

## ONWARD, CHRISTIAN SOLDIERS

The military-like culture of early universities is also described by historian David Noble, who describes how young men attending medieval universities were like marauding soldiers: The students – all seminarians – roamed the streets bearing arms, assaulting women, and generally creating mayhem. Noble traces the history of Western science and of universities to joint origins in the Christian Church. The scientific revolution, he shows, was created by religious devotees setting up monastery-like institutions devoted to learning. Early universities were seminaries, and early scientists were either clergy or devoutly religious individuals who led monk-like lives. (Until as recently as 1888, fellows at Oxford were expected to be unmarried.)

That Western science is rooted in the Christian Church helps explain why our approach to knowledge tends to be conceived as a metaphorical battle: The Christian Church, Noble shows, has origins and early forms rooted in the military. Many early monks had actually been soldiers before becoming monks. Not only were obedience and strict military-like discipline required, but monks saw themselves as serving 'in God's knighthood,' warriors in a battle against evil. In later centuries, the Crusades brought actual warrior-monks.

The history of science in the Church holds the key to understanding our tradition of regarding the search for truth as an enterprise of oral disputation in which positions are propounded, defended, and attacked without regard to the debater's personal conviction. It is a notion of truth as objective, best captured by formal logic, that Ong traces to Aristotle. Aristotle regarded logic as the only trustworthy means for human judgment; emotions get in the way: 'The man who is to judge would not have his judgment warped by speakers arousing him to anger, jealousy, or compassion. One might as well make a carpenter's tool crooked before using it as a measure.'

This assumption explains why Plato wanted to ban poets from education in his ideal community. As a lover of poetry, I can still recall my surprise and distress on reading this in *The Republic* when I was in high school. Not until much later did I understand what it was all about. Poets in ancient Greece were wandering bards who traveled from place to place performing oral poetry that persuaded audiences by moving them emotionally. They were like what we think of as demagogues: people with a dangerous power to persuade others by getting them all worked up. Ong likens this to our discomfort with advertising in schools, which we see as places where children should learn to think logically, not be influenced by 'teachers' with ulterior motives who use unfair persuasive tactics.

## SHARING TIME: EARLY TRAINING IN SCHOOL

A commitment to formal logic as the truest form of intellectual pursuit remains with us today. Our glorification of opposition as the path to truth is related to the development of formal logic, which encourages thinkers to regard truth seeking as a step-by-step alternation of claims and counterclaims. Truth, in this schema, is an abstract notion that tends to be taken of context. This formal approach to learning is taught in our schools, often indirectly.

Educational researcher James Wertsch shows that schools place great emphasis on formal representation of knowledge. The common elementary school practice of 'sharing time' (or, as it used to be called, 'show-and-tell') is a prime arena for such training. Wertsch gives the example of a kindergarten pupil named Danny who took a piece of lava to class. Danny told his classmates, 'My mom went to the volcano and got it.' When the teacher asked what he wanted to tell about it, he said, 'I've always been taking care of it.' This placed the rock at the center of his feelings and his family: the rock's connection to his mother, who gave it to him, and the attention and care he has lavished on it. The teacher reframed the children's interest in the rock as informational: 'Is it rough or smooth?' 'Is it heavy or light?' She also suggested they look up 'volcano' and 'lava' in the dictionary. This is not to imply that the teacher harmed the child; she built on his personal attachment to the rock to teach him a new way of thinking about it. But the example shows the focus of education on formal rather than relational knowledge – information about the rock that has meaning out of context, rather than information tied to the context: Who got the rock for him? How did she get it? What is his relation to it?

Here's another example of how a teacher uses sharing time to train children to speak and think formally. Sarah Michaels spent time watching and tape-recording in a first-grade classroom. During sharing time, a little girl named Mindy held up two candles and told her classmates, 'When I was in day camp we made these candles. And I tried it with different colors with both of them but one just came out, this one just came out blue and I don't know what this color is.' The teacher responded, 'That's neat-o. Tell the kids how you do it from the very start. Pretend we don't know a thing about candles.

OK, what did you do first? What did you use?' She continued to prompt: 'What makes it have a shape?' and 'Who knows what the string is for?' By encouraging Mindy to give information in a sequential manner, even if it might not seem the most important to her and if the children might already know some of it, the teacher was training her to talk in a focused, explicit way.

The tendency to value formal, objective knowledge over relational, intuitive knowledge grows out of our notion of education as training for debate. It is a legacy of the agonistic heritage. There are many other traces as well. Many Ph.D. programs still require public 'defenses' of dissertations or dissertation proposals, and oral performance of knowledge in comprehensive exams. Throughout our educational system, the most pervasive inheritance is the conviction that issues have two sides, that knowledge is best gained through debate, that ideas should be presented orally to an audience that does its best to poke holes and find weaknesses, and that to get recognition, one has to 'stake out a position' in opposition to another.

## INTEGRATING WOMEN IN THE CLASSROOM ARMY

If Ong is right, the adversarial character of our educational institutions is inseparable from their all-male heritage. I wondered whether teaching techniques still tend to be adversarial today and whether, if they are, this may hold a clue to a dilemma that has received much recent attention: that girls often receive less attention and speak up less in class. One term I taught a large lecture class of 140 students and decided to take advantage of this army (as it were) of researchers to answer these questions. Becoming observers in their own classrooms, my students found plenty of support for Ong's ideas.

I asked the students to note how relatively adversarial the teaching methods were in their other classes and how the students responded. Gabrielle DeRouen-Hawkins's description of a theology class was typical:

The class is in the format of lecture with class discussion and participation. There are thirteen boys and eleven girls in the class. In a fifty-minute class:

Number of times a male student spoke: 8

Number of times a female student spoke: 3

. . . In our readings, theologians present their theories sur-rounding G-D, life, spirituality and sacredness. As the pro-fessor (a male) outlined the main ideas about the readings, he posed questions like 'And what is the fault with /Smith's/ basis that the sacred is individualistic?' The only hands that went up were male. Not one female *dared* challenge or refute an author's writings. The only questions that the females asked (and all female comments were questions) involved a problem they had with the content of the reading. The males, on the other hand, openly questioned, criticized, and refuted the readings on five separate occasions. The three other times that males spoke involved them saying something like: '/Smith/ is very vague in her theory of XX. Can you explain it further?' They were openly argumentative.

This description raises a number of fascinating issues. First, it gives concrete evidence that at least college classrooms proceed on the assumption that the educational process should be adversarial: The teacher invited students to criticize the reading. (Theology, a required course at Georgetown, was a subject where my students most often found adversarial methods – interestingly, given the background I laid out earlier.) Again, there is nothing inherently wrong with using such methods. Clearly, they are very effective in many ways. However, among the potential liabilities is the risk that women students may be less likely to take part in classroom discussions that are framed as arguments between opposing sides – that is, debate – or as attacks on the authors – that is, critique. (The vast majority of students' observations revealed that men tended to speak more than women in their classes – which is not to say that individual women did not speak more than individual men.)

Gabrielle commented that since class participation counted for 10 percent of students' grades, it might not be fair to women students that the agonistic style is more congenial to men. Not only might women's grades suffer because they speak up less, but they might be evaluated as less intelligent or prepared because when they did speak, they asked questions rather than challenging the readings.

I was intrigued by the student's comment '/Smith/ is very vague in her theory of XX. Can you explain it further?' It could have been phrased 'I didn't understand the author's theory. Can you explain it to me?' By beginning 'The author is vague in her theory,' the questioner blamed the author for his failure to understand. A student who asks a question in class risks appearing ignorant. Prefacing the question this way was an excellent way to minimize that risk.

In her description of this class, Gabrielle wrote that not a single woman '*dared* challenge or refute' an author. She herself underlined the word 'dared.' But in reading this I wondered whether 'dared' was necessarily the right word. It implies that the women in the class wished to challenge the author but did not have the courage. It is possible that not a single woman *cared* to challenge the author. Criticizing or challenging might not be something that appealed to them or seemed worth their efforts. Going back to the childhoods of boys and girls, it seems possible that the boys had had more experiences, from the time they were small, that encouraged them to challenge and argue with authority figures than the girls had.

This is not to say that classrooms are more congenial to boys than girls in every way. Especially in the lowest grades, the requirement that children sit quietly in their seats seems clearly to be easier for girls to fulfill than boys, since many girls frequently sit fairly quietly for long periods of time when they play, while most boys' idea of play involves at least running around, if not also jumping and roughhousing. And researchers have pointed out that some of the extra attention boys receive is aimed at controlling such physical exuberance. The adversarial aspect of educational traditions is just one small piece of the pie, but it seems to reflect boys' experiences and predilections more than girls'.

A colleague commented that he had always taken for granted that the best way to deal with students' comments is to challenge them; he took it to be self-evident that this technique sharpens their minds and helps them develop debating skills. But he noticed that women were relatively silent in his classes. He decided to try beginning discussion with relatively open questions and letting comments go unchallenged. He found, to his amazement and satisfaction, that more women began to speak up in class.

Clearly, women can learn to perform in adversarial ways. Anyone who doubts this need only attend an academic conference in the field of women's studies or feminist studies – or read Duke University professor Jane Tompkins's essay showing how a conference in these fields can be like a Western shoot-out. My point is rather about the roots of the tradition and the tendency of the style to appeal initially to more men than women in the Western cultural context. Ong and Noble show that the adversarial culture of Western science and its exclusion of women were part and parcel of the same historical roots – not that individual women may not learn to practice and enjoy agonistic debate or that individual men may not recoil from it. There are many people, women as well as men, who assume a discussion must be contentious to be interesting. Author Mary Catherine Bateson recalls that when her mother, the anthropologist Margaret Mead, said, 'I had an argument with' someone, it was a positive comment. 'An argument,' to her, meant a spirited intellectual interchange, not a rancorous conflict. The same assumption emerged in an obituary for Diana Trilling, called 'one of the very last of the great midcentury New York intellectuals.' She and her friends had tried to live what they called 'a life of significant contention' – the contention apparently enhancing rather than undercutting the significance.

## LEARNING BY FIGHTING

Although there are patterns that tend to typify women and men in a given culture, there is an even greater range among members of widely divergent cultural backgrounds. In addition to observing adversarial encounters in their current classrooms, many students recalled having spent a junior year in Germany or France and commented that American classrooms seemed very placid compared to what they had experienced abroad. One student, Zach Tyler, described his impressions this way:

> I have very vivid memories of my junior year of high school, which I spent in Germany as an exchange student. The class-room was very debate-oriented and agonistic. One particular instance I remember well was in physics class, when a very

confrontational friend of mine had a heated debate with the teacher about solving a problem. My friend ran to the board and scribbled out how he would have solved the problem, completely different from the teacher's, which also gave my friend the right answer and made the teacher wrong.

STUDENT: 'You see! This is how it should be, and you are wrong!'

TEACHER: 'No! No! No! You are absolutely wrong in every respect! Just look at how you did this!' (He goes over my friend's solution and shows that it does not work.) 'Your solution has no base, as I just showed you!'

STUDENT: 'You can't prove that. Mine works just as well!'

TEACHER: 'My God, if the world were full of technical idiots like yourself! Look again!' (And he clearly shows how my friend's approach was wrong, after which my friend shut up.)

In Zach's opinion, the teacher encouraged this type of argument. The student learned he was wrong, but he got practice in arguing his point of view.

This incident occurred in high school. But European classrooms can be adversarial even at the elementary school level, according to another student, Megan Smyth, who reported on a videotape she saw in her French class:

Today in French class we watched an excerpt of a classroom scene of fifth-graders. One at a time, each student was asked to stand up and recite a poem that they were supposed to have memorized. The teacher screamed at the students if they forgot a line or if they didn't speak with enough emotion. They were reprimanded and asked to repeat the task until they did it perfectly and passed the 'oral test.'

There is probably little question about how Americans would view this way of teaching, but the students put it into words:

After watching this scene, my French teacher asked the class what our opinion was. The various responses included: French schools are very strict, the professor was 'mean' and didn't have respect for the students, and there's too much emphasis on memorization, which is pointless.

If teaching methods can be more openly adversarial in European than American elementary and high schools, academic debate can be more openly adversarial there as well. For example, Alice Kaplan, a professor of French at Duke University, describes a colloquium on the French writer Céline that she attended in Paris:

> After the first speech, people started yelling at each other. 'Are you suggesting that Céline was fascist!' 'You call that evidence!' 'I will not accept ignorance in the place of argument!' I was scared.

These examples dramatize that many individuals can thrive in an adversarial atmosphere. And those who learn to participate effectively in any verbal game eventually enjoy it, if nothing else than for the pleasure of exercising that learned skill. It is important to keep these examples in mind in order to avoid the impression that adversarial tactics are always destructive. Clearly, such tactics sometimes admirably serve the purpose of intellectual inquiry. In addition to individual predilection, cultural learning plays a role in whether or not someone enjoys the game played this way.

## GRADUATE SCHOOL AS BOOT CAMP

Although the invective Kaplan heard at a scholarly meeting in Paris is more extreme than what is typical at American conferences, the assumption that challenge and attack are the best modes of scholarly inquiry is pervasive in American scholarly communities as well. Graduate education is a training ground not only for teaching but also for scientific research. Many graduate programs are geared to training young scholars in rigorous thinking, defined as the ability to launch and field verbal attacks.

Communications researchers Karen Tracy and Sheryl Baratz tapped into some of the ethics that lead to this atmosphere in a study of weekly symposia attended by faculty and graduate students at a major research university. When they asked participants about the purpose of the symposia, they were told it was to 'trade ideas' and 'learn things.' But it didn't take too much discussion to uncover the participants' deeper concern: to be seen as intellectually competent. And here's the rub: To be seen as competent, a student had to ask 'tough and challenging questions.'

One faculty member commented, when asked about who participated actively in a symposium,

> Among the graduate students, the people I think about are Jess, Tim, uh let's see, Felicia will ask a question but it'll be a nice little supportive question.

'A nice little supportive question' diminished the value of Felicia's participation and her intelligence – the sort of judgment a student would wish to avoid. Just as with White House correspondents, there is value placed on asking 'tough questions.' Those who want to impress their peers and superiors (as most, if not all, do) are motivated to ask the sorts of questions that gain approval.

Valuing attack as a sign of respect is part of the argument culture of academia – our conception of intellectual interchange as a metaphorical battle. As one colleague put it, 'In order to play with the big boys, you have to be willing to get into the ring and wrestle with them.' Yet many graduate students (and quite a few established scholars) remain ambivalent about this ethic, especially when they are on the receiving rather than the distribution end. Sociolinguist Winnie Or tape-recorded a symposium at which a graduate student presented her fledgling research to other students and graduate faculty. The student later told Or that she left the symposium feeling that a truck had rolled over her. She did not say she regretted having taken part; she felt she had received valuable feedback. But she also mentioned that she had not looked at her research project once since the symposium several weeks before. This is telling. Shouldn't an opportunity to discuss your research with peers and experts fire you up and send you back to the isolation of research renewed and reinspired? Isn't something awry if it leaves you not wanting to face your research project at all?

This young scholar persevered, but others drop out of graduate school, in some cases because they are turned off by the atmosphere of critique. One woman who wrote to me said she had been encouraged to enroll in graduate school by her college professors, but she lasted only one year in a major midwest university's doctoral program in art history. This is how she described her experience and her decision not to continue:

> Grad school was the nightmare I never knew existed . . . Into the den of wolves I go, like a lamb to slaughter . . . When, at the end of my first year (masters) I was offered a job as a curator for a private collection, I jumped at the chance. I wasn't cut out for academia – better try the 'real world.'

Reading this I thought, is it that she was not cut out for academia, or is it that academia as it was practiced in that university is not cut out for people like her. It is cut out for those who enjoy, or can tolerate, a contentious environment.

(These examples remind us again of the gender dynamic. The graduate student who left academia for museum work was a woman. The student who asked a 'nice little supportive question' instead of a 'tough, challenging one' was a woman. More than one commentator has wondered aloud if part of the reason women drop out of science courses and degree programs is their discomfort with the agonistic culture of Western science. And Lani Guinier has recently shown that discomfort with the agonistic procedures of law school is partly responsible for women's lower grade point averages in law school, since the women arrive at law school with records as strong as the men's.)

## THE CULTURE OF CRITIQUE:
## ATTACK IN THE ACADEMY

The standard way of writing an academic paper is to position your work in opposition to someone else's, which you prove wrong. This creates a *need* to make others wrong, which is quite a different matter from reading something with an open mind and discovering that you disagree with it. Students are taught that they must disprove others' arguments in order to be original, make a contribution, and demonstrate their intellectual ability. When there is a *need* to make others wrong, the temptation is great to oversimplify at best, and at worst to distort or even misrepresent others' positions, the better to refute them – to search for the most foolish statement in a generally reasonable treatise, seize upon the weakest examples, ignore facts that support your opponent's views, and focus only on those that support yours. Straw men spring up like scarecrows in a cornfield.

Sometimes it seems as if there is a maxim driving academic discourse that counsels, 'If you can't find something bad to say, don't say anything.' As a result, any work that gets a lot of attention is immediately opposed. There is an advantage to this approach: Weaknesses are exposed, and that is surely good. But another result is that it is difficult for those outside the field (or even inside) to know what is 'true.' Like two expert witnesses hired by opposing attorneys, academics can seem to be canceling each other out. In the words of policy analysts David Greenberg and Philip Robins:

> The process of scientific inquiry almost ensures that competing sets of results will be obtained . . . Once the first set of findings are published, other researchers eager to make a name for themselves must come up with different approaches and results to get their studies published.

How are outsiders (or insiders, for that matter) to know which 'side' to believe? As a result, it is extremely difficult for research to influence public policy.

A leading researcher in psychology commented that he knew of two young colleagues who had achieved tenure by writing articles attacking him. One of them told him, in confidence, that he actually agreed with him, but of course he could not get tenure by writing articles simply supporting someone else's work; he had to stake out a position in opposition. Attacking an established scholar has particular appeal because it demonstrates originality and independence of thought without requiring true innovation. After all, the domain of inquiry and the terms of debate have already been established. The critic has only to say, like the child who wants to pick a fight, 'Is not!' Younger or less prominent scholars can achieve a level of attention otherwise denied or eluding them by stepping into the ring with someone who has already attracted the spotlight.

The young psychologist who confessed his motives to the established one was unusual, I suspect, only in his self-awareness and willingness to articulate it. More commonly, younger scholars, or less prominent ones, convince themselves that they are fighting for truth, that they are among the few who see that the emperor has no clothes. In the essay mentioned earlier, Jane Tompkins describes how a young scholar-critic can work herself into a passionate conviction that she is morally obligated to attack, because she is fighting on the side of good against the side of evil. Like the reluctant hero in the film *High Noon*, she feels she has no choice but to strap on her holster and shoot. Tompkins recalls that her own career was launched by an essay that

> began with a frontal assault on another woman scholar. When I wrote it I felt the way the hero does in a Western. Not only had this critic argued *a*, *b*, and *c*, she had held *x*, *y*, and *z*! It was a clear case of outrageous provocation.

Because her attack was aimed at someone with an established career ('She was famous and I was not. She was teaching at a prestigious university and I was not. She had published a major book and I had not.'), it was a 'David and Goliath situation' that made her feel she was 'justified in hitting her with everything I had.' (This is analogous to what William Safire describes as his philosophy in the sphere of political journalism: 'Kick 'em when they're up.')

The claim of objectivity is belied by Tompkins's account of the spirit in which attack is often launched: the many motivations, other than the search for truth, that drive a critic to pick a fight with another scholar. Objectivity would entail a disinterested evaluation of all claims. But there is nothing disinterested about it when scholars set out with the need to make others wrong and transform them not only into opponents but into villains.

In academia, as in other walks of life, anonymity breeds contempt. Some of the nastiest rhetoric shows up in 'blind' reviews – of articles submitted to journals or book proposals submitted to publishers. 'Peer review' is the cornerstone of academic life. When someone submits an article to a journal, a book to a publisher, or a proposal to a funding institution, the work is sent to established scholars for evaluation. To enable reviewers to be honest, they remain anonymous. But anonymous reviewers often take a tone of derision such as people tend to use only when talking about someone who is not there – after all, the evaluation is not addressed to the author. But authors typically receive copies of the evaluations, especially if their work is rejected. This can be particularly destructive to young scholars just starting out. For example, one sociolinguist wrote her dissertation in a firmly established tradition: She tape-recorded conversations at the company where she worked part-time. Experts in our field believe it is best to examine conversations in which the researcher is a natural participant, because when strangers appear asking to tape-record, people get nervous and may change their behavior. The publisher sent the manuscript to a reviewer who was used to different research methods. In rejecting the proposal, she referred to the young scholar 'using the audiotaped detritus from an old job.' Ouch. What could justify the sneering term 'detritus'? What is added by appending 'old' to 'job,' other than hurting the author? Like Heathcliff, the target hears only the negative and – like Heathcliff – may respond by fleeing the field altogether.

One reason the argument culture is so widespread is that arguing is so easy to do. Lynne Hewitt, Judith Duchan, and Erwin Segal came up with a fascinating finding: Speakers with language disabilities who had trouble taking part in other types of verbal interaction were able to participate in arguments. Observing adults with mental retardation who lived in a group home, the researchers found that the residents often engaged in verbal conflicts as a means of prolonging interaction. It was a form of sociability. Most surprising, this was equally true of two residents who had severe language and comprehension disorders yet were able to take part in the verbal disputes, because arguments have a predictable structure.

Academics, too, know that it is easy to ask challenging questions without listening, reading, or thinking very carefully. Critics can always complain about research methods, sample size, and what has been left out. To study anything, a researcher must isolate a piece of the subject and narrow the scope of vision in order to focus. An entire tree cannot be placed under a microscope; a tiny bit has to be separated to be examined closely. This gives critics the handle of a weapon with which to strike an easy blow: They can point out all the bits that were not studied. Like family members or partners in a close relationship, anyone looking for things to pick on will have no trouble finding them.

All of this is not to imply that scholars should not criticize each other or disagree. In the words of poet William Blake, 'Without contraries is no progression.' The point is to distinguish constructive ways of doing so from nonconstructive ones. Criticizing a colleague on empirical grounds is the beginning of a discussion; if researchers come up with different findings, they can engage in a dialogue: What is it about their methods, data, or means of analysis that explains the different results? In some cases, those who set out to disprove another's claims end up proving them instead – something that is highly unlikely to happen in fields that deal in argumentation alone.

A stunning example in which opponents attempting to disprove a heretical claim ended up proving it involves the cause and treatment of ulcers. It is now widely known and accepted that ulcers are caused by bacteria in the stomach and can be cured by massive doses of antibiotics. For years, however, the cure and treatment of ulcers remained elusive, as all the experts agreed that ulcers were the classic psychogenic illness caused by stress. The stomach, experts further agreed, was a sterile environment: No bacteria could live there. So pathologists did not look for bacteria in the stomachs of ailing or deceased patients, and those who came across them simply ignored them, in effect not seeing what was before their eyes because they did not believe it could be there. When Dr Barry Marshall, an Australian resident in internal medicine, presented evidence that ulcers are caused by bacteria, no one believed him. His findings were ultimately confirmed by researchers intent on proving him wrong.

The case of ulcers shows that setting out to prove others wrong can be constructive – when it is driven by genuine differences and when it motivates others to undertake new research. But if seeking to prove others wrong becomes a habit, an end in itself, the sole line of inquiry, the results can be far less rewarding.

## BELIEVING AS THINKING

'The doubting game' is the name English professor Peter Elbow gives to what educators are trained to do. In playing the doubting game, you approach others' work by looking for what's wrong, much as the press corps follows the president hoping to catch him stumble or an attorney pores over an opposing witness's deposition looking for inconsistencies that can be challenged on the stand. It is an attorney's job to discredit opposing witnesses, but is it a scholar's job to approach colleagues like an opposing attorney?

Elbow recommends learning to approach new ideas, and ideas different from your own, in a different spirit – what he calls a 'believing game.' This does not mean accepting everything anyone says or writes in an unthinking way. That would be just as superficial as rejecting everything without thinking deeply about it. The believing game is still a game. It simply asks you to give it a whirl: Read *as if* you believed, and see where it takes you. Then you can go back and ask whether you want to accept or reject elements in the argument or the whole argument or idea. Elbow is not recommending that we stop doubting altogether. He is telling us to stop doubting exclusively. We need a systematic and respected way to detect and expose strengths, just as we have a systematic and respected way of detecting faults.

Americans need little encouragement to play the doubting game because we regard it as synonymous with intellectual inquiry, a sign of intelligence. In Elbow's words, 'We tend to assume that the ability to criticize a claim we disagree with counts as more serious intellectual work than the ability to enter into it and temporarily assent.' It is the believing game that needs to be encouraged and recognized as an equally serious intellectual pursuit.

Although criticizing is surely part of critical thinking, it is not synonymous with it. Again, limiting critical response to critique means not doing the other kinds of critical thinking that could be helpful: looking for new insights, new perspectives, new ways of thinking, new knowledge. Critiquing relieves you of the responsibility of doing integrative thinking. It also has the advantage of making the critics feel smart, smarter than the ill-fated author whose work is being picked apart like carrion. But it has the disadvantage of making them less likely to learn from the author's work.

---

## THE SOCRATIC METHOD – OR IS IT?

---

Another scholar who questions the usefulness of opposition as the sole path to truth is philosopher Janice Moulton. Philosophy, she shows, equates logical reasoning with the Adversary Paradigm, a matter of making claims and then trying to find, and argue against, counterexamples to that claim. The result is a debate between adversaries trying to defend their ideas against counterexamples and to come up with counterexamples that refute the opponent's ideas. In this paradigm, the best way to evaluate someone's work is to 'subject it to the strongest or most extreme opposition.'

But if you parry individual points – a negative and defensive enterprise – you never step back and actively imagine a world in which a different system of ideas could be true – a positive act. And you never ask how larger systems of thought relate to each other. According to Moulton, our devotion to the Adversary Paradigm has led us to misinterpret the type of argumentation that Socrates favored: We think of the Socratic method as systematically leading an opponent into admitting error. This is primarily a way of showing up an adversary as wrong. Moulton shows that the original Socratic method – the *elenchus* – was designed to convince others, to shake them out of their habitual mode of thought and lead them to new insight. Our version of the Socratic method – an adversarial public debate – is unlikely to result in opponents changing their minds. Someone who loses a debate usually attributes that loss to poor performance or to an adversary's unfair tactics.

---

## KNOWLEDGE AS WARRING CAMPS

---

Anne Carolyn Klein, an American woman who spent many years studying Tibetan Buddhism, joined a university program devoted to women's studies in religion. It was her first encounter with contemporary feminist theory, which she quickly learned was divided into two warring camps. In one camp are those who focus on the ways that women are different from men. Among these, some emphasize that women's ways are equally valid and should be respected, while others believe that women's ways are superior and should be more widely adopted. Both these views – called 'difference feminism' – contrast with those in the other camp, who claim that women are no different from men by nature, so any noticeable differences result from how society treats women. Those who take this view are called 'social constructionists.'

Klein saw that separating feminist theory into these two camps reflects the Western tendency to rigid dichotomies. Recalling how Buddhist philosophy tries to integrate disparate forces, she shows that there is much to be gained from both feminist views – and, in any case, both perspectives tend to coexist within individuals. For example, even though the constructionist view of gender has won ascendancy in academic theory (that's why we have the epithet 'essentialist' to describe those who hold the view that is in disfavor but no commonly used epithet to sneer at the constructionist view), 'feminists still struggle to recognize and name the commonalities among women that justify concern for women's lives around the world and produce political and social alliances.' Klein asks, 'Why protest current conditions unless the category "women" is in some way a meaningful one?' She shows, too, that the very inclination to polarize varied views of women and feminism into two opposing camps is in itself essentialist because it reduces complex and varied perspectives to simplified, monolithic representations. This also makes it easy to dismiss – and fight about – others' work rather than think about it.

Reflecting this warring-camps view, journalist Cynthia Gorney asked Gloria Steinem, 'Where do you stand in the current debate that the feminist world has divided into "equity" feminism versus "difference" feminism – about whether women are to be treated like men or as different from men?' This question bears all the earmarks of the adversarial framework: the term 'debate' and the separation of a complex domain of inquiry into two opposed sides. Steinem responded:

> [*Sighs.*] Of course, you understand that I've turned up in every category. So it makes it harder for me to take the divisions with great seriousness, since I don't feel attached to any of them – and also since I don't hear about the division from women who are not academics or in the media. The idea that there are two 'camps' has not been my experience. The mark to me of a constructive argument is one that looks at a specific problem and says, 'What shall we do about this?' And a nonconstructive one is one that tries to label people. 'Difference' feminist, 'gender' feminist – it has no meaning in specific situations.

In this short comment, Steinem puts her finger on several aspects of the argument culture. First, she identifies academics and journalists as two groups that have a habit of – and a stake in – manufacturing polarization and the appearance of conflict. Second, she points out that this view of the world does not describe reality as most people live it. Third, she shows that polarizing issues into 'a debate' often goes along with 'labeling' the two sides: Lumping others together and sticking a label on them makes it easy to ignore the nuances and subtleties of their opinions and beliefs. Individuals are reduced to an oversimplification of their ideas, transformed into the enemy, and demonized.

The phenomenon could be observed in the coverage the British media gave to the publication of Natasha Walter's *The New Feminism* in January 1998. Though there was indeed much debate over whether or not the feminism Natasha Walter advocated was new or even still necessary, some of the headlines fanned the flames of division, though actually there were a multitude of views and individual voices: 'Today, the backlash begins' shouted *The Observer*.

False dichotomies are often at the heart of discord.

## QUESTION THE BASIC ASSUMPTION

My aim is not to put a stop to the adversarial paradigm, the doubting game, debate – but to diversify: Like a well-balanced stock portfolio, we need more than one path to the goal we seek. What makes it hard to question whether debate is truly the only or even the most fruitful approach to learning is that we're dealing with assumptions that we and everyone around us take to be self-evident. A prominent dean at a major research university commented to me, 'The Chinese cannot make great scientists because they will not debate publicly.' Many people would find this remark offensive. They would object because it generalizes about all Chinese scientists, especially since it makes a negative evaluation. But I would also question the assumption that makes the generalization a criticism: the conviction that the only way to rest and develop ideas is to debate them publicly. It may well be true that most Chinese scientists are reluctant to engage in public, rancorous debate. I see nothing insulting about such a claim; it derives from the Chinese cultural norms that many Chinese and Western observers have documented. But we also know that many Chinese have indeed been great scientists. The falsity of the dean's statement should lead us to question whether debate is the only path to insight.

## CONSENSUS THROUGH DISSENSION?

The culture of critique driving our search for knowledge in the scientific world of research is akin to what I have described in the domains of politics, journalism, and law. In those three institutions, an increasingly warlike atmosphere has led many people already in those professions to leave, and many who would have considered entering these professions in the past are now choosing other paths. Those who remain are finding it less fun; they don't look forward to getting up and going to work in the same way that they and others used to. And in all these areas, raised voices and tempers are creating a din that is drowning out the perhaps more numerous voices of dialogue and reason. In law, critics of the principle of zealous advocacy object on the grounds of what it does to the souls of those who practice within the system, requiring them to put aside their consciences and natural inclinations toward human compassion – just what some among the press say about what aggression journalism is doing to journalists.

Forces affecting these institutions are intertwined with each other and with others I have not mentioned. For example, the rise of malpractice litigation, while prodding doctors to be more careful and providing deserved recompense to victims, has also made the doctor-patient relationship potentially more adversarial. At the same time, physicians are finding themselves in increasingly adversarial relationships with HMOs and insurance companies – as are the patients themselves, who now need the kind of advice that was offered under the headline 'When Your HMO Says No: How to Fight for the Treatment You Need – and Win.'

People in business, too, report an increasingly adversarial atmosphere. There are, of course, the hostile takeovers that have become common, along with lawsuits between companies and former employees. But there is also more opposition in the day-to-day doing of business. A man who works at a large computer company in Silicon Valley told me that he sees this daily. Disagreement and verbal attack are encouraged at meetings, under the guise of challenging assumptions and fostering creativity. But in reality, he observes, what is fostered is dissension. In the end, the company's ability to do business can be threatened. He has seen at least one company virtually paralyzed by trying to seek consensus after assiduously stirring up dissension.

## WHO WILL BE LEFT TO LEAD?

If this seems to describe an isolated phenomenon in a particular industry, take note: A comparable situation exists in our political life. The culture of critique is threatening our system of governance. Norman Ornstein, a political analyst at the American Enterprise Institute, articulates how.

Ornstein offers some astonishing statistics: Between 1975 and 1989, the number of federal officials indicted on charges of public corruption went up by a staggering 1,211 percent. During the same period, the number of nonfederal officials indicted doubled. What are we to make of this? he asks. Does it mean that officials during that decade were far more corrupt than before? Not likely. Every systematic study, as well as all anecdotal evidence, suggests just the opposite: Public officials are far less corrupt now; fewer take bribes, get drunk in the middle of their duties, engage in immoral conduct, and so on.

What we have is the culture of critique. The press is poised to pounce on allegations of scandal, giving them primacy over every other kind of news. And the standards by which scandals are judged have declined. Allegations make the news, no matter where they come from, often without proof or even verification. (Remember the ruckus that accompanied reports that planes were forced to circle and travelers were delayed while President Clinton got a haircut on Air Force One in the Los Angeles airport? And that George Bush did not know what a supermarket scanner was? Both turned out to be false.) Political opponents seize on these allegations and use them to punish or bring down opponents. The sad result is that laws designed to improve ethics have not improved ethics at all. Instead, they have made government almost impossible. Allegations trigger long investigations that themselves damage reputations and suggest to the public that terrible things are going on even when they aren't.

Prosecutors, too, are part of the web, Ornstein continues. In the past, an ambitious prosecutor might set out to snare a criminal on the FBI's ten most wanted list. Now the temptation is to go after a senator or cabinet member – or a vice president. That's where attention is paid; that's where the rewards lie.

The threat is not only to those at the highest levels of government but to public servants at every level. I spoke to someone prominent in the arts who was invited to join a federal commission. But first there was a questionnaire to fill out – pages and pages of details requested about the prospective nominee's personal, professional, and financial life. Special request was made for anything that might be embarrassing if it became public. The person in question simply declined the invitation.

The artist I spoke to typified a situation Ornstein described: It is becoming almost impossible to get qualified people to serve in public positions, from the highest executive nominations to part-time or even honorary appointments. Leaving private life for public service has always required personal sacrifice: Your family life is disrupted; you take a pay cut. But now those contemplating such a move must be willing to make an even greater sacrifice: putting their personal reputation at risk. Instead of enhancing reputations, going into public services now threatens them, whether or not the officials have done anything to be ashamed of.

Disruption of family life is intensified, too, by the inordinate delay, Ornstein explained. While a nominee waits to be confirmed, life goes on hold: A spouse's job is in limbo; children await a change in schools; houses must – but can't – be found or rented or bought or sold. What is causing the delays to become so much more protracted than they were before? Every step in the process: Presidents (and their staffs) must take much more time in choosing potential nominees, to make absolutely sure there is nothing in their lives or backgrounds that could embarrass not just the nominee but the president. Once people are selected, the FBI takes weeks or months longer than it used to for background checks, because it too wants to make sure it is not embarrassed later. Finally, the nomination goes to the Senate, where political opponents of the president or the nominee try to go for the jugular on ethics charges.

The result of all these forces is a much smaller pool of qualified people willing to consider public service, long periods when important posts are left vacant, a climate of suspicion that reinforces public doubts about the ethics of people in government, and real disruption in the running of our country.

We have become obsessed with the appearance of impropriety, as Peter Morgan and Glenn Reynolds show in a book with that title. Meanwhile, real impropriety goes unnoticed. We have to ask, as Ornstein does, whether the price we're paying to have pristine individuals fill every public post is worth what we're getting – and he (like Morgan and Reynolds) doubts that what we're getting is less impropriety.

---

## THE COST IN HUMAN SPIRIT

---

Whatever the causes of the argument culture – and the many causes I have mentioned are surely not the only ones – the most grievous cost is the price paid in human spirit: Contentious public discourse becomes a model for behavior and sets the tone for how individuals experience their relationships to other people and to the society we live in.

Recall the way young boys on Tory Island learned to emulate their elders:

> All around milled little boys imitating their elders, cursing, fluffing, swaggering, threatening. It was particularly fascinating to see how the children learned the whole sequence of behavior. Anything that the men did, they would imitate, shouting the same things, strutting and swaggering.

Tory Island may be an especially ritualized example, but it is not a totally aberrant one. When young men come together in groups, they often engage in symbolic ritual displays of aggression that involve posturing and mock battles. Without pressing the parallel in too literal a way, I couldn't help thinking that this sounds a bit like what journalists and lawyers have observed about their own tribes: that the display of aggression for the benefit of peers is often more important than concrete results.

Consider again law professor Charles Yablon's observation that young litigators learn to value an aggressive stance by listening to their elders' war stories about 'the smashing victories they obtained during pretrial discovery in cases which ultimately were settled.' Litigators

> derive job satisfaction by recasting minor discovery disputes as titanic struggles. Younger lawyers, convinced that their future careers may hinge on how tough they *seem* while conducting discovery, may conclude that it is more important to look and sound ferocious than to act cooperatively, even if all that huffing and puffing does not help (and sometimes harms) their cases.

Against this background, recall too the observations made by journalists that their colleagues feel pressured to ask tough questions to get peer approval. Kenneth Walsh, for example, commented that 'it helps your stature in journalism' if you ask challenging questions because that way 'you show you're tough and you're independent.' Just as litigators trade war stories about how tough they appeared (whether or not that appearance helped their client), Walsh points out that a journalist who dares to challenge the president takes on a heroic aura among his peers. He recalled a specific incident to illustrate this point:

> Remember Brit Hume asking the question . . . about the zigzag decision-making process of President Clinton? And of course President Clinton cut off the questions after that one question because he felt it was not appropriate. That's what we all remember about the Ruth Bader Ginsburg period, is that Brit asked that question.

Let's look at the actual exchange that earned Brit Hume the admiration of his peers. President Clinton called the press conference to announce his nomination of Judge Ruth Bader Ginsburg to the Supreme Court. After the president introduced her, Judge Ginsburg spoke movingly about her life, ending with tributes to her family: her children, granddaughter, husband, and, finally, her mother, 'the bravest and strongest person I have known, who was taken from me much too soon.' Following these remarks, which moved listeners to tears, journalists were invited to ask questions. The first (and, as it turned out, also the last) asked by correspondent Hume was this:

> The withdrawal of the Guinier nomination, sir, and your apparent focus on Judge Breyer and your turn, late, it seems, to Judge Ginsburg, may have created an impression, perhaps unfair, of a certain zigzag quality in the decision-making process here. I wonder, sir, if you could kind of walk us through it and perhaps disabuse us of any notion we might have along those lines. Thank you.

This question reminded everyone – at the very moment of Judge Ginsburg's triumph and honor – that she was not the president's first choice. It broke the spell of her moving remarks by shifting attention from the ceremonial occasion to the political maneuvers that had led up to the nomination – in particular, implying criticism of the president not from the perspective of substance (whether Judge Ginsburg would make a good Supreme Court justice) but strategy (the decision-making process by which she was chosen). Remarking, 'How you could ask a question like that after the statement she just made is beyond me,' the president closed the event.

The answer to how Brit Hume could have asked a question like that lies in Walsh's observation that journalists value a display of toughness. In this view, to worry about Judge Ginsburg's feelings – or those of the viewing audience – would be like an attorney worrying about the feelings of a witness about to be cross-examined. But public ceremonies play a role in the emotional lives not only of participants but also of observers, an enormous group in the era of television. Viewers who were moved by Judge Ginsburg's personal statement shared in the ceremony and felt connected to the judge and, by implication, to our judicial system. Such feelings of connection to public figures whose actions affect our lives is a crucial element in individuals' sense of community and their feeling of well-being. Breaking that spell was harmful to this sense of connection, contributing a little bit to what is often called cynicism but which really goes much deeper than that: alienation from the public figures who deeply affect our lives and consequently from the society in which we live.

In this sense, the valuing of the appearance of toughness is related to another theme running through all the domains I discussed: the breakdown in human connections and the rise of anonymity. Lieutenant Colonel Grossman points out that this, too, was one of many ways that the experience of serving in Vietnam was different for American soldiers than was the experience of serving in previous wars. Remember my Uncle Norman, who at the age of eighty-seven was still attending annual reunions of the 'boys' he had served with in World War II? This was possible because, as Grossman describes, soldiers in that war trained together, then went to war and served together. Those who were not killed or wounded stayed with the group until they all went home together at the end of the war. No wonder the bonds they forged could last a lifetime. Vietnam, in contrast, was a 'lonely war' of individuals assigned to constantly shifting units for year-long tours of duty (thirteen months for Marines). Grossman's description is graphic and sad:

> In Vietnam most soldiers arrived on the battlefield alone, afraid, and without friends. A soldier joined a unit where he was an FNG, a 'f—ing new guy,' whose inexperience and incompetence represented a threat to the continued survival of those in the unit. In a few months, for a brief period, he became an old hand who was bonded to a few friends and able to function well in combat. But then, all too soon, his friends left him via death, injury, or the end of their tours ... All but the best of units became just a collection of men experiencing endless leavings and arrivals, and that sacred process of bonding, which makes it possible for men to do what they must do in combat, became a tattered and torn remnant of the support structure experienced by veterans of past American wars.

Though this pattern is most painful in this context, it parallels what we have seen in all the other domains of public dialogue. Recall attorney Susan Popik's observation 'You don't come up against the same people all the time. That encouraged you to get along with them because you knew that in six months, you would be across the table from them again.' Recall journalists' lamenting that the present White House press corps is a large group, often unknown to aides and leaders, kept at a distance from the leaders they are assigned to cover: confined in a small room, in the back of the president's plane, behind ropes at public events. Contrast this with the recollections of those old enough to remember a small White House press corps that had free run of official buildings and lots of private off-the-record meetings with public officials, including the president and first lady, so that they actually got to know them – as people. And recall departing Senator Heflin's regret about the decline of opportunities for legislators of opposing parties to socialize, which led to friendships developed 'across party and ideological lines' that 'led to more openness and willingness to discuss issues on a cordial basis' and to finding 'common ground.' We could add the demise of the family doctor who came to your home, replaced by an overworked internist or family practitioner – if not an anonymous emergency room – and, if you're unlucky enough to need them but lucky enough to get to see them, a cadre of specialists who may not talk to each other or even much to you, or surgeons who may spend hours saving your life or limb but hardly ever see or speak to you afterward.

In all these domains, wonderful progress has been accompanied by more and more anonymity and disconnection, which are damaging to the human spirit and fertile ground for animosity.

## GETTING BEYOND DUALISM

At the heart of the argument culture is our habit of seeing issues and ideas as absolute and irreconcilable principles continually at war. To move beyond this static and limiting view, we can remember the Chinese approach to yin and yang. They are two principles, yes, but they are conceived not as irreconcilable polar opposites but as elements that coexist and should be brought into balance as much as possible. As sociolinguist Suzanne Wong Scollon notes, 'Yin is always present in and changing into yang and vice versa.' How can we translate this abstract idea into daily practice?

To overcome our bias toward dualism, we can make special efforts not to think in twos. Mary Catherine Bateson, an author and anthropologist who teaches at George Mason University, makes a point of having her class compare *three* cultures, not two. If students compare two cultures, she finds, they are inclined to polarize them, to think of the two as opposite to each other. But if they compare three cultures, they are more likely to think about each on its own terms.

As a goal, we could all try to catch ourselves when we talk about 'both sides' of an issue – and talk instead about 'all sides.' And people in any field can try to resist the temptation to pick on details when they see a chance to score a point. If the detail really does not speak to the main issue, bite your tongue. Draw back and consider the whole picture. After asking, 'Where is this wrong?' make an effort to ask 'What is right about this?' – not necessarily *instead*, but *in addition*.

In the public arena, producers can try to avoid, whenever possible, structuring public discussions as debates. This means avoiding the format of having two guests discuss an issue, pro and con. In some cases three guests – or one – will be more enlightening than two.

An example of the advantage of adding a third guest was an episode of *The Diane Rehm Show* on National Public Radio following the withdrawal of Anthony Lake from nomination as director of central intelligence. White House Communications Director Ann Lewis claimed that the process of confirming presidential appointments has become more partisan and personal. Tony Blankley, former communications director for Newt Gingrich, claimed that the process has always been rancorous. Fortunately for the audience, there was a third guest: historian Michael Beschloss, who provided historical perspective. He explained that during the immediately preceding period of 1940 to 1990, confirmation hearings were indeed more benign than they have been since, but in the 1920s and the latter half of the nineteenth century, he said, they were also 'pretty bloody.' In this way, a third guest, especially a guest who is not committed to one side, can dispel the audience's frustration when two guests make opposite claims.

Japanese television talk shows provide a window on other possibilities. Sociolinguist Atsuko Honda compared three different current affairs talk shows televised in Japan. Each one presents striking contrasts to what Americans take for granted in that genre. (The very fact that Honda chose to compare three – not two – is instructive.) The Japanese shows were structured in ways that made them less likely to be adversarial. Within each structure, participants vigorously opposed each other's ideas, yet they did so without excessively polarizing the issues.

Consider the formats of the three shows: *Nichiyoo Tooron* (*Sunday Discussion*) featured a moderator and four guests who discussed the recession for an hour. Only the moderator was a professional news commentator; two guests were associated with research institutes. The two other shows Honda examined concerned Japanese involvement in a peacekeeping mission in Cambodia. *Sunday Project* featured three guests: one magazine editor and two political scientists; the third show was a three-and-a-half-hour discussion involving fourteen panelists sitting around an oval table with a participating studio audience composed of fifty Japanese and Cambodian students. Viewers were also invited to participate by calling or faxing. Among the panelists were a history professor, a military analyst, a movie director, a scholar, a newscaster, and a legislator.

It is standard for American shows to provide balance by featuring two experts who represent contrasting political views: two senators or political consultants (one Republican, one Democrat), two journalist commentators (one on the left, one on the right), or two experts (one pro and one con). These Japanese shows had more than two guests, and the guests were identified by their expertise rather than their political perspectives. Another popular Japanese show that is often compared to ABC's *Nightline* or PBS's *Jim Lehrer News Hour* is called *Close-up Gendai*. Providing thirty minutes of nightly news analysis, the Japanese show uses a format similar to these American TV shows. But it typically features a single guest. Japanese shows, in other words, have a wide range of formats featuring one guest or three or more – anything but two, the number most likely to polarize.

The political talk shows that Honda analyzed included many disagreements and conflicts. But whereas moderators of American and British talk shows often provoke and stoke conflict to make their shows more interesting, the Japanese moderators – and also the other guests – expended effort to modulate conflicts and defuse the spirit of opposition, but not the substance of disagreement. One last example, taken from Honda's study, illustrates how this worked.

In the long discussion among fourteen panelists, a dispute arose between two: Shikata, a former executive of the Japanese Self-Defense Forces, supported sending these forces to Cambodia. He was opposed by Irokawa, a historian who believed that the involvement of these forces violated the Japanese constitution. This exchange comes across as quite rancorous:

SHIKATA: Why is it OK to send troops to the protecting side but not OK to the protected side?

IROKAWA: Because we have the Japanese Constitution.

SHIKATA: Why is it so, if we have the Constitution?

IROKAWA: Well, we have to abide by the Constitution. If you don't want to follow the Constitution, you

> should get rid of your Japanese nationality and go
> somewhere else.

These are pretty strong words. And they were accompanied by strong gestures: According to Honda, as Shikata posed his question, he was beating the table with his palms; as Irokawa responded, he was jabbing the air toward Shikata with a pen.

Yet the confrontation did not take on a rancorous tone. The television cameras offered close-ups of both men's faces – smiling. In Japanese and other Asian cultures, smiling has different connotations than it does for Americans and Europeans: It tends to express not amusement but embarrassment. And while Shikata and Irokawa smiled, other panelists rushed to add their voices – and everyone burst out laughing. The laughter served to defuse the confrontation. So did the loud cacophony of voices that erupted as several panelists tried to speak at once. When individual voices finally were distinguished, they did not take one side or the other but tried to mediate the conflict by supporting and criticizing both sides equally. For example, Ohshima, a movie director, said:

OHSHIMA:  I think that both parties overestimate or underesti-
          mate the realities for the sake of making a point.

Atsuko Honda found this to be typical of the televised discussions she analyzed: When a conspicuous conflict arose between two parties, other participants frequently moved in with attempts to mediate. In this way, they supported the Japanese ideal of avoiding winners and losers and helped everyone preserve some measure of 'face.' This mediation did not prevent varying views from being expressed; it resulted in different kinds of views being expressed. If two sides set the terms of debate and subsequent comments support one side or the other, the range of insights offered is circumscribed by the original two sides. If the goal instead is to mediate and defuse polarization, then other panelists are more likely to express a range of perspectives that shed nuanced light on the original two sides or suggest other ways of approaching the issue entirely.

## MOVING FROM DEBATE TO DIALOGUE

Many of the issues I have discussed are also of concern to Amitai Etzioni and other communitarians. In *The New Golden Rule*, Etzioni proposes rules of engagement to make dialogue more constructive between people with differing views. His rules of engagement are designed to reflect – and reinforce – the tenet that people whose ideas conflict are still members of the same community. Among these rules are:

- Don't demonize those with whom you disagree.
- Don't affront their deepest moral commitments.
- Talk less of rights, which are nonnegotiable, and more of needs, wants, and interests.
- Leave some issues out.
- Engage in a dialogue of convictions: Don't be so reasonable and conciliatory that you lose touch with a core of belief you feel passionately about.

As I stressed in earlier chapters, producers putting together television or radio shows and journalists covering stories might consider – in at least some cases – preferring rather than rejecting potential commentators who say they cannot take one side or the other unequivocally. Information shows might do better with only one guest who is given a chance to explore an idea in depth rather than two who will prevent each other from developing either perspective. A producer who feels that two guests with radically opposed views seem truly the most appropriate might begin by asking whether the issue is being framed in the most constructive way. If it is, a third or fourth participant could be invited as well, to temper the 'two sides' perspective.

Perhaps it is time to reexamine the assumption that audiences always prefer a fight. In reviewing a book about the history of *National Geographic*, Marina Warner scoffs at the magazine's policy of avoiding attack. She quotes the editor who wrote in 1915, 'Only what is of a kindly nature is printed about any country or people, everything unpleasant or unduly critical being avoided.' Warner describes this editorial approach condescendingly as a 'happy-talk, feel-good philosophy' and concludes that 'its deep wish not to offend has often made it dull.' But the facts belie this judgment. *National Geographic* is one of the most successful magazines of all time – as reported in the same review, its circulation 'stands at over 10 million, and the readership, according to surveys, is four times that number.'

Perhaps, too, it is time to question our glorification of debate as the best, if not the only, means of inquiry. The debate format leads us to regard those doing different kinds of research as belonging to warring camps. There is something very appealing about conceptualizing differing approaches in this way, because dichotomies appeal to our sense of how knowledge should be organized.

Well, what's wrong with that?

What's wrong is that it obscures aspects of disparate work that overlap and can enlighten each other.

What's wrong is that it obscures the complexity of research. Fitting ideas into a particular camp requires you to oversimplify them. Again, disinformation and distortion can result. Less knowledge is gained, not more. And time spent attacking an opponent or defending against attacks is not spent doing something else – like original research.

What's wrong is that it implies that only one framework can apply, when in most cases many can. As a colleague put it, 'Most theories are wrong not in what they assert but in what they deny.' Clinging to the elephant's leg, they loudly proclaim that the person describing the elephant's tail is wrong. This is not going to help them – or their readers – understand an elephant. Again, there are parallels in personal relationships. I recall a man who had just returned from a weekend human development seminar. Full of enthusiasm, he explained the main lesson he had learned: 'I don't have to make others wrong to prove that I'm right.' He experienced this revelation as a liberation; it relieved him of the burden of trying to prove others wrong.

If you limit your view of a problem to choosing between two sides, you inevitably reject much that is true, and you narrow your field of vision to the limits of those two sides, making it unlikely you'll pull back, widen your field of vision, and discover the paradigm shift that will permit truly new understanding.

In moving away from a narrow view of debate, we need not give up conflict and criticism altogether. Quite the contrary, we can develop more varied – and more constructive – ways of expressing opposition and negotiating disagreement.

We need to use our imaginations and ingenuity to find different ways to seek truth and gain knowledge, and add them to our arsenal – or, should I say, to the ingredients for our stew. It will take creativity to find ways to blunt the most dangerous blades of the argument culture. It's a challenge we must undertake, because our public and private lives are at stake.

# NOTES

*Note:* Sources referred to by short form are cited in full in the References.

## PREFACE TO THE BRITISH EDITION

2. 'I started it by introducing Paula Jones to the world. Now I'm trying to stop it': David Brock, *Esquire*, April, 1998.

## 1. FIGHTING FOR OUR LIVES

10. *'culture of critique'*: I first introduced this term in an op-ed essay, 'The Triumph of the Yell,' *The New York Times*, Jan. 14, 1994, p. A29.

10. *'There are moments'*: Charles Simic, 'In Praise of Invective,' *Harper's*, Aug. 1997, pp. 24, 26–27; the quote is from p. 26. The article is excerpted from *Orphan Factory* (Ann Arbor: University of Michigan Press, 1997). I am grateful to Amitai Etzioni for calling this article to my attention.

10. Both the term 'agonism' and the phrase 'programmed contentiousness' come from Walter Ong, *Fighting for Life*.

13. *'the great backpacking vs. car camping debate'*: Steve Hendrix, 'Hatchback vs. Backpack,' *The Washington Post Weekend*, Mar. 1, 1996, p. 6.

13. *creationism:* See, for example, Jessica Mathews, 'Creationism Makes a Comeback,' *The Washington Post*, Apr. 8, 1996, p. A21.

13. *'People dispute that'*: Lipstadt, *Denying the Holocaust*, p. 15. Lipstadt cites *Esquire*, Feb. 1983, for the interview with Mitchum.

14. *Gallo had to spend:* See Nicholas Wade, 'Method and Madness: The Vindication of Robert Gallo,' *The New York Times Magazine*, Dec. 26, 1993, p.

12, and Elaine Richman, 'The Once and Future King,' *The Sciences*, Nov.–Dec. 1996, pp. 12–15. The investigations of Gallo were among a series of overly zealous investigations of suspected scientific misconduct – all of which ended in the exoneration of the accused, but not before they – had caused immense personal anguish and professional setbacks. Others similarly victimized were Gallo's colleague Mika Popovic, immunologist Thereza Imanishi-Kari, and her coauthor (not accused of wrongdoing but harmed as a result of his defense of her) Nobel Prize winner David Baltimore. On Popovic, see Malcolm Gladwell, 'Science Friction,' *The Washington Post Magazine*, Dec. 6, 1992, pp. 18–21, 49–51. On Imanishi-Kari and Baltimore, see *The New Yorker*, May 27, 1996, pp. 94–98ff.

16. *potentially endless list:* Randy Allen Harris, *The Linguistics Wars* (New York: Oxford University Press, 1993); 'The Science Wars,' *Newsweek*, Apr. 21, 1997, p. 54; 'The Mammogram War,' *Newsweek*, Feb. 24, 1997, p. 54; 'Party Wars,' *New York*, June 2, 1997, cover. The subhead of the latter reads, 'In the battle to feed New York's elite, the top caterers are taking off their white gloves and sharpening their knives.'

16. 'DEMOCRATS SEND CLINTON': *The New York Times*, Aug. 29, 1996, p. A1.

17. *'We risk imposing'*: Keller, *Reflections on Gender and Science*, p. 157. Another such case is explained by paleontologist Stephen Jay Gould in his book *Wonderful Life* about the Burgess shale – a spectacular deposit of 530-million-year-old fossils. In 1909, the first scientist to study these fossils missed the significance of the find, because he 'shoehorned every last Burgess animal into a modern group, viewing the fauna collectively as a set of primitive or ancestral versions of later, improved forms' (p. 24). Years later, observers looked at the Burgess shale fossils with a fresh eye and saw a very different reality: a panoply of life forms, far more diverse and numerous than what exists today. The early scientists missed what was right before their eyes because, Gould shows, they proceeded from a metaphoric understanding of evolution as a linear march of progress from the ancient and primitive to the modern and complex, with humans the inevitable, most complex apex. Accepting the metaphor of 'the cone of increasing diversity' prevented the early scientists from seeing what was really there.

18. *'Showdown at Lincoln Center'*: Peter Watrous, 'The Year in the Arts: Pop & Jazz/1994,' *The New York Times*, Dec. 25, 1994, sec. 2, p. 36.

19. *'the face-off between'*: Jack Kroll, 'And in This Corner . . .,' *Newsweek*, Feb. 10, 1997, p. 65.

20. *a fight between two skaters:* Though Harding was demonized somewhat more as an unfeminine, boorish 'Wicked Witch of the West' (George Vecsey, 'Let's Begin the Legal Olympics,' *The New York Times*, Feb. 13, 1994, sec. 8, p. 1.), Kerrigan was also demonized as cold and aloof, an 'ice princess.'

20. *'long-anticipated figure-skating shootout'*: Jere Longman, 'Kerrigan Glides Through Compulsory Interview,' *The New York Times*, Feb. 13, 1994, sec. 8, p. 9.

20. *'the rivalry surrounding'*: Paul Farhi, 'For NBC, Games Not Just for Guys; Network Tailors Its Coverage to Entice Women to Watch,' *The Washington Post*, July 26, 1996, p. A1.

22. *'I haven't much time':* *The Washington Post Book World,* June 16, 1996, p. 14.

24. *even judges:* *Washingtonian,* June 1996, ranked judges.

24. *Ohio State University protested:* Letter to the editor by Malcolm S. Baroway, Executive Director, University Communications, *Time,* Oct. 3, 1994, p. 14.

24. Overlaid on the talk show example is the gender issue: The woman who called wished she had the courage to stand up to a man and saw her habitual way of speaking as evidence of her insecurity. This interpretation is suggested by our assumptions about women and men. Many people, researchers included, start from the assumption that women are insecure, so ways they speak are scrutinized for evidence of insecurity. The result is often a failure to understand or appreciate women's styles on their own terms, so women are misinterpreted as defective men.

25. *'Always provocative, sometimes infuriating':* Jill Nelson, 'Fighting Words,' review of Ishmael Reed, *Airing Dirty Laundry, The New York Times Book Review,* Feb. 13, 1994, p. 28.

26. *In this spirit:* John Krich, 'To Teach Is Glorious: A Conversation with the New Dean of Cal's Journalism School,' Orville Schell, *Express,* Aug. 23, 1996, pp. 1, 14–16, 18, 20–22. The remark is from p. 15.

26. *Many cultures have rituals:* See Schlegel and Barry, *Adolescence.*

27. *'Democracy begins in conversation':* *Dialogue on John Dewey,* Corliss Lamont, ed. (New York: Horizon Press, 1959), p. 88. Thanks to Pete Becker for this reference.

28. *In dialogue, there is:* This insight comes from Walter Ong, who writes, 'There is opposition here but no head-on collision, which stops dialogue. (Of course, sometimes dialogue has to be stopped, but that is another story.)' (*Fighting for Life,* p. 32).

---

## 2. BOTH SIDES COME OUT FIGHTING: THE ARGUMENT CULTURE AND THE PRESS

29. The 'TAKE A SIDE' ad appeared in *The Washington Post,* Feb. 24, 1997. The *Crossfire* ad appeared in *Newsweek,* May 6, 1996.

30. *'When you think "Guggenheim"':* *Newsweek,* Jan. 13, 1997, pp. 68–70; the quote is from p. 69.

31. 'A CLASSIC MATCHUP': *Newsweek,* Feb. 10, 1997, pp. 47, 49.

31. *A single issue: Newsweek,* Mar. 10, 1997. Quotations are from pp. 39, 48, and 45.

32. Lingua Franca *debates:* Janny Scott, 'At Home With: Jeffrey Kittay: Whipsawing the Groves of Academe,' *The New York Times,* Dec. 12, 1996, p. C1.

32. *'The middle ground':* Howard Kurtz, *Hot Air,* p. 4.

32. *The combative attitude:* 'The Clare v Liz turf war,' *Independent on Sunday,* February 8, 1998, p. 4.

32. *'at each other's throats':* 'Furious Prescott, the tunnel chief and 5bn fiasco,' *Evening Standard,* January 29, 1998, p. 9.

33. *'the debate turned out'*: Edward Wyatt, 'Mutual Funds: Why Fidelity Doesn't Want You to Shop at Schwab,' *The New York Times*, July 14, 1996, p. F7.

33. *Almost any topic:* 'The Mel Gibson of the potting shed meets his mulcher,' *The Independent on Sunday*, September 21, 1997.

33. *the Library of Congress:* Personal communication with James Billington. For a news story, see Marc Fisher, 'Under Attack, Library Shelves Freud Exhibit,' *The Washington Post*, Dec. 5, 1995, p. A1.

34. For reports of my appearance with Robert Bly, see: Esther B. Fein, 'Book Notes,' *The New York Times*, Oct. 30, 1991, p. C20; Esther B. Fein, 'Battle of the Sexes Gets Fuzzy as Authors Meet,' *The New York Times*, Nov. 3, 1991, p. L44; 'Speaking Softly, Carrying No Stick,' *Newsweek*, Nov. 11, 1991, p. 66; 'Great Debates: Bill and Coo,' *The Economist*, Nov. 9–15, 1991, pp. 107, 108.

36. *'Relations between him'*: Carroll Bogert, 'Richardson for the U.N.: Slicker Than He Looks,' *Newsweek*, Feb. 10, 1997, p. 29.

36. *James Fallows recounts: Breaking the News*, pp. 164–65.

37. Quotations from Johnson and Broder, *The System*, come from pp. 634, 633, and 231 respectively.

39. *'Controversy has become'*: Cosmo Landesman, 'Shocked but not stirred,' *Sunday Times*, Section 10, February 12, 1995, p. 10.

40. On Randall Kennedy, see Ellis Cose, 'No Labels Need Apply,' *Newsweek*, June 2, 1997, p. 71.

41. The Buffalo student editor is quoted in Lipstadt, 'The Fragility of Memory,' p.26. The Montel Williams Show is described in Lipstadt, *Denying the Holocaust*, p. 2.

42. *'a special radioactive power'*: *Newsweek*, Sept. 6, 1993, p. 31.

42. *'one-sided Jewish propaganda'*: Philip Gourevitch, 'What They Saw at the Holocaust Museum,' *The New York Times Magazine*, Feb. 12, 1995, pp. 44–45; the quote is from p. 45.

42. The *Georgetown Record* editor is quoted in Lipstadt, 'The Fragility of Memory,' p. 26.

43. *The magazine's publisher:* T. R. Reid, 'Tokyo Magazine Shut For Denying Holocaust,' *The Washington Post*, Jan. 31, 1995, p. A20. This seems to reflect the more highly developed Japanese senses of shame and responsibility. The magazine's employees were given other jobs in the same corporation.

43. The Gelbspan quotation is from *The Heat Is On*, p. 9.

44. *The resulting 'debate':* I have taken this from Alan Ehrenhalt's review of David Gelernter, *Drawing a Life*, *The New York Times Book Review*, Sept. 21, 1997, p. 8.

45. 'POLL ON ABORTION': Condit, p. 329.

45. *'two-faced, unreliable, and'*: I would add that the strategy focus of reporting plays into the tendency to polarize. Asking 'Why does this candidate or leader hold this belief?' would more likely lead to an evaluation of the belief, but asking 'What is this candidate or officeholder trying to accomplish politically by taking this stance?' would more likely suggest that taking an equivocal position is waffling and deceptive.

47. *'smarter prohibition'*: Christopher S. Wren, 'New Voice in Drug Debate Seeks to Lower the Volume,' *The New York Times*, Sept. 1, 1997, p. A10.

48. My article on apologizing appeared in *The New York Times Magazine*, July 21, 1996, pp. 34–35.

51. *'Politics is theater'*: Kelsey Menehan, '"D.C. Politics & Government Hour" starring Derek McGinty, Mark Plotkin, and a Cast of Thousands,' *WAMU Newsletter*, April/May 1995, pp. 2–3; quotes from p. 2.

51. *'sheer, raucous aggression'*: 'Just shout' (leading article), *Daily Telegraph*, September 29, 1997.

51. *confrontational interview technique*: 'Why our interviewers should stop sneering and start to listen,' *The Times*, February 4, 1995, p. 16.

51. *'a compelling blood sport'*: Simon Jenkins, 'Taking a risk with vox pop,' *The Times*, March 18, 1995, p. 18.

52. Kurtz, *Hot Air*, pp. 21, 22, 23. The quotation from Eleanor Clift is changed slightly based on personal communication.

53. *television sports announcers*: See Goldstein and Bredemeier, 'Socialization.'

53. *'sports and violence'*: Quotations from Bryant, 'Viewers' Enjoyment of Televised Sports Violence,' come from pp. 270, 271, and 272. Bryant attributes the Dave Brown quotation to E. M. Swift, 'Hockey? Call It Sockey,' *Sports Illustrated*, Feb. 17, 1986, pp. 12–17; the quote is from p. 15.

55. The radio talk show on which Rosenthal appeared was *The Diane Rehm Show*, Mar. 25, 1997.

56. *'We are very good'*: 'Taking on Paxman and Humphrys,' *Daily Telegraph*, June 10, 1997.

56. *'complementary schismogenesis'*: See Gregory Bateson, *Steps to an Ecology of Mind*. I have shown how this works in personal relationships in several books; see *That's Not What I Meant!*, pp. 129–31, and *You Just Don't Understand*, p. 282.

---

### 3. FROM LAPDOG TO ATTACK DOG: THE AGGRESSION CULTURE AND THE PRESS

58. *'constantly chomping at'*: Larry Sabato, comments at an American Forum symposium 'President Clinton and the Press: Is It Better the Second Term Around?' American University, Washington, D.C., Apr. 14, 1997.

59. *Former Republican Senator*: Alan Simpson, *Right in the Old Gazoo: A Lifetime of Scrapping with the Press* (New York: William Morrow, 1997), p. 6.

59. Brit Hume is quoted in Kenneth Walsh, *Feeding the Beast*, p. 12.

60. Jill Abramson's remarks were made on *All Things Considered*, National Public Radio, June 18, 1997.

60. *'Some journalists'*: 'Its effect on our democracy': Michael Leapman, *Treacherous Estate* (Hodder and Stoughton, 1992), p. 245.

60. David Remnick on Katharine Graham: 'Citizen Kay,' *The New Yorker*, Jan. 20, 1997, pp. 60–71; the Graham quote is on pp. 70–71.

61. *When a grand jury*: Attorney General Elliot Richardson and his deputy,

Alexander Ruckleshaus, both resigned rather than follow the order, so it fell to Solicitor General Robert Bork to fire Cox. He did not, however, fire the rest of the prosecution team, and the president did eventually deliver the tapes, which proved his complicity in the cover-up and sealed his fate. My source for these details is a National Public Radio series aired on the twenty-fifth anniversary of Watergate, June 16–20, 1997. Daniel Schorr's remarks were made on NPR, *Talk of the Nation*, June 17, 1997.

62. *a June 1997 poll:* The CNN/USA Today/Gallup survey, taken May 30 and June 1, 1997, appears on the CNN/Time All Politics Web page.

62. Paul Begala made these remarks as part of the American Forum symposium 'President Clinton and the Press: Is It Better the Second Term Around?' American University, Washington, D.C., Apr. 14, 1997.

62. Bay Buchanan's remarks were also made at the American Forum symposium, Apr. 14, 1997.

63. *'a kind of weird':* Gopnik, 'Read All About It,' p. 99.

63. *'adding opinion or "edge"':* Walsh, *Feeding the Beast*, p. 7.

63. *'snarl':* Fallows, *Breaking the News*, p. 178.

63. *'Pieces that are harsh':* Fallows, *Breaking the News*, p. 179.

63. *'Yesterday's edge becomes':* Gopnik, 'Read All About It,' p. 90.

63. *'Reporters feel pressured':* Walsh, *Feeding the Beast*, p. 286.

63. ABC reporter Charles Peters is quoted in Fallows, *Breaking the News*, p. 180.

64. *'equal-opportunity sneering':* Overholser, 'Tell the Story,' *The Washington Post*, Apr. 13, 1997, p. C6.

64. *This conviction was stated:* Howell Raines, *The New York Times*, Feb. 25, 1996, p. E14.

65. *'Journalists are taught':* Richard Folkers, 'When Our Worlds Collide,' *U.S. News & World Report*, Sept. 15, 1997, p. 40.

66. Kathryn Ruud cites German linguist Siegfried Bork as the source for Hitler's use of 'whining.' She notes the same manipulation in right-wing talk radio references to 'whining liberals.'

66. *Diana 'was not above':* Matthew Cooper, 'Was the Press to Blame?,' *Newsweek*, Sept. 8, 1997, pp. 36–38; the quote is from p. 37.

66. *'The press is ferocious':* Matthew Cooper, 'Was the Press to Blame?' *Newsweek*, Sept. 8, 1997, p. 37. Just two weeks before her death, a commentator wrote in *The New York Times* that Diana 'has recently been called a mindless "fruit" who thinks nothing of flying 160 miles by helicopter to consult her psychic.' (Youssef M. Ibrahim, 'Outside the Faith, Big Time, and Highly Entertaining,' Aug. 17, 1997, p. E5).

66. The text of Earl Spencer's remarks was published in *The New York Times*, Sept. 7, 1997, sec. 1, p. 11.

67. *the teenage daughter:* News of the World, February 1, 1998.

67. *'a glorified sort':* *The Diane Rehm Show*, May 28, 1996. The same point is also made by Kenneth Walsh in *Feeding the Beast*, Fallows in *Breaking the News*, and panelists at the American Forum symposium.

67. Gergen's remarks were made on *The Diane Rehm Show*, May 28, 1996. So were his and Kenneth Walsh's following comments.

68. *an informal system of contact*: Leapman, *op. cit.*, p. 242.

69. The American University symposium was 'An American Forum: President Clinton and the Press: Is It Better the Second Term Around?' Washington, D.C., Apr. 14, 1997.

69. *'knew we were being used'*: The source of Patricia O'Brien's comments is personal communication.

70. Interview with Elizabeth Dole: Richard Stengel, 'Liddy Makes Perfect,' *Time*, July 1, 1996, p. 32.

71. *This aggressive technique*: 'Still rabbiting on': *Independent on Sunday* (Sunday Review), May 6, 1990.

71. *could be autobiographical*: 'Confessions of an axewoman': *Sunday Times*, April 28, 1991.

72. *secondhand criticism:* A chapter in my book *That's Not What I Meant!*, called 'The Intimate Critic,' is devoted to the topic of criticism in daily life.

73. *All that remained:* I have taken the accounts of the contexts of Hillary Clinton's two remarks from Jamieson, *Beyond the Double Bind*, pp. 24–25. Jamieson uses these examples to show that the press's treatment of Hillary Clinton is a Rorschach test for the double binds women are in.

73. *a* New York Times/*CBS News poll:* See, for example, Alessandra Stanley, 'Democrats in New York: A Softer Image for Hillary Clinton,' *The New York Times*, July 13, 1992, pp. B1, B4; the poll is referred to on p. B1.

74. *what would be the point:* Jamieson, *Dirty Politics.*

75. *'Although Redgrave has'*: Frank Bruni, 'Under a Bare Bulb,' *The New York Times Magazine*, Feb. 16, 1997, pp. 22–25; the quote is from p. 22.

78. *he had, after all:* Gitta Sereny, *Albert Speer: His Battle with Truth* (New York: Knopf, 1995). I have taken this account from the review by Claudia Koonz in *The New York Times Book Review*, Oct. 8, 1995, pp. 11–12.

78. Nick Kotz's detailed account of Admiral Boorda's suicide: 'Breaking Point,' *The Washingtonian*, Dec. 1996, pp. 95–121.

81. The awards Col. Hackworth removed were 'a cloth patch known as a ranger tab and one of two Distinguished Flying Crosses' (*The New York Times*, May 16, 1977, p. 22). *Newsweek* (May 26, 1997, p. 34) described them as 'an oak-leaf cluster to the Distinguished Flying Cross and an Army Ranger tab.'

81. *'I never wanted'*: Quoted in Kotz, 'Breaking Point,' p. 102.

81. *'It is possible'*: Jonathan Alter, 'Beneath the Waves,' *Newsweek*, May 27, 1996, pp. 30–31. The quote is from p. 31.

82. The Hackworth and Thomas quotes are from Kotz, 'Breaking Point,' p. 113. The Turner quote is from 'Liar's Poker,' *New York*, July 29, 1996, pp. 12–13, p. 13. It is also of interest that Thomas used the word 'opposition' for what I think most would regard as the 'competition.'

83. *'Unless you're a public figure'*: Gerike, *Old Is Not a Four-Letter Word*, p. 103.

84. *'all American institutions'*: Cokie Roberts made these remarks at the

American Forum symposium, Apr. 14, 1997.

84. *'Temporizing, moderate figures'*: Gopnik, 'Read All About It,' p. 94.

85. *they might as well be as cynical:* This point is made by Fallows in *Breaking the News*.

85. *a study of the 1974 elections:* Arthur Miller, Edie Goldenberg, and Lutz Erbring, 'Type-set Politics: Impact of Newspapers on Public Confidence,' p. 80, cited in Michael J. Robinson and Margaret A Sheehan, *Over the Wire and on TV: CBS and UPI in Campaign '80* (New York: Russell Sage Foundation, 1983), p. 264.

85. The review of Cappella and Jamieson, *Spiral of Cynicism: The Press and the Public Good*, is by Douglas A. Sylva, *The New York Times Book Review*, May 18, 1997, p. 20.

86. *'This was a guy'*: 'Inman Quits, Leveling Charges,' Ann Devroy, *The Washington Post*, Jan. 19, 1994, pp. A1, A8; the quote is from p. A8.

86. *Inman also referred:* In his remarks, Inman talked at length about columnist William Safire and maintained that coverage had been fair overall, with the exception of columns in *The New York Times* and *The Boston Globe*. *The Washington Post* also mentioned columnists Anthony Lewis and Ellen Goodman (Jan. 19, 1994, pp. A1, A8).

87. Inman's remarks were published in full in *The New York Times*, Jan. 19, 1994, p. A14.

87. *Reports of Inman's withdrawal:* 'Mystified' comes from R.W. Apple, Jr., 'Inman Withdraws as Clinton Choice for Defense Chief,' *The New York Times*, Jan. 19, 1994, pp. A1, A13. 'Stunned,' 'astonishment,' and 'puzzlement' come from Eric Schmitt, 'In Inman's Wake, Astonishment, and a Scramble,' *The New York Times*, Jan. 19, 1994, p. A15. 'Extraordinary' comes from Linda Greenhouse, 'Inman Says "New McCarthyism" in the Nation's Press Led to His Withdrawal,' *The New York Times*, Jan. 19, 1994, p. A13.

87. *'I know he doesn't like'*: Schmitt, 'In Inman's Wake,' p. A15.

88. *'After Watergate'*: Overholser is quoted in Maxwell McCombs, 'Explorers and Surveyors: Expanding Strategies for Agenda-setting Research,' *Journalism Quarterly*, 69(4) (1992), pp. 813–24; the quote is from p. 819.

88. The New York Times *summed up: 'In fact . . .'*: Apple, 'Inman Withdraws,' p. A13.

88. *The front-page profile:* Barton Gellman, 'Critical Spotlight Stings Behind-the-Scenes Man,' *The Washington Post*, Jan. 19, 1994, pp. A1, A8.

89. *'They have no skins'*: Geneva Overholser told me this quote from Edward R. Murrow. Many other journalists have noted the glass-house sensitivity of journalists to criticism; see 'An Author's Ethics' by Iver Peterson, quoting Suzanne Braun Levine; the 'Fools for Scandal' letter exchange (*The New York Times Book Review*, Aug. 25, 1996, sec. F, p. 4); and a *New Yorker* article on press responses to James Fallows's book (David Remnick, 'Scoop,' Jan. 29, 1996, pp. 38–42).

89. *'ruining people is'*: Quoted in Dan Balz, *The Washington Post*, 'Inman's Accusations Echo Foster's Attacks on Washington Process,' Jan. 19, 1997, p. A6.

89. *'I sense elements'*: Quoted in Ann Devroy, 'Inman Quits, Leveling Charges,' *The Washington Post*, Jan. 19, 1994, p. A1.

90. Guinier was quoted in Balz, 'Inman's Accusations . . .,' p. A6. See also Laurel Leff, 'From Legal Scholar to Quota Queen,' *The Columbia Journalism Review*, 32 (Sept.–Oct. 1993), pp. 36–41.

90. *She cites a book:* The book is *Lingua Tertii Imperii: Sprache des Dritten Reiches* (*LTI: Language of the Third Reich*). (Random House is scheduled to publish an English translation of Klemperer's diaries in 1998.) Ruud's article, unpublished at the time of this writing, is called 'Liberal Chiggers and Other Creepers.'

91. The quotations from Fallows are from *Breaking the News*, p. 203.

92. *'The viewers are responsible'*: Attributed to Marlene Sanders, in Max Frankel, 'To Pry or Not to Pry,' *The New York Times Magazine*, Nov. 3, 1996, pp. 34, 36; the quote is from p. 36.

93. *'We're losing a whole generation'*: Kenneth Walsh, comments at American Forum symposium, Apr. 14, 1997.

94. Jill Abramson was speaking on *All Things Considered*, June 18, 1997.

94. *'When I first started'*: The *Diane Rehm Show*, May 28, 1996.

94. The comments by Maxwell McCombs come from personal communication as well as his article 'Explorers and Surveyors: Expanding Strategies for Agenda-setting Research.'

94. Sabato's comment comes from the American Forum symposium, Apr. 14, 1997.

95. Details of the suit against *The Wall Street Journal* come from Larry Reibstein, 'One Heck of a Whupping,' *Newsweek*, Mar. 31, 1997, p. 54.

95. Orville Schell's remarks are from John Krich, 'To Teach Is Glorious: A Conversation with the New Dean of Cal's Journalism School, Orville Schell,' *Express*, Aug. 23, 1996, pp. 1, 14–16, 18, 20–22; the quotes are from pp. 15 and 18.

97. Ronald Ostrow's remarks were made on *Talk of the Nation*, June 17, 1997.

97. Studs Terkel's remarks were made on *Talk of the Nation*, Sept. 11, 1997.

97. *Overholser believes that:* 'Tell the Story,' *The Washington Post*, Apr. 3, 1997, p. C6. I interviewed Overholser, but her views on anonymity are also expressed in columns published in *The Washington Post* on Dec. 3, 1995; Feb. 18, 1996; and Mar. 10, 1996.

98. Jonathan Alter's article: 'Beneath the Waves,' *Newsweek*, May 27, 1996, p. 31.

99. On Auletta, see *At Random*, no. 17 (Spring-Summer 1997), p. 43.

99. The initiative of the American Society of Newspaper Editors' is described on their home page.

99. *a group of prominent journalists:* Howard Kurtz, 'An "Eye" Toward the Bottom Line,' *The Washington Post*, Sept. 1, 1997, p. D3. The signers include David Halberstam, Carl Bernstein, Robert MacNeil, Geneva Overholser,

and Bob Herbert. Tom Rosenstiel and Bill Kovach are 'spearheading the effort.'

---

## 4. 'A PLAGUE ON BOTH YOUR HOUSES!':
## OPPOSITION IN OUR POLITICAL LIVES

100. *In contrast, the average:* Ornstein, *Lessons and Legacies*, p. ix. The quotation from Ornstein appears on p. xi; quotations from Senator Exon appear on p. 57; from Senator Simon on p. 172; and from Senator Heflin on pp. 76, 79, and 81–82.

100. Among those voluntarily retiring from the House were 4 of the 47 women (out of a total of 435 House members): Pat Schroeder (Dem., Colo.), Jan Meyers (Rep., Kans.), Cardiss Collins (Dem., Ill.), and Barbara Vucanovich (Rep., Nev.).

103. The quotations from Senator Rudman appear in *Combat*, pp. 250, 243, and 245.

104. *'Mr Clinton also fears':* Adam Clymer, 'No Deal: Politics and the Dead Art of Compromise,' *The New York Times*, Oct. 22, 1995, pp. 1, 3. The quotation is from p. 3.

104. *'The extreme elements':* Heflin, quoted in Ornstein, *Lessons and Legacies*, p. 82.

105. Dr Elders's remarks are from Claudia Dreifus, 'Joycelyn Elders,' *The New York Times Magazine*, Jan. 30, 1994, pp. 16–19; the quote is from p. 18.

105. *'We have much':* Beschloss made this comment on *The Diane Rehm Show*, Mar. 31, 1997.

106. Leahy's and McCain's comments both appear in Helen Dewar, 'Nominees Now Face "Trial by Fire": Senate Confirmation Process Has Evolved into Political Warfare,' *The Washington Post*, Mar. 23, 1997, p. A10.

106. *'It's the politics':* Gunderson and Morris, *House and Home*, p. 221.

106. *In reality, the furlough:* Kathleen Hall Jamieson, *Dirty Politics*. Jamieson dissects in detail the misrepresentations and machinations of this and other political advertising campaigns.

108. *'We've got a homo':* Gunderson and Morris, *House and Home*, p. 11.

109. *'because it can create':* Krauss, 'Conflict in the Diet,' p. 246.

109. *'More and more':* Rudman, *Combat*, p. 243.

110. *'They have become friends':* Krauss, 'Conflict in the Diet,' p. 275. The later quote is from p. 255.

110. *'informal togetherness among':* Sen. Heflin, quoted in Ornstein, *Lessons and Legacies*, p. 86.

110. *'Once they were friends':* Matthew Cooper, 'The Trouble with Newt,' *Newsweek*, Jan. 20, 1997, p. 34.

111. Sen. Kassebaum made this comment on *The Diane Rehm Show*, Dec. 14, 1995.

111. *'Worried that the':* Gunderson and Morris, *House and Home*, pp. 321–22. Later quotations are from pp.188, 189, and 166.

113. *'When I grow up':* The cartoon appeared in *The New Yorker*, Aug. 19,

1996, p. 25. The cartoonist is Lee Lorenz.

114. *They didn't know:* Johnson and Broder, *The System*, p. 632.

115. *'The very fact':* 'Blair rounds on "useless, pathetic" Hague over sleaze': *Independent*, January 29, 1998, p. 6.

115. *'A Government licensed lynch mob':* 'Labour mob storms Palace of Westminster': *Daily Telegraph*, February 5, 1998, p. 2.

117. *The Horton case:* Sabato and Simpson, *Dirty Little Secrets*, p. 161.

117. *Radosh shows that:* Radosh, *Divided They Fell*. This summary is taken from a review in *The Washington Post Book World*, Sept. 8, 1996, p. 4.

117. *'big-government social right':* Gunderson and Morris, *House and Home*, p. 188.

120. *Few major newspapers:* Howard Kurtz, 'Times for a Change,' *The Washington Post*, Feb. 14, 1997, p. B2. Ironically, those who do not give 'too political' as the reason for not carrying Mrs Clinton's column claim instead that it is not political enough – 'too soft.' This article reports that the ultraconservative *Washington Times* was beginning to carry the column; however, the circulation of that paper in the nation's capital is minuscule compared to that of *The Washington Post*.

122. The panel discussion was on *The Diane Rehm Show*, Feb. 5, 1997. The caller was identified as Imogene from Kensington.

122. *The 'opposition party':* In this and other remarks taken from talk shows, I have deleted the occasional repetitions and false starts that characterize spontaneous talk but give a misleading impression of hesitance and disorganization when printed.

125. *'The focus on':* Sen. Heflin, in Ornstein, *Lessons and Legacies*, p. 79. Journalists' eagerness to see big divisive issues aired is not so different in spirit from campaign consultants' advice to seek out 'wedge issues' about which people have strong emotions.

129. *For example, phony 'pollsters':* According to Sabato and Simpson, the decision to use the push-poll was made and implemented not by Bennett's opponent, Democrat John Baldacci, but by the Maine Democratic Party, which thought that Baldacci's refusal to use such tactics was naïve (Sabato and Simpson, *Dirty Little Secrets*, p. 263). Other push-poll examples come from pp. 264–65.

130. Gaylord is quoted in Dionne, Hess, and Mann, 'Curing the Mischief of Disengagement,' p. 7.

131. *'In hindsight, that':* Sabato and Simpson, *Dirty Little Secrets*, p. 159.

131. On Paula Jones see, for example, Jeffrey Toobin, 'Casting Stones,' *The New Yorker*, Nov. 3, 1997, pp. 52–61.

132. On Whitewater, see Lyons, *Fools for Scandal*. The book's main thesis is reflected in its subtitle: *How the Media Invented Whitewater*. A review of this book appeared in *The New York Times Book Review*, Aug. 4, 1996, p. 15, written by Phil Gailey, who was 'a reporter for *The New York Times* from 1981 to 1987.' The review lambasted *Fools for Scandal* as 'a nasty book . . . because it assaults the integrity of the journalists who did the reporting. It is a smear job unworthy of any fair-minded critic of the press. Surely the newspapers got *something* right.' A letter to the editor, published Aug. 25, 1996, p. 4, signed 'Roy Reed,' refereed:

Phil Gailey and I both worked for The Times some years ago, and I have high regard for him. But I have to disagree with his review of Gene Lyons's 'Fools for Scandal.' He seems to believe that Mr Lyons's criticism of The Times for its Whitewater coverage is flawed because an institution like The Times is simply too good to make such mistakes. I am a native of Arkansas and have reported on this part of the country off and on for 40 years. I have a pretty good idea of how Arkansas works and who its villains are. It grieves me to say it, Phil, but our old paper got it wrong ... Mr Lyons's book is the best reporting I've seen on the subject. His tone is more polemical than I would have chosen, but he has the facts right.

132. *'His boss, Floyd Brown'*: Lieberman, 'Churning Whitewater,' p. 27.

133. *The investigation, in contrast*: Toni Locy, 'Ex-Agriculture Secretary Indicted,' *The Washington Post*, Aug. 28, 1997, p. A1.

133. *hardly anyone remembers*: Kim Isaac Eisler, 'And Then There Was Janet,' *Washingtonian*, April 1997, pp. 43–46.

133. *there is no accountability*: Jeffrey Rosen, 'Kenneth Starr Trapped,' *The New York Times Magazine*, June 1, 1997, pp. 42–47; the quote is from p. 47.

133. *'elevator music'*: Sabato is quoted in John Harwood, 'Missouri Town's Election Scandal Shows System's Ills,' *The Wall Street Journal*, Aug. 5, 1997, p. A20.

134. *In 1994 ... twice*: Fallows, *Breaking the News*, p. 132.

134. *polls repeatedly find*: For example, *The Washington Post*, Aug. 29, 1997, pp. A1, A28, reported Clinton's approval rating had 'slipped' from 64 percent to 58 percent but was greater than 50 percent for the twentieth time in a row, making him 'about as popular as Ronald Reagan was at the height of his presidency.'

135. *'an era in which'*: Greenfield, 'When the Cops Come,' *Newsweek*, Feb. 10, 1997, p. 74.

135. *'a vicious, witless'*: Howard Kurtz, 'Newsweek Regrets Role in Keeping "Anonymous" Secret,' *The Washington Post*, July 19, 1997, pp. B1, B2; *'overzealous, blood-thirsty'*: Howard Kurtz, 'True Colors: The Man Behind Anonymous,' *The Washington Post*, Aug. 8, 1996, pp. C1, C6; the quote is from p. C6; *'rude and ugly'*: Richard Turner, 'Liar's Poker,' *New York*, July 29, 1997, pp. 12–13; the quote is from p. 12.

135. *'The ensuing maelstrom'*: Joe Klein, 'A Brush with Anonymity,' *Newsweek*, July 29, 1996, p. 76; *'an inquisition'* also comes from this source.

136. *'Cynicism is a'*: Sen. Simpson, in Ornstein, *Lessons and Legacies*, p. 186.

137. *The attack consisted*: Imran Ghori, 'Alioto, Riggs Come Out Slugging,' *The Napa Valley Register*, Sept. 6, 1997, pp. 1A, 8A.

## 5. 'LITIGATION IS WAR'

139. *Everyone is entitled*: She was speaking for her profession. Georgetown University legal ethicist David Luban quotes an 1854 publication by George Sharswood: 'The lawyer, who refuses his professional assistance because in his

judgment the case is unjust and indefensible, usurps the function of both judge and jury.' Luban notes that this is the view held by most lawyers today (Luban, 'The Adversary System Excuse,' p. 84).

139. *the German and French systems:* See John Langbein, 'The German Advantage in Civil Procedure.'

140. *A leading critic:* Material in these two paragraphs comes from Carrie Menkel-Meadow, 'The Trouble with the Adversary System in a Postmodern, Multicultural World,' and from an interview with her.

141. *'I remember back':* The panel discussion appears in *U.S. Business Litigation* 2(6) (Jan. 1997), pp. 24.

141. *According to Georgetown:* This section is based on an interview with David Luban. See also his essays, especially 'The Adversary System Excuse.'

143. *Even those who:* Stephan Landsman, *The Adversary System.*

143. *Though fewer than 1 percent:* This statistic comes from Marc Galanter, 'The Regulatory Function of the Civil Jury,' p. 63.

144. *Lawyers do not:* One of the most outspoken defendants of the adversary system and its ethical implications is Hofstra University law professor Monroe Freedman, who maintains that the adversary system 'often requires an affirmative answer' to the question 'Should you cross-examine a prosecution witness whom you know to be accurate and truthful, in order to make the witness appear to be mistaken or lying?' (*Lawyers' Ethics in an Adversary System,* p. viii).

144. *the cross-examining attorney:* Gregory Matoesian shows in *Reproducing Rape* that reframing rape as consensual sex is the standard tactic used by defense attorneys.

144. *A young woman:* Although trial transcripts are part of the public record, I have not provided the case citation in order to protect the privacy of the victim. For obvious reasons, I have telescoped my summary of the case, leaving out many of the details that Magenau provides.

145. *If you fight:* This advice has been questioned. Gary Kleck and Susan Sayles found that in many circumstances, fighting back lessens the chances of being raped. Equally important, having resisted seems to make it easier for the woman to put her life back together afterward.

150. *But the outcome:* David Luban believes that lawyers should not try to discredit rape victims if they believe the victims are telling the truth, but he says few if any lawyers agree with him.

150. *The percentage of:* Gregory Matoesian cites studies that examined conviction rates in rape cases (*Reproducing Rape,* pp. 14–15). The defendants in this case were appealing the verdict at the time of this writing.

150. *'In an infamous':* Luban, 'Twenty Theses on Adversarial Ethics.' Stephan Landsman tells me the case referred to is *Her Majesty the Queen v. Ernst Zundel.*

151. *'lackluster performance inside':* Peter Annin, 'Defending McVeigh,' *Newsweek,* May 26, 1997, pp. 36–37.

152. *Monroe Freedman, former:* Freedman, 'Kinder, Gentler, But Not So Zealous,' pp. 8, 9. In a similar spirit, when Judge Judith Kaye of New York's Court of Appeals proposed a code of civility, divorce lawyer Raoul Lionel Felder objected that her proposal 'reflects a misreading of what lawyers are hired to be

– adversaries – and a misreading of what the legal profession is about – conflict.'
(Felder, 'I'm Paid to Be Rude,' *The New York Times*, July 17, 1997, p. A29).

153. *moral nonaccountability:* The phrase was coined by Murray Schwartz. See his articles 'The Professionalism and Accountability of Lawyers' and 'The Zeal of the Civil Advocate.'

153. *'An advocate':* Luban, 'The Adversary System Excuse,' p. 86; the quotation is from J. Nightingale, ed., *Trial of Queen Caroline*, 3 vols. (London: J. Robins & Co., Albion Press, 1820–21), vol. 2, p. 8.

154. *'every thesis is':* Luban, 'Twenty Theses on Adversarial Ethics.'

154. *Almost all criminal:* Dershowitz, *The Best Defense*, p. xvi.

154. *'Before we will':* Freedman, *Lawyers' Ethics in an Adversary System*, p. 3.

155. *I have written:* 'I'm Sorry, I Won't Apologize,' *The New York Times Magazine*, July 21, 1996, pp. 34–35.

155. *'She wants the Robins':* Ronald Bacigal, *The Limits of Litigation*, p. 125.

156. *'There is rarely':* Philips, 'Dominant and Subordinate Gender Ideologies in Tongan Courtroom Discourse,' p. 595.

156. *Spiro Agnew accepted:* 'Vice President Agnew Resigns, Fined for Income Tax Evasion,' by Laurence Stern, *The Washington Post*, Oct. 11, 1973, p. A1.

156. *a 1984 book:* Tom Alibrandi with Frank H. Armani, *Privileged Information*.

157. *'Not only did':* Freedman, *Lawyers' Ethics in an Adversary System*, pp. 1–2.

158. *'attorneys … routinely twist':* Judge Peter Fay of the Eleventh Circuit, quoted in Bartlett H. McGuire, 'Rambo Litigation: A Losing Proposition,' p. 39.

158. Description of the case between Philip Morris and ABC comes from Benjamin Wittes, 'Quite a Discovery: Philip Morris' Papers in ABC Libel Case Leave Foes Fuming,' *Legal Times*, May 1, 1995, pp. 1, 22.

159. *a later court decision:* Judge Markow, Circuit Court of Richmond, Virginia, May 5, 1995.

159. *'an inevitable result':* Charles Yablon, 'Stupid Lawyer Tricks,' p. 1619.

159. *Other tactics include:* Sources that name dirty tricks include the *U.S. Business Litigation* panel; Yablon, 'Stupid Lawyer Tricks'; Jim Ritter, 'ABA to Lawyers: Mind Your Manners,' *Chicago Sun-Times*, Aug. 7, 1995, p. 7; and James Barron, 'Thou Shalt Not Yell at the Judge,' *The New York Times*, July 13, 1997, p. 19.

160. *Here's another example:* Susan Popik, *U.S. Business Litigation* panel.

161. *The Dalkon Shield class action suit:* Bacigal, *The Limits of Litigation*, pp. 19–20. Thanks to David Luban for calling this example to my attention.

163. *'In the Ninth Circuit':* Arthur Gilbert, 'Civility: It's Worth the Effort,' p. 108.

163. *'The lack of civility':* Roger Abrams, 'Law Schools Must Teach Professionalism – Now,' *New Jersey Law Journal*, Dec. 4, 1995, p. 27.

163. The quotations from Cooper are from 'President's Message: Courtesy Call,' p. 8. Cooper's example of the lawyer holding a deposition is also discussed in his article, 'Beyond the Rules: Lawyer Image and the Scope of Professionalism.'

164. *'You don't come up'*: Susan Popik was a member of the *U.S. Business Litigation* panel.

164. *'Behavior seems better'*: Arthur Garwin is quoted in Jim Ritter, 'ABA to Lawyers: Mind Your Manners,' *Chicago Sun-Times*, Aug. 7, 1995, p. 7.

165. Cotchett made this comment on the *U.S. Business Litigation* panel.

165. *creating a physical exhaustion:* Joan Williams, personal communication.

166. *As of May 1997:* Jeffrey Toobin, 'Spinning Timothy McVeigh,' *The New Yorker*, May 19, 1997, pp. 42–48; see p. 44.

166. *'people might be finding'*: Abrams, 'Law Schools Must Teach Professionalism – Now,' p. 28.

166. *'It's hard to'*: Cornelia Honchar, quoted in Jim Ritter, 'ABA to Lawyers: Mind Your Manners,' *Chicago Sun-Times*, Aug. 7, 1995, p. 7.

166. *Marcia Clark:* Clark with Theresa Carpenter, *Without a Doubt* (New York: Viking, 1997), p. 5.

166. *'in all branches'*: Glendon, *A Nation Under Lawyers*, p. 15. The same conclusion was reached at a conference sponsored by the American Bar Association and laid out in a report ominously titled *At the Breaking Point* (American Bar Association, 1991).

167. *'courtesy and decency'*: McGuire, quoted in Martha Middleton, '7th Circuit Court OK's Rules on Civility,' *National Law Journal*, Jan. 11, 1993, p. 18.

167. *She interviewed women lawyers:* Harrington, *Women Lawyers*.

167. *'Seldom does uncivil'*: Falk made this comment on the *U.S. Business Litigation* panel.

168. *'derive job satisfaction'*: Yablon, 'Stupid Lawyer Tricks,' p. 1639.

168. *'These days'*: Yablon, 'Stupid Lawyer Tricks,' p. 1641.

169. *a 60 percent reduction:* This statistic comes from *U.S. News & World Report*, which also notes, 'Since 1993, the overall crime rate in New York City has plunged to its lowest level in three decades' (John Marks, 'New York, New York,' Sept. 29, 1997, pp. 44–49; the quotation is from pp. 47–48).

169. *Following the arrest:* Tony Mauro and Haya El Nasser, 'Legal System in France Differs Widely from USA's,' *USA Today*, Sept. 4, 1997, pp. A1–2.

169. *'ethically and emotionally'*: Paul J. Spiegelman, 'Integrating Doctrine, Theory and Practice in the Law School Curriculum: The Logic of Jake's Ladder in the Context of Amy's Web.'

170. *'I predict that'*: Derek Bok, 'Law and Its Discontents,' *Bar Leader*, March–April 1983, pp. 21, 28, quoted in Leonard L. Riskin, 'Mediation in the Law Schools.'

170. *'Discourage litigation'*: This quote from Lincoln is used by Carrie Menkel-Meadow to open her essay 'The Silences of the Restatement of the Law Governing Lawyers: Lawyering as Only Adversary Practice.' It is also quoted in Glendon, *A Nation Under Lawyers*, p. 55.

171. *alternative dispute resolution:* Like any system, ADR can be abused. Michael Gottesman, for example, knew of a case in which a sexual harassment complaint went to a board of three male peers of the person against whom the complaint was made. Others see ADR as a second-tier system of justice for poorer people. Also, the less structured environment of mediation can enable the more powerful party to overwhelm the weaker one; Trina Grillo, for example, showed that women

often fare worse when their divorces are handled by mediation ('Mediation – Process Dangers for Women'); see also Carrie Menkel-Meadow, 'What Trina Taught Me: Reflections on Mediation, Inequality, Teaching and Life.'

171. *the best hope:* This section is based on conversations with Professor Menkel-Meadow and her article 'Toward Another View of Legal Negotiation: The Structure of Problem Solving.'

172. The illustration of two people in a boat comes from Paul Watzlawick, John Weakland, and Richard Fisch, *Change: Principles of Problem Formation and Problem Resolution* (New York: Norton, 1974), p. 37.

---

## 6. BOYS WILL BE BOYS: GENDER AND OPPOSITION

---

174. *The forces of gender:* In addition to gay men and lesbians, there are transgendered and transsexual people: women and men who either take hormones and undergo surgery or simply present themselves to the world to make their outward appearance better conform to their inward experience of gender. There are also intersexuals, people whose bodies cannot easily be assigned at birth to either sex.

178. *'sits back on his heels':* Sheldon, 'Preschool Girls' Discourse Competence,' p. 531. The complete transcript of the girls' dispute that Sheldon analyzes is longer than the excerpts I include.

181. *'double-voice discourse':* Another example, though – a dispute over a plastic pickle that also comes from Sheldon's research, one that I discuss in *You Just Don't Understand* – showed girls negotiating very much like the girls in this example do, but the boys' argument over the pickle involved one boy threatening to take the pickle away from a second boy in order to give it to a third. In other words, he was struggling for someone else, not himself.

185. *Some years ago:* The experiment was modeled on one designed by Bruce Dorval in which he had asked me to participate. My analysis of his tapes of friends talking is written up in an essay, 'Gender Differences in Conversational Coherence: Physical Alignment and Topical Cohesion,' in *Gender and Discourse* and also in the chapter 'Look at Me When I'm Talking to You!: Cross Talk Across the Ages' in *You Just Don't Understand*. The patterns I describe apply to Dorval's tapes as well. Patricia O'Connor helped me set up this experiment.

191. Petronio is quoted by Mary Geraghty, 'Strategic Embarrassment: The Art and Science of Public Humiliation,' *The Chronicle of Higher Education*, Apr. 4, 1997, p. A8. See also Bradford and Petronio, 'Strategic Embarrassment.'

192. *A Greek woman:* Anthropologist Ernestine Friedl observed that Greek parents routinely tease their children, beginning in infancy.

194. *A stock scene:* This should not be confused with another stock scene in which a man tries to embrace a woman who at first tries to fight him off. He grabs her against her protests, and she continues punching him – doing no damage – until her wan pounding of fists against his back gradually slows and transmogrifies into caresses. It has been rightly observed that such scenes

reinforce the dangerous assumption that when a woman says no she really means yes, but she wants to be forced.

196. *'duck-walking across campus'*: Anne Matthews, 'Hazing Days,' *The New York Times Magazine*, Nov. 3, 1996, p. 50.

196. *In a memoir*: The memoir, *In Contempt*, is by Darden, one of the prosecutors in the O.J. Simpson trial, and coauthor Jess Walter; see pp. 72–75.

197. *'A leader of the'*: Susan Faludi, 'The Naked Citadel,' p. 67.

198. [hazing] *has reached a peak*: Anthropologist Peggy Reeves Sanday shows a connection between fraternity hazing, in which pledges are degraded as if they were women, and the literal degradation of women in the practice of gang rape.

198. *'like soldiers at war'*: Darden, *In Contempt*, p. 92.

198. *A recent exposé*: This practice is reported briefly in *Newsweek*, 'Hazing in the Ranks,' Feb. 10, 1997, p. 36.

201. *'Maybe when you'*: David Margolis, 'The Reunion,' in *The Time of Wandering* (Jerusalem: Bright Idea Books, 1996), pp. 43–67; the quote is from p. 54.

201. *'arouses warm emotions'*: William H. McNeill, *Keeping Together in Time*, p. 2.

202. *Just a few cultures*: See Dundes, Leach, and Özkök, 'The Strategy of Turkish Boys' Verbal Dueling Rhymes'; Abrahams, 'Playing the Dozens'; Doukanari, 'The Presentation of Gendered Self in Cyprus Rhyming Improvisations'; Ayoub and Barnett, 'Ritualized Verbal Insult in White High School Culture'; and McDowell, 'Verbal Dueling.'

202. *ritual laments*: See Sherzer, 'A Diversity of Voices.'

202. *One study*: Kluwer, Heesink, and van de Vliert, 'Marital Conflict About the Division of Household Labor and Paid Work.'

203. *that often puzzle women*: By the same token, men are often puzzled by the concern women show for being left out. A man who wrote to me commented that women are petty, an opinion he supported by the following example: A group of women in his office tended to go out to lunch together. When one woman discovered the group had gone out without inviting her, she talked about it for days. He could not believe anyone could be so worked up over something so trivial as being left out of lunch, an omission he figured was probably just an oversight. But among girls, being left out of a gathering is a very serious sign of ostracization: the equivalent of not being invited to a birthday party. So for women, being left out of a group gathering is less likely to be an oversight than to portend a major realignment of social relations.

205. *One of these referred*: This letter was signed Richard F. Riley Jr. The letters appeared in the *The New York Times Book Review*, Feb. 12, 1995.

206. *children's computer games*: Cassell cites Robert William Kubey and Reed Larson, 'The Use and Experience of the New Video Media Among Children and Young Adolescents,' for the finding that 80 percent of computer game playing among nine- to fifteen-year-olds is by boys. Her other observations are based on articles collected in *From Barbie to Mortal Kombat: Gender and Computer Games*.

207. *women were more likely*: Just one of many articles to make this point is Gail Collins, 'Those Gender-Gap Blues,' *The New York Times*, Nov. 10, 1996, p. 12.

207. *A study of children's television:* 'The State of Children's Television: An Examination of Quantity, Quality, and Industry Beliefs,' conducted by Amy B. Jordan under the direction of Kathleen Hall Jamieson, The Annenberg Public Policy Center, University of Pennsylvania, June 17, 1996.

208. *'Aristocratic men and women':* Noble, *A World Without Women*, p. 193.

208. *'The appropriate duties':* Campbell and Jerry, 'Woman and Speaker,' p. 124.

209. *'The fearful idea':* This and the later quote from Madeleine Kunin come from *Living a Political Life*, p. 63.

210. *Governor Kunin's experience:* The women's movement has long been aware of the exclusion of women from public life, and among its great achievements has been the breaking down of many of these barriers, as witness the increasing number of women in law and politics. But in this regard, attention has focused, I think, more on the very real external barriers to women's participation and less on the role played by gender differences relating to agonism, such as those discussed here.

211. *on a roadway outside Washington:* The crash, which took place at 6:15 A.M. on the George Washington Memorial Parkway in Virginia on Apr. 17, 1996, was reported in Steve Vogel and John W. Fountain, 'Drivers' Duel Blamed After 3 Die in GW Parkway Crash,' *The Washington Post*, Apr. 18, 1996, pp. A1, A14. The statements by Dr Martinez were aired on an NBC News *Dateline* episode, Jan. 7, 1997.

212. The interview with Kareem Abdul-Jabbar is by Claudia Dreifus, 'Making History Off the Court,' *The New York Times Magazine*, Oct. 13, 1996, p. 50.

212. *Many cultures:* In his book *The Sibling Society*, Robert Bly also notes the rise of an ethos that enshrines opposition to authority characteristic of unsupervised youth. When Bly and I appeared together at New York's Open Center, he put this in a pithy way: Unless a society finds a way to channel young men's aggressive impulses, he said, 'they'll burn your city down for you.'

213. *compared children playing:* Whiting and Whiting, *Children of Six Cultures*. The cultures were in Okinawa, the Philippines, India, Kenya, Mexico, and the United States. A different pair of researchers carried out the observations in each culture. The Whitings cite a study by Carol Ember for the finding about boys in Kenya; see p. 150.

213. *Chinese parents would never:* Wolf, quoted in Bond and Sung-Hsing, 'China,' (p. 60), who also cite (p. 62) Ryback, Sanders, Lorentz, and Koestenblatt, 'Child-rearing Practices Reported by Students in Six Cultures' and (pp. 62–63) Niem and Collard, 'Parental Discipline of Aggressive Behaviors in Four-year-old Chinese and American Children.'

---

## 7. WHAT OTHER WAYS ARE THERE?: LISTENING TO OTHER CULTURES

---

216. *Jewish tradition requires:* Sam Lehman-Wilzig explores this general tradition

in 'Am K'shei Oref,' and Gabriella Modan examines its effects on a group of Jewish women in 'Pulling Apart Is Coming Together.' Deborah Schiffrin explores 'Jewish Argument as Sociability.'

216. *A linguist who spent:* The linguist is A. L. Becker.

217. *why Americans and Germans:* Byrnes, 'Interactional Style in German and American Conversations.' See also Carolyn Straehle, 'German and American Conversational Styles.'

219. *Here, Jones explains:* Kimberly Ann Jones, 'Conflict in Japanese Conversation.'

220. *'as a great leader':* Yamada, *Different Games, Different Rules*, p. 110.

221. *Nicholas Kristof:* Kristof, 'Too Polite for Words,' *The New York Times Magazine*, Sept. 24, 1995, pp. 22, 24.

222. *'The moment that':* Smith, *Chinese Characteristics*, pp. 219–21, cited in Bond and Sung-Hsing, 'China,' p. 67.

224. *one guest expressed:* Carbaugh, *Talking American*, p. 87.

225. *'For example, if it':* Henry Home, Lord Kames, *Essays on the Principles of Morality and Natural Religion* (Edinburgh: R. Fleming, for A. Kincaid and A. Donaldson, 1751), pp. 77–78.

226. *'as complementary and necessary':* Bodde, *Harmony and Conflict in Chinese Philosophy*, p. 69.

226. *'constantly revolving':* Young, *Crosstalk and Culture in Sino-American Communication*, p. 121.

226. *'intersex' babies:* Biologist Anne Fausto-Sterling notes in *The Sciences* (Mar. – Apr. 1993) that the frequency of intersex births is not definitively known. She cites one specialist's belief that it may be as high as 4 percent of births. According to Dr George Szasz, a physician specializing in such cases, 'A major hospital such as Vancouver's Children's Hospital would see about one case a month' (Ian Mulgrew, 'Controversy Over Intersex Treatment,' *Vancouver Sun*, Apr. 7, 1997, p. A1). Cheryl Chase, founder of the Intersex Society of North America, cites experts who conclude, 'About one in a hundred births exhibit some anomaly in sex differentiation' while 'about one in two thousand is different enough to render problematic the question, "Is it a boy or a girl?"' ('Hermaphrodites with Attitude,' p. 1).

226. *'You can dig':* Melissa Hendricks, 'Is It a Boy or a Girl?,' *Johns Hopkins Magazine*, Nov. 1993, pp. 10–16. I have taken the reference from Chase, 'Hermaphrodites with Attitude,' p. 2.

226. *The wisdom of this:* There is currently burgeoning attention to and awareness of intersexuality, thanks to the activism of adults who underwent surgery as children. The Intersex Society of North America, headquartered in San Francisco, has a Web site (http://www.isna.org) that offers much information. See also a special issue of *Chrysalis* 2(4) (1997); the work of Anne Fausto-Sterling (her article 'The Five Sexes: Why Male and Female Are Not Enough,' and her forthcoming book *Building Bodies*); and Natalie Angier, 'New Debate Over Surgery on Genitals,' *The New York Times*, May 13, 1997, p. B7.

227. *among the Zuni:* Roscoe, *The Zuni Man-Woman*, p. 4.

227. *'They are leaders':* Clifford Geertz, *Local Knowledge*, p. 82. Geertz

(drawing on an article by Robert Edgerton in *American Anthropologist*) uses the phenomenon of intersexuality to show that what people regard as 'common sense' differs drastically from one culture to the next. So as not to imply that all cultures handle everything better than ours does, I should mention that Geertz also describes an East African tribe, the Pokot, among whom 'frequently, intersexed children are killed, in the offhand way one discards an ill-made pot ..., but often they are allowed, in an equally offhand way, to live' (p. 83).

228. *'avoided, mitigated, muted'*: Ashkenazi, 'Religious Conflict in a Japanese Town,' p. 193.

229. *this interference leads:* Lebra, 'Nonconfrontational Strategies for Management of Interpersonal Conflicts,' p. 56. The source for her quotation from Ronald Dore is *Land Reform in Japan*, p. 343.

231. *Many cultures of the Pacific:* See Watson-Gegeo and White, eds., *Disentangling*.

232. nemawashi: I discuss this practice in *Talking from 9 to 5*, drawing on Yamada's description in *Different Games, Different Rules*.

233. *the elite regard:* This is how Geertz puts it: 'The elite, which is not itself so very puritan, worries about the poor, ignorant peasant gambling all his money away, about what foreigners will think, about the waste of time better devoted to building up the country. It sees cockfighting as "primitive," "backward," "unprogressive," and generally unbecoming an ambitious nation' ('Deep Play,' p. 414).

237. *'Well, and wasn't that':* Fox, 'The Inherent Rules of Violence,' p. 142. Subsequent quotations come from pp. 141 and 139 respectively.

238. *'militant posturing':* Ben-Ari, 'Ritual Strikes, Ceremonial Slowdowns,' p. 105.

239. *a 'designated strike':* Hanami, *Labor Relations in Japan Today*, p. 106.

239. *'General meetings are accompanied':* Rohlen, *For Harmony and Strength*, p. 186, quoted in Ben-Ari, 'Ritual Strikes, Ceremonial Slowdowns,' p. 106.

240. *'Ordinary warriors may leap':* Norbeck, *African Rituals of Conflict*, p. 1262. The Yao are described on the same page.

---

## 8. FAST FORWARD: TECHNOLOGICALLY
## ENHANCED AGGRESSION

247. *a troubled Vietnam veteran:* Patrick Rogers and Michael Haederle, 'Men at Peace,' *People*, Dec. 16, 1996, pp. 47–51.

251. *instant responses:* This point is also made by Fallows in *Breaking the News*, and I have heard it made by commentators in other discussions of politicians and the press as well.

251. *Thanks to word processors:* Yablon, 'Stupid Lawyer Tricks,' p. 1621.

252. *'Henderson called a colleague':* Ann O'Hanlon and Mike Mills, 'Now, Anyone's Got Your Number,' *The Washington Post*, July 5, 1996, p. D1.

253. *An extensive survey of soldiers:* The direct quotations are from Grossman, *On Killing*, pp. 4, 302, and 310.

254. *'films specially designed'*: Grossman pp. 306–307, quoting Peter Watson, *War on the Mind*.

257. *Sufferers from chronic*: Linton Weeks, 'Hysteria Book Hits a Raw Nerve: Sufferers Attack Author Who Says It's All in Their Heads,' *The Washington Post*, Apr. 12, 1997, p. D1.

257. *because their communication*: James Brooke, 'Anti-Fur Groups Wage War on Mink Farms,' *The New York Times*, Nov. 30, 1996, p. 9.

258. *'The poster distanced himself'*: Susan Herring, 'Bringing Familiar Baggage to the New Frontier,' ms. p. 145.

258. *'represented themselves as aligned'*: Herring, 'Two Variants of an Electronic Message Schema,' p. 103.

258. *'I am somewhat puzzled'*: Herring provided this example to me.

259. *'female users are more'*: Herring, 'Two Variants of an Electronic Message Schema,' p. 103.

260. *'This is precisely'*: Herring, 'Bringing Familiar Baggage to the New Frontier,' p. 145.

260. *his attitude toward agonism*: Herring uses this example in two articles: 'Bringing Familiar Baggage to the New Frontier,' p. 148, and 'Posting in a Different Voice,' p. 121.

261. *Following a tragic incident*: Robert Hanley, '15-Year-Old Held in Young Fund-Raiser's Slaying,' *The New York Times*, Oct. 2, 1997, pp. A1, B2; Steven Levy, 'Did the Net Kill Eddie?,' *Newsweek*, Oct. 13, 1997, p. 63.

## 9. THE ROOTS OF DEBATE IN EDUCATION AND THE HOPE OF DIALOGUE

264. *going back to the ancient Greeks*: This does not mean it goes back in an unbroken chain. David Noble, in *A World Without Women*, claims that Aristotle was all but lost to the West during the early Christian era and was rediscovered in the medieval era, when universities were first established. This is significant for his observation that many early Christian monasteries welcomed both women and men who could equally aspire to an androgynous ideal, in contrast to the Middle Ages, when the female was stigmatized, unmarried women were consigned to convents, priests were required to be celibate, and women were excluded from spiritual authority.

264. *Ong credits the ancient Greeks*: There is a fascinating parallel in the evolution of the early Christian Church and the Southern Baptist Church: Noble shows that the early Christian Church regarded women as equally beloved of Jesus and equally capable of devoting their lives to religious study, so women comprised a majority of early converts to Christianity, some of them leaving their husbands – or bringing their husbands along – to join monastic communities. It was later, leading up to the medieval period, that the clerical movement gained ascendancy in part by systematically separating women, confining them in either marriage or convents, stigmatizing them, and barring them from positions of power within the church. Christine Leigh Heyrman, in *Southern Cross: The Beginnings of the Bible Belt*, shows that a similar trajectory characterized the Southern Baptist movement.

At first, young Baptist and Methodist preachers (in the 1740s to 1830s) preached that both women and blacks were equally God's children, deserving of spiritual authority – with the result that the majority of converts were women and slaves. To counteract this distressing demography, the message was changed: Antislavery rhetoric faded, and women's roles were narrowed to domesticity and subservience. With these shifts, the evangelical movement swept the South. At the same time, Heyrman shows, military imagery took over: The ideal man of God was transformed from a 'willing martyr' to a 'formidable fighter' led by 'warrior preachers.'

265. *'incompatible with the decorum'*: Ong, *Fighting for Life*, p. 122. Ong's source, on which I also rely, is Oliver, *Communication and Culture in Ancient India and China*. My own quotations from Oliver are from pp. 259.

266. *Many early monks*: Pachomius, for example, 'the father of communal monasticism . . . and organizer of the first monastic community, had been a soldier under Constantine' and modeled his community on the military, emphasizing order, efficiency, and military obedience. Cassian, a fourth-century proselytizer, '"likened the monk's discipline to that of the soldier," and Chrysostom, another great champion of the movement, "sternly reminded the monks that Christ had armed them to be soldiers in a noble fight"' (Noble, *A World Without Women*, p. 54).

266. *'The man who is'*: Aristotle, quoted in Oliver, *Communication and Culture in Ancient India and China*, p. 259.

266. *Not until much later*: I came to understand the different meaning of 'poet' in Classical Greece from reading Ong and also *Preface to Plato* by Eric Havelock. These insights informed many articles I wrote about oral and literate tradition in Western culture, including 'Oral and Literate Strategies in Spoken and Written Narratives' and 'The Oral/Literate Continuum in Discourse.'

267. *regard truth seeking as*: Moulton, 'A Paradigm of Philosophy'; Ong, *Fighting for Life*.

267. The example of Danny and the lava: Wertsch, *Voices of the Mind*, pp. 113–14.

268. *girls often receive*: See David and Myra Sadker, *Failing at Fairness*.

268. *'The class is in'*: Although my colleagues and I make efforts to refer to our students – all over the age of eighteen – as 'women' and 'men' and some students in my classes do the same, the majority refer to each other and themselves as 'girls' and 'boys' or 'girls' and 'guys.'

271. *'one of the very last'*: Jonathan Alter, 'The End of the Journey,' *Newsweek*, Nov. 4, 1996, p. 61. Trilling died at the age of ninety-one.

273. *'After the first speech'*: Kaplan, *French Lessons*, p. 119.

274. *'Among the graduate students'*: Tracy and Baratz, 'Intellectual Discussion in the Academy as Situated Discourse,' p. 309.

276. *'The process of scientific'*: Greenberg and Robins, 'The Changing Role of Social Experiments in Policy Analysis,' p. 350.

277. *'began with a frontal'*: These and other quotes from Tompkins appear in her essay 'Fighting Words,' pp. 588–89.

277. *'Kick 'em when they're up'*: Safire is quoted in Howard Kurtz, 'Safire Made No Secret of Dislike for Inman,' *The Washington Post*, Jan. 19, 1994, p. A6.

279. *'Without contraries is no progression'*: I've borrowed the William Blake quote from Peter Elbow, who used it to open his book *Embracing Contraries*.

279. *His findings were ultimately confirmed*: Terence Monmaney, 'Marshall's Hunch,' *The New Yorker*, Sept. 20, 1993, pp. 64–72.

280. *'We tend to assume'*: Elbow, *Embracing Contraries*, p. 258.

281. *'subject it to'*: Moulton, 'A Paradigm of Philosophy,' p. 153.

282. *'social constructionists'*: Social constructionists often deride the ideas of those who focus on differences as 'essentialist' – a bit of academic name-calling; it is used only as a way of criticizing someone else's work: 'Smith's claims are repugnant because they are essentialist.' I have never heard anyone claim, 'I am not an essentialist,' though I have frequently heard elaborate self-defenses: 'I am not an essentialist!' Capturing the tendency to use this term as an epithet, *Lingua Franca*, a magazine for academics, describes 'essentialist' as 'that generic gender studies *j'accuse!*' See Emily Nussbaum, 'Inside Publishing,' *Lingua Franca*, Dec. – Jan. 1997, pp. 22–24; the quote is from p. 24.

282. *'Why protest current conditions'*: Klein, *Meeting the Great Bliss Queen*, pp. 8–9.

283. *The phenomenon could be observed*: Natasha Walter, *The New Feminism* (Little, Brown 1998).

283. *'Chic chick chicken':Observer*, January 18,1998.

283. *'Of course, you understand'*: Cynthia Gorney, 'Gloria,' *Mother Jones*, Nov. – Dec. 1995, pp. 22–27; the quote is from p. 22.

284. *But we also know*: See, for example, Needham, *Science and Civilization in China*.

285. *'When Your HMO Says No'*: Ellyn E. Spragins, *Newsweek*, July 28, 1997, p. 73.

285. *Norman Ornstein, a political analyst*: This section is based on an interview with Ornstein. See also Ornstein's article, 'Less Seems More.'

286. The story behind the haircut story is told by Gina Lubrano, 'Now for the Real Haircut Story . . .,' *The San Diego Union-Tribune*, July 12, 1993, p. B7. That the supermarket scanner story was not true was mentioned by George Stephanopoulos at a panel held at Brown University, as reported by Elliot Krieger, 'Providence Journal/Brown University Public Affairs Conference,' *The Providence Journal-Bulletin*, Mar. 5, 1995, p. 12A.

288. *'All around milled'*: Fox, 'The Inherent Rules of Violence,' p. 141.

288. *'derive job satisfaction'*: Yablon, 'Stupid Lawyer Tricks,' p. 1639.

289. *'Remember Brit Hume'*: Kenneth Walsh made this comment on *The Diane Rehm Show*, May 28, 1996.

291. *'In Vietnam most soldiers'*: Grossman, *On Killing*, p. 270.

291. Susan Popik made this comment on the *U.S. Business Litigation* panel.

292. Suzanne Wong Scollon: Personal communication.

292. Mary Catherine Bateson: Personal communication.

293. *White House Communications Director*: At the time of this show, Ms Lewis was deputy communications director.

294. *Another popular Japanese show*: Yoshiko Nakano helped me with observations of *Close-up Gendai*.

296. *His rules of engagement:* Etzioni, *The New Golden Rule*, pp. 104–106. He attributes the rule 'Talk less of rights . . . and more of needs, wants, and interests' to Mary Ann Glendon.

296. *In reviewing a book:* Marina Warner, 'High-Minded Pursuit of the Exotic,' review of *Reading National Geographic* by Catherine A. Lutz and Jane L. Collins in *The New York Times Book Review*, Sept. 19, 1993, p. 13.

297. *'Most theories are wrong':* I got this from A. L. Becker, who got it from Kenneth Pike, who got it from . . .

British examples by Michael Leapman appear on pages 31, 32, 33, 39, 51, 54, 56, 60, 61, 64, 66, 67, 71, 77, 93, 97, 99, 101, 114, 118, 128, 169, 191, 211, 283.

# REFERENCES

Abrahams, Roger D. 'Playing the Dozens.' *Journal of American Folklore* 75 (1962), pp. 209–20.

Abrams, Roger. 'Law Schools Must Teach Professionalism – Now.' *New Jersey Law Journal* (Dec. 4, 1995), pp. 27, 36.

Alibrandi, Tom, with Frank H. Armani. *Privileged Information* (New York: Dodd, Mead, 1984).

Ashkenazi, M. 'Religious Conflict in a Japanese Town: Or Is It?' In *Japanese Models of Conflict Resolution*, S. N. Eisenstadt and Eyal Ben-Ari, eds. (New York: Kegan Paul International, 1990), pp. 192–209.

Atkinson, Rob. 'How the Butler Was Made to Do It: The Perverted Professionalism of *The Remains of the Day*.' *The Yale Law Journal* 105 (1995), pp. 177–220.

Ayoub, Millicent R., and Stephen A. Barnett. 'Ritualized Verbal Insult in White High School Culture.' *Journal of American Folklore* 78 (1965), pp. 337–44.

Bacigal, Ronald. *The Limits of Litigation: The Dalkon Shield Controversy* (Durham, N.C.: Carolina Academic Press, 1990).

Bateson, Gregory. *Steps to an Ecology of Mind* (New York: Ballantine, 1972).

Bateson, Mary Catherine. *With a Daughter's Eye: A Memoir of Margaret Mead and Gregory Bateson* (New York: William Morrow, 1984).

Ben-Ari, Eyal. 'Ritual Strikes, Ceremonial Slowdowns: Some Thoughts on the Management of Conflict in Large Japanese Enterprises.' In *Japanese Models of Conflict Resolution*, S. N. Eisenstadt and Eyal Ben-Ari, eds. (New York: Kegan Paul International, 1990), pp. 94–126.

Bly, Robert. *The Sibling Society* (Reading, Mass.: Addison-Wesley, 1996).

Bodde, Derk. 'Harmony and Conflict in Chinese Philosophy.' In *Studies in Chinese Thought*, Arthur F. Wright, ed. (Chicago: University of Chicago Press, 1953).

Boggs, Stephen T., and Malcolm Naea Chun. '*Ho'oponopono:* A Hawaiian Method of Solving Interpersonal Problems.' In *Disentangling: Conflict Discourse in Pacific Societies*, Karen Ann Watson-Gegeo and Geoffrey M. White, eds. (Stanford, Calif.: Stanford University Press, 1990), pp. 122–60.

Bolinger, Dwight. *Language – The Loaded Weapon: The Use and Abuse of Language Today* (London and New York: Longman, 1980).

Bond, Michael H., and Wang Sung-Hsing. 'China: Aggressive Behavior and the Problem of Maintaining Order and Harmony.' In *Aggression in Global Perspective*, Arnold P. Goldstein and Marshall H. Segall, eds. (New York: Pergamon Press, 1983), pp. 58–74.

Bradford, Lisa, and Sandra Petronio. 'Strategic Embarrassment: A Culprit of Emotions.' In *Handbook of Communication and Emotion: Research, Theory, Applications, and Contexts*, Peter A. Andersen and Laura K. Guerrero, eds. (San Diego: Academic Press, 1998), pp. 99–121.

Brenneis, Donald. 'Dramatic Gestures: The Fiji Indian *Pancayat* as Therapeutic Discourse.' In *Disentangling: Conflict Discourse in Pacific Societies*, Karen Ann Watson-Gegeo and Geoffrey M. White, eds. (Stanford, Calif.: Stanford University Press, 1990), pp. 214–38.

Bryant, Jennings. 'Viewers' Enjoyment of Televised Sports Violence.' In *Media, Sports, and Society*, Lawrence A. Wenner, ed. (Newbury Park, Calif.: Sage, 1989), pp. 270–89.

Bryant, Jennings, and Dolf Zillman. 'Sports Violence and the Media.' In *Sports Violence*, Jeffrey H. Goldstein, ed. (New York: Springer, 1983), pp. 195–211.

Byrnes, Heidi. 'Interactional Style in German and American Conversations.' *Text* 6(2) (1986), pp. 189–206.

Campbell, Karlyn Kohrs, and E. Claire Jerry. 'Woman and Speaker: A Conflict in Roles.' In *Seeing Female: Social Roles and Personal Lives*, Sharon S. Brehm, ed. (New York: Greenwood Press, 1988), pp. 123–33.

Cappella, Joseph N., and Kathleen Hall Jamieson. *Spiral of Cynicism: The Press and the Public Good* (New York: Oxford University Press, 1997).

Carbaugh, Donal. *Talking American: Cultural Discourses on* Donahue (Norwood, N.J.: Ablex, 1988).

Cassell, Justine, and Henry Jenkins, eds. *From Barbie to Mortal Kombat: Gender and Computer Games* (Cambridge, Mass.: MIT Press, forthcoming).

Chase, Cheryl. 'Hermaphrodites With Attitude: Mapping the Emergence of Intersex Political Activism" *GLQ* 4(2)(1988).

Clift, Eleanor, and Tom Brazaitis. *War Without Bloodshed: The Art of Politics* (New York: Scribner's, 1996).

Condit, Celeste Michelle. 'Two Sides to Every Question: The Impact of New Formulas on Abortion Policy Options.' *Argumentation* 8(4) (1994), pp. 237–336.

Cooper, N. Lee. 'President's Message: Courtesy Call: It Is Time to Reverse the Decline of Civility in Our Justice System.' *ABA Journal* 83 (Mar. 1997), p. 8.

—— 'Beyond the Rules: Lawyer Image and the Scope of Professionalism.' *Cumberland Law Review* 26 (1995), pp. 923–40.

Darden, Christopher A., with Jess Walter. *In Contempt* (New York: ReganBooks, 1996).

Deby, Jeff. 'Language as Agonistic Resource in Televised Ice-Hockey Commentary.' Paper presented at the 96th Annual Meeting of the American Anthropological Association, Nov. 19–23, 1997, Washington, D.C.

Dershowitz, Alan. *The Best Defense* (New York: Vintage, 1983).

Dionne, E. J., Jr., Stephen Hess, and Thomas E. Mann. 'Curing the Mischief of Disengagement: Politics and Communication in America.' 'Future Strategies of Political Communication,' German-American Workshop of the Bertelsmann Foundation, Berlin, Feb. 5, 1997.

Dore, Ronald Phillip. *Land Reform in Japan* (London: Oxford University Press, 1959).

Doukanari, Elli. 'The Presentation of Gendered Self in Cyprus Rhyming Improvisations: A Sociolinguistic Investigation of *Kipriaka Chattista* in Performance.' Ph.D. dissertation, Georgetown University, Washington, D.C., 1997.

Dower, John W. *War Without Mercy: Race and Power in the Pacific War* (New York: Pantheon, 1986).

Dundes, Alan, Jerry W. Leach, and Bora Özkök. 'The Strategy of Turkish Boys' Verbal Dueling Rhymes.' In *Directions in Sociolinguistics: The Ethnography of Communication*, John J. Gumperz and Dell Hymes, eds. (New York: Holt, Rinehart and Winston), 1972), pp. 130–60.

Eder, Donna. 'Serious and Playful Disputes: Variation in Conflict Talk Among Female Adolescents.' In *Conflict Talk*, Allen Grimshaw, ed. (Cambridge, England: Cambridge University Press, 1990), pp. 67–84.

Ekman, Paul. *Telling Lies* (New York: Norton, 1992).

Elbow, Peter. *Embracing Contraries: Explorations in Learning and Teaching* (New York and Oxford: Oxford University Press, 1986).

Etzioni, Amitai. *The New Golden Rule: Community and Morality in a Democratic Society* (New York: Basic, 1996).

Fallows, James. *Breaking the News: How the Media Undermine American Democracy* (New York: Pantheon, 1996).

Faludi, Susan. 'The Naked Citadel.' *The New Yorker*, Sept. 5, 1994, pp. 62–81.

Fausto-Sterling, Anne. 'The Five Sexes: Why Male and Female Are Not Enough.' *Sciences*, Mar./Apr. 1993, pp. 20–25.

Fox, Robin. 'The Inherent Rules of Violence.' In *Social Rules and Social Behaviour*, Peter Collett, ed. (Totowa, N.J.: Rowman and Littlefield, 1976), pp. 132–49.

Freedman, Monroe H. *Lawyers' Ethics in an Adversary System* (Indianapolis: Bobbs-Merrill, 1975).

—— 'Kindler, Gentler, But Not So Zealous.' *The Recorder*, Aug. 23, 1995.

Friedl, Ernestine. *Vasilika: A Village in Modern Greece* (New York: Holt, Rinehart and Winston, 1962).

Funderburg, Lise. *Black, White, Other: Biracial Americans Talk About Race and Identity* (New York: William Morrow, 1994).

Galanter, Marc. 'The Regulatory Function of the Civil Jury.' In *Verdict: Assessing the Civil Jury System*, Robert E. Litan, ed. (Washington: Brookings, 1993), pp. 61–102.

Geertz, Clifford. 'Deep Play: Notes on the Balinese Cockfight.' In *The Interpretation of Cultures* (New York: Basic, 1973), pp. 412–53.

——. *Local Knowledge: Further Essays in Interpretive Anthropology* (New York: Basic, 1983).

Gelbspan, Ross. *The Heat Is On: The High Stakes Battle over Earth's Threatened Climate* (Reading, Mass.: Addison-Wesley, 1997).

Gelernter, David. *Drawing Life: Surviving the Unabomber* (New York: Free Press, 1997).

Gerike, Ann E.; illustrations by Peter Kohlsaat. *Old Is Not a Four-Letter Word: A Midlife Guide* (Watsonville, Calif.: Papier-Mache Press, 1997).

Gilbert, Arthur. 'Civility: It's Worth the Effort.' *Trial* (Apr. 1991), pp. 106–10.

Glendon, Mary Ann. *A Nation Under Lawyers: How the Crisis in the Legal Profession Is Transforming American Society* (New York: Farrar, Straus and Giroux, 1994).

Goldstein, Jeffrey H., and Brenda J. Bredemeier. 'Socialization: Some Basic Issues.' *Journal of Communication* 27(3) (1977), pp. 154–59.

Goodwin, Marjorie Harness. *He-Said-She-Said: Talk as Social Organization Among Black Children* (Bloomington: Indiana University Press, 1990).

——. '¡Ay Chillona!: Stance-Taking in Girls' Hop Scotch.' In *Cultural Performances: Proceedings of the Third Berkeley Women and Language Conference*, Mary Bucholtz, A. C. Liang, Laurel A. Sutton, and Caitlin Hines, eds. (Department of Linguistics, University of California, Berkeley: Berkeley Women and Language Group, 1994), pp. 232–41.

Gopnik, Adam. 'Read All About It.' *The New Yorker*, Dec. 12, 1994, pp. 84–102.

Gould, Stephen Jay. *Wonderful Life: The Burgess Shale and the Nature of History* (New York: W. W. Norton, 1989).

Greenberg, David H., and Philip K. Robins. 'The Changing Role of Social Experiments in Policy Analysis.' *Journal of Policy Analysis and Management* 5:2 (1986), pp. 340–62.

Grillo, Trina. 'Mediation – Process Dangers for Women.' 100 *Yale Law Journal* (1991), pp. 1544–1610.

Grossman, Dave. *On Killing: The Psychological Cost of Learning to Kill in War and Society* (Boston: Little, Brown, 1995).

Guinier, Lani, Michelle Fine, and Jane Balin, with Ann Bartow and Deborah Lee Stachel. 'Becoming Gentlemen: Women's Experiences at One Ivy League Law School.' 143 *University of Pennsylvania Law Review* (Nov. 1994), pp. 1–110.

Gunderson, Steve, and Rob Morris with Bruce Bawer. *House and Home* (New York: Dutton, 1996).

Hacker, Andrew. *Money: Who Has How Much and Why* (New York: Scribner's, 1997).

Hanami, T. *Labor Relations in Japan Today* (Tokyo: Kodansha, 1979).

Harr, Jonathan. *A Civil Action* (New York: Vintage, 1995).

Harrington, Mona. *Women Lawyers: Rewriting the Rules* (New York: Knopf, 1994).

Hasund, Kristine. 'Colt Conflicts: Reflections of Gender and Class in the

Oppositional Turn Sequences of London Teenage Girls.' (Bergen, Norway: University of Bergen, Hovedfag thesis).

Havelock, Eric A. *Preface to Plato* (Cambridge, Mass.: Belknap Press, Harvard University Press, 1963).

Herdt, Gilbert. 'Introduction: Third Sexes and Third Genders.' In *Third Sex, Third Gender: Beyond Sexual Dimorphism in Culture and History*, Gilbert Herdt, ed. (New York: Zone, 1994), pp. 21–81.

Herring, Susan. 'Bringing Familiar Baggage to the New Frontier: Gender Differences in Computer-mediated Communication.' In *CyberReader*, Victor Vitanza, ed. (Boston: Allyn & Bacon, 1996), pp. 144–54.

——. 'Posting in a Different Voice: Gender and Ethics in Computer-mediated Communication.' In *Philosophical Approaches to Computer-mediated Communication*, Charles Ess, ed. (Albany: SUNY Press, 1996), pp.115–45.

——. 'Two Variants of an Electronic Message Schema.' In *Computer-mediated Communication: Linguistic, Social and Cross-Cultural Perspectives*, Susan Herring, ed. (Philadelphia: Benjamins, 1996), pp. 81–106.

Herzfeld, Michael. *The Poetics of Manhood: Contest and Identity in a Cretan Mountain Village* (Austin: University of Texas Press, 1985).

——. *Portrait of a Greek Imagination: An Ethnographic Biography* (Chicago: University of Chicago Press, 1997).

Hewitt, Lynne E., Judith F. Duchan, and Erwin M. Segal. 'Structure and Function of Verbal Conflicts Among Adults with Mental Retardation.' *Discourse Processes* 16(4) (1993), pp. 525–43.

Heyrman, Christine Leigh. *Southern Cross: The Beginnings of the Bible Belt* (New York: Knopf, 1997).

Honda, Atsuko. 'Conflict Management in Japanese Public Affairs Talk Shows.' Dissertation in progress, Georgetown University.

Jamieson, Kathleen Hall. *Dirty Politics: Deception, Distraction, and Democracy* (New York: Oxford University Press, 1992).

——. *Beyond the Double Bind: Women and Leadership* (New York: Oxford University Press, 1995).

Jamison, Kay Redfield. *Touched with Fire: Manic-Depressive Illness and the Artistic Temperament* (New York: Free Press, 1993).

Johnson, Haynes, and David S. Broder. *The System: The American Way of Politics at the Breaking Point* (Boston: Little, Brown, 1996).

Jones, Kimberly Ann. 'Conflict in Japanese Conversation.' Ph.D. dissertation, University of Michigan, Ann Arbor, 1990.

Jordan, Amy B., under the direction of Kathleen Hall Jamieson. 'The State of Children's Television: An Examination of Quantity, Quality, and Industry Beliefs.' The Annenberg Public Policy Center, University of Pennsylvania, June 17, 1996.

Kaplan, Alice. *French Lessons: A Memoir* (Chicago: University of Chicago Press, 1993).

Keller, Evelyn Fox. *Reflections on Gender and Science* (New Haven: Yale University Press, 1985).

Kleck, Gary, and Susan Sayles. 'Rape and Resistance.' *Social Problems* 37 (1990), pp. 149–62.

Klein, Anne Carolyn. *Meeting the Great Bliss Queen: Buddhists, Feminists, and the Art of the Self* (Boston: Beacon Press, 1995).

Kluwer, Esther S., Jose A. M. Heesink, and Evert van de Vliert. 'Marital Conflict About the Division of Household Labor and Paid Work.' *Journal of Marriage and the Family* 58 (1996), pp. 958–69.

Kolb, Deborah M. 'Women's Work: Peacemaking in Organizations.' In *Hidden Conflict in Organizations: Uncovering Behind-the-Scenes Disputes*, Deborah Kolb and Jean Bartunek, eds. (Newbury Park, Calif.: Sage, 1992), pp. 63–91.

Konner, Melvin. 'The Aggressors.' *The New York Times Magazine*, Aug. 14, 1988, pp. 33–34.

Krauss, Ellis S. 'Conflict in the Diet: Toward Conflict Management in Parliamentary Politics.' In *Conflict in Japan*, Ellis S. Krauss, Thomas P. Rohlen, and Patricia G. Steinhoff, eds. (Honolulu: University of Hawaii Press, 1984), pp. 244–93.

Krich, John. 'To Teach Is Glorious: A Conversation with the New Dean of Cal's Journalism School, Orville Schell.' *Express*, Aug. 23, 1996, pp. 1, 14–16, 18, 20–22.

Kubey, Robert William, and Reed Larson. 'The Use and Experience of the New Video Media Among Children and Young Adolescents.' *Communication Research* 17 (1990), pp. 105–30.

Kulick, Don. 'Speaking as a Woman: Structure and Gender in Domestic Arguments in a New Guinea Village.' *Cultural Anthropology* 8:4 (1993), pp. 510–41.

Kunin, Madeleine. *Living a Political Life* (New York: Knopf, 1994).

Kurtz, Howard. *Hot Air: All Talk, All the Time* (New York: Times Books, 1996).

Landsman, Stephan. *The Adversary System: A Description and Defense* (Washington, D.C.: American Enterprise Institute for Public Policy Research, 1984).

Langbein, John H. 'The German Advantage in Civil Procedure.' *University of Chicago Law Review* 52 (1995), pp. 823–28.

Leapman, Michael. *Treacherous Estate* (London: Hodder and Stoughton, 1992).

Lebra, Takie Sugiyama. 'Nonconfrontational Strategies for Management of Interpersonal Conflicts.' In *Conflict in Japan*, Ellis S. Krauss, Thomas P. Rohlen, and Patricia G. Steinhoff, eds. (Honolulu: University of Hawaii Press, 1984), pp. 41–60.

Lehman-Wilzig, Sam. '"Am K'shei Oref": Oppositionism in the Jewish Heritage.' *Judaism* 40(1) (1991), pp. 16–38.

Lieberman, Trudy. 'Churning Whitewater.' *Columbia Journalism Review* 33:1 (May-June 1994), pp. 26–30.

Lindstrom, Lamont. 'Straight Talk on Tanna.' In *Disentangling: Conflict Discourse in Pacific Societies*, Karen Ann Watson-Gegeo and Geoffrey M. White, eds. (Stanford, Calif.: Stanford University Press, 1990), pp. 373–411.

Lipstadt, Deborah. *Denying the Holocaust: The Growing Assault on Truth and Memory* (New York: Free Press, 1993).

———. 'The Fragility of Memory: Reflections on the Holocaust.' Address and response at the inauguration of the Dorot Chair of Modern Jewish and Holocaust Studies, Department of Religion, Emory University, Atlanta, 1994.

Loftus, Elizabeth F., and John C. Palmer. 'Reconstruction of Automobile Destruction: An Example of the Interaction Between Language and Memory.' *Journal of Verbal Learning and Verbal Behavior* 13 (1974), pp. 585–89.

Luban, David, ed. *The Good Lawyer: Lawyers' Roles and Lawyers' Ethics* (Totowa, N.J.: Rowman & Allanheld, 1983).

——. 'The Adversary System Excuse.' In *The Good Lawyer: Lawyers' Roles and Lawyers' Ethics* (Totowa, N.J.: Rowman & Allanheld, 1983), pp. 83–122. Reprinted in *The Ethics of Lawyers*, David Luban, ed. (Aldershot, England: Dartmouth Publishing, 1994), pp. 139–78.

——. 'Twenty Theses on Adversarial Ethics.' In *Beyond the Adversarial System*, H. Stacy and M. Lavarch, eds. (Sydney, Australia: Federation Press, forthcoming).

Lyons, Gene, and the Editors of *Harper's* Magazine. *Fools for Scandal: How the Media Invented Whitewater* (New York: Franklin Square Press, 1996).

Magenau, Keller S. 'Framing, Contest, and Consent: Questioning in the Cross-Examination of a Rape Victim.' Paper presented at the 96th Annual Meeting of the American Anthropological Association, Nov. 19–23, 1997, Washington, D.C.

Matoesian, Gregory M. *Reproducing Rape: Domination Through Talk in the Courtroom* (Chicago: University of Chicago Press, 1993).

McCombs, Maxwell. 'Explorers and Surveyors: Expanding Strategies for Agenda-Setting Research.' *Journalism Quarterly* 69:4 (1992), pp. 813–24.

McDowell, John H. 'Verbal Dueling.' In *Handbook of Discourse Analysis*, vol. 3, Teun A. van Dijk, ed. (London: Academic Press, 1985), pp. 203–11.

McGuire, Bartlett H. 'Rambo Litigation: A Losing Proposition.' *The American Lawyer* (May 1996).

McNeill, William H. *Keeping Together in Time: Dance and Drill in Human History* (Cambridge, Mass.: Harvard University Press, 1995).

Menkel-Meadow, Carrie. 'Toward Another View of Legal Negotiation: The Structure of Problem Solving.' *UCLA Law Review* 31 (1984), pp. 754–842.

——. 'The Trouble with the Adversary System in a Postmodern, Multicultural World,' *William and Mary Law Review* 38 (Oct. 1996), pp. 5–44.

——. 'What Trina Taught Me: Reflections on Mediation, Inequality, Teaching and Life.' *Minnesota Law Review* 81 (June 1997), pp. 1413–28.

——. 'The Silences of the Restatement of the Law Governing Lawyers: Lawyering as Only Adversary Practice.' *Georgetown Journal of Legal Ethics* 10 (forthcoming 1997).

Michaels, Sarah. '"Sharing time": Children's Narrative Styles and Differential Access to Literacy.' *Language in Society* 10:3 (1981), pp. 423–42.

Millar, Frank E., Edna L. Rogers, and Janet Beavin Bavelas. 'Identifying Patterns of Verbal Conflict in Interpersonal Dynamics.' *Western Journal of Speech Communication* 48(3) (1984), pp. 231–46.

Miller, Arthur H., Edie N. Goldenberg, and Lutz Erbring. 'Type-Set Politics: Impact of Newspapers on Public Confidence.' *American Political Science Review* 73 (1973), pp. 67–84.

Modan, Gabriella. 'Pulling Apart Is Coming Together: The Use and Meaning of Opposition in the Discourse of Jewish-American Women.' In *Cultural Performances: Proceedings of the Third Berkeley Women and Language Conference*, Mary

Bucholtz, A. C. Liang, Laurel A. Sutton, and Caitlin Hines, eds. (Department of Linguistics, University of California, Berkeley 1994), pp. 501–508.

Morgan, Peter W., and Glenn H. Reynolds. *The Appearance of Impropriety: How Ethics Wars Have Undermined American Government, Business, and Society* (New York: Free Press, 1997).

Moulton, Janice. 'A Paradigm of Philosophy: The Adversary Method.' In *Discovering Reality*, Sandra Harding and Merrill B. Hintikka, eds. (Dordrecht, Holland: Reidel, 1983), pp. 149–64.

Nakano, Yoshiko. 'Frame Analysis of A Japanese-American Contract Negotiation.' Ph.D. dissertation, Georgetown University, 1995.

Needham, Joseph. *Science and Civilization in China* (Cambridge, England: Cambridge University Press, 1956).

Niem, Tien-Ing Chyou, and Roberta R. Collard. 'Parental Discipline of Aggressive Behaviors in Four-Year-Old Chinese and American Children.' In *Proceedings of the Annual Convention of the American Psychological Association* 7 (1972), pp. 95–96.

Niyekawa, Agnes M. 'Analysis of Conflict in a Television Home Drama.' In *Conflict in Japan*, Ellis S. Krauss, Thomas P. Rohlen, and Patricia G. Steinhoff, eds. (Honolulu: University of Hawaii Press, 1984), pp. 61–84.

Noble, David. *A World Without Women: The Christian Clerical Culture of Western Science* (New York and Oxford: Oxford University Press, 1992).

Norbeck, Edward. 'African Rituals of Conflict.' *American Anthropologist* 65(6) (1963), pp. 1254–79.

Oliver, Robert T. *Communication and Culture in Ancient India and China* (Syracuse, N.Y.: Syracuse University Press, 1971).

Omoniyi, Tope. 'Song-lashing as a Communicative Strategy in Yoruba Interpersonal Conflicts.' *Text* 15:2 (1995), pp. 299–315.

Ong, Walter J. *Fighting for Life: Contest, Sexuality, and Consciousness* (Ithaca, N.Y.: Cornell University Press, 1981).

Or, Winnie Wing Fung. 'Agonism in Academic Discussion.' Paper presented at the 96th Annual Meeting of the American Anthropological Association, Nov. 19–23, 1997, Washington, D.C.

Ornstein, Norman J. 'Less Seems More: What to Do About Contemporary Political Corruption.' *The Responsive Community* 4:1 (Winter 1993–94), pp. 7–22.

——. *Lessons and Legacies: Farewell Addresses from the Senate* (Reading, Mass.: Addison-Wesley, 1997).

Patterson, Thomas E. *Out of Order* (New York: Knopf, 1993).

Philips, Susan U. 'Dominant and Subordinate Gender Ideologies in Tongan Courtroom Discourse.' In *Cultural Performances: Proceedings of the Third Berkeley Women and Language Conference*, Mary Bucholtz, A. C. Liang, Laurel A. Sutton, and Caitlin Hines, eds. (Berkeley: Linguistics Department, University of California, Berkeley Press, 1994), pp. 593–604.

Radosh, Ronald. *Divided They Fell: The Demise of the Democratic Party, 1964–1996* (New York: Free Press, 1996).

Riskin, Leonard L. 'Mediation in the Law Schools.' *Journal of Legal Education* 34 (1984), pp. 259–97.

Rohlen, Thomas P. *For Harmony and Strength: Japanese White-Collar Organization in Anthropological Perspective*. (Berkeley: University of California Press, 1974).

Roscoe, Will. *The Zuni Man-Woman* (Albuquerque: University of New Mexico Press, 1991).

Rose, Jonathan. 'The Legal Profession in Medieval England: A History of Regulation.' *Syracuse Law Review* 48 (forthcoming 1997).

Rosof, Patricia J. F. 'Beyond Rhetoric.' *The History Teacher* 26(4) (1993), pp. 493–97.

Rudman, Warren B. *Combat: Twelve Years in the U.S. Senate* (New York: Random House, 1996).

Ruud, Kathryn. 'Liberal Chiggers and Other Creepers.' Unpublished manuscript.

Ryback, David, Arthur L. Sanders, Jeffrey Lorentz, and Marlene Koestenblatt. 'Child-Rearing Practices Reported by Students in Six Cultures.' *Journal of Social Psychology* 110 (1980), pp. 153–62.

Sabato, Larry J., and Glenn R. Simpson. *Dirty Little Secrets: The Persistence of Corruption in American Politics* (New York: Times, 1996).

Sadker, Myra, and David Sadker. *Failing at Fairness: How America's Schools Cheat Girls* (New York: Scribner's, 1994).

Sanday, Peggy Reeves. *Fraternity Gang Rape: Sex, Brotherhood, and Privilege on Campus* (New York: New York University Press, 1990).

Schiffrin, Deborah. 'Jewish Argument as Sociability.' *Language in Society* 13(3) (1984), pp. 311–35.

Schlegel, Alice, and Herbert Barry III. *Adolescence: An Anthropological Inquiry* (New York: Free Press, 1991).

Schwartz, Murray. 'The Professionalism and Accountability of Lawyers.' *California Law Review* 66 (1978), pp. 669–97.

——. 'The Zeal of the Civil Advocate.' In *The Good Lawyer*, David Luban, ed. (Totowa, N.J.: Rowman & Allanheld, 1983), pp. 150–71.

Sheldon, Amy. 'Preschool Girls' Discourse Competence: Managing Conflict.' *Locating Power: Proceedings of the Second Berkeley Women and Language Conference*, vol. 2, Kira Hall, Mary Bucholtz, and Birch Moonwomon, eds. (Berkeley: Berkeley Women and Language Group, Linguistics Department, University of California, Berkeley, 1992), pp. 528–39.

Sherry, Michael S. *In the Shadow of War: The United States Since the 1930's* (New Haven: Yale University Press, 1995).

Sherzer, Joel. 'A Diversity of Voices: Men's and Women's Speech in Ethnographic Perspective.' In *Language, Gender and Sex in Comparative Perspective*, Susan U. Philips, Susan Steele, and Christine Tanz, eds. (Cambridge, England: Cambridge University Press, 1987), pp. 95–120.

Shillony, Ben-Ami. *Politics and Culture in Wartime Japan* (New York: Oxford University Press, 1981).

Showalter, Elaine. *Hystories: Hysterical Epidemics and Modern Culture* (New York: Columbia University Press, 1997).

Smith, Arthur Henderson. *Chinese Characteristics* (New York: Barnes & Noble, 1972 [1900]).

Spiegelman, Paul J. 'Integrating Doctrine, Theory and Practice in the Law School

Curriculum: The Logic of Jake's Ladder in the Context of Amy's Web.' *Journal of Legal Education* 38 (1988), pp. 243–70.

Straehle, Carolyn A. 'German and American Conversational Styles: A Focus on Narrative and Agonistic Discussion as Sources of Stereotypes.' Ph.D. dissertation, Georgetown University, Washington, D.C., 1997.

Tannen, Deborah. 'Oral and Literate Strategies in Spoken and Written Narratives.' *Language* 58(1) (1982), pp. 1–21.

——. 'The Oral/Literate Continuum in Discourse.' In *Spoken and Written Language: Exploring Orality and Literacy*, Deborah Tannen, ed. (Norwood, N.J.: Ablex, 1982), pp. 1–16.

——. *Conversational Style: Analyzing Talk Among Friends* (Norwood, N.J.: Ablex, 1984).

——. *That's Not What I Meant!: How Conversational Style Makes or Breaks Relationships* (New York: William Morrow, 1986).

——. *You Just Don't Understand: Women and Men in Conversation* (New York: William Morrow, 1990).

——. *Gender and Discourse* (New York: Oxford University Press, 1994).

Tenner, Edward. *Why Things Bite Back: Technology and the Revenge of Unintended Consequences* (New York: Knopf, 1996).

Thornburg, Elizabeth. 'Metaphors Matter: How Images of Battle, Sports, and Sex Shape the Adversary System.' *Wisconsin Women's Law Journal* 10 (1995), pp. 225–81.

Tompkins, Jane. 'Fighting Words: Unlearning to Write the Critical Essay.' *Georgia Review* 42 (1988), pp. 585–90.

Toobin, Jeffrey. *The Run of His Life: The People v. O. J. Simpson* (New York: Random House, 1996).

Tracy, Karen, and Sheryl Baratz. 'Intellectual Discussion in the Academy as Situated Discourse.' *Communication Monographs* 60 (1993), pp. 300–20.

Turow, Joseph. 'Hidden Conflicts and Journalistic Norms: The Case of Self-Coverage.' *Journal of Communication* 44:2 (Spring 1994), pp. 29–46.

Walsh, Kenneth T. *Feeding the Beast: The White House Versus the Press* (New York: Random House, 1996).

Watson, Peter. *War on the Mind: The Military Uses and Abuses of Psychology* (New York: Basic, 1978).

Watson-Gegeo, Karen Ann, and David W. Gegeo. 'Shaping the Mind and Straightening Out Conflicts: The Discourse of Kwara'ae Family Counseling.' In *Disentangling: Conflict Discourse in Pacific Societies*, Karen Ann Watson-Gegeo and Geoffrey M. White, eds. (Stanford, Calif.: Stanford University Press, 1990), pp. 161–213.

Watson-Gegeo, Karen Ann, and Geoffrey M. White, eds. *Disentangling: Conflict Discourse in Pacific Societies* (Stanford, Calif.: Stanford University Press, 1990).

Watzlawick, Paul, John Weakland, and Richard Fisch. *Change: Principles of Problem Formation and Problem Resolution* (New York: W. W. Norton, 1974).

Wertsch, James V. *Voices of the Mind: A Sociocultural Approach to Mediated Action* (Cambridge, Mass.: Harvard University Press, 1991).

Whiting, Beatrice B., and John W. M. Whiting, in collaboration with Richard Longabaugh; based on data collected by John and Ann Fischer, et al. *Children of Six Cultures: A Psycho-cultural Analysis* (Cambridge, Mass.: Harvard University Press, 1975).

Wolf, Margery. 'Child Training and the Chinese Family.' In *Family and Kinship in Chinese Society*, Maurice Freeman, ed. (Stanford, Calif.: Stanford University Press, 1970), pp. 37–62.

Wright, Robert. 'Hyperdemocracy: Washington Isn't Dangerously Disconnected from the People; The Trouble May Be It's Too Plugged In.' *Time*, Jan. 23, 1995, pp. 14–21.

Yablon, Charles. 'Stupid Lawyer Tricks: An Essay on Discovery Abuse.' *Columbia Law Review* 96 (1996), pp. 1618–44.

Yamada, Haru. *Different Games, Different Rules: Why Americans and Japanese Misunderstand Each Other* (New York: Oxford University Press, 1997).

Young, Linda W. L. *Crosstalk and Culture in Sino-American Communication* (Cambridge, England: Cambridge University Press, 1994).

# PERMISSIONS

Grateful acknowledgment is made to the following for permission to reprint previously published material:

*Columbia Law Review* AND CHARLES YABLON: Excerpts from 'Stupid Lawyer Tricks: An Essay on Discovery Abuse' by Charles Yablon. This article originally appeared in *Columbia Law Review* 96 (1996), p. 1618. Reprinted by permission of *Columbia Law Review* and Charles Yablon.

STEPHEN D. CORRSIN: Excerpt from a letter by Stephen D. Corrsin which appeared in the February 12, 1995, issue of *The New York Times Book Review*. Reprinted by permission of Stephen D. Corrsin.

*Cumberland Law Review:* Excerpts from 'Beyond the Rules' by N. Lee Cooper, *Cumberland Law Review* 26. Reprinted by permission.

SANDRA DIJKSTRA LITERARY AGENCY: Excerpt from 'The Naked Citadel' by Susan Faludi. Copyright © 1993 by Susan Faludi. As first appeared in *The New Yorker*. Reprinted by permission of the author and the Sandra Dijkstra Literary Agency.

*East Bay Express:* Excerpt from 'To Teach is Glorious' by John

Krich, *Express* 18, August 23, 1996, p. 15. Copyright © 1996 by Express Publishing Co. Reprinted by permission.

LOREN D. ESTLEMAN: Excerpt from a letter by Loren Estleman from the June 16, 1996, issue of *The Washington Post Book World*. Reprinted by permission of Loren Estleman.

*Los Angeles Daily Journal:* Excerpt from 'Civility: It's Worth the Effort' by Arthur Gilbert. Copyright © 1991 by Daily Journal Corp. Reprinted with permission.

*Mother Jones:* Excerpt from 'Gloria' by Cynthia Gorney, November/December 1995, p. 22. Copyright © 1995 by Foundation for National Progress. Reprinted with permission from *Mother Jones*.

NATIONAL PUBLIC RADIO: Excerpt from *Talk of the Nation*. This news report by NPR's Ray Suarez was originally broadcast on National Public Radio's *Talk of the Nation* on March 4, 1997, and is reprinted with the permission of National Public Radio, Inc. Copyright © 1997 by National Public Radio, Inc. Any unauthorized duplication is strictly prohibited.

*The New York Times:* Excerpt from article in *The New York Times Magazine*, January 30, 1994; excerpt from 'The Year in the Arts' by Peter Watrous, December 25, 1994; excerpt from 'Under a Bare Bulb' by Frank Bruni, February 16, 1997. Copyright © 1994, 1997 by The New York Times Company. Reprinted by permission.

*Newsweek:* Excerpt from 'A Brush with Anonymity' by Joe Klein, from *Newsweek*, July 29, 1996. Copyright © 1996 by Newsweek, Inc. Excerpt from 'Richardson for the U.N.' by Carroll Bogert from *Newsweek*, February 10, 1997. Copyright © 1997 by Newsweek, Inc. Excerpt from 'And in This Corner . . .' by Jack Koll from *Newsweek*, February 10, 1997. Copyright © 1997 by Newsweek, Inc. All Rights Reserved. Reprinted by permission.

ROY REED: Excerpt from a letter by Roy Reed from the August 25, 1996, issue of *The New York Times Book Review*. Reprinted by permission of Roy Reed.

RICHARD F. RILEY, JR: Excerpt from a letter by Richard F. Riley, Jr, from the February 12, 1996, issue of *The New York Times Book Review*. Reprinted by permission of Richard F. Riley, Jr.

JUDY SEIGEL: Excerpt from a letter by Judy Seigel from the February 12, 1996, issue of *The New York Times Book Review*. Reprinted by permission of Judy Seigel.

*Time:* Excerpt from 'Liddy Makes Perfect' from the July 1, 1996,

# TALKING FROM 9 TO 5
## Women and Men at Work: Language, Sex and Power

Deborah Tannen

**'Deborah Tannen confirms that what is true in the bedroom is also true in the boardroom . . . men and women speak different languages'** – *Observer*

Deborah Tannen looks at the role played by talk 'from 9 to 5', focusing in particular on the differing conversational rituals that typify men and women. Those common among men involve opposition such as banter, joking and playful put-downs; common among women are ways of maintaining the appearance of equality, avoiding boasting and downplaying authority. Arguing that no one style is superior, Tannen shows that when conventions are taken literally, there are negative results for both sides. She illuminates the different ways men and women make decisions, ask for information and delegate. Then shows how these styles affect how we are judged in the workplace. *Talking from 9 to 5* is a brilliantly incisive book that offers powerful new ways of understanding what's really going on at work.

# YOU JUST DON'T UNDERSTAND
## Women and men in Conversation

Deborah Tannen

**'Tannen combines a novelist's ear for the way people speak with a rare power of original analysis . . . fascinating' – Oliver Sacks**

Why do so many women feel that men don't tell them anything, but just lecture and criticise? Why do so many men feel that women nag them and never get to the point? In this pioneering book Deborah Tannen shows us how women and men talk in different ways, for profoundly different reasons. While women use language to make connections and reinforce intimacy, men use it to preserve their status and independence.

## Now you can order superb titles directly from Virago

| | | | |
|---|---|---|---|
| ☐ | You Just Don't Understand | Deborah Tannen | £8.99 |
| ☐ | Talking from 9-5 | Deborah Tannen | £8.99 |
| ☐ | City of Dreadful Delight | Judith Walkowitz | £12.99 |
| ☐ | Of Woman Born | Adrienne Rich | £8.99 |
| ☐ | When she was Bad | Patricia Pearson | £9.99 |
| ☐ | The Age of Anxiety | Sarah Dunant and Roy Porter (ed) | £7.99 |
| ☐ | The Female Malady | Elaine Showalter | £9.99 |
| ☐ | The Haunting of Sylvia Plath | Jacqueline Rose | £8.99 |
| ☐ | Christina Rossetti | Frances Thomas | £8.99 |
| ☐ | The Drama of Being a Child | Alice Miller | £7.99 |

Please allow for postage and packing: **Free UK delivery.**
Europe; add 25% of retail price; Rest of World; 45% of retail price.

To order any of the above or any other Virago titles, please call our credit card orderline or fill in this coupon and send/fax it to:

**Virago, 250 Western Avenue, London, W3 6XZ, UK.**
Fax 0181 324 5678   Telephone 0181 324 5516

☐ I enclose a UK bank cheque made payable to Virago for £ ...........
☐ Please charge £.............. to my Access, Visa, Delta, Switch Card No.

☐☐☐☐☐☐☐☐☐☐☐☐☐☐☐☐☐☐☐

Expiry Date ☐☐☐☐   Switch Issue No. ☐☐

NAME (Block letters please) .................................................................

ADDRESS .................................................................................................

..................................................................................................................

..................................................................................................................

Postcode ...............................Telephone ...........................................

Signature .................................................................................................

Please allow 28 days for delivery within the UK. Offer subject to price and availability.

Please do not send any further mailings from companies carefully selected by Virago ☐